HOMETOWN HEROES

THE HISTORY OF THE AUBURN FIRE DEPARTMENT

KATHY DEJOY-GENKOS

SCOTT DEJOY

Auburn, NY

© 2016 Kathy DeJoy-Genkos & Scott DeJoy

All rights reserved. No part of this book may be used or reproduced in any manner whatsoever without written permission except in the case of brief quotations embodied in critical articles and reviews.

Back cover photography by Sarah Jean Condon.

Downtown Books Publishing
66 Genesee Street
Auburn, NY 13021
downtownbooksandcoffee.com

ISBN: 978-0-69274-923-4

Dedicated to Dad and Mom, who always led by example.
We miss you more than words can say.

CONTENTS

Beginnings	1
Fire Companies & Facilities	17
Chiefs	49
Fire Force	95
Apparatus	107
Fire Alarms	139
Animals	157
Fires	169
Charitable and Community-Oriented Events	309
Firefighter Stories	315
Hot Spots	351
Acknowledgements	393
References	395

HOMETOWN HEROES

THE HISTORY OF THE AUBURN FIRE DEPARTMENT

BEGINNINGS

Top: 1890, Auburn Fire Department First Paid Company
Bottom: AFD Spider

1880, Auburn Fire Department Hose 1

Auburn's history is steeped with many historical people and events. The history of its fire department is no exception. From its earliest inception and continuing through the years and into the present day, the Auburn Fire Department has always been a source of community pride. A firefighter must possess that singular ability to cast aside natural human instinct to run away from fire and, instead, run toward it, focusing on a plan of action and carrying out the duties necessary to rescue others and extinguish flames. Surrounded by the sounds of a roaring inferno, dense and impenetrable smoke and true dangers all around, a firefighter maintains a clear mental vision of the job to be done. Their strength must be both physical and analytical in nature, always dynamic to the evolving fire scene. Each and every member is part of a unique family; one in which lives depend on another 'brother' or 'sister'. More times than not, they are humble and righteous. They are a rare breed and have true grit. Their career is complex, and the experiences are cumulative and become engrained within them. Detroit Firefighter Dave Parnell said it best; "I wish my head could forget what my eyes have seen in 32 years of firefighting."

It only makes sense that the Maltese Cross is used throughout the Fire Service in the United States as a symbol of Honor, Courage, and Dedication. The history of the Maltese Cross proves fitting for modern day firefighters and dates back to the eleventh century. A courageous band of crusaders, known as the Knights of St. John, fought the Saracens for possession of the holy land. They encountered a new weapon unknown to European warriors. It was a simple, but horrible device of war, and wrought excruciating pain and agonizing death upon the brave fighters for the cross. The Saracen's weapon was fire. As the crusaders advanced on the walls of the city, they were struck by glass bombs containing naphtha. When they became saturated with the highly flammable liquid, the Saracens hurled a flaming torch into their midst. Hundreds of the knights were burned alive; others risked their lives to save their brothers-in-arms from dying painful, fiery deaths. Thus, these men became the first of a long list of courageous firefighters. Their heroic efforts were recognized by fellow crusaders who awarded each hero a badge of honor; a cross similar to the one firefighters wear today. Since the Knights of St. John lived for close to four centuries on a little island in the

Mediterranean Sea named Malta, the cross came to be known as the Maltese Cross. The Maltese Cross is an eight-point cross and symbolizes protection. Firefighters who wear this cross are willing to lay down their lives just as the crusaders sacrificed their lives for their fellow man so many years ago.

Auburn began taking steps to provide the community fire protection in 1815, the same year Auburn was incorporated as a village. The village board passed a series of ordinances and included fire protection measures among them. In August 1815, the board resolved to purchase "a good, sizeable fire engine and one hundred fire buckets as soon as may be convenient." Four Fire Wardens were appointed; Ansel Howland, Abijah Keeler, Abel Terry and Ezekiel Williams Jr. On November 20, 1815, village officials recognized the danger of fire when they approved an ordinance that ordered "every dwelling house, store or mechanic shop less than three stories high within said village, shall be supplied with a good substantial ladder of sufficient length to reach from the ground to the height of four feet above the eaves of the building; and that every dwelling house, store or mechanic shop of three stories high or upwards shall have a scuttle hole through the roof at least three feet square, with a convenient pair of stairs leading to the same; and it is further ordered, that the occupant of every dwelling house, store or mechanic shop, shall provide the necessary ladder or scuttle hole as above directed before the first of January next, and every person who shall fail to comply with this order shall forfeit the sum of $5 to be recovered with costs of suit." These critical steps toward fire protection were, at least in part, a deciding factor in building a prison in Auburn. It was during this same time that the State was evaluating sites. Construction of the north wing of the prison began in 1816.

The trustees of the village of Auburn ordered that good, substantial leather fire buckets be provided by property owners. Fire protection was similar to other villages and consisted of fire buckets and a bucket engine or tub. The fire buckets mandated for all property owners held three gallons of water and were made of leather. They relied on wells and cisterns for their water supply. Wells were dug by hand and cisterns were constructed and located at various locations in the city to provide water to extinguish flames. Water from the outlet was also used in battling fires. In May of 1817, the village board identified a standardized process to sound the fire alarm and outlined the conduct of firemen at a fire. When the alarm was sounded, firemen would run to the fire. Buckets from nearby properties were given to the men working the fire. They would form two bucket brigade lines and from the nearest water source, one line would pass up full buckets of water to be used against the fire and the other line would pass down empty buckets to be filled. If the fire was of a large proportion or there were not enough men, the women would fall in line and assist the bucket brigade. Firemen were required to provide themselves with leather hats or caps, as identified and directed by the president, and were required to wear them "at all times when called out on actual duty or for exercise; and to respond immediately on alarm of fire to the engine, convey it to or near the fire, and work and manage the same fire engine hose and other instruments and implements thereto belonging with all their skill and power." If any fireman "willfully or negligently" failed to attend any fire, or to perform his duty when there, or left his engine without permission, or failed to "do his duty in washing, working or exercising his engine when lawfully required," he should "for the first offense forfeit and pay $3", and for the second "be removed from his station, and such removal, and the cause thereof, be published in all the newspapers printed in said village."

The 1820 census for the village indicated that Auburn had 2,333 inhabitants. In the years that followed, Auburn quickly grew, adding many businesses and manufacturers. Auburn was the home of many noteworthy citizens; scientists, innovators, artists, writers, military heroes, industrialists, physicians, musicians and the list goes on and on. The Village of Auburn flourished. As expansion continued, fire protection became glaringly important in order to protect the ever-growing population and buildings of the village. The village experienced several large conflagrations and continued to identify additional needs in terms of apparatus and processes. The citizens of Auburn recognized the need for "modern day" fire systems and took steps toward that protection. In the first decades of service, the fire companies of the village dealt with many events that challenged their equipment and manpower. The village's fire response system required men to literally run from the fire company where the engines were housed to the scene of the fire, carrying equipment and pulling and lugging engines over the unpaved and rough roads of the village. Men had to be in top physical condition and able to endure potentially long journeys to a fire. On top of that, they then had to exert great physical efforts to extinguish the flames that they encountered upon arrival.

In 1848, Auburn was chartered as a City. In the years that followed, Auburn fire companies continued to adopt new techniques and innovative equipment. Due to the physical and demanding nature of their role, the turnover rate for fire company personnel ran high. Due to membership problems and continuing rivalry between fire companies, reorganization was deemed necessary to band together the disparate entities. In 1856, the Fire Department leadership consisted of a chief engineer, a first and second assistant and aldermen who acted as fire wardens within their wards, of which there were four at the time. For those who found their niche within the fire companies of Auburn, their determination to advance fire protection and their firefighting abilities was readily observable.

In 1870, the Common Council elected George H. Battams Chief Engineer of the Auburn fire companies. Battams began his association in fire service as a torch boy in 1849, under Aurelian Conklin, Foreman of Old "Gooseneck" No. 1 and Mayor of Auburn in 1850 and 1851, and worked his way through the ranks until becoming Chief Engineer. In January of 1874, George Battams withdrew from active duty. The Common Council elected Joseph H. Morris as Chief Engineer to replace Battams in 1874.

The Firemen's Association of the State of New York (FASNY) was organized and formed in Auburn, New York in 1872. The organization cites on their website that FASNY was an idea that was sparked by an Auburn firefighter (whose name was not formally documented at the time) during a State convention of a benevolent organization meeting and parade that took place in Auburn, New York. He suggested a firemen's convention. The vision and forward-thinking of the Auburn firefighters was impressive. On September 2, 1872, members of the Auburn Fire Department met at the courthouse. After "much free and uninterrupted discussion" it was agreed that each of the six fire companies at their next monthly meetings would select three members to act as a committee. This steering committee was to meet with the officers of the department to present the report relative to forming a national firemen's association.

The origin of FASNY is documented on their website and in local newspapers at the time as follows: Three members each from Logan Hook and Ladder Co. No. 1, Neptune Hose Co. No. 1, Auburn Hose Co. No. 2, Niagara Hose Co. No. 3, Cayuga Hose Co. No. 4 and Union Hose Co. No. 5 were selected at the regular monthly meetings of the companies. This committee met the next evening and prepared a report, which was presented at the September 6th meeting of the entire fire department. The report was in the form of a resolution stating that the object of the association be "co-operative in nature and with the view to improve the general government of the fire departments, the discussion and adoption of modern and improved fire apparatus, as well as a general interchange of ideas and a discussion of important questions pertaining to the various duties of firemen." The resolution also called for the appointment of an executive committee of three, with full power, and subordinate committees on finance, entertainment, and reception. It stated that at the convention there shall preside a president, six vice-presidents, one corresponding secretary and one recording secretary, also that each company in all fire departments be entitled to one representative in the convention, his expenses to be defrayed by his respective company.

The committee members were:

FINANCE COMMITTEE

George Milk, Logan Hook and Ladder Co.

Joseph H. Morris, Neptune Hose Co.

George Friend, Auburn Hose Co.

Nicholas D. Kierst, Niagara Hose Co.

S. Wright Milk, Cayuga Hose Co.

Charles Tallowday, Union Hose Co.

ENTERTAINMENT COMMITTEE

George Smith, Logan Hook and Ladder Co.

Albert Sanford, Niagara Hose Co.

S. Wright Milk, Cayuga Hose Co.

Lewis Montgomery, Union Hose Co.

William McEwan, Logan Hook and Ladder Co.

Joseph Furness, Neptune Hose Co.

H. P. Brown, Cayuga Hose Co.

It was decided during a meeting of the executive committee that the first annual Convention of the Firemen's National Association be held in the City of Auburn on Tuesday and Wednesday, October 1 and 2, 1872. Every fire company in every fire department in the United States would be invited to send a delegate. As the convention grew closer, it seemed that the project had much interest, and eleven states sent letters indicating their interest in sending delegates. However, when the convention opened, Paterson, New Jersey, and Des Moines, Iowa, were the only two states outside New York that had representation. The

State of New York, however, was well represented at the convention, with fire companies from many New York municipalities present. The first day of the convention included many speakers addressing those gathered and a Grand Inauguration Ball in the evening at the Academy of Music. A large and well-attended parade took place the second day. There were also exhibitions, competitions and tests among the fire companies and a half mile race between Hose Co. No. 7 of Ithaca and Niagara Hose Co. No. 3 of Auburn. The 49th Regiment Band played music for the spectators and visiting firemen. At the end of the convention, the chairman of the Business Committee presented a report, in the form of a resolution, indicating "The Firemen of Auburn did a wise and beneficent act in organizing the Convention" and that given the assembly of representation, "Therefore, Be It Resolved: That this body be known as the Firemen's Association of the State of New York." So began the long and rich history of the Firemen's Association of the State of New York (FASNY). The first President was an Auburn man, Thomas Towne. Clarence Day was the first Secretary, also an Auburn man. Albert F. Smith, of Oswego, was first Treasurer. Over the years, the conventions continued to be very popular and well attended. The convention would be held in Auburn again in 1880.

In 1878, the Auburn Fire Department organization was equipped with 6,450 feet of linen hose, 100 feet of leather hose and 155 feet of rubber hose. The city had 212 fire hydrants and 19 fire alarm boxes. The department had a hose tower designed to dry the hose for all fire companies. It was sixty feet high, and a large stove supplied the heat to dry the hose. Two thousand feet of hose could be hung up at once. The hoisting apparatus was made up of ten pulleys with an arm in the form of the letter 'S' attached to each pulley. On each of the arms they would hang two lengths of hose. The butts were held in place with clamps. A brick well about four feet deep was used to wash the hose.

In 1879, the City of Auburn revised its charter and provided a Board of Fire Commissioners. The new City Charter resulted in the appointing of three Fire Commissioners by the Common Council. The initial appointment terms were staggered, with the first Commissioner appointed for a term of one year, a second for a term of two years and a third for a term of three years. The Commissioners were given power and exclusive control and management of the fire department. The Auburn Fire Commissioners ordered 200 silver-plated badges to be made by Anderson & Jones of New York City. The badges were numbered and had a raised "A. F. D" monogram on them. Three of the numbered badges were gold-plated and identified for the three Fire Commissioners.

In 1880, the 64th Annual Auburn Fire Department Parade and 8th Annual Convention of the New York State Firemen's Association took place in Auburn, New York. Amid the festivities, and on the day before the parade was to take place, the public was shocked to learn that Auburn's Chief Engineer, Joseph H. Morris, had died. Chief Morris roomed in the

McCrea block on State Street. His room adjoined that of his friend, Thomas McCrea. For almost a week Mr. Morris had been unable to sleep due to his nervousness. He paced back and forth at night and kept his friend and fellow lodger, Mr. Tom McCrea, awake. He had also suffered seizures in the past. Chief Morris had lost one of his men during a fire just two months previous; firefighter Lewis Chadderdon died at the Osborne House Fire on June 17th. With little time to grieve the loss, and many responsibilities for the upcoming parade and convention, Mr. Morris worked diligently to ensure the success of the convention and parade, but was worried about the preparations. He felt the success or failure of the event was his respon-

Joseph H. Morris

sibility exclusively. Thoughts of the parade and worry about it being a failure weighed so heavily on him, that Mr. Morris took his own life. Mr. Morris was a second generation firefighter; his father, also Joseph Morris, was a member of Hose Company No. 4 prior to his death in 1869. Joseph Morris' interest in fire fighting began at an early age. He started as a torch boy and held many different positions in the fire company before becoming Chief Engineer. Joseph Morris was known for his impartial manner and was well liked. His popularity with firemen across the state was such that it was rumored that he might have been elected President of the State Firemen's Association. This information also worried him and he expressed to a newspaper reporter that he much preferred to occupy a humble position among his brethren, and he could not see why his friends insisted that he should accept a position so distasteful to him.

On the morning of August 18th, Mr. McCrea found Chief Engineer Joseph Morris in a closet, lying face down in a pool of blood. Examination at the scene by the undertaker revealed a gash extending ear to ear, deep enough to expose vertebrae. Beneath his left shoulder and under his body was a sharp razor. The event was described as a sad and tragic ending to a useful career of a gallant chief. Mr. Morris was 37 years old. On August 19th, the coroner's jury concluded that Mr. Morris died as the result of a self-inflicted wound to the neck using a razor. His death occurred in the room adjoining his lodging on the third story of 12 State Street on the morning of August 18th, between the hours of 2-7:30am, while in a condition of temporary insanity. It was assumed his actions were the result of extreme nervousness and foreboding regarding the possibility that the State Association of Firemen, in session in Auburn, would not receive proper accommodations from the citizens. He felt the full weight of this responsibility was on him and would be blamed for any failure.

In spite of the horrific death of Mr. Morris, the parade took place on August 19th, and was greatly received by the citizens of Auburn and by those in areas across the state. Chief Engineer Morris' death overshadowed the events, and people were frequently heard uttering "Poor Joe!" The success of the convention and parade was attributed, in large part, to Chief Morris. It was reported that well more than twenty-five thousand people crowded the streets to see the parade and attend the festivities. There were public and private displays in celebration of the event. City Hall was decorated with almost 400 yards of cloth in holiday fashion. A floral bell and horseshoe were suspended from an arch constructed at the junction of North, South and Genesee Streets. Private residences were decorated for the event in grand fashion with flowers, flags, bunting, lanterns and other ornaments. Also present were emblems of mourning and displays of black bunting in honor and remembrance of the late Chief Morris. The streets filled up early on the morning of the 19th with spectators for the parade. There were peanuts, lemonade, watermelon and one-cent candies galore! All of the Auburn fire companies held open houses throughout the day. The rain that was present that morning cleared in time for the parade. At noon a signal from an alarm bell notified all fire companies to gather at their assigned locations at the beginning of the parade. The streets leading into Franklin Street near the junction of Lewis Street were used. At 2:30pm, another signal was given and the procession began. The Forty-Ninth Regimental Band followed the Acting Chief Engineer and a Platoon of Police. The march was approximately seven miles in length. The route followed Franklin to North Street, South to Mayor Osborne's residence, countermarch to Elizabeth Street, Elizabeth to Steel Street, Steel to Grover Street, Grover to South Street, South to William Street, William to

1946, Ornate spider in Auburn parade

Genesee Street, Genesee to Jefferson Street, Jefferson to Clark Street, Clark to State Street, State to VanAnden Street, VanAnden to North Street, North to Seymour Street, Seymour to Fulton Street, Fulton to Genesee Street, Genesee to Washington Street and countermarch to North Street. The procession was dismissed at 6pm, after marching for more than four hours. All Auburn fire companies presented in fine fashion and were well appointed. Various other cities were also represented in the convention and subsequent procession.

The procession included:

- Auburn's Neptune Hose Company No. 1 attired in red shirts, black pantaloons and fatigue caps. Spanning the reel of their "spider" was a beautiful arch of flowers and a floral bell suspended from the center.

- Binghamton Alert Hose 2 was noted to have a handsome carriage; their attire included red shirts, white fire hats and black pantaloons.

- The Sexton Extinguisher Company of Clyde was nicely uniformed in white shirts and red fire hats.

- Letchworth Hose Company No. 2 was attired in red shirts, black pantaloons and black fire hats. A ferocious looking dog covered with a blanket marched between the ropes.

- The Protectives of Clyde wore blue shirts and black hats.

- The Red Rovers of Seneca Falls were attired in red shirts, blue fatigue caps and black pantaloons.

- Neptune Hose 1 of Dryden had a splendid carriage presented in the march.

- The Protectives of Auburn were one of the finest looking companies in line. Their uniforms were new and made of white flannel and white hats. They had a floral banner of white flowers with "Protective" in red flowers running the entire length of their carriage.

- Ahwaga 6 of Owego had a steamer that was polished as bright as a mirror and was drawn by two stately horses.

- Wiltwyck Hose of Kingston were described as one of the best looking companies in the line.

- Hamilton White's "Chemical" was drawn by a pair of gray horses and the crowd applauded as they passed.

- The Hose Company from Weedsport marched with the precision of veteran soldiers.

- Hydrant Hose of Lockport drew the attention of all eyes and was admired as they marched in wheel and square formations that were beautifully executed and with such precision that it appeared to be almost automatic.
- Cayuga Hose No. 4 had their new uniforms of blue flannel and fatigue caps and displayed their handsome "spider" apparatus.
- Torrent Hose of Ithaca was handsomely uniformed in white fatigue caps and grey shirts and attracted a great deal of attention.
- Steamer No. 1 of Horseheads wore blue dress coats and black fatigue caps; their nickel-plated steamer drawn by a pair of magnificent gray horses.
- One of the most interesting features was the Torrent Engine Company of Skaneateles who brought their old goose neck drawn by four gray horses followed by their "jumper" with a horse attached.
- C. N. Ross Hose Company No. 5 wore red shirts and white fire hats. The citizens in the "west end" took great interest in this group, as did the entire city.
- The Z. C. Priest Steamer Company of Little Falls had a handsome parade cart and was greatly admired.
- Wide Awake Hose Company of Mexico was uniformed in blue shirts and helmet hats.
- Ontario Steamer 3 of Canandaigua was one of the finest fire organizations in the State, and their steamer was drawn by Alderman Webster's pair of sorrels.
- The old Volunteer fire department of Oswego, clad in citizen's dress, brought up the rear of the second division.
- Emerald Hose of Cortland was the first company in the third division and were dressed in gray dress coats and fatigue caps and was greatly admired for their drill, performing the different maneuvers with military precision.
- Alert Hose Company No. 6 wore red shirts and black fire hats and presented in fine appearance.
- Steam and Hose 1 of Palmyra took the prize for their excellence in drill at the convention in Canandaigua the year before. Their drilling in 1880 won the admiration of all and they were applauded throughout the march.
- Independent Hose and Active Hose of Lyons were excellent companies.
- Rescue Steamer of Ithaca looked fine in their red shirts and blue fatigue caps; their steamer was drawn by a pair of large bay horses.

- Defiance Hook and Ladder members of Owego were clad in blue sack coats with brass buttons, fatigue caps and white pantaloons; they were one of the finest appearing companies in the procession.
- Logan Hook and Ladder of Auburn, thought to be the second oldest company in the procession (Neptune Hose of Auburn being the oldest), wore black fire hats and red shirts. They had their newly painted truck with two coach dogs walking between the front and back wheels.
- Susquehanna Steamer 1 of Owego had a large machine and was drawn by a team of horses.
- Crystal Hose of Binghamton had a $6,000 carriage that was a mirror on wheels. It was beyond description. One word was said to cover all that could be said about it, "Beautiful". The men were attired in gray uniforms and had white fire hats. They were greatly admired and received with applause all along the long route.

On the evening of August 19th, a grand dinner and concert was held at the National Hotel to celebrate the convention and provide a venue for the various fire companies to gather. A portrait of Chief Morris was draped in mourning decorations and suspended over his empty chair in the dining room. His chair and the mourning decorations remained in place for thirty days. A very large fireworks display was provided in the evening hours.

At a meeting of Chief Engineers at the Osborne Hotel on August 20th, action was taken on the death of Chief Morris. The following resolutions of regret at the death of Chief Morris were adopted.

The Firemen's Association of the State of New York:

Whereas, This association has received with profound sorrow the sad intelligence of the death of Joseph H. Morris, Chief Engineer of the Auburn Fire Department, a delegate to this convention and a member of the executive committee, it becomes our mournful duty to express our sense of the deep loss which the association and the fire service in general has sustained in this sudden and unexpected bereavement. Recognizing the inadequacy of words to fully express the grief with which we are overwhelmed, we cannot, nevertheless, let pass this occasion when so many of his old comrades and friends are assembled, without placing on record a faint expression of our sense of the magnitude of the loss we have sustained. Therefore be it

Resolved, That inasmuch as it has pleased the Supreme Ruler of the universe to strike down our friend and comrade in the flower of his manhood and in the midst of his usefulness, at a moment when he was surrounded by a great number of brother fireman who knew him well, and loved him for his many noble qualities, we bow our heads in heartfelt sorrow to the decree of the Supreme Wisdom that governs all things best, and will strive to school our hearts to respond "It is well."

Resolved, That in the death of Chief Morris the fire service has lost an able and efficient officer and one who commanded the love and respect of all with whom he came in contact, that while fully appreciating his ability as a fireman and an executive officer of a prominent department, we also have a thorough appreciation of the many noble qualities of his head and heart, his genuine manhood, his genial, pleasant disposition, his courteous manners and his thorough unselfishness in sacrificing his own personal comforts at any time to contribute to the pleasure and enjoyment of his friends.

Resolved, That in the manner of our comrade's death we recognize that in his anxiety to cater to the entertainment of his friends on the occasion of the present convention of this association and the annual parade of his department, he overtaxed his mental and physical strength; that it was observed by his friends that for several days his spirits have been depressed and his mind affected, least the arrangements for our entertainment should miscarry in some respect that to the over taxation of his resources is to be attributed the fact of his temporary insanity, in which condition of mind his death occurred.

Resolved, That we recognize the fact that any words to which we can give utterance must fail to assuage the grief of the relations and immediate friends of the deceased, for under the shock of so great an affliction the heart is dumb; nevertheless, we tender to these our heartfelt sympathy and our sincere condolences.

Resolved, That the Recording Secretary cause a copy of these resolutions to be suitably engraved and presented to the Auburn Fire Department as a token of the estimation in which the lamented chief was held by the Association.

W. S. Newman,

Frank C. Plumb

S. A. Smyth,

Henry W. Mathews,

Clifford Thompson.

A new Board of Fire Commissioners for the City of Auburn was organized on March 1, 1890. At that time the Fire Department consisted of seven companies. An appropriation of $5,000 was provided in order to cover expenses for salaries, repairs, apparatus, hose and all other expenses relating to the Fire Department. Prior to the establishment of the Board of Fire Commissioners, the City was responsible for many of the expenses and debts incurred by the department. The beginnings of a paid fire department commenced in 1890, with six paid permanent firefighters employed at the onset. There were an additional 185 volunteer firefighters on the membership rolls. It was a time of transition and a move away from complete reliance on volunteer services, with steps toward a paid permanent Fire Department.

In 1892, The Fire Commissioners approved a resolution that established uniforms for all permanent members of the Auburn fire companies. The uniform consisted of a double-breasted sack coat of dark blue cloth with inside pockets and five metal 'F. D.' buttons on each breast and two on sleeves at the cuff. Their shirts were dark blue flannel and they wore a black silk necktie. The cap was dark blue cloth and of regulation pattern with a badge on the front. They wore white straw hats during the summer. Officers had three buttons on their coat sleeves; the vest and pants were the same cloth and the vest had a rolling collar and six small metal buttons. They could wear a white linen or flannel shirt. Their caps had an insignia of rank in place of a badge on their caps. The uniforms had to be worn when on duty. However, when they were cleaning the quarters, they were allowed to wear their civilian clothing. There was no smoking allowed by uniformed members while visitors were in the quarters.

In 1893, the National Board of Fire Underwriters made an examination and inspection of the Auburn fire companies. Their report to the Auburn Board of Fire Commissioners recommended that Auburn form a paid department to remedy and improve the service and fire protection, and that the volunteer department in existence at that time, be changed into a paid department. Auburn had a large manufacturing component, many business interests and the city's population was continuing to grow. After reviewing the report and completing additional studies on the matter, the Auburn Board of Fire Commissioners concluded that a paid permanent fire department should be formed. The Neptune Hose Company No. 1, Chemical Company No. 1 and Hook and Ladder Company No. 1 were formed and officially organized into full-time paid fire companies. In the Annual Report of the Fire Department for the year ending February 28, 1893, the Board of Fire Commissioners noted that there were 162 men in the Fire Department, eight of them paid, permanent firemen. While the volunteers were willing and enthusiastic, it was felt that a number of trained men who were always ready would be better. A response five minutes in the incipient stages of a fire was worth hours of time after. The growth and conversion to a paid department would continue throughout 1893.

The Auburn Fire Department was established as a full-time, paid department on January 1, 1894. Edward J. Jewhurst, who was appointed Chief in 1880 by D. M. Osborne, became the first paid Fire Chief of the Auburn Fire Department January 1, 1894. Active Hose Company No. 7 was added to the rolls of the Auburn Fire Department as Active Hose Company No. 3. There were four paid companies; Cayuga Chemical Company, Neptune Hose Company No. 1, Active Hose Company No. 3 and Logan Hook and Ladder Company.

All Auburn Fire Department companies at that time had horse-drawn apparatus within their companies. By March of 1894, the Auburn Fire Department had 18 permanent firemen, 11 men in the call force and 59 volunteers.

For more than 122 years, the City of Auburn has been protected by the members of the Auburn Fire Department, 24 hours a day 7 days a week! It is a staggering testimony to the bravery, dedication and efficiency of the department and its members. The protection and security of the residents of Auburn has been a constant effort and has resulted in lives saved, fires extinguished, structures protected and residents educated in fire prevention. It has also afforded the City of Auburn high fire protection ratings for many, many years, resulting in lower fire insurance premiums.

FIRE COMPANIES & FACILITIES

Top: AFD Hook & Ladder

Bottom: c. 1909-1913, AFD Hose 2
L to R: Morgan Olmstead, William Maywalt, Patrick "Paddy" Ryan, Dayton Smith, John Maywalt, Clarence Whiting, Augustus "Gus" Hemrick; Driver, Fred Haskell

Bottom: 1904

Top: 1919, AFD Combination 3

Bottom: Truck: George Bishop, Edward Lyons / Hose Wagon: William Kehoe, Louis Spaide, Fred Hoyt, Charles Hawelka / Engine: Joseph Anton, Theodore Hamilton, Patrick Morrissey

Identifying the various fire companies, their locations and name changes proves to be a challenging task, as many individuals we spoke to can attest. In the early years there were numerous volunteer companies and they were not always well documented or formally organized. They tended to operate independently. Not every Hose Company number reflects a single, continuous service company. Therefore, we have attempted to identify individual fire companies based upon continuous service. If a company was disbanded and not replaced for years, we have represented it as a separate company. If a company was renamed and continued in service, we have viewed it as a single company. As with any undertaking that involves scores of handwritten records, newspaper accounts and historical recollections, we have faced some conflicting information (years, names, etc.). What follows is what we have determined to be an accurate representation of the history of fire companies within the Auburn Fire Department.

In its infancy, Auburn's firefighting force consisted solely of Bucket Brigades; men of the village whose primary tools were buckets. Vaguely referenced in records and newspaper accounts, they continued to exist, albeit in a dwindling capacity, thru the 1840s. During the volunteer years, there were numerous fire companies that started and disbanded. Some lasted only weeks and others took roots and endured for years. Some of the early volunteer fire companies in Auburn, not otherwise mentioned in the list that follows, include the Auburn Hose Company No. 2, Cataract Engine Company No. 2 and Hope Fire Company No. 4.

Early records show that many of the companies made records for themselves. At the 1856 Firemen's Tournament in Syracuse, the men of Neptune Company No. 1 took first place and won a magnificent silver trumpet, valued at $125. The Engine that brought them to victory was built by Mr. James Smith of New York. The engine was said to be the most powerful fire engine in the United States, as testimony from some of the best mechanics present at the event indicated. Each company in the competition filled a tank with water. The tank was 6' 9" at the base and 6' 2 ¾" at the top and was 80 inches deep. The tank was positioned a distance from the apparatus. Using a 10-inch cylinder, the men of Neptune Company No. 1 threw 51 inches of water into the tank, using just over 1,086 gallons of water, in four minutes. The Jordan Fire Company placed second in the tournament. Neptune's silver trumpet was beautiful and confirmed to be made of pure silver. It was placed on display at Harbottle & Smith's Jewelry store on Genesee Street before being brought back to Neptune's quarters, next to the "Big Machine".

Niagara Hose Company No. 3 held the record for years for making the fastest one-half mile run with apparatus. Neptune Hose Company No. 1 had claimed the reputation of out-pumping any engine in the state. Cayuga Hose Company No. 4 also had a reputation for speed, having run a quarter of a mile, laid 300' of hose, broke couplings and attached pipe in 1 minute, 28 seconds. The Logan Hook and Ladder Company placed second in a large drill competition held in Buffalo in August of 1886, and won a $200 cash prize. The Logan Hook & Ladder No. 1 held a Grand Gala Day at Seward Avenue Park on September 12, 1873, with more than one thousand people in attendance. Game winners included: Thomas Mansell for the running hop, step and jump; Billy Manning for the wheelbarrow race; M. Burns for the 250 yard foot race; William Crawford and his sister and partner, Miss Crawford, shared honors for the best dancer of round dances. A greased pig was supplied by Chief Engineer Battams and Joseph H. Morris as a prize to the party who succeeded in seizing the animal and throwing it over his shoulder. The pig race was wildly attended by spectators. The pig was described as rather eccentric in his movements that day, as it scurried through the neighboring gardens with almost seven hundred men and boys in pursuit! Billy Manning won the event when he managed to capture the pig as it attempted to root through a corner of a fence. Auburn Hose No. 2 held their Grand Gala Day at Seward Avenue Park on September 15, 1873, during which they held "Fool Races", wheelbarrow races, and a greased pig race. Tickets to the event were 25 cents; women and children were free.

Neptune Company No. 1

With its roots in 1816 as Auburn Fire Company No. 1, Neptune Company No. 1 was officially organized on May 2, 1817, after the 1815 ordinance was repealed and a new fire company formed. Neptune Company No. 1 represented the very beginning of Auburn's Fire Department. Neptune, God of the Waters, was a fire company composed of 25 leading citizens of Auburn. Neptune Company No. 1 was located on Market Street near North Street. Neptune Co. kept a handwritten record book from 1817-1840 that detailed the early days of the Fire Department. In 1817, the company chose Archy Kasson as Foreman, John Hunter as Assistant Foreman and C. Ten Eyck as Secretary and Treasurer. In 1868, it was renamed Neptune Hose Company No. 1. Neptune Hose Company was incorporated into Auburn's permanent paid Fire Department on January 1, 1894. By 1899, it was known as Hose Company No. 1. Remaining on Market Street, it was later renamed Engine Company No. 1. Engine Company No. 1 was disbanded in 1971, due to the anticipated increased manning that would be required to maintain four engine companies and one ladder company.

November 1872, Neptune Hose Company 1

Chief George Battams, Foreman Joseph Morris, Assistant Foremen George Wilson and Joseph Furness, Secretary Walter Bray.

Members in photo; Al Kilburn, George Long, Watson Hutson, Ralph Stalker, Joseph French, John Winsor, Ed Schoonmaker, Thomas Finn, Joe Havens.

Police Chief Harrison Daniels, Mr. Coddington, Secretary of Hook and Ladder Company Clarence Day, Auburn Policeman J. E. Bennett, Police Justice A. L. Sisson, Alderman A. L. Purdy, Honorary Neptune Hose Member Walter Weed, Former Chief David Schoonmaker.

Logan Hook & Ladder No. 1

Logan Hook and Ladder Company was organized June 24, 1824. Their members were known as "The Logans" and "Hooks". In October of 1874, the City of Auburn held a large semi-centennial event to commemorate and celebrate their long history in the department. In parades and exhibitions, the company often displayed a likeness of "Logan", the famous Cayuga Indian Chief. They also had a full length oil portrait of a Cayuga Indian Chief in their quarters. Their motto: "Useful but not ornamental". A source of pride in the community, the "Hooks" usually brought up the rear in parades and were seen as the highlight of many events. Their unique abilities and equipment were often called upon during a fire call. They were reorganized on January 1, 1894, as Hook and Ladder No. 1 and were located on Market Street. It remains housed on Market Street to this day.

Assistant Foreman

Letchworth Hose Company No. 2

Letchworth Hose Company No. 2 was organized in 1847, and reorganized November 17, 1873. It was originally located in an old blacksmith shop on Owasco Street near the woolen mill, where the superintendent lived. It later moved to a different Owasco Street location near Fulton Street. From there, it was relocated in February 1884 to 9 Fulton Street (what is now the Utopia Club). It was reorganized again on January 1, 1894, and April of 1899. A new fire station was built in 1898 on the corner of Mill and Owasco Streets (57 Owasco Street) and it was renamed 'Hose Company No. 2' as part of the Auburn Fire Department. The Owasco Street station remained in service for many years, but time took a toll on the building. In 1960, the 62-year-old doors of the station were replaced when it was discovered that the framework was loose and weakened and presented a hazard. Modernized equipment and apparatus were much heavier than the equipment used in the 19th century, and the repairs that would have been necessary would have cost an estimated $100,000. The Owasco Street station's advanced age and weakened physical condition required it to be closed. In 1966, the lot at 5 Frederick Street was purchased by the City of Auburn from Mr. and Mrs. Herbert Steigerwald for $12,000. The Frederick Street location was chosen in order to maximize fire protection for the city. A new fire station was constructed during 1966, and was put into service on November 21, 1966. Engine Co. 2 was housed there. It remained at that location until it was closed in 2008.

1889, AFD Letchworth Hose Company 2

Back Row L to R: Isaac Moore, Edward Corfield, Joseph Hahn, Patrick Ryan, John Frank, George Morse, Michael McCartin, William Fulton, Nicholas Hahn, Edward Perrigo, William Morse.

Front Row L to R: James Lattimore, John Elder, William Corfield, George Houser, John Farrar, Thomas Woods, George Bain, Augustus Hemrick, John McAlpine, John Willman, Charles Sanford, Michael Carmody.

Top: *AFD Hose Company 2, Owasco Street*
Bottom: *Plaque, AFD Engine 2, Frederick Street Fire Station*

Niagara Hose Company No. 3

Niagara Hose Company No. 3 was organized June 1, 1847, and was located on William Street near Genesee Street (two doors down). Their original motto, "We hope to save," was later changed to the more confident, "We strive to save." In December of 1879, the Niagara Hose Company No. 3 unanimously resolved to disband after long contemplation. The organization resolved itself into a social society and became known as the "Niagara Social Club". In that capacity they hosted many social events in Auburn. The Protective Hose Company No. 3 (which originated as the Exempt Hose Company) would later supersede Niagara Hose Company in that part of Auburn in 1880.

Cayuga Hose Company No. 4

Cayuga Hose Company No. 4 was organized June 26, 1856, and was located on Franklin Street, east of the City Hall. They were reorganized June 28, 1872. In 1884, they were organized as Cayuga Fire Patrol Company No. 1 and were located on Franklin Street at the rear of City Hall. Other names observed for this company over the years include; Patrol Extinguisher, Cayuga Patrol (~1886-1888), Cayuga Hose, Seward Hose Company (1870-1872), and Patrol Chemical Co. No. 1. In 1890, Cayuga Chemical Engine Company No. 1 was organized and remained at its location on Franklin Street. In 1907, they became Hose Company No. 4. In later years it became Engine Company No. 4 and was located on Market Street, where it remains today.

Left: Cayuga Fire Patrol Company No. 1, c. 1884-1889
(From the collection of the Cayuga Museum of History and Art)
Right: Photo courtesy of Michael Deyneka

Union Fire Company No. 5

Union Fire Company No. 5 was organized on July 8, 1869. They were housed in a blacksmith shop on Wall Street just below Division Street. The company remained in that location until October 6, 1869, when they moved to the blacksmith shop owned by E. P. Babcock at the junction of Wall Street and Aurelius Avenue. They housed their apparatus in the lower portion of the building and the attic was used as a session room. The water mains reached that section of the city in August of 1871. On September 6, 1871, Alderman Pearson presented the company with an elegant banner with gilt fringe trimming and tassels that was supported with an ebony bar. The banner was embellished with a fine oil painting by Lieutenant Colonel Terance J. Kennedy, modeled after "The American Eagle Guarding the Spirit of Washington" by Thomas Rogers. The painting represented an eagle gazing upon the rising sun through the misty atmosphere. The rock, from behind which the sun was rising, delineated the head of George Washington and the one upon which the bird was perched outlined the features of Washington. Above the picture were the words "Union Fire Co. No. 5, Auburn, NY." On the reverse side the banner

Top: Photo courtesy of Anita Luisi Colvin
Bottom: Union Fire Company No. 5

read "Union fire Co. 5, presented by Ald. D. S Pearson, 1871." The City constructed a new house for the fire company. On December 13, 1871, the Union Hose Company No. 5 moved into a new two-story building on Wall Street, between Division and Aurelius Avenue.

On October 7, 1874, the name of the organization was changed to the C. N. Ross Hose Company No. 5 in honor of Charles N. Ross, Mayor of Auburn, and in later years, New York State Treasurer. The company was presented a solid silver trumpet by Alderman Charles F. Galon. The Ross Hose Company was said to have a "loud talker" in its ranks; a miniature cannon was mounted and kept on reserve for special occasions. It was said that when the cannon 'spoke', everyone listened. The company's motto was "Ever on alert." It was disbanded in May of 1897, and later sold and turned into the Italian Club House.

Steamer Engine Company No. 1

Steamer Engine Company No. 1 was organized December 31, 1902, and was located at 27 Market Street. It was later renamed to Hose Company No. 5/Engine Company No. 5. The Auburn Fire Department had the distinct privilege of utilizing the oldest brick building in the city, and one that was rich with historical relevance. The original settler, Col. John Hardenbergh, built a log cabin on the site. He later built a brick building to replace the log cabin on the same site. For many years it was used as a residence prior to being sold. The building was located on the same area of Market Street that held City Hall, on the banks of the Owasco River. It was part of the original Hardenbergh property, and was purchased by the City around 1880 for approximately $6,000. The building was originally secured because the Fire Department needed a storehouse for hay, grain and supplies. In 1902,

Hose Company No. 5
(From the collection of the Cayuga Museum of History and Art)

when it became necessary for an additional firehouse, the building was converted for use by Steamer and Hose/Engine Company No. 5. An addition was added later so that the hook and ladder truck could be housed in the building. Over the years the building began to show its age. It needed new floors, the front wall was bulging, and bracing became necessary as well as other structural concerns. It remained in that location until it was disbanded on July 1, 1931.

Good Will Hose Company No. 6

Good Will Hose Company No. 6 was organized in 1874 and located on Wall Street, near State Street. In 1879, the company was renamed Alert Hose Company No. 6. Alert Hose Company moved to a building on the west side of State Street. Also known as the 5th Ward Hose House, Alert Company had a new hose house built on the southeast corner of State and VanAnden Streets by Auburn contractors, George Mason and Don Springstead (Mason & Springstead), at a cost of $1,600. Original plans had the hose house as a two-story brick building, but the plans were modified and a two-story wood hose house was finalized. Each story of the 22' x 40' hose house was eleven feet in height. It was constructed of southern hemlock with double outside doors that opened out and had bronze bolts. The roof and tower were covered with MF tin. The hose house had an interior water closet with a marble wash basin and slab ends. The building was painted a rich chocolate shade of brown and had a slate roof. The City owned the building that housed the fire company and leased the property from the New York Central Railroad for 99 years at $10 a year. Alert Hose Company No. 6 remained in that location for almost 18 years before being disbanded in 1898.

Photo courtesy of Michael Deyneka

Hose Company No. 6

In 1911, Fire Commissioner Burgess made a motion to the common council for a new fire station in the northwest part of Auburn due to the increased manufacturing and business interests in that section of the city. After consideration and discussion, the council unanimously passed and carried the motion. A search for a suitable location was conducted and $2,000 was paid to John and Catherine Marr for property located at 184 State Street. Hose Company No. 6 was organized January 1, 1912. The State Street fire station was sold November 16, 1931, to the Polish Meat and Grocery Company, Inc. for $10,000. Hose 6 moved to Franklin Street and was later renamed Engine Company No. 6.

Active Hose Company No. 7

Active Hose Company No. 7 (aka: 8th Ward Hose Company) was located on the corner of Jefferson and Clark Streets and was in existence as early as 1879. The exact year of its organization is not known. In 1880, Active Hose Company No. 7 occupied a newly constructed two-story, 40' x 22', brick hose house built by contractors Sisson and Ocobock, of Auburn. Active Hose Company was disbanded in February of 1894 and was replaced on March 1, 1894, with a reorganized Hose Company No. 3 as part of the permanent paid Auburn Fire Department. It was later renamed to Engine Company No. 3. The fire station located at 129 Clark Street opened in 1912, and was situated at the foot of Jefferson Street. Clark Street had to be regraded to make a proper site for the Hose Company's apparatus. The Engine 3 station house was known to be very cold. Some of the old timers shiver, even

Active Hose Company No. 7

today, when they recollect waking up in the morning with snow literally accumulated on their bunks! In 1956, it was discovered that the floor joists had become weakened. The old Knox truck, originally housed in the station, weighed over 2 ½ tons. The pumper parked in the station in 1956 weighed 14 tons! Actions were immediately taken to strengthen the floor. There were so many 4"x4" posts installed in the basement to shore up the floor, it was referred to as the Enchanted Forest by its members. The Clark Street fire station is remembered today by those who worked there. The memories include the challenges that the station provided. The firemen had to be strategic in maneuvering apparatus in and out of the Clark Street station; there was only a six inch clearance on each side of the doorway to fit the truck in. The Clark Street station was demolished due to the East-West Arterial that was being built through the center of the city. The fire station was directly in the path of the arterial plan. The new station was built two blocks away on the corner of Clark and Columbus Streets and opened August 1, 1974. It was built with two solid ground support truck bays to allow for possible expansion, a dormitory and kitchen. It was built to be an easily accessible station. It remains in that location today.

1918, AFD Hose Company No. 3, Clark Street Station

Clapp Hose Company

Clapp Hose Company was a private fire company owned by E. D. Clapp, owner of E. D. Clapp Manufacturing and E. D. Clapp Wagon Company. It was organized in 1887 and located on Genesee Street. Equipment and apparatus was lacking when Clapp Hose was first formed. During their initial year of service, the men within the company gathered pieces and parts that had been thrown away or otherwise deemed unusable around the city. The men of the E. D. Clapp Company made their own firefighting machine. Every man in the company had a hand in its design and completion. They surprised many with their homemade wagon which was somewhat lacking on flair. It was meant for service and in that capacity it performed adequately and the members of the Clapp Hose Company were proud. The Clapp Hose Company did not fall under the Fire Chief's regulations, however, Mr. Clapp instructed his men to follow orders from the Auburn Fire Chief Engineer or the Chief in Charge in order to maintain continuity of services.

Exempt Hose Company

Exempt Hose Company (aka: X.M.T. Hose Company) was organized May 2, 1867, and had 74 charter members. A group of veterans organized the hose company after the Civil War. Chief Jewhurst had a book of records from the Exempt Hose Company which listed the charter members. Records of the Exempt Hose Company indicated that General William H. Seward and General Clinton D. MacDougall were among its charter members. Many leading men in Auburn at the time were on the list, including Robert Dyer, Horace Knapp (Knapp, Peck & Thomson), and Gorton W. Allen (Henry & Allen). Later members included

1889, Protective Hose Company No. 3 (From the collection of the Cayuga Museum of History and Art)
Front Row L to R: Acting First Assistant Lou Tournier, Foreman F. W. Milliear, Second Assistant G. C. Smith.
Rear Row L to R: Firemen Haines, Boyle, Wickes, Morris, Meaker, Gard, Hughson, Titus, Thomas, Wassman, O'Brien, Hamilton, Bunnell, Cameron, French.

Henry D. Titus and George H. Nye. The fire company became incorporated in 1868, by NYS Legislature, and was located on Exchange Street near South Street. A petition was signed by a large group of Auburn citizens in March of 1880, and was presented to the Auburn Fire Commissioners for consideration. The Exempt Hose Company was received into the Auburn Fire Department and reorganized as the Protective Hose Company No. 3. Upon entry into the Auburn Fire Department, they requested to remain in the hose house on Exchange Street. Protective Hose Company No. 3 was active until August 29, 1893, when it was discharged from service.

Eagle Fire Company No.4/No.2

Photo courtesy of Michael Deyneka

The Eagle Fire Company No. 4 existed as far back as the 1840s in Auburn. The exact date of organization is not known. In 1856, the Eagle Fire Company fought the Auburn House fire. The Auburn House was a hotel located on East Genesee Street. The fire that evening was large and it brought many fire company members and citizens to its rescue. Sixteen members of Eagle Company were present. Eight members of the company worked inside the burning building to extinguish the flames. In 1868, it was reorganized as the Eagle Hose Company No. 2 and was located on the Paddock Block; on the corner of Lewis and Franklin Streets. John C. Winsor, born in 1850, was a member of the Eagle Hose Company No. 2. He would later go on to become a fireman in the paid department and achieved the rank of Captain with Hose Company No. 2 before his death in 1909. The company voted to disband by "mutual consent" in April of 1871. The Common Council officially disbanded Eagle Hose Company No. 2 in May of 1871. The contents of the hose house were moved to the Exempt Hose Company firehouse.

Westfall Hose Company

The Westfall Hose Company was an independent volunteer fire company named after Sidney Westfall with a hose house located at 34 Grant Avenue. Westfall Hose was organized in December of 1887. Sidney J. Westfall was born in September 1844, in Niles, NY. He was a Civil War veteran and fought with General William H. Seward's Ninth New York Heavy Artillery. During the Battle of Cedar Creek he received injuries to his arm necessitating amputation. Following his recovery and muster out of the military in 1865, Mr. Westfall taught school in the Town of Owasco. He was later appointed clerk of the Board of Supervisors, and in 1872, he was appointed as a deputy clerk. He was elected Cayuga County Clerk in 1875. Mr. Westfall was elected as Alderman in the City of Auburn in 1890-1891, and represented the 10th ward. He also served as Water Commissioner for the City of Auburn. Mr. Westfall made possible the organization of the Westfall Hose Company, which responded to fire alarms, participated in parades and attended exhibitions with the likes of the Logan Drum Corps. In 1887, they acquired a new, four wheeled hose cart. The spider cart weighed 815 lbs. and carried 600 feet of hose. It was purchased from the New England Hose Company. During a march to show off their new cart, the company carried a banner that read, "Westfall Hose, time nine minutes, but we got there just the same. Last but not least. Next time look out." The Westfall Hose Company disbanded in May 1892.

Auburn Prison Hose Company

The State of New York and the City of Auburn made an agreement that if there were any fires within the Prison walls, Auburn firefighters would respond. With the security at the prison and a delay in getting Auburn equipment into the prison, the State of New York purchased a pumper that was manned by the civilians living close to the prison. It was housed in a building adjacent to the prison. Response to fires in the prison was poor. The Warden had to give permission before the Auburn Prison Hose was allowed entrance to the institution. The warden waited until he could complete an evaluation of the fire before he would render a decision as to whether or not to admit the company. Today, the Auburn Correctional Facility has its own fire house and engine within the walls of the prison. A Correctional Officer is the Chief and one Correctional Officer is assigned for each shift to be in charge of a company made up of inmates. The Auburn Fire Department will still respond to a call at the request of the Warden.

Exempt Firemen's Association

An Act of Legislature in relation to firemen in cities and villages of New York State was passed on March 18, 1848, and amended and passed again on April 5, 1848. It provided qualified firemen who served for a specific period of time to be exempt from serving as a juror and from militia and military duty, except in case of insurrection or invasion. The Exempt Firemen's Association of the City of Auburn, NY was organized on January 5, 1882, with 37 members. Any firemen who served in a fire company for the necessary term of five years entitled him to an honorable discharge and qualified him for membership in the association. Evidence of qualification, usually in the form of an exempt certificate, provided the individual scrutiny by an investigating committee and an election for membership. If elected, membership continued throughout his life or until he withdrew his name or was suspended or expelled. The Exempt Firemen's Association was social in nature with a formalized mission and protocols. The association held regular meetings on the first Friday of each month, barring holidays. There was a joining fee incurred by those in membership; in 1890, the annual membership fee was 50 cents. The group sought to conduct themselves in honorable ways and with dignity, promoting the association's usefulness and the welfare of all its members.

In 1878, after many complaints by firemen and the public regarding the main quarters of the Auburn fire companies and of the condition of the hose house and requests for a new one, the matter was formally reviewed. On April 22, 1878, Alderman Horace M. Whipple introduced a resolution in the common council that the Committee on City Buildings examine the old hose house located in the rear of City Hall to consider a new house. The resolution was adopted. At the May 6th meeting, the committee reported that the old house was not suitable for the Fire Department. The roof was found to be in poor condition and leaked substantially, the rooms were narrow and contracted, the house as a whole was damp and musty and the overall condition was not found to be worth investing in repairs. On June 17th a motion was adopted that the Fire Department Committee be added to the Committee on City Buildings and look into a hew hose house to be built in the rear of City Hall. Plans and specifications were developed and approved. In January of 1879, a contractor was awarded the project. Several of the firemen were present at the common council meeting and as soon as they heard the good news they ran out of the council chamber to the hose house to celebrate and share the news with their fellow firemen. The men were elated at the prospect of having a new hose house. Within a few minutes there were holes large enough to admit a man punctured in the partitioned walls that separated the different quarters, and as some of the men indicated later, they had a runway between the rooms before the council had even adjourned their meeting! On the same night, Logan Hook and Ladder and Neptune Hose No. 1 marched into the old tannery on Market Street and on the following day Cayuga Hose No. 4 established their headquarters at Exempt Hose House on Exchange Street. Demolition began and within a few days, the old building was razed to the ground. The building of the new hose house progressed slowly due to the limited supply of bricks available in the city. An extension was provided to the contractor. The new central fire headquarters covering Market and Franklin Street was completed in March of 1880 (dedicated in 1879). The house held Neptune Hose Co. No. 1, Hook & Ladder Company Co. 1, Cayuga Hose Company No. 4, as well as the Chief.

During annual parades, conventions and inspections held in Auburn, the fire companies hosted visiting fire companies from other cities and provided accommodations, entertainment, friendship and camaraderie. For events held in other cities, Auburn fire companies were often extended the same accommodations by the hosting fire companies. The partnerships that formed across the fire companies of the various cities lasted years and fostered a sense of family that extended beyond the city limits. That feeling of camaraderie between fire companies remained evident years later during the CANUSA/CANUS games that began in 1976. Auburn, NY and Orillia, Ontario, Canada joined in a Sister City program that included athletic competitions between the two cities, the location of which alternated annually between the two cities. Many of us remember and participated in the city-to-city events. Many city departments joined their sister departments, and the Auburn Fire Department was no exception. Auburn Fire Department families travelled en masse to Orillia, Ontario, Canada. Orillia Fire Department families provided accommodations at their houses for the visiting Auburn families and others joined together with them at area campgrounds. We fondly remember our family traveling to the Orillia games that first year and in subsequent years. Friendships were made among the firefighter families. The games included a range of athletic competitions and sports. The event also included softball games between the two fire departments. The two fire departments exchanged mementos and tokens of friendship that remain a source for fond reflection of our time with the sister city.

Public Safety Building – Fire Department Headquarters, Police Station and City Jail

In 1930, after 50 years of service, it was decided that the Fire Department headquarters needed to be replaced. Safety had become a concern and the condition of the existing building was considered unsafe. Additionally, the evolution of fire apparatus and technology was such that the logistics of maneuvering the trucks in and out became problematic. The building had been laid out during a time when the department had horses and motorized equipment did not yet exist. It was time to modernize and construct a building that was more efficient and could better meet the needs of the department. The new public safety building would house the Fire Department headquarters, Police station and City Jail. The property on which it would be located would replace the old City Hall, adjacent fire house and the block acquired from Hollister & Noble. It would encompass areas of North, Franklin and Market Streets. The building would remain located on the original Hardenbergh property; a historic location, to be sure. During a Common Council meeting in January 1930, prior to the official opening of the new City Hall, it was decided to employ an architect to prepare plans and specifications, along with an estimated cost of the project. Since they had already planned and designed the new City Hall, the firm of Coolidge, Shepley, Bulfinch & Abbott, of Boston, Massachusetts, was also chosen as the architects for the new public safety building.

Coolidge, Shepley, Bulfinch & Abbott were world renowned engineers and architects. The founder of the company, Henry Hobson Richardson, was known for his collaborative design and approach to detail. They designed Boston's Trinity Church and the first buildings at Stanford University. The firm operated as Coolidge, Shepley, Bulfinch & Abbott from 1924-1952. During that period they designed projects for the Rockefeller Institute in New York and New Jersey. They also designed a new medical school for the University of Virginia. They had continuing work at Harvard University, including the seven Harkness River Houses, of which Dunster House, with its distinctive form, is considered the most notable. Today the firm operates as Shepley Bulfinch, and their architectural designs remain innovative and award-winning with a history that includes designs of many notable buildings across the nation.

The plans for a new public safety building were completed in July 1930 and were in keeping with the City Hall on South Street as much as possible. The exterior designs were similar in style and material, while the interior was planned to align with the services each department would provide. The estimated maximum cost of the project was $325,000. They were to be designed in a similar fashion and style. The heads of each department approved the building specifications. The Auburn Fire and Police Chiefs approved their designated areas, and the NYS Department of Corrections approved the jail design. Before finalizing and adopting the plans, Mayor Osborne called for a public hearing to be held the following week. Three people spoke at the public hearing held on July 22, 1930; Charles Heiser of Mattie Street, Charles Holihan of State Street and Francis Marshall. Mr. Heiser spoke on behalf of a local union of the Brotherhood of Electrical Workers and felt the city needed a new building and requested that all labor be completed by Auburn citizens wherever possible. Mr. Holihan, a former alderman, felt the proposition should be submitted to a referendum. Mr. Marshall, on behalf of the Central Labor Union and representing organized labor, felt the estimated cost was too high, but requested the use of Auburn contractors and labor if the project moved forward. Mayor Osborne indicated that, as much as possible, local labor would be used. He anticipated construction would employ many people. He informed those present that the cost per cubic foot showed that the estimated cost was not exorbitant. The plans were approved and adopted by the end of July 1930.

During construction, the Fire Department operated out of the city garage on Franklin Street. The old buildings on the site were razed beginning in August 1930. The Police station was built facing North Street with a small park in front. The entire complex was built in the colonial style, as was City Hall. Just as City Hall, it was constructed using the same water-struck brick, also known as "Harvard" brick. Such bricks are molded by water instead of sand processes. Both City Hall and the public safety complex had slate roofs installed, copper cornices and a cupola. The original design of the police and fire station building included large pillars of colonial design, but these were modified as the plans were finalized.

The Police Department portion of the building was a three-story construction. The basement was designed to hold a rifle and pistol range, a tramps room, utilities and storage. On the first floor, entering from North Street, a main corridor led to the offices of the City recorder, City judge, stenographer, clerk and courtroom on the left. On the right side were the offices of the Chief of Police, the police clerk, the file room, the captain's office and the radio room. In the rear of the Police Department building was a three-car garage, arranged so that an offender could be driven into the garage, taken to the docket room, booked and locked up in the jail. The garage faced Market Street. On the Franklin Street side, opposite the garage was the city jail. From the outside, passersby could not discern the area to be a jail. There were no bars on the outside windows. The garage and jail formed a connecting link between the Police and Fire Department. The second floor held a police gymnasium, locker room, lounge, showers and lavatories. There was also a meeting room. The third floor provided a smaller footprint and allowed for some storage.

The Fire Department portion of the building was built with three stories. The basement held the boiler room, utilities, hose drying racks and a lift, as well as Fire Department and Public Works storage areas. The main portion on the first floor consisted of one large

Relic found in wall during bathroom renovation years later.

Officers Desk, Bunk and Sliding Pole

room capable of housing eight pieces of fire apparatus. The building was constructed as a pillarless, suspended construction. The only poles in the room were the six along the walls which were installed to permit the firemen to slide down from the floors above when the alarm sounded. The six sliding poles were constructed of brass. There were four large doors facing Market Street and Franklin Street so that the fire trucks could be driven in through either side. East of the main room, facing Market Street was the instrument room which held the switchboard and the recording equipment of the fire alarm system. To the rear of that room was the repair shop with pits. The repair shop was large enough to hold any of the fire apparatus. A separate section was designed for the office of the Fire Chief. The second floor was built with 32 windows and housed a dormitory, locker room, drying room, storage room, sleeping quarters and showers and lavatories. Separate rooms were constructed for the Assistant Chiefs and Captains. The third floor was designed to be a large open area to afford the department flexibility in the use of the space. The Fire Department building ended 30 feet from the Ramsey feed store. The space between the two was used to create an inclined concrete driveway from Market Street to Franklin Street. There are basements under both buildings and an attic space as well. The original plans were such that trucks could drive into the basement through service entrances from Franklin Street and remove ashes and other debris from the basements of both the Police and Fire Departments.

The building was completed before the end of 1931. The Fire Department headquarters housed five fire companies and their apparatus. The Police Station address was 46 North Street and the Fire Department address was 19 Market Street (23 Market Street today). The

total cost of the building was $317,130.89, including construction, architect fees, partial equipment and interest on loans. The building was to be dedicated December 21, 1931. A horrific fire in the Hislop Block, which resulted in the death of Lieutenant Irving Dwyer and nearly a half million dollars in damages, occurred on the day the new Public Safety Building was to be formally dedicated. Mayor Osborne stated "These men have dedicated these buildings by giving their lives in the fulfillment of duty and our sadness at the news makes it seem to me desirable that we call off the formal ceremonies we had planned." Major John Warner, head of the New York State Police, who was to have been the principal speaker, commented on the new building, stating "This building can and will stand alone. Its construction, its architecture and its beauty will remain for years. The Police and Fire Departments housed within it must struggle, each and every man, to maintain a standard of dignity, efficiency and attention to duty in keeping with the demands of the people as expressed in this building." In lieu of a formal dedication ceremony, the new Public Safety Building was opened for inspection by the public.

The Thomas Mott Osborne statue that stands outside the Police Department entrance today, was moved to that location in 1949. It was originally installed on the grounds of East High School on Franklin Street in 1930. The statue was the target of several acts of vandalism, and it was decided to move it to the Public Safety Building.

Thomas Mott Osborne, 1859-1926
Prophet and Pioneer of Prison Reform

Over the course of the last decade, the City of Auburn has spent a significant amount of money on upgrades, maintenance repairs and improvements on the current police and fire station headquarters building. Faced with a significant predicted financial need to maintain a safe and effective environment for the public safety departments, the City is forced to accept the possibility that the current building may no longer be able to sustain the Police and Fire Departments' needs. The significant renovations required and the cost of the repairs may add up to more than development of a new building. The strength of the Fire Department floor is of particular concern. It was designed and built in an era when fire engines were much lighter and had fewer components. Cracks have developed and some have led to leaks into a lower floor of the facility. A working group was formed and conducted a series of meetings and site visits with various City and County departments including, but not limited to; Fire, Police, City Courts, Emergency Management office (EMO) and Probation. Through a joint

City and County project committee, an inventory and assessment of current building infrastructure and operating needs was completed during 2015. The City released a Request For Proposal (RFP) for development and construction of a public safety building. While there is much work to be done to bring any plan to fruition, it seems probable that Auburn may have a new Public Safety Building in its future.

Training Towers / Facilities

A firefighter's training never ends. From the first day through the last, education and training elements are ongoing and evolving with new technologies, hazards and management skills. Frank Hughson was an instrumental part of Auburn's initial fire instruction and training program. He was sent to New York City for six weeks to learn training techniques and became a lead instructor for the department. Chief Edward Jewhurst contributed primary design elements to the plans for a new training facility. Chief Jewhurst and Fire Commissioner Haeffner traveled to Syracuse and directly observed the firemen complete their daily training. It became apparent that the City of Auburn would benefit from a multi-story structure in order to drill on ladder scaling and rescue techniques, along with movement and drills within the building itself. In 1906, a five-story training tower was constructed on Franklin Street behind the main station. The training tower was constructed of wood and was 63 feet high and 15 feet square. It provided firemen a chance to train

1948, Training Tower

and learn their trade. They would practice pulling hose lines from the ground to the top floor, ladder raising by hand and using ropes, and climbing of the pompier ladders. They learned how to descend the building with ropes, jump into the safety nets and practiced rescue techniques. They practiced use of their smoke masks and artificial "breathers". The tower proved to be extremely valuable to the men. The training tower reinforced the firefighters' skills and kept them fine-tuned. By 1915, the building was beginning to show its age, and was determined by local authorities to be unsafe, and had to be razed. The plan was to erect a new training tower on the site using steel from the Groton Bridge Company. However, when the new fire station headquarters was built in 1930, there was no room for a training tower. Chief Washburn advocated publically regarding the need for a training facility. It would be more than three decades before the Auburn Fire Department had another formal training facility.

The need for a fire training facility in the city was expressed by Fire Department officers and personnel many times over the years. The logistics of location, funding, etc. seemed to thwart any movement toward making the training area a possibility. However, in 1966, a training facility became a reality for the Auburn Fire Department. The old Bowen Products factory on Canal Street was out of business and their buildings were owned by the City. With the support of the City Manager, along with City Council members and other city departments, the former Bowen Products location became a possibility. The upper area was cleared to expose the hydrant and the road was leveled and made to be accessible by fire engines. This area was a good location for pumper training and testing. The lower area was worked on and provided access to one of the buildings for ladder training and rappelling. The sprinkler system was activated in a large room of one building with the assistance of one of the firemen who had a plumbing background. Parts and pieces for a

1966, Canal Street Training School

sprinkler system were taken from other parts of the abandoned building in order to make the one area functional. The old metal house was transformed into a smoke training school. With the help of several firemen who had carpentry backgrounds, movable lightweight partitions were installed in the building, creating obstacles for the training experience. The movable partition enhanced the training experience since the configuration was always changing. Due to its location so close to downtown and with buildings so close by, the metal house was not used for actual fire training, as it would have introduced a hazardous risk that the department and City were not willing to accept. The smoke training in the house was very effective.

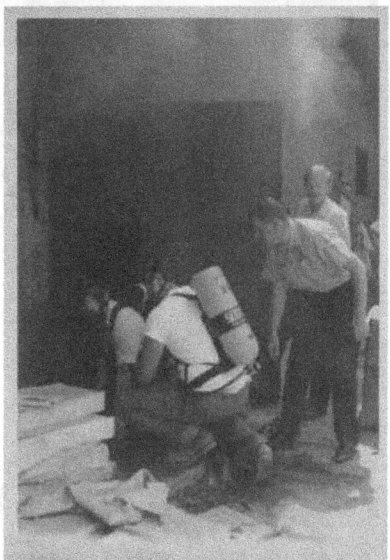

Top: c. 1968, AFD Training Class
Bottom: Training Officers Bill Jacobs and Mike Harmon conducting instruction session

Over the years many firefighters received training and benefitted from the Canal Street training facility. It was an asset to the department, but its days were numbered, when in 1977 it fell at the hands of arsonists. Auburn had suffered four fires in June of 1977 that were identified as "suspicious". One of those fires claimed the training facility on Canal Street. Two 16-year-old teens were subsequently charged with setting the facility on fire. Arson cost the Fire Department its physical structure and established programming from that location. The training facility was lost and would not be replaced for many years.

The current Cayuga County Training Center and Fire Tower site opened in 2003 and is located on Quarry Road in Auburn. The site provides advanced training for Auburn Fire Department personnel and surrounding municipality first responders in Cayuga County. Training is essential to firefighters and is an ongoing process throughout their careers. The minimum standards of training are extensive and cover a wide range of fire science. Emergency Medical Services (EMS), fire pump systems, hazardous material handling, vehicle extraction, rope rescue, high angle rescue, building collapse rescue, trench rescue,

Top: Cayuga County Training Center and Fire Tower
Bottom: Lt. Jeff Clark at Training Center with Firemen Brian Donovan, Jeff Hutchinson, Dan Guzalak

confined space rescue and construction materials and methods learning take place. Thermal imaging cameras, foam, ventilation techniques, use of new tools and safety techniques are also part of the training received. The composition and behavior of fires changes as new materials and technologies are used in residential and commercial settings. Firefighters must study and learn how such new materials react and how best to stop them. The training center provides firefighters from Auburn and surrounding areas with crucial education and opportunities to enhance their skills.

The City of Auburn Fire Department currently has an Insurance Services Office (ISO) Class 2 rating. The ISO collects information on fire-protection efforts in communities throughout the United States, which also proves useful in many aspects of insurance underwriting. The ISO takes into account many factors when determining the local fire suppression rating; staffing, apparatus, capabilities, documented training, pre-fire planning, water supply and response times are among them. A community's investment in fire mitigation is a proven and reliable predictor of future fire losses. The ISO Class rating often assists in determining a homeowner's or business's cost on fire insurance premiums. The Auburn Fire Department is in the top 1% of the 2,517 New York fire departments graded by ISO.

Propane Tank Live Fire Training

Photo courtesy of Anita Luisi Colvin

CHIEFS

Engine 3 Far Left: Charles Zambito, Francis Bunnell (Driver), Ernest Porter, Tomas Burke.
Engine 4 Rear Truck: Captain James Monahan, John Burger, James Turner, Richard Walsh.
Front Left: Asst. Chief, Chief Bergan, Paul Kierst, Frederick Smart, Thomas Gard.
Front Right – Drivers and line of firemen: Robert Chabau, George Reidy, Richard Gunger, Bernard Oury, William Maywalt, Charles Hardy, Charles Conboy, Leonard Bochenek, Glen Adams Jr.

Edward J. Jewhurst

Edward J. Jewhurst was born in Auburn, New York on July 20, 1853. He was the son of Edward B. and Jane (Lynd) Jewhurst. He had two sisters, Mary and Sarah, and one brother, Joseph. His father was born in England and lived in Syracuse for a time before coming to Auburn. He had a large stable of horses and was a prominent horse dealer and devotee of horse racing. He was well-known among turfmen. Edward B. Jewhurst held the mile record in the city with a horse known as "Sorrel Dapper" in 1865; as a result, he became known as "Dapper" Jewhurst. He trained horses for years and was the lessee of a track in Auburn and also of a driving park in Syracuse. Edward's mother, Jane Lynd, was born in Ireland and moved to Auburn when she was still a child. His brother, Joe, was a Captain in the Auburn Fire Department and had 30 years of service. He was quiet and unassuming and very well-liked by his fellow firemen. Edward J. Jewhurst attended public schools and worked in the printing business. He worked on the Northern Christian Advocate, the Bulletin and also worked in the offices of the Advertiser for several years. He married Helen Steele and had five children; Jennie, William, Mary, John and Alice. They lived on Lincoln Street and later moved to Steel Street. Edward J. Jewhurst started his own print business with a fellow printer, Frank E. Plumb; "Jewhurst and Plumb Printing" at 3 State Street. They completed book and print job services in Auburn. When the First National Bank of Auburn failed, it resulted in the subsequent failure of the printing business due to lack of capital.

Photo courtesy of Anita Luisi Colvin

Edward J. Jewhurst began as a torch boy with the Logan Hook and Ladder Fire Company in 1869. In 1872, he became a firefighter with the Cayuga Hose Company. Jewhurst was elected First Assistant of Cayuga Hose Company No. 4 in 1875. During the Centennial year of 1876, Jewhurst traveled to Philadelphia with Chief Engineer Morris, S. W. Milk, Lansing D. Wilder and John Davie, on a ten-day trip to explore the City of Brotherly Love. While there, they made stops at historical landmarks and relics and visited fire companies throughout the area. In 1879, he was promoted to Assistant Chief of the Auburn Fire Department. At the time of election to his new post, a dinner was held in his honor at the newly opened Cosgrove and Miller's hotel, located at 6 State Street. A variety of friends, Cayuga Hose members, Chief Engineer Morris and others gathered in the dining room and listened as Fire Commissioner Wilder addressed the group. He spoke kindly of Edward Jewhurst and indicated that he was a man whose frequent calls to public service had been a source of pride to his fellow members of Hose Four and other friends. He expressed pride in the fact that he had been elected from their ranks to the position of First Assistant of the Fire Department. Jewhurst was presented with a silver service trumpet and a gold badge, inscribed "First Assistant Engineer, Auburn Fire Department" as a token of their high regard for him. Edward Jewhurst was rapidly gaining the respect and trust of his fellow firefighters, City officials and other officers in the department. In 1880, the Fire Commissioners appointed Edward J. Jewhurst as the successor to the late Chief Engineer Morris. He continued as Chief, and on January 1, 1894, became Auburn's first paid Fire Department Chief. He remained in that position until his retirement in 1926, after 54 years of service, 45 of them as Fire Chief. Department documents have him recorded as being 5'10" tall, 220 pounds.

Often referred to by his comrades as "The Grand Old Man", Chief Jewhurst was an efficient firefighter. He was a strict disciplinarian, but tempered his commands with common sense and compassion. His men followed his instructions to the letter, putting their best work into their tasks. He was a chief to the firefighters, but also balanced an element of friendship and respect that produced cooperation across the department. He exhibited true leadership skills and always directed in such a way that his "boys" followed him. He was known never to ask a fireman to take a risk that he would not have taken himself and often endangered his own life rather than detail one of his men. He was like a father to the department and was always alert for their safety. His management of the department produced harmony in and confidence from his men.

Edward Jewhurst was one of the original organizers of the Auburn Lodge of Elks. During the 1922 Firemen's Convention, a reception was given in the Elks' Temple in honor of Chief Jewhurst. During the reception, he was presented with a mounted Elks' emblem. It was an elk tooth set in solid gold with embossed emblems and an elk's head in platinum with a diamond; two rubies served as eyes. George Benham of the Auburn Lodge of Elks gave a second presentation, a life card bound in gold, making Edward Jewhurst a lifetime member. In acceptance of the presentations, Chief Jewhurst humbly thanked those gathered and told of the beginning of his association with a local Auburn fire company as a torch boy prior to his becoming a firefighter in 1872. Chief Jewhurst was also a member of the Knights of Pythias.

Chief Jewhurst often told stories of his time spent in Pennsylvania. He left Auburn around 1870, to find fame and fortune in the oil business in Pennsylvania. He had no such luck, but he came away with some entertaining stories of his adventures. In Titusville, PA he was a boarder at the American Hotel. He told of hobnobbing with J. D. Archbold, the

American capitalist and one of the country's earliest oil refiners. He also told of one particular encounter with J. D. Rockefeller, the business magnate and co-founder of Standard Oil Company. The story was told numerous times over the years and while the details sometimes differed, the essential portions remained consistent. The incident happened when "John D." was a hard-working man and while the Eddie Jewhurst was seeking his fortune among the oil fields of Pennsylvania. Edward Jewhurst loved oranges, but was always a bit timid about ordering them in restaurants, as he felt amateurish in manipulating a spoon, lacking confidence in himself in some of the finer points of table manners. He was quoted as saying,

> "I was eating all my meals in restaurants and finally decided to master the art of eating an orange or die in the attempt. One day I purchased a dozen of the fruit, took them to my room and began practicing. By the time I had eaten five or six, I felt experienced enough to meet the best orange eater in the world. Accordingly, the next morning, confident in my newly acquired accomplishment, I sauntered into the restaurant and boldly asked for an orange. The place was empty except for a few waiters standing about. Before my waiter returned with my orange, a stranger entered and sat opposite me at my table. He picked up the menu and scanned it. My waiter brought me my orange. I picked up a spoon and launched the attack. I was full of confidence. I had no more than started when, 'zip', something happened. A good-sized stream of orange juice suddenly shot out of my orange and raced across the table and hit the stranger straight in the eye. 'Good shot, young man,' said the stranger. I found out later he was John D. Rockefeller."

Mr. Jewhurst was working as a foreman in the press room of the Auburn Advertiser at the time of his appointment as Chief in 1880. He said that he had a gong hitched up to the fire alarm system and kept an extra pair of boots in the composing room to be ready in case of fire. He would chuckle as he told the story and recalled that there was a hack stand across from the newspaper office on State Street and they would keep a horse on hand in case the Chief had to go to a fire.

Chief Jewhurst also relayed a story of a time shortly after he became Chief, when he had just returned to the press room of Auburn Advertiser after attending a fire in the foundry of the Osborne plant. He was busily at work setting the print when Mayor Osborne walked into the press room praising the department for the efficient work that had been conducted at the plant. He extended his hand to shake the Chief's hand. Chief Jewhurst explained to the Mayor that he wouldn't want to shake hands with him and stretched out his hands to reveal printer's ink covering them. The Mayor replied, "Give it here. I always like to shake a hand soiled by honest toil." As they shook hands, another fire alarm was sounded and the Chief had to run off.

Chief Jewhurst loved horses and he recorded the name, age and amount paid for every horse he purchased for the department. He took after his father in his love for horses. He was a great judge of a horse's strength and usefulness. He could recollect the names and characteristics of each of the horses in the department at any given time; at times there were upwards of almost 50 horses in the department. He was often heard advising people about the risk of purchasing an old fire horse. He would tell of a time he was following a fire truck to a fire and saw one of the old fire horses drawing a load of wood along the street. The horse heard the clanging of the fire wagon bell, bolted on his driver and raced off to the scene of the fire. It would appear that you cannot take the fire service out of a horse!

On January 7, 1885, following a business meeting of the Cayuga Fire Patrol, about 50 people were invited to gather together in the Cayuga Fire Patrol parlor; the purpose was to recall the career of "Eddie" Jewhurst. The group reviewed Chief Jewhurst's career, the various companies he was a member of (Logan Hook & Ladder as a torch boy, Seward Hose/Cayuga Hose) and his progression through the department. They presented him with a badge as a token of their fondness for him as a fireman. It was reported to be a most expensive and elegant badge, made by Braxum and was composed of a bar engraved with his name and a pendant disc that read "Chief Engineer, Auburn, N.Y." In the center of the badge were multiple fire department symbols, finely engraved. The group then retired to the carriage house of the hose company and a casual sharing of stories ensued. Healy Burlingame played his banjo for the group. They called for John E. Tarte to tell a story. He got up and spoke of several funny incidents from Jewhurst's younger days. He explained a funny story about how Eddie James Jewhurst earned a doughnut when he was a small youngster. He also told a tale of how Eddie had literally plastered the billiard bald head of an ancient uncle. Another member of the group illustrated the baldness that Jewhurst's uncle had when he waved his hand in a gesture toward and around George B. Wright's head. Wright, a neighbor, jumped to his feet in frustration. He huffed and said that he enjoyed a good story, thought that it was funny himself and didn't blame the company for laughing, but that he did object to being made the illustrious example, a living illustration, in the bald-headed story. At this display, the group laughed even louder.

In his Annual Report of 1893 to the City Council, just prior to the department becoming paid, Chief Jewhurst outlined the shortcomings of the department's apparatus and number of volunteer men responding. He pointed out that a paid department, with trained men who would be ready to respond at any hour, would be more effective to the City. The Council was alerted to the fact that, with few exceptions, Auburn was one of the only cities among those with comparable populations, which still primarily used hand-drawn apparatus. He encouraged steps to be taken to modernize and better protect the property and lives in Auburn.

Chief Jewhurst was a man who encouraged, supported and participated in a 'hands on' approach to tasks around the Fire Department. Firemen cared for the horses, did carpentry work and repairs within the department and their quarters and any other tasks that were required. In 1899, the Fire Department was given old bricks by the City of Auburn. Chief Jewhurst had the firefighters use the old bricks to pave the entrance to headquarters on the Franklin Street side. It was a great improvement and the community took pride in their accomplishment.

Chief Jewhurst implemented a series of regulations for his men to ensure the integrity of the department and the respect of its men. In 1905, he established a rule that forbade members of the department from frequenting saloons while in uniform except in the strict discharge of public duty. Also in 1905, Chief Jewhurst inaugurated a system of monthly inspections of the manufacturing plants in the city by Captains in the Fire Department. During the inspections, reports were made to provide information regarding ingress and egress, fire escapes and any other information that would be beneficial in case of fire. The documentation that resulted from these inspections would prove invaluable for future fires.

In its early years, the Auburn Fire Department consisted of permanent firemen and callmen. Permanent firefighters worked 24 hours a day, except 48 hours a month. A fireman lived at the fire company and was all but denied a family and home of his own to enjoy. Callmen were required to sleep in the fire quarters at night and were expected to respond during the day when an alarm was sounded. Chief Jewhurst understood and acknowledged the hardships of such a work configuration. He advocated for, and implemented, a platoon system during his tenure. The platoon system was a schedule where a fireman worked four days, had 24 hours off and then worked four nights. This ensured adequate staffing and helped alleviate fatigue. The platoon underwent several modifications, and the system remains in use today in the Auburn Fire Department. Current firefighters work two days, then two nights, followed by four days/nights off.

Chief Jewhurst saw the Auburn Fire Department develop from hand drawn engines to horse drawn engines to motorized equipment. He was a forward-thinking man who embraced the growth and development of his department through the adoption of new techniques, equipment and other innovative solutions. In 1907, Chief Jewhurst was one of the first chiefs in the country to have a motorized car to go to fires. The famous old

Cameron, known as "red devil", made its first appearance in Auburn as Chief Jewhurst's car. It was used from 1907-1909. The Cameron was a four cylinder car and it had a reputation within the department. It only failed to get to one fire. Many stories are told of amusing incidents that occurred while leading the way to fires. In 1910, Chief Jewhurst removed the Cameron from service and replaced it with a Buick, four cylinder speedster. The Buick was old, but reliable, and made it to all the fires.

Miniature replica of business sections in Auburn

During 1909, Chief Edward Jewhurst came up with an idea for the members of the Auburn Fire Department to create a miniature reproduction of the City of Auburn, New York, focusing on the business sections. The idea was not brought forward by Mr. Jewhurst as a novelty. His idea for the miniature city was to provide value to himself and the men of the department when they were called to fight a fire. The construction of the miniature provided the firefighters accurate knowledge and awareness of the buildings, shops and manufacturing plants. It became a visual reference of the business sections and buildings in Auburn. He thought if the city could be reproduced in miniature, then the men would have a chance, when not otherwise engaged, to make a study of the buildings they might be called on someday for a fire. He brought the idea to Captain Frank Hughson who was the drillmaster for the Pompier life-saving corps and to other members of the department. All were in agreement regarding the benefits that could be gained by such an exercise. The work began and most of the men of the department participated in the project. It included the business sections between Market and Genesee Streets on the east and Court Street on the west. The southern boundary line ran to Lincoln Street, south on South Street to the Women's Educational and Industrial union and ran north down State Street and North Streets to include the bulk of the blocks of that part of Auburn. The miniature city was made of wooden blocks and all other types of suitable material, and was built to scale. Every inch on the miniature represented 25 feet of the city as it stood. Construction included every window, identification of elevator shafts, all exits and doors, scuttle holes and chimneys. The exterior of the buildings corresponded to the actual buildings. The 'build' took approximately one year and was completed in 1910. The business districts of Auburn had blocks adjoining blocks and factories and shops close to each other. There were many difficulties to contend with in the event of a fire. They were not able to do away with such obstacles, but were able to study them in their miniature city and able to thoroughly familiarize themselves with the conditions as they existed. The miniature city was studied regularly and proved to be very beneficial.

July, 1910, Convention Photo (Chief Jewhurst, front row second from left).

Chief Jewhurst worked to institute preventative requirements into the local codes for the city, including requirements of fire walls and monthly inspections of factories and businesses. He was primarily responsible for a fire tower built on Market Street that was used to train the firefighters in scaling and rescuing tactics as well as net work and window-to-window ladder work. He requested fire alarm telegraph registers be placed in each fire station to ensure greater certainty in the receiving of alarms. He supported the purchase of a smoke protector for the department. The protector was a helmet that was fitted with an air tube and connection so that a fireman was able to stay within a building longer and not be forced to evacuate as quickly due to smoke conditions. The helmet was purchased from the Meyer Supply Company of St. Louis, Missouri for $175. In 1919, Chief Jewhurst acquired an experimental smoke mask which the department had occasion to use during a fire at the Advertiser-Journal plant fire. The mask allowed the fireman to move through the smoke-filled rooms of the Advertiser-Journal building and he did not suffer from the suffocating black smoke. The mask was known as an army smoke mask, but differed from the ones used by service men, in that it had no nose or mouth piece. It fit securely over the face. A canister containing chemicals purified the air being breathed in by the firemen. The purified air proved useful against gases and smoke as well. The only gas that the mask was found to be ineffective against was ammonia. The masks were found to be simplistic and comfortable. The unit was not bulky and the men could breathe easily in the mask. They proved so beneficial that the chief ordered 12 smoke masks for use by the department companies. Once acquired, the chief ensured successful implementation of the new devices by identifying one man in each platoon assigned to the position of "gas hound". The gas hound used the mask and provided instruction and gas mask drills for other "gas hounds", captains and lieutenants within each company. Chief Jewhurst frequently took opportunities to educate the public regarding fire prevention activities and precautions that citizens could take to avoid fires.

During World War I, Chief Jewhurst recognized the increasing price of bluestone and zinc as a result of war-time use. Bluestone and zinc were necessary for the fire alarm telegraph system, and the price for these resources had more than doubled and was expected to go up even higher. Chief Jewhurst repeatedly requested the installation of a storage battery system. He acknowledged that the initial startup cost was large but that the cost of maintenance after purchase and installation would be almost non-existent. The electric light utility agreed to furnish the city with the necessary electricity free of charge. He appealed to the City to give up the "old-fashioned gravity system" and make the move toward the storage battery system.

During his time in the Fire Department, Chief Jewhurst compiled a collection of data relating to Auburn fires, dating back to 1816. He gathered fire information from the infancy of the Auburn Fire Companies and recorded it for future generations. The first entry in his collection was December 21, 1816, for a fire at "Samuel Dill's Saw and Carding Mill, near big dam E. side, destroyed". His historical collection continued with an entry for each of the fire alarms the department responded to during his tenure. His log book of Auburn Fire Department 'runs' begins in March of 1879, and ends December of 1925. It is a handwritten journal outlining details of every fire call from the time he was promoted to Assistant Chief until his retirement. For each fire call, the log includes; date, hour, box (fire alarm box # or method of notification), location/address, description (structure type), owner, occupant, origin, loss (buildings/contents), insurance paid (buildings/contents), hours and minutes on duty, hose laid (feet of fire/chemical), ladders used (feet), chemical charges (engine/hand), apparatus used (companies), attendance (companies) and remarks. Each entry carefully documented in his neat handwriting, Chief Jewhurst guaranteed that the history of the Auburn Fire Department would be preserved. He took pride in his collection and documentation; it was a cherished record book then and remains a prized possession in the department today.

The Chief retired in January of 1926, and wintered in Lakeland, Florida for a few months at the beginning of his retirement. He was known to stop by the local fire headquarters in Lakeland and visit, swapping stories with the firefighters. They would discuss antique and modern firefighting methods, and he would always tell them about the Auburn firefighters.

During his time as Auburn Fire Department Chief, Edward Jewhurst commanded many large fires, including the 1903 Garden Street fire that damaged the high school and 14 other buildings, The 1904 J. H. Osborne residence, the 1906 fire at the Temple Court Building and Columbus block, the Twine Factory of International Harvester in 1907, the 1910 Lincoln Flats fire, and the Cayuga County Court House in 1922. One of his mottos was "Get to the fire before the fire gets you."

Upon and after his retirement, Chief Jewhurst received many accolades and a variety of receptions and events were held in his honor. On June 21, 1926, a reception was held at headquarters. The event included the engine corps, regular firefighters, call members, city officials and the new Chief, Frank B. Hughson. The former Chief Jewhurst was presented with a gold watch and his wife received a set of Roger's silver. A luncheon was served, songs were sung by Captain Patrick Morrissey's son, Billy Morrissey, and he was accompanied by Freddy Webb. Mayor Roy A. Weld spoke: "We are gathered to pay our respects to honor and welcome back from the south, former Chief Edward J. Jewhurst who sits with smiling face among us. By hard work and study of his duty, he became one of the greatest fire chiefs of the country. His methods have been copied by other departments, a great tribute to his ability. You boys are doing the right thing. It shows that your hearts are in the proper place. From the boys, Chief, I present this token of affection, esteem and best wishes. I present this watch with the good wishes of all of us for your future happiness."

Chief Jewhurst's response was brief and emotional: "Mr. Mayor and brother firemen, I never expected this. I am really obligated to you for many favors received which I think were not deserved. I appreciate this gift coming from the source it does. I shall always prize it. I'm really not deserving of all this boys. You're too good to me. I'll never forget it. Never."

Chief Hughson followed up, saying: "We of the Fire Department know differently. We know that the hard part of many a rocky road was smoothed over for us by Edward J.

Jewhurst. Whatever the Fire Department of Auburn is today is due to his efforts. Whatever the Fire Department of Auburn will be for years to come will also be due to his efforts. No structure is any stronger than the foundation on which it rests. Edward J. Jewhurst built well. We have got a solid foundation and it will stand secure for years to come."

At a Kiwanis Club Dinner in August of 1926, Edward J. Jewhurst was the honored guest. During the evening, Chief Jewhurst said, "I did not relinquish my trust entirely because of age, as termed nowadays. I wouldn't call myself an old fellow. I have had my ups and downs and carry scars as a reminder of my firefighting days, but I am happy to say that fortune has been good to me, and so far, my physical health. I ask no odds of anyone."

When the new City Hall was opened and dedicated in April of 1930, Edward Jewhurst was believed to be the only living survivor of the men who served under the administration of David Munson Osborne, whose memory was being perpetuated by the living monument of the new City Hall for future generations to come. D. M. Osborne was the Mayor of Auburn, New York from 1879-1880. D. M. Osborne appointed Edward Jewhurst to the position of Chief of the Auburn Fire Department after he had been recommended by the Board of Fire Commissioners. Chief Jewhurst served under 16 mayors:

- David M. Osborne (1879-1880)
- Cyrenus Wheeler, Jr. (1881-1886)
- Mortimer V. Austin (1887-1888)
- Cyrenus Wheeler, Jr. (1889-1990)
- David Wadsworth, Jr. (1891-1892)
- John E. McIntosh (1893-1894)
- Orlando Lewis (1895-1900)
- William C. Burgess (1901-1902)
- Thomas M. Osborne (1903-1905)
- E. Clarence Aiken (1906-1907)
- C. August Koenig (1908-1909)
- Thomas H. O'Neill (1910-1913)
- Charles W. Brister (1915)
- Mark L. Koon (1916)
- Adam P. Burkhart (1920-1921)
- Roy A. Weld (1924-1927)

Regarding the retirement of Chief Jewhurst, City Manager John P. Jaeckel, issued a statement,

> "He has performed the duties of a fireman in the City of Auburn, volunteer and permanent, and held every active position in the department from private to chief for a period of 54 years and as chief for 45 years. This record of fire service is unusual in the long years which it covers and exemplary in its faithfulness and devotion to public interest. Its parallel cannot be found in the entire country. As administrative head of the Fire Department, I have been in daily contact with Chief Jewhurst for six years. I have been in accord with him always in all of his undertakings for the betterment of department efficiency. His ideals for an efficient firefighting organization have been realized during the past six years in the complete motorization of department equipment and the adoption of the two platoon system. He retires with satisfaction of having by his own efforts built up this splendid organization. In his retirement, the city loses a conscientious, able public servant. His reputation as a fire chief is nation-wide. He is known from Maine to California and his counsel has been sought by many cities in matters pertaining to fire department problems. As evidence of the esteem in which he has been held, I cite his continuous service under all administration of whatever political faith. Administrations of the city government have been fairly equally divided between the two political parties during the past three decades. Chief Jewhurst has not only been kept in the service, but has always had the cooperation of all administrations. This long meritorious service is a bright spot in the history of our city government."

Edward J. Jewhurst had a stroke on November 22, 1935, and died less than 24 hours later at his home on Steel Street. He was survived by his wife, Mrs. Helen Steele Jewhurst, two sons and three daughters, one sister, five grandchildren and two great-grandchildren. During Chief Jewhurst' funeral, the historic Old Wheeler bell tolled. The flag at Richardson Square was flown at half-mast in honor of the gallant firefighter and chief. Many city officials, delegations of fire chiefs and firemen from all around New York State, friends and people who had admired "Ed" were present. He was laid in repose at the family home, surrounded by countless floral tributes. The services were simple. A platoon of firemen from the Auburn Fire Department who were off duty attended the funeral and acted as escort of honor to the cemetery. Honorary bearers were: George Benham, Mortimer Clark, Frank Hendrick, John Bell, John Jaeckel, Dr. A. J. Tuxill, James Murphy, and Arthur Brayer. Active bearers were members of the Auburn Fire Department and included: Chief Fred Washburn, Capt. James Doyle, Capt. Edward Lyons, Lt. John Maywalt, Thomas Frost, Martin O'Neill. The "Grand Old Man" was laid to rest at Fort Hill Cemetery. He left behind a personal and professional legacy that will never be equaled.

Frank B. Hughson

Frank Blair Hughson was born in October of 1868, in Auburn, New York, the son of Sylvester and Eliza (Weed) Hughson. Sylvester Hughson was a veteran of the Civil War. The family lived on Wall Street in 1880. Frank had one brother, George. At age 12, Frank applied to work in the press room of the Auburn Daily Advertiser. The foreman, Edward J. Jewhurst, hired him and taught him the trade. Several years later Mr. Jewhurst left his position and Frank became foreman at the Advertiser. In 1885, Frank joined Protective Hose No. 3 at the suggestion of his former boss, Edward J. Jewhurst, who was then Chief of the Auburn Fire Department. Frank married Mabel Vickery in 1892, and they had two daughters, Leida and Nellie. The family lived on Walnut Street, Steel Street and later moved to Capitol Street.

Frank Hughson was appointed as a call man in the Auburn Fire Department in 1893. He became a permanent firefighter in April of 1894, with the Chemical Co. at the age of 26. He was promoted to Captain of the Chemical Co. in April of 1899. Department documents have him recorded as being 5' 11 ½" tall, 180 pounds. In August 1906, he was sent to the New York City Fire Department to attend a school of instruction under the famed Chief of the New York City Fire Department, Edward Croker. Captain Hughson spent approximately six weeks in New York City before returning to Auburn to put many of the ideas and improved methods he had learned into the daily operations of the Auburn Fire Department. While attending training, the Fire Department of New York City was so impressed with Captain Hughson, they attempted to get him to take a permanent position in their ranks. He turned them down and returned to Auburn. The Auburn Fire Department Instruction School was formally implemented in 1906. Captain Hughson became the first fireman instructor for the Auburn Fire Department and continued its great tradition of modern firefighting methods using advanced ideas. He was promoted to Drill Master in 1906. The Fire Department's training school, conducted under the direction of Captain Frank Hughson, resulted in greater efficiencies noted within the department. A training tower was constructed for use in instructing and drilling firefighters. Training included ladder practice, hose work, rapid changes and coupling work with nozzles, use of deluge sets, 'siamese twin' connections (hose splitter plug cap) and Eastman nozzle holders. The men were trained at high altitudes in order to reinforce their confidence through increased experience. Instruction school took place at the 65-foot high practice tower on Franklin Street. During the course of 1907, men in the Auburn Fire Department received weekly assignments to the school. One man from each fire company was always present at the school. They became very adept at raising ladders from ground to roof using what was described as a "ladder roller" technique. Another piece of apparatus that the crews were trained on was the "life gun and outfit", also known as the "Lyle Gun". The life gun and outfit was a line-throwing gun which had a short carbine which fired an 'arrow' from a barrel and carried a light line coiled in a special box that could feed easily. The men were taught to shoot the arrow into windows at any height. The gun was proved, in New York City, to be shot into windows 18 stories from the ground. Once the arrow took hold, a heavier line was drawn up, which could be used to escape from a burning building. The men were also training on proper knot techniques and received instruction for the rolling knot, single and double half-hitch knots, clove knot and boiling knot. A boiling knot was used to lower a person from varying heights.

The Auburn Pompier Corps was instituted under Frank Hughson's direction in 1907. The Corps was named after the Pompier ladder, which was a simple, but effective tool for scaling buildings and saving lives. The pompier ladder resembled a 'clothes-tree' ladder, but at the top it had a large iron hook with teeth to dig into a window sill firmly. The hook was shaped like a question mark and was driven hook first into the window above the firefighter. The teeth and would dig into the sill as it was pulled by the firefighter. The men would climb to the window, straddle the sill, raise the ladder to the next floor and repeat the process until they reached their destination. Climbing a pompier ladder required a good sense of balance and much skill, as they had a tendency to shift from side to side. In order to achieve a level of expertise, the men of the Pompier Corps drilled constantly, perfecting their techniques and increasing their speed. Pompier ladders (scaling) came in varying lengths of 12, 14 and 16 feet. A fireman used a special service belt that had a hook to fasten him to the ladder in order to work at high altitudes with both hands free. While receiving instruction on the use of the pompier ladders in Auburn, Captain Hughson's men had a large net stretched beneath them to guard against injuries from accidents. The Auburn Pompier Corps excelled in their field and became experts in life-saving techniques using the equipment. Before long, the Auburn Pompier Corps was in high demand

1907, Auburn Pompier Corps

at firemen's conventions around the area and completed many demonstrations and instructions to showcase their skills. They put on wildly popular exhibition events and built up a reputation as a premiere group of firefighters. Crowds of people would gather around to catch even a glimpse of the demonstrations given by the Pompier Corps. They would take ladders from ground to roof in single and double stands, make diagonal swings from windows out of line and would take up a 25 foot straight ladder to the roof in order to show how the men were able to go from the roof to higher altitudes by taking up a plain wall ladder. The men would carry each other from the top story of a building or tower to the ground using a rope. The firemen would slide down a rope from the top of a building, shoot a line over the building and haul up a line of hose. They would take men and boys from the crowd and position them in windows of buildings at varying heights and then carry them down a ladder or slide down a rope. They completed many nail-biting feats of perilous rescue work and often ended with a thrilling leap from a roof into fire nets at ground level. Their skill, however, was not isolated to showmanship and exhibitions. They used their techniques in the line of duty. The Pompier Corps, under the leadership of Frank Hughson, saved a number of lives at fires in Auburn and they were considered top-notch firemen. The Auburn Pompier Corps were a source of pride to Auburn residents.

As the City began to replace horse-drawn engines with motorized equipment, Captain Hughson kept pace with the times. He took a special course in the mechanical care of motor apparatus. He saved the City much money by having repairs completed primarily in-house. He had acquired knowledge of the operation and repair of the motorized apparatus. He embraced the technology and spoke at many events regarding the efficiencies of and long-term cost savings achieved with the implementation of motorized apparatus. Frank Hughson was promoted to First Assistant Chief in July of 1920. He continued to promote fire prevention and fire education services. He and Fred Washburn worked with members of the Cayuga County Council of Boy Scouts to provide classes to award the Firemanship Merit Badge to the top five participants in each of the five classes they taught.

On January 1, 1926, Frank B. Hughson was appointed Chief of the Auburn Fire Department after the retirement of Edward J. Jewhurst. Chief Hughson was known to be a strong advocate of fire prevention. He ensured the department observed National Fire Prevention Week and he spoke often regarding fire prevention topics at a variety of events and gatherings. In 1926, he spoke several times warning of common household fire hazards including the gathering and storing of large amounts of letters, photographs, clothes etc. in an attic in an unsafe manner, and about the danger of using an oiled rag for dusting and then storing it in an atmosphere that made it susceptible to combustion. He warned residents who were forced to burn soft coal in the winter of 1925-1926 due to the lack of anthracite, that their chimneys had buildups of soot that would need to be addressed, as they were fire hazards. Chief Hughson conducted fire drills in the Auburn schools and established the standard system used by the Board of Education. Regular fire drills became routine in schools.

On September 22, 1927, at the age of 59, Frank B. Hughson died at his home. He was surrounded by family at the time of his death, along with doctors and Assistant Chief Fred Washburn. He had battled an abdominal condition for several months and underwent surgery in the spring of 1927. He had returned to his position at the Fire Department, however, the surgery had revealed that Chief Hughson had a cancerous condition that could not be treated. Flags at all the fire stations were at half-mast; black and white bunting was draped across the headquarters of every company. His funeral was largely attended by Auburn citizens and firemen from all around Central New York. The funeral procession was headed by a platoon of Auburn Police composed of Sgt. Daniel Randall, Patrolmen Thomas Monahan, John O'Brien, Robert Bobbett, Edward Arnold, Michael Linnenbach and Louis Pelton. Next was the Fire Department's big red car, in which Chief Hughson was often seen on his way to fires. The car was driven by Harry Orman, the chief's driver. In the vacant seat of the car, where the Chief would normally sit, were Hughson's fire helmet and other equipment. Auburn and Syracuse firemen followed in uniform. There were also automobiles carrying family members and close friends. When the funeral cortege approached the municipal buildings, the old Wheeler bell tolled and delegations of city officials and members of the Auburn and visiting fire departments and Sons of Veterans marched from the municipal buildings to the church. Pall bearers included Captain Clarence Whiting, Lt. John Maywalt, Lt. Timothy Ryan, Firemen Paul Flynn, Joseph Flynn and Leon Miner. The Central New York Volunteer Firemen's Association was represented as well; eight past Presidents of the association were present for the funeral. Frank B. Hughson was buried in Soule Cemetery.

The following memorial on the death of Frank B. Hughson, Chief of the Fire Department, was presented by Mayor Weld and adopted by the City Councilmen:

"This council records with regret the severance by death of the relationship between Frank B. Hughson, Chief of the Fire Department, and the City of Auburn, which has extended over a period of upwards of 40 years. From an early manhood until death, Frank B. Hughson has been closely and intimately associated with the Fire Department of the city – from 1885 to 1894 with the volunteer service, and from 1894 until his death with the paid department.

He has served the department in all capacities: as a member of the old volunteer Protective Hose No. 3; as a member of the original Chemical Company; and from 1899 down as Captain and Chief. His service in building up the efficiency and morale of our Fire Department has been exceptional and has been characterized by an unrelenting diligence and thoroughness which has materially assisted in advancing it to a position well up among the leading fire departments in the state.

As an expression of its appreciation of this unfailing loyalty, and devotion to our Fire Department for upwards of 40 years, this Council directs that this minute be spread in the records of its proceedings, and a copy forwarded by the clerk to the family of Chief Hughson."

Many tributes were offered to Frank Hughson following his death:

"I feel deeply the loss of Chief Hughson. His appointment as Chief of our fire fighting forces was a fitting climax to many years of faithful service in this department. The city has lost an efficient public officer. The sympathy of our people is with his family." –R. A. Weld, Mayor

"I have known Chief Hughson since he was a boy, and have known him as a real man— loyal, dependable and true to his department. When fighting a fire, he never said to his men, 'Go in there,' rather than that, he said 'Come on, boys'. He was one of the most enthusiastic firemen I have ever known." –George Coneybear, Fire Marshal

"In the death of Chief Hughson, I feel it as a personal loss and after an acquaintance and association with him as an officer and member of the Fire Department for more than 40 years, gave me an opportunity to judge of his valuable work in the advancement of the fire service and leaves a place in the Fire Department that will be hard to fill. To a few of us, it is a privilege given to knowing how dear to his heart was the Fire Department and what a labor of love it was to him, and the time and devotion which he gave to the department will probably never be appreciated to its fullest value. He was a real fire fighter in the highest sense of the term and always ready and on the job to do anything to advance the welfare of the department. When I look back at the number of years of service and agreeable intercourse between myself and Chief Hughson, I feel that one of my best friends has gone, a man who was loyal from every point of life." –Former Chief, Edward J. Jewhurst

Assistant Fire Chief Fred Washburn, who was present at the deathbed of Chief Hughson, was nearly overcome with grief over the loss of his superior, to whom he had become very close to during his years as a firefighter. "In describing my feelings over the death of Chief Hughson, he was a great friend, a great man and a great firefighter. The city has suffered a heavy blow."

Fred J. Washburn

Fred J. Washburn was born November 10, 1875, to Charles and Jennie (Pollock) Washburn. He had one brother, Lewis, and one sister, Jennie. Fred Washburn worked as a railroad man before joining the Auburn Fire Department. He was employed by the Lehigh Valley and the Auburn & Syracuse Electric Railroads. He was a conductor-motorman for the Auburn street railroad company. He also worked for four years as a "one man crew" on an electric street car. Fred Washburn married Cora M Harvey and they lived on Franklin Street before later moving to Liberty Street. Fred J. Washburn became an Auburn firefighter in May of 1900, at the age of 24. He started at Hose Co. 3 and was transferred to Chemical Co. during the same year. In August of 1907, he was promoted to Captain of Hose Company No. 1. Captain Washburn continued to develop his career and leadership skills. He became Assistant Chief in October of 1921. He was appointed Chief of the Auburn Fire Department on October 5, 1927, following the death of Chief Frank Hughson. Department documentation has him recorded as being 5' 11 ½" tall, 160 pounds.

As Auburn Fire Department Chief, Washburn commanded the fire companies during the July 1929 riot at Auburn Prison, the 1931 Hislop block blaze that enveloped numerous buildings and resulted in the loss of one of his men, and the Masonic Building fire in 1932. The famous electric chair that saw the first electrocution in history was destroyed during the riot at the Auburn Prison in July of 1929. The marble slab on which the chair sat was removed and a piece was preserved in a glass case in Chief Washburn's office at Auburn

Fire Department headquarters. It remained there until his death.

In March of 1930, Chief Washburn experienced a narrow escape when he and Fireman Harry Orman faced a fire in the Cuykendall block of Moravia. Chief Washburn and Harry Orman were buried under falling timbers and rubble and both men were squeezed by a large timber. Their precarious position became even more treacherous when the beam that had them pinned in place shifted and pushed their heads into several inches of water that covered the floor. They feared they would drown. Both men were able to escape. Washburn sustained abrasions and cuts around his left eye and a chest wound. Orman was hospitalized for treatment of his injuries. Both men were able to return to work without much delay.

During February of 1931, Chief Washburn faced public criticism and a request for his resignation from the City Manager, John Donovan, who cited a failure to enforce discipline in the department and a lack of morale. Actions were taken at the same time to suspend two firefighters due to misconduct charges. City Manager Donovan publically released his letter requesting the resignation of Chief Washburn and cited several cases to reinforce his demand. Chief Washburn conducted himself in a civil and respectable manner throughout the investigation. He commented that Mr. Donovan was his superior officer and that any statements should come from him. He indicated that his job was to fight fires and not to get into discussions regarding the matter in question. He indicated that he had not and would not attempt to take any actions to enlist allies in his support. He continued to perform his duties with professionalism. The City Council convened as a committee and completed an investigation into the matter. The committee found that some members of the department had ignored basic principles and rules of discipline and had lapsed into conduct which had resulted in violations of the department and of law and ordinances. The committee's findings showed that a strict interpretation of the rule of the department formed a sufficient basis for the resignation request of Chief Washburn. However, the committee acknowledged the Chief's distinguished service to the city and afforded him the opportunity to correct matters himself. Chief Washburn did not resign. He ensured that his command of the department was without further reproach.

Washburn's years as Chief saw blazes touched off by the Hackney 'Gang' of boys. Each year during 'The Night Before' celebration of Independence Day, the Fire Department would respond to a variety of calls in Auburn, many of which were in the Hackney area. In 1931, the department was kept busy with fires at the dump on Cottage Street, Nicht's Feed Store on Water Street, a tree fire on Owasco Street and a confectionary store on Genesee Street. Bonfires raged out of control that year. Among the objects piled on the blazes were an old tin lizzie automobile and a coal wagon. The traditional Hackney Bonfire Brigade caused the Fire Department much trouble over the years. In 1937, they were called to North Division Street at the site of the new sewer construction, where planks and other material were set ablaze. They were also detailed to Chapman Avenue for a bonfire consisting of hay, boxes, boards and other flammable materials. All five companies were called to Myrtle Avenue, where a shed had been set on fire and spread to a nearby barn. The property was owned by F. Edwin Parker; a theme that was common over the years. F. Edwin Parker was a well-known Wall Street businessman (Wall Street, Auburn, as opposed to Wall Street, New York City). They were called to two locations on Wall Street, one of which was owned by F. Edwin Parker as well. A storehouse owned by F. Edwin Parker was also torched. In 1940, a vacant house on Wadsworth Street, owned by F. Edwin Parker, was set on fire. Due to the incendiary nature of the blaze, an investigation was conducted. Precautions were taken every year by the Police and Fire Departments in anticipation of 'The Night Before' events, but many times the Hackney boys found other ways to complete their mission.

Chief Washburn owned a cottage on Cayuga Lake and enjoyed spending time there when not working. He was an ardent fisherman and hunter. He very much enjoyed talking about fishing and hunting with others but seldom spoke about his experiences as a firefighter. Close friends said that he often remarked, "The big boss lets results speak".

For almost two years prior to his death, Chief Washburn experienced several medical conditions that required a number of hospitalizations. In January of 1942, he collapsed while in the Auburn Fire Headquarters and was hospitalized. In February of 1942, he was hospitalized again after being discovered unconscious at his home on Liberty Street. He suffered a stroke in 1943, and was hospitalized for treatment. His medical absences required that James S. Doyle step in as acting department chief. During his hospitalizations, the department and hospital received many phone calls from concerned people. Regardless of his seemingly fragile medical condition, the Chief continued to attend almost all alarms. Physicians advised him to maintain bed rest, but he chose to respond to fire alarms. As is the case with so many chiefs, Washburn wanted to be an active part of department operations and stubbornly insisted on being present for each fire call.

It was reported that on April 13, 1944, Fire Chief Fred J. Washburn died as he wanted to die, with his boots on. He was at his desk when he collapsed. Fireman Harry Orman was present in the office with the Chief when he suddenly slumped over in his chair. Orman quickly leapt to the Chief and prevented him from falling to the floor. Washburn was placed in a car and rushed to the hospital immediately. He died shortly after arrival at the hospital. His devotion to duty in spite of his illnesses was admirable. For approximately one month prior to this death, the Chief answered all fire calls and personally directed his men. Just a week prior to his death he had responded to and commanded the fire at the Welch-Allyn-Gleason Avery Factory on Clark Street. He climbed ladders and entered the smoke-filled buildings and remained at the scene until all was clear. Members of the Fire Department recalled that the Chief had often said, "If and when it comes, I hope I'll be in the harness". He had been with the Auburn Fire Department for almost 44 years. He was often called upon by other departments around the state for advice in firefighting methods. Beyond the medical illnesses he had experienced at the end of his career, he was known to rarely miss a day of work. His skill as a fireman brought him many complimentary letters over the years. Among his prized possessions were letters of praise for the department during their service in the rioting and fires at the Auburn Prison in July of 1929.

Following his death, the flags in Richardson Square, the park in front of the Police and Fire Headquarters, as well as Memorial City Hall and all the fire stations in the city were flown at half-mast. The Wheeler bell tolled its requiem in remembrance of Washburn. Many tributes were given to him by city officials, fire organization members and fellow firefighters. His funeral was attended by a large delegation of fire departments from across Central New York. A resolution of respect to the late Fire Chief Fred J. Washburn was adopted by the Central New York Firemen's Association. Chief Fred J. Washburn was laid to rest at Lake View Cemetery in Skaneateles, New York.

James S. Doyle

James S. Doyle was born October 1, 1878, in Cobourg, Canada, the son of Daniel and Mary Doyle. His family moved to Auburn, New York when James was about three years old. He attended Auburn schools. He married Helen (aka: Nellie) and had five children; four daughters and one son and resided on Grant Avenue. James was a bricklayer prior to joining the Fire Department. James Doyle became a call man June 14, 1909, with Hose Company No. 4 at the age of 30. On June 8, 1912, he became a permanent firefighter with the same company. In 1913, he was transferred to Hose Co. 1. After gaining further experience in the department, James Doyle was promoted to Lieutenant on July 12, 1920, with Hose Co. 2 on Owasco Street. He continued  his climb through the ranks and was swiftly advanced to Captain on November 1, 1921, and took command of Engine Co. 1. He remained in that position for almost 19 years and became Assistant Fire Chief on July 8, 1940. Assistant Chief Doyle fulfilled his job duties and provided services as "Acting Chief" for almost a year during Chief Washburn's medical absence. He was no stranger to the duties of the Chief position when he was appointed Auburn Fire Department Chief on May 3, 1944, following the death of the Chief Fred J. Washburn. Department documentation has him recorded as being 5' 7 ¾" tall, 152 pounds. James Doyle was known for his efficient services and vast experience as a firefighter and completed tasks satisfactorily while providing the duties of the Chief.

Chief Doyle was not an "office chief"; he worked at the front of the action. He was described by many as the first up the ladder and was no stranger to fighting fires. As was the practice of chiefs before Doyle, he never sent a firefighter where he would not go himself first. His vast experience and skilled efficiencies as a firefighter were known by many people, and he was a well-liked Chief. Morale ran high during his time at the helm.

Chief Doyle advocated to obtain higher wages for the firefighters, and provided data and planning documents to support his requests. Chief Doyle promoted for more stringent fire protection laws in the city. He proposed existing ordinances be revised to include requirements for owners and occupants to comply with fire inspection citations. He expressed a need for sprinkler systems, fire escapes and alarm systems within public buildings and areas. After repeatedly observing the difficulties of his men being able to efficiently respond to alarms due to motorists, Chief Doyle brought the issue forward to the City Manager, George F. Train. He expressed concern over the practices of motorists, including failing to give the right of way, parking within close range of a fire and blocking the fire engines and possibly causing delay in their ability to respond to subsequent calls. Firemen had been injured and fire hose and equipment damaged in the street due to cars running into and over them. Chief Doyle spoke up about the need to protect his firefighters and the public during response to and work on a fire. The City Manager issued warnings to the public and the Auburn Police worked to enforce the vehicle and traffic laws concerning emergency responses.

Chief James S. Doyle retired from the Auburn Fire Department on July 1, 1950. His last official alarm response with the department was on June 30, 1950. An automobile owned by Salvatore Mana had a seat cushion catch fire on Clark Street. The fire was put out without further incident. A retirement dinner was held at headquarters, and for the first time in 24 years, the entire Auburn Fire Department personnel were assembled together in one group. During the event, arrangements had been made to ensure adequate coverage; Aurelius Fire Department went to the Clark Street station to cover and the Owasco Fire Department was standing by for any emergency.

In spite of his retirement, James Doyle remained directly involved in fire department and emergency services. In February of 1951, former Chief James S. Doyle was appointed Chief of Auxiliary Firemen in the city's Civil Defense Organization by Defense Director and Chief of Police, Chester J. Bills. His duties included the recruitment, organizing and training of auxiliary firemen in the city in case of emergency. He worked with the assistance of the regular Fire Department in completing these tasks. The auxiliary firemen would be called in the event of an attack and would provide immediate response. Volunteers were enlisted and recruited for the auxiliary firemen at the city's fire stations. The goal of the program was to enlist 500 auxiliary firemen throughout the city's ten Civil Defense zones. The auxiliary firemen were provided with preliminary and fundamental courses and training and attended meetings within their zone.

James S. Doyle died May 31, 1959, at Auburn Memorial Hospital following a long illness. He is buried in St. Joseph's cemetery. Upon learning of the death of Chief Doyle, Mayor Herbert T. Anderson stated:

> "He had a long and full and highly creditable life. I have known Chief Doyle for a great many years. He was one of the old timers who contributed a lot to the safety and protection of the city during the years when modern firefighting equipment was unheard of. He, with the other members of the department, had to do it the hard way."

Bernard F. Rooney

Bernard Francis Rooney was born June 18, 1883, in Ovid, New York, the son of Thomas and Mary Rooney. Bernard was the oldest of five children; he had three brothers and one sister. Bernard's father, Thomas, died June 23, 1895, at the age of 50 due to cancer. Bernard was just 12 years old. His mother was left to raise five children. Bernard moved to Auburn in 1902 and worked in the Shipping Room of the D. M. Osborne plant. He became a molder in 1903 and worked at the Osborne Works until he became a fireman. Bernard was a boarder at the Grant Avenue residence of Michael Doyle, also a molder at the Osborne Works. Mr. Rooney married Emma Doyle, daughter of Michael and Margaret Doyle, on April 26, 1905. Together they had five children. One son, Thomas Vincent, died as an infant. They had another son, Joseph, and three daughters; Mildred, Mary and Bernadine. Bernard and Emma's son, Joseph J. Rooney, would later become a City Judge in Auburn. In 1908, Bernard built a house on Grant Avenue. Bernard F. Rooney became a call man with Hose Company No. 4 in the Auburn Fire Department in 1908, at the age of 25. In 1909, he became a substitute fireman. On September 30, 1910, he was a permanent fireman and continued to rise through the ranks, becoming Captain of the Hook and Ladder Company in 1920. On October 7, 1944, he was named Assistant Chief. During World War II, Assistant Chief

Rooney worked two jobs. In addition to his position in the Fire Department he worked at the Columbian Rope Company for two years. When he worked nights at the fire house, he worked days at Columbian Rope and vice versa. After the retirement of Chief James S. Doyle, Bernard F. Rooney was appointed Acting Chief, effective July 1, 1950, pending a Civil Service examination and appointment of a permanent chief. Bernard F. Rooney's first run as Acting Chief was on July 1, 1950, the same day as his appointment. The department responded to an alarm at the Marian Margaret candy and ice cream store at 7 South Street, where an electric motor had caught fire. In August, Acting Chief Rooney was appointed Deputy Director of the Civil Defense in charge of Fire Services Division by Director of the local Civil Defense organization and Chief of Police, Chester J. Bills. As Deputy Director, Acting Chief Rooney's duties included Fire Department coordination and expansion of the auxiliary fire volunteers.

During Acting Chief Bernard Rooney's time as commander of the Fire Department, Auburn staged one of its largest, most comprehensive, fire and emergency drills on June 27, 1951. The event was huge and Acting Chief Rooney served as the Incident Commander. The drill included not only all of Auburn's firemen and emergency services personnel, but also neighboring towns and villages in Cayuga County. The test was sponsored by the Cayuga County Fire Advisory Board with cooperation from the Civil Defense Directors, Police Department and Sheriff Department. Approximately 80 individuals were actively involved in the drill, which was being conducted to test the ability to cope with a big fire in the event of a bombing attack. The drill was a scenario in which the City Water Works had been bombed and much of the Auburn Fire Department equipment was unavailable due to enemy action. It was designed to test the coordinated efforts of the Civil Defense plan between the City of Auburn and the surrounding towns and villages. Police Department and auxiliary police blocked off the area of State and Water Streets in which the drill took place, stationed at strategic locations to keep traffic and onlookers from the area while firemen worked the fires. Acting Chief Rooney sent out a call for outside aid through the control center. Firefighter Harry Orman, positioned at the County control center, called the towns to dispatch their equipment to the scene. The other towns and villages involved included Owasco, Throop, Sennett, Fleming and Aurelius. During the drill, the Mutual Aid Board ensured the protection of the responding towns while their equipment responded to the drill emergency. Boy Scouts played an active role in the drill too. Ten Boy Scouts of an emergency division, under the direction of Jay L. Harter of Owasco, ran messages between the fire chiefs on the scene. They were later praised by Wendell Linnenbach as having done a fine job. Permanent Auburn firefighters, neighboring village and town firefighters and some seventy auxiliary firemen responded to the drill. Outside fire departments responded to the scene with their tankers full of water. The Owasco River was also used as a source of water for the drill. Sennett firemen, Merritt and Roscoe Tucker, were responsible for keeping a suction line clear of mud and other debris. The Sennett hose line was connected to their engine which in turn pumped through nearly a thousand feet of hose to State Street. At the mid-point of the long hose from the river, Aurelius Truck No. 1 maintained inspection as one of the lines passed through an Aurelius pumper and was relayed to another engine further along State Street. The firemen all worked together efficiently and smoothly to demonstrate how a fire could be controlled without the regular water supply system. For drill purposes, the water taken from the outlet was sprayed back into the outlet. Throop firemen used their clever new rig to supply water when their tanker ran dry. They used a basin made from three ladders and a tarpaulin which was filled from the outlet using a portable pump. It has become an accepted practice and still used today; it is referred to as a porta-pond. It proved successful for the circumstances. The Auburn Fire Department used their engine to throw a stream of water 100 feet into the outlet. Four hose lines were connected with it to supply the necessary amount of water. At the conclusion of the event, Acting Chief Bernard Rooney and Captain Wendell Linnenbach stated that the demonstration had gone off perfectly. City Manager George Train was present during the drill, and in a short talk over the public address system, he praised the cooperation on the part of the local municipalities and the Auburn Fire Department. He stated, "This makes me proud to be a citizen of Auburn." A huge undertaking, the drill exhibited the abilities necessary to successfully respond to such an emergency situation.

By all accounts, Bernard Rooney had a razor-sharp memory and a subtle sense of humor. During an interview in 1951, Mr. Rooney presented as a humble and cooperative man. He was reported to have a hearty handshake and a friendly smile. He told of a time in early 1911, when he rescued a woman from the third floor of a burning building at 36 Water Street. He was with Engine 1 at the time, and while his vehicle was racing down Water Street, he noticed a woman screaming for help from a third story window. The Hook and Ladder truck was on the scene and setting up the rescue ladder. Bernard was rather new on the job and decided to go get her. As soon as the fire wagon was stopped, he jumped off and ran up the ladder that had been set up. The rescue was swift and successful. It seemed that Acting Chief Rooney had an adventurous side to him.

Chief Bernard Rooney retired in December of 1951, after 42 years as a permanent member of the Auburn Fire Department. A banquet was held in his honor at headquarters. There were a number of speakers present. Assistant City Manager and Comptroller John A. Keller spoke of him as "a good chief, neighbor and father." Reverend E. Leo McMannus, former assistant pastor of St. Mary's Church and the former Catholic chaplain of the Fire Department, returned from Rochester to attend the event. In his tribute, he indicated "You appreciate the fine spirit of friendliness which exists in Auburn, especially after you leave here. Nobody exemplifies that spirit better than Mr. Rooney. What he has done he has done well and we all respect him for it." Mayor Edward T. Boyle, during his speech, indicated "Chief Rooney is one of the finest men to get along with that I know and you have a great spirit here in the department. Auburn Fire Department is one of the finest of any city of its size. Chief Rooney is one of the youngest old men that I know and a credit to himself and to the city." The new chief, Luke J. Bergan, also spoke, echoing the sentiments of so many speakers before him and characterized Chief Rooney as "a swell fellow to work with and has never refused a favor." Chief Rooney thanked all present and said he would miss the men and the fire hall. He was presented with a retirement pin, a $50 check, a complete pipe set and a billfold.

Following his retirement, Bernard Rooney flew to Miami in February 1952 for vacation. He was an ardent baseball fan and attended as many exhibition games as possible at the training camps in Florida. Mr. Rooney was also an active member of the Auburn Lions Club. In September of 1973, he was honored by that group in celebration of his 90th birthday in June. He was the oldest member of the Auburn Lions Club and was cited as possibly being the oldest Lions member in the United States at that time. He was presented with a gold key to the city by Mayor Paul W. Lattimore. Bernard F. Rooney died March 6, 1975, at the age of 91. He is buried at St. Joseph's cemetery.

Luke J. Bergan

Luke J. Bergan was born in Auburn, New York, October 22, 1895, to Kieran and Mary (Kinsella) Bergan. The family had eight children; four boys and four girls. They lived on Cornell Street. The family later moved to Mary Street. Luke attended St. Mary's grammar school. He joined the U.S. Army May 25, 1918. He became a Corporal in September of 1918, and was promoted to Sergeant in October. He was honorably discharged December 14, 1918, at the end of the war. Luke Bergan was 5'9" tall and weighed 172 lbs. He had red hair and blue eyes.

Luke Bergan actively supported and participated in many local baseball leagues. In a 1985 Auburn Citizen newspaper article, Leo Pinckney told of a group of veteran athletes in Auburn, 'OldTimers', getting together and reminiscing about early softball leagues in Auburn. Softball popularity took off in the 1930s at Gasoline Alley, a popular spot opposite Springside Inn on Westlake Road. Several families owned cottages in the area and they would gather there to play softball on the driveway and the sand in front of the

Fire-Police Ball Game

camps. The Conboys, Bergans and Shamons were among the families involved. Most of the players were also members of the Knights of Columbus. Luke Bergan and Joe Conboy organized a K-of-C team. In later years, Conboy and Bergan also instituted the Firemen and Policemen softball rivalry which remained popular for many years. The Fire Department vs. Police Department ball games were usually the season openers and many in Auburn looked forward to the friendly competition between the two. Luke Bergan was an avid baseball fan and was one of the organizers and the first President of the 'Little Bigger League' in Auburn, later known as the Babe Ruth League. Henry "Buddy" West, later an Auburn Fireman, was an original member of the Little Bigger League and was known as a heck of player. Luke Bergan served as President of the league for a total of five years. He attended many Auburn baseball games as an observer in his later years.

Luke Bergan became a fire fighter for the Auburn Fire Department in February 1927 after scoring 93.5 on the civil service test. In October 1936, he married Mary Twyne. Together they had three children; Helen, William and Patricia. They lived at 45

Fire-Police Ball Game; Chief Bergan, John Schlegel, Murphy

Mattie Street. In June of 1941, Luke was promoted to Lieutenant in the Auburn Fire Department. During World War II Bergan was a training officer for the Civil Defense Fire Auxiliary. Several hundred civilians received training from Lt. Bergan from 1941–1945. Toward the end of the war, the city took advantage of Lt. Bergan's vast skillset and training background and appointed him as a Training Instructor and Drill Master, with the rank of Assistant Chief, in 1944. In 1948, he was appointed as the first Fire Instructor for Cayuga County under the Fire Safety Division of the NYS Division of Safety. He played a key role in the development of a training manual for the New York State Fire Training Program. He continued providing fire safety instruction and training for many years in his career. He conducted training classes and instruction on a regular basis throughout Cayuga County and the surrounding areas. On December 26, 1951, Luke Bergan took over the reins from Bernard F. Rooney and became Chief of the Auburn Fire Department. He was sworn in at Memorial City Hall with family and friends surrounding him, along with former Chiefs Rooney and Doyle and several city officials. City Manager, George F. Train, pinned the Fire Chief badge on Luke Bergan and indicated that the administration was most fortunate to have had two chiefs such as James Doyle and Bernard Rooney, and still more fortunate to add the name of Luke Bergan to an already impressive list. George Shamon, City Clerk, administered the oath of office. Mayor Boyle spoke of Chief Bergan and indicated that it was an honor to elevate him to the highest office within the department. He indicated that the Auburn Fire Department was one of the finest in any city of its size in the country. He went on to say that the new chief's courage, honesty and ability were unquestioned and that he entrusted the lives of the people in Auburn and their property to Chief Bergan.

Chief Bergan was the people's chief and was very popular throughout the community. He was a strong advocate for the Fire Department and the firefighters. His annual reports were detailed and carefully researched. He made recommendations for additional firefighters to be hired, apparatus to be purchased and fire station improvements to be made. During a time when the hours of the firemen were in adjustment, it became necessary and financially prudent to hire additional firefighters to ensure the full strength of the department. He advocated for the Owasco and Clark Street stations to be replaced with new stations that would better meet their needs and alleviate the aging conditions that were becoming more concerning in the two stations. As a result, a new fire station was approved to be built for Engine #2 to be located on Frederick Street. During his years in the Fire Department he saw the Auburn prison riot and fire, the Hislop fire, the Masonic Block fire, and the tragic gasoline explosion at the corner of South and Lincoln Streets that claimed five lives.

Chief Luke Bergan was particularly interested in fire prevention and education. Fire Prevention Week occurs every October. In 1959, the Chamber of Commerce formed a Fire Prevention Committee with Clarence Nolan as the Chair. Under the leadership of the committee, and in collaboration with the Auburn Fire Department, the city instituted several new and innovative methods to educate the public. Many firefighters contributed to the fire prevention activities. Fire prevention messages were transmitted via radio. One of the most popular fire prevention week activities involved a decommissioned fire alarm box that was installed downtown at the corner of North Street and Genesee Street. It was assembled in such a way that firefighters and other participants were staged in a second story location with a line of sight to the fire alarm box. They would speak into a microphone that would transmit to the alarm box and broadcast the fire prevention messages to passersby. The talking fire alarm box generated much interest. Many of the messages gave "personalized" fire prevention tips using the individual's name or a reference to a particular fire hazard or education element that may apply. People were stunned and stymied by the messages that they heard come out of the fire alarm box. Chief Bergan spent time talking on the box every day during Fire Prevention Week. The "talking fire box" was used for years for a variety of fire education purposes.

In 1960, more than 1,000 Auburnians visited the fire station on Market Street during Fire Prevention Week. They were able to see demonstrations of equipment and firefighting techniques. A mock fire and rescue scenario was also set up at a three-story building across the street from the station. The Truck Company raised its extension ladder to the roof of the building and simulated fighting a mock fire at that location. Lieutenant John Delaney, dressed as a woman and holding a doll, called for "help" from a second story window and jumped from the ledge of the building into a safety net held by fellow firemen below. It was a rousing and popular feat. In 1965, Lt. Bernard Simmons explained the "talking fire box" to visiting school classes and taught students fire safety and prevention rules.

Other activities also took place during Fire Prevention week. Store window displays were setup during the week with staged fire hazards and there was a contest for citizens to try to identify all the hazards. Stores displayed smoking in bed hazard, overloaded electrical outlets, matches and lighters, gasoline and many other hazards. A prize was awarded to the individual who identified the most hazards. There were a variety of catchphrases introduced into the community; "The ash you drop may be your own," "Don't clown around with fire," "Fire hurts everyone." The department sponsored essay contests for elementary and middle school children, which resulted in prizes, publicity, and for some a trip to Elmira to tour the American LaFrance factory. The Fire Department brought fire engines to the schools to give fire prevention and education instructions. Many Auburnians today can still remember the firemen who showed up at their school educating them and allowing close proximity to the fire trucks, wearing a helmet, trying on boots, etc. At headquarters on Market Street, the department gave rescue and fire demonstrations and provided instructions for coping with a variety of fires. Auburn's Fire Prevention program received national recognition and Chief Bergan was proud of his department and their efforts.

In April 1954, the Woman's Home Companion rated Auburn, New York as "Good" from a fire loss standpoint; the scale ranged from Fair, Poor to Good – Good being the highest rating. Cities across the country were reviewed and scored. The rating was based on the average fire loss per person between 1946 and 1952. According to the National Fire Protection Association, this was a fair measure of firefighting effectiveness for a community. The national average fire loss per person was $3.44 in 1952. In order to achieve the rating of "Good", a city had to have an average loss per person under $2.50. Auburn's Fire Department was rated to be among the best of the best!

Chief Bergan retired November 1, 1965, after 38 years of service. His last official response to a fire alarm was on September 28, 1965, when the department responded to 52 South Street on a report of a malfunction in a natural gas furnace. The furnace had a delayed ignition, causing a small explosion. There was smoke present and damage was described as moderate. A retirement banquet was held at headquarters for Chief Bergan in December 1965. More than 100 firemen, city officials, friends and family were present. William Maywalt, the new chief, was the master of ceremonies for the evening. Mayor Schwartz spoke of Bergan, indicating he was always a gentleman and had the respect of the community. He wished him many happy years of health and retirement. Congratulations and well wishes were expressed by City Manager Oliver Taylor, Councilman Karpinski, Councilman Greene, Councilman Miskell, Rev. Dr. James Stuart, Assistant Fire Chief Ralph Quill, Assistant Chief Timothy Ryan, Assistant Fire Chief Peter Mentillo and County Fire Coordinator, Dr. Percy Bryan, as well. The retiring Chief was presented with many gifts. Among them, a lamp with a fire hydrant shaped base that was painted bright red with a street light globe similar to the ones used at the turn of the century. In his speech, Luke Bergan quoted something he had heard from Chief Mentillo many years previous, "When you first come on the job, retirement looks a long ways away, but when you get there it doesn't seem so long." During his years with the department he responded to 2,521 fire alarms. He thanked the firemen for their cooperation during his term as chief and said to Chief Maywalt, "You're getting good men and a good department."

Luke Bergan was a 50-year member of the Auburn Council, Knights of Columbus, and served as the Grand Knight 1946-1947. He was named the Knights of Columbus Man of the Year in 1962, and as the Lions Club Citizen of the Year in 1966. He was one of the founders and President of the Cayuga County Muscular Dystrophy Association.

Fire Chief Luke J. Bergan died at his home on Mattie Street on December 12, 1966, at the age of 71 after suffering a heart attack. He remained active during his brief retirement. Just two weeks prior to his death he was at the fire house assisting with the annual Muscular Dystrophy drive. Chief Maywalt spoke of his mentor on the occasion of his death, indicating "He was an excellent employer who instilled confidence in everyone who ever worked for him. Chief Bergan was well known and highly respected throughout the state. And the reason for this was probably his complete calmness." Richard Walsh remembered his friend, stating "The Fire Department has lost a truly great friend and a fireman who can never be surpassed." Mayor Maurice Schwartz spoke of Chief Bergan, indicating "A friend for a great many years, I personally will feel his loss. I have known Chief Bergan for about 60 years. The last time I saw him was at the firemen's annual ball. The people of Auburn will miss 'The Chief'. He was one of the finest people connected with the city administration." The sentiments expressed by countless others who knew him used similar words to describe his character; capable, cooperative, fair, a great inspiration, nice, fine fire chief, a good friend. Perhaps retired Assistant Chief Timothy Ryan summed it up best, "Luke was a great leader of men and a friend to everyone."

William D. Maywalt

William D. Maywalt was born May 18, 1916, the son of William F. and Elizabeth (Ringwood) Maywalt. He later had a stepmother, Metha (Holdgrum) Maywalt. Bill's father was a member of the Auburn Fire Department, beginning his career in 1908 as a call man for the department. He served as a firefighter for over 30 years and was the first to drive a motorized truck in the department. Following his father's death in 1939, Bill helped to raise his brothers and sister and was determined to following in his father's footsteps and become a firefighter. The Maywalt family was no stranger to the Auburn Fire Department, with members that dated back to 1905, when John E.

Maywalt was appointed to the department. John was the father of Francis "Bud" Maywalt and the uncle of William D. Maywalt. Bud Maywalt joined the department in 1943, and retired with almost 30 years of service and had achieved the rank of Assistant Chief.

William D. Maywalt married Jean Miller and the couple lived on Elizabeth Street. They raised five children; two daughters and three sons. William D. Maywalt became a temporary firefighter in June of 1941, and a permanent firefighter in March of 1942. He spent time briefly with Engine 6 and Engine 1 prior to being permanently assigned to Engine 3. He was 5' 10 ½" tall and weighed 150 lbs.

Bill Maywalt enlisted in the United States Navy April 3, 1944, and completed his basic training at the U.S. Naval Training Station (USNTS Sampson) on the east side of Seneca

Lake. He received Landing Ship Tank (L.S.T.) training at the Little Creek Base in Virginia. While there, Bill was identified as a fireman and removed from the group and reassigned to the Navy Fire Station on base. The base had two fire engines, a Pirsch and a Seagrave. Bill acclimated himself to the Navy fire station engines and apparatus. During his time in the Navy, Maywalt first experienced a self-breathing mask, which was new technology at the time. The mask circulated air through a canister, where it was cooled, had oxygen added and then was re-introduced to the wearer. The masks were cumbersome to use due to the artificial lung component that was mounted on the front of the mask. Bill Maywalt was part of a group that was also privy to demonstration of another new style mask, the demand-type mask. The group agreed that the demand-type mask would be well-suited for municipal and military use. William Maywalt was honorably discharged from the U.S. Navy at the beginning of 1946.

After discharge from the Navy, Maywalt returned to Auburn and the Fire Department to continue his career. He became a Lieutenant in 1950, a Captain in 1954, and made Assistant Chief in 1959. Assistant Chief Maywalt wrote an article published in the nationally-circulated magazine, "Fire Engineering", in September of 1964. The article, *'Gimmicks' Sell Fire Prevention Week*, told of the City's innovative Fire Prevention Week activities that began in 1959, and continued through the years. In his article he described the revamped fire prevention program and the results of the department's efforts. He explained how the 'gimmicks' and catchphrases used during fire prevention week stuck with people and they remembered not only the circumstances but the messages themselves. Bill Maywalt played a key role in the fire prevention activities that took place in the city.

William Maywalt was one of the the coordinators of the first Fire Science Program at Auburn Community College (ACC), the first in New York State. He taught a fire science course at the college that introduced students to the Associate's Degree program in Fire Science. New York State Fire Training Instructors, George Bannon and Joe Graney, also Auburn firefighters, were major contributors to the program's success.

Community service was very important to Bill Maywalt. He was a board member of the Boy Scouts of America and performed camp safety and fire inspections many times. He facilitated the acquisition of merit badges by boy scouts, and himself received the prestigious Silver Beaver award, recognizing his exceptional character and distinguished service within a council. He was involved in the Muscular Dystrophy Association and the United Way Program.

William D. Maywalt was appointed Chief of the Auburn Fire Department on November 1, 1965. Chief Maywalt led the department and was instrumental in acquiring new fire engines, introduction and adoption of large diameter, 5" intake supply hose, replacement of the demand masks and replacement of other aging department equipment. Auburn was second only to Niagara Falls for implementation of the 5" intake supply hose in New York State. As the Fire Chiefs before him, Chief Maywalt advocated for a training facility for the department and saw it become a reality during his time at the reins. He played a crucial role in the approval and development of the Canal Street training facility.

Chief Maywalt wrote many articles over the years which were published in a variety of publications. In 1977, Bill traveled to England to study the British Fire Service at their National Fire College and the London Fire Brigade. In 1980, Chief Maywalt published another article in Fire Engineering Magazine, titled *"Cooperation Blends Security with Fire Safety in Prison"*. His article provided insight into fighting fires in a maximum security setting, cell fires and arson. He told of the procedures the Fire Department used in accessing and exiting the prison as well as extinguishing and evacuation processes. He told of the existing cooperation between prison officials and the city's Fire Department. The article provided valuable information and insight into a unique firefighting situation. In 1985, Chief Maywalt was elected to the position of Director for the New York State Fire Chief's Association.

William D. Maywalt retired from the Auburn Fire Department in January of 1986, after more than 44 years in the department. A retirement dinner was held for Chief William D. Maywalt on January 26, 1986, at the Holiday Inn. The event was attended by numerous friends, family, fellow firefighters and city officials. The night included several speakers who acknowledged and praised Chief Maywalt's dedication and service to the Auburn Fire Department. Following his retirement, Senator Lloyd Stephen Riford Jr. introduced Resolution No. 114 entitled: "Legislative Resolution commending William D. Maywalt upon the occasion of his retirement from forty-five years of service in the Auburn Fire Department."

After retirement Chief Maywalt continued to write and have his work published. He was also a skilled woodworker and was often seen at area art and craft events selling his beautiful candle holders. William D. Maywalt passed away July 18, 2006. He is buried at Maple Grove Cemetery in Jordan, New York. He is remembered by many to have been a skilled firefighter and a great Chief.

Frank A. Calarco

Frank A. Calarco was born October 11, 1934, to Michael and Rose (Buttaro) Calarco in Auburn, New York. Frank grew up in Auburn and was a Navy veteran of the Korean War. Frank "Chubby" Calarco joined the Auburn Fire Department in May of 1960. Calarco was one of three firefighters hired following the deadly gas station explosion that claimed five lives; three of them firefighters. During his career he served as President of the Fire Fighters Local 1446 Union. On January 1, 1974, he was promoted to Lieutenant. In 1975, he married Deborah Sanders and the two lived on Orchard Street and raised 5 children. On December 12, 1980, he became Captain and in March of 1985, Assistant Chief. Calarco served as a Cayuga County legislator until January 1, 1986, when he left his seat. On January 5, 1986, Frank Calarco was appointed as the Department Chief, replacing William Maywalt upon his retirement. Of his predecessor, Frank indicated he learned to remain calm no matter what the problem might be. When Chief Calarco took over the department there were 90 firefighters, three pumper companies and one ladder company.

During 1986, the City solicited proposals from consultants to conduct a management study of the Police and Fire Departments in the city. The study was conducted to identify ways for the departments to operate more efficiently. Cresap, McCormick and Paget, a Washington, D. C.-based company, completed the study at a cost of $25,000. Upon presentation of the 30-page study findings at a City Council meeting, it was suggested that savings could be found by reducing the Fire Department personnel by 24 positions and the police force by 10 positions. The study also recommended relocating two of the three fire stations (Frederick Street and Clark Street) to more centralized areas of the city. Renovation of headquarters was also part of the plan presented. The Fire Department's efficiencies at the time were acknowledged and Calarco's leadership and increased morale within the department were noted. Upon hearing of the management study suggestions, Chief Calarco expressed his concern and disagreement with the results. He had been Fire Chief for one year at the time the study was concluded, and indicated that the morale of the department, which he had worked hard to facilitate, was destroyed in one night upon hearing the recommendations. The department had already experienced a loss of ten positions a few years previously, and the idea of further reductions was unfathomable. The backlash of criticism from firefighters and many others was immediate and strong. The report provided by Cresep, McCormick and Paget seemed to indicate that the Auburn Fire Department was functioning well but could shrink the department without affecting services to the community. Mayor Edward Lauckern Jr. praised the study but also indicated that he stuck to the philosophy, "If it's not broke, don't fix it. It looks to me this department is not broke." Management studies were often completed in the 1980s by companies and municipalities. This study was believed to be Auburn's first formalized management study. As in any scrutiny that results in suggestions to cut personnel or increase taxes, there will be those who are not satisfied with the results. There were calls for the City Council to conduct management studies on all City departments and City Hall, itself.

During 1989, the County's five fire dispatchers worked out of Auburn Fire headquarters on Market Street. The radio system in use at the time was in need of upgrading to improve communication throughout the county. As part of the county's new radio system plans, it was proposed that the dispatchers be moved to the new Cayuga County jail that was opened in Sennett. There was concern and opposition from the dispatchers, city officials, legislators and Chief Calarco regarding the move. City firefighters at headquarters provided backup services to the dispatchers when needed. The fire dispatchers were to share space with the Sheriff dispatchers. Concerns centered on the proposed space that would be shared, the types of calls that each received and the specialized skillset that required to handle each entities calls. Ultimately, the dispatchers were moved to County House Road. The development of the Cayuga County Association of Emergency Services has resulted in, among many other things, an E-911 Emergency Communications Department that provides timely and appropriate responses to requests for public safety assistance throughout Cayuga County.

Chief Calarco retired as the Chief of the Auburn Fire Department in April of 1994. Frank Calarco died May 24, 2006. One of Chief Calarco's sons, Michael, joined the Auburn Fire Department in February of 2005, citing his father as a primary reason for his career choice.

R. Michael Harmon III

R. Michael Harmon III was born in Auburn on December 19, 1943. The son of R. Michael Harmon II and Ruth (Aiken) Harmon, he was raised in Weedsport, New York and moved to Auburn in 1962. R. Michael "Mike" Harmon married the former MaryAnn Walowsky and together they have one daughter, Melissa, and two sons, James and Dennis. Mike Harmon worked at a television factory for three years before he pursued a career as a firefighter. He had taken several Civil Service tests and scored well on the Firefighter exam. Harmon became a firefighter in October of 1966, at the age of 22. As a firefighter, Mike quickly demonstrated his natural instinct and  abilities in the field. A humble man, he is not one to boast about his many achievements over the years, but those who know him relay many accomplishments and examples that illustrate his qualities, earning him the respect of many. It's no wonder that Mike Harmon rose through the ranks of the Fire Department over the years. In 1976, he was promoted to Lieutenant. He became a Training Officer and relished the activities associated with education of the Auburn Fire Department force.

In 1977, Lt. Harmon responded to an alarm that proved to be the most difficult one of his career. At 4:30pm on June 6, 1977, a call was received for a man trapped in a cement mixer at Auburn Cement Products on Perrine Street. A co-worker at the cement plant had accidentally turned on the mixer while a 57-year-old worker at the plant was inside. Upon arrival on the scene, it was discovered that the man inside the mixer had lost both his legs. He was bleeding and in pain and whispered to Lt. Harmon, "Get me out of here." Lt. Harmon was quoted in a newspaper article, saying "He died in my arms on the way to the hospital. That man was my father." When the alarm came into the Fire Department that afternoon, Harmon feared that it could be his father. As soon as the fire engine arrived at the cement plant, his worst fear was confirmed when he was told his father was the victim. One cannot imagine the anguish of a firefighter responding to a call for a family member, let alone a call that involves such a horrific accident that results in the death of a father.

Harmon was promoted to Captain in 1985, and continued his Training Officer duties as well. He became Assistant Chief of the department in 1987. R. Michael Harmon III became Chief of the Auburn Fire Department in April of 1994. By all accounts he was a Chief who had the perfect combination of immense fire science knowledge, compassion for the firefighters and the department as a whole, as well as personal values to which he always remained true. As Fire Chief, Harmon was instrumental in appointing two Assistant Chiefs. He upgraded the firefighter training program and reorganized the department and created an incident command system. Chief Harmon also hired the first female firefighter in the history of the Auburn Fire Department.

Chief Harmon submitted his resignation as the Auburn Fire Chief in early 1995. His retirement announcement took the department members and city officials by surprise. Citing personal reasons, his retirement took effect February 27, 1995, after being in the position of Chief for nine months. Fire Department personnel were shocked and saddened to hear of Harmon's resignation. He had been a leading force within the department and was highly respected. William Weller, Firefighters' Union Local 1446 President, was quoted in response to the Chief's resignation, saying "It's a real sad day for the department. Few times in our lives does the right man come along at the right time – at a point when morale was low – he gave us the leadership we needed in our ever-changing profession. He is well-respected by every firefighter on the job. And to those who know him well, his dedication and his convictions were something we knew would be hard for City Hall to deal with. He's not someone who could be asked to compromise his beliefs." During the next City Council meeting, Auburn Mayor Guy Cosentino accepted his resignation and indicated that Chief Harmon had done an excellent job and regretted his leaving the position. Councilor Chris DeAngelis spoke of Harmon during the meeting, "It's not very often a person of such honesty, integrity and compassion comes along, but while this news deeply saddens me, this is what the Chief has chosen to do, and I respect that. He has the respect of all his firefighters and the entire community, and I wish him well."

Following his retirement, Mike Harmon went to work for the Federal Emergency Management Agency (FEMA). He provided disaster response and recovery services as part of a team deployed to areas experiencing catastrophic damage and loss. In 1998, he was part of a response team for the straight line wind disaster that struck the New York State Fairgrounds. He also spent two months in Puerto Rico in response to a devastating hurricane. Harmon's team searched surrounding and remote areas to identify those in need and facilitated getting the necessary resources and assistance to the victims. Mike also traveled to New Jersey as part of the response team for a flood disaster.

Upon leaving the FEMA team, Mike Harmon drove for Centro for several years. He is currently enjoying retirement and time spent with family, especially his grandchildren. He and MaryAnn have long enjoyed their camping trips and continue to travel.

Michael D. Quill

Michael D. Quill was born in Auburn, New York March 2, 1949, to Ralph and Anna (Salata) Quill. He is the oldest of nine children. A lifelong resident of Auburn, Quill's family has a long-established connection with the Auburn Fire Department. Mike's father, Ralph P. Quill, was a member of the Auburn Fire Department for more than 35 years and had achieved the rank of Assistant Chief prior to his retirement in 1985. Ralph Quill is described by Mike as a tough, but fair, Assistant Chief. He had a unique combination of brains and brawn. He could take apart a complex item, figure out how it worked and reassemble it with ease. He had an ability to lead a crew of firefighters, calling upon his knowledge of fire strategies to implement effective attacks.

In fact, several generations of the Quill family were members of the Auburn Fire Department. His youngest brother, Matthew, is currently a Lieutenant on the Auburn Fire Department. A nephew, Mark Quill, is currently a Lieutenant in Ridge Road Fire District. The Quill family has deep roots in the Auburn community that span many generations. His grandfather, James Quill, was an Auburn City Councilman for twenty years. His great-grandfather, Jeremiah Quill, was a member of the Cayuga County Board of Supervisors. Michael Quill is a Marine Corps Vietnam veteran. He is married to the former Joan McDonald and the couple has two children, Michael Jr. and Colleen. Mike did not initially set out to carry on the family firefighting tradition; he had considered several other career choices following his service in the Marines. After careful consideration, Michael Quill decided that he would follow in his father's footsteps. A Civil Service test for the firefighting position was announced and Mike took advantage of the opportunity. It was decision that forever shaped his future, and it was one that he never regretted.

Photo Courtesy of Michael D. Quill

Michael D. Quill joined the Auburn Fire Department in November of 1973. He walked into the fire station on his first day and never looked back. His first call to a fire was in January of 1974, during a particularly frigid night. An alarm came in for a basement fire in a residence. Mike Quill and Ed Laraway, both members of Engine 4, were gearing up when Laraway said to Quill, "Pull the flaps down." Quill, who was still a rookie and trying to remember everything that he had learned about the Fire Department, was not sure what Laraway was referring to. Mike had just finished serving in the Marine Corps and had been accustomed to working on planes; "flaps", historically, had a different connotation to him. He gave Laraway a quizzical look. Ed Laraway said, "Your helmet! Pull the flaps down!" Down went the flaps! Upon arrival at the scene, smoke was billowing from the first floor windows and the basement. Electric service was cut and the firefighters battled the flames. The two-alarm fire resulted in no reported injuries and was confined to the lower portion of the home.

In 1978, Quill responded to a fire alarm on VanAnden Street with Assistant Chief George Bannon. Mike Quill was the Chief's driver that night. They arrived first on the scene and were informed that there were two children in the residence trapped on the second floor. Fire was evident and flames were visible. They entered the house and Quill made his way to the second floor, where he saw movement out of the corner of his eye. He realized it was the two children and yelled to Bannon as he reached for the huddled kids. He scooped them up into his arms and carefully and quickly carried them from the smoke-filled bedroom, shielding them from the smoke and flames as much as possible. Assistant Chief Bannon met Quill at the top of the stairway and took one of the children. As they reached the bottom of the stairs, the flames had become too intense to exit out the front door. They ran to the back of the house, found a door and emerged from the burning house with two lives saved. The Auburn Lions Club honored both Assistant Chief George Bannon and Firefighter Michael Quill for their heroic actions that night on VanAnden Street when they saved the lives of two children. They were each presented a plaque at the ceremony. To this day, Mike Quill remains humble about his actions that night, indicating that he and Bannon had been at the right place at the right time, and that anyone would have done the same thing. The truth is that their particular actions that night were heroic and resulted in a positive outcome to what could easily have been a fatal fire.

Mike Quill was initially assigned to Engine 4, then Truck Company, before he found a home at Engine 2 on Frederick Street. Among the officers he worked for, Andrew Guter was one of his Captains. Many years prior, Quill's kindergarten class visited the fire station and Guter was working there at the time! The two would joke about it periodically. Richard "Dick" Walsh was also a standout officer. As many relay, Dick Walsh was a gem of a firefighter and a great officer. In 1980, Quill was promoted to Lieutenant. In 1986, he became Captain, and in August of 1994, he became Assistant Chief. One of his favorite fire trucks was the 1946 Mack. It was an old, open cab truck that they would use for leaf fire detail in the fall. It had to be double-clutched and was a bit finicky.

Michael D. Quill became Chief of the Auburn Fire Department in February of 1995, following the retirement of former Chief Mike Harmon. Mike referred to the firefighters he oversaw, saying "They're my heroes. Not sports figures or actors or actresses. They risk their lives every day for people they don't even know."

In January of 1999, Fire Chief Michael D. Quill established the Auburn Fire Department Medal of Valor Award. There were great things being done within the department and Chief Quill felt it was important to have them widely recognized. The award acknowledges heroic acts and deeds above and beyond the call of duty by Auburn Fire Department personnel.

During his time as Chief of the Auburn Fire Department, Mike Quill led the Fire Department transition into a more computerized unit. Prior to electronic reporting, every incident had to have a handwritten report completed. In fact, two copies had to be handwritten, and the use of carbon paper was not allowed. If a crew responded to 50 or 100 leaf fires in a night, a separate incident report had to be completed for each. It was tedious and time consuming. The department was required to use the National Fire Incident Report System (NFIRS) reporting system, a federal reporting system necessary for mandated report and data collection as well as grant applications. The Fire Department and Cayuga County had adopted use of the New World Systems' AEGIS Public Safety System. AEGIS (Greek word for 'shield') was identified to be an easy-to-use recording system that collected everything a fire department needs in order to manage and access information critical to responding quickly and safely to incidents. As in any organization, change is sometimes met with resistance. Some of the firefighters who had no experience with computerized systems or electronic reporting were apprehensive about the new reporting method. Others embraced it immediately. The introduction of information technology into the department presented some challenges, but was ultimately successful. The AEGIS Fire Management Reporting system streamlined and shortened the time it took personnel to enter information and gather necessary data as required for National Fire Incident Report Systems (NFIRS) reporting. Documenting daily log information, inventory, incident reporting, maintenance checks and other items was effective and comprehensive. Implementation of AEGIS increased the efficiency of the reporting documentation process within the department.

In 2003, Chief Quill was asked to testify as an expert witness by Congressman Sherwood L. Boehlert. On June 4, 2003, he testified in front of the House Committee on Science in regard to H. R. 1118: Staffing for Adequate Fire and Emergency Response (SAFER) Act of 2003. Congressman Boehlert requested the Chief to, "Give us your perspective from the front lines of service." The Chief testified on staffing and the need for federal funding; he told the effects that varying staffing levels had throughout his 30+ years of service. The SAFER Act authorizes grants to career, volunteer and combination fire departments for the purpose of increasing the number of firefighters to help communities to meet industry minimum standards and attain 24-hour staffing to provide adequate protection from fire and fire-related hazards. The SAFER Act was signed into law on November 24, 2003. In 2013, Chief Dygert, along with the City, applied for and received a SAFER Grant. After many discussions, and with the support of Mayor Mike Quill, the City implemented the Grant in August of 2014, and six new firefighters were hired. The grant totaled nearly one million dollars.

Chief Michael Quill retired from the Auburn Fire Department in June of 2006. In his 32½ years with the Auburn Fire Department, Fire Chief Michael Quill never got to "tiller" the back end of a tiller ladder truck. He mentioned to his colleagues that was the one thing he wished he had done before retiring. On Chief Quill's last day, he got his wish. The Auburn Fire Department arranged for the Aurora Fire Department to bring up their 1956 Pirsch fire truck for Quill to drive. The fire truck was, in fact, previously in service with the Auburn Fire Department. Mike Quill points to his years in the Fire Department as teaching him valuable lessons that he continues to call upon to this day.

In 2007, Michael D. Quill threw his hat in the political ring and won the Auburn mayoral election. He has served as Auburn's 55th Mayor since 2008, and was re-elected in 2015 to a third term in office. When Mayor Quill initially took office, he felt it was important to be accessible to all people. He created "Monday's with Mike", an informal question-and-answer style meeting that allows city residents the opportunity to ask questions or present concerns that they have pertaining to their specific neighborhood or city issues in general.

In the spring of 2011, Mayor Quill was appointed to the New York Conference of Mayor's Nominating Committee (NYCOM). The nominating committee was responsible for assembling the slate of officers to be elected during the Annual Meeting in Saratoga Springs. The Conference of Mayors has been in existence since 1910 and represents 590 cities and villages in New York State.

Mayor Quill is an active member of a number of committees. His New York State Governor appointments include the Regional Economic Development council, State Workforce Investment Board, and the New York Municipal Insurance Reciprocal (NYMIR) Board of Governors. His county appointments include the Cayuga Economic Development Agency and his city involvement includes Auburn Industrial Development Authority, Auburn Local Development Committee and the Auburn Municipal Power Authority. He is also a member of the Syracuse Regional Airport Authority (SRAA).

Throughout and beyond his firefighting career, Mayor Quill has recognized and valued the outstanding service of the Auburn Fire Department. In 2015, Mike was re-elected Mayor of the City of Auburn and will continue to serve the citizens of Auburn, New York.

C. Michael Hammon

C. Michael Hammon, "Mike", became a firefighter with the Auburn Fire Department in 1987. He left the department in 1999. He became a Battalion Chief for the Batavia Fire Department. He was recruited back to Auburn by City Manager, Mark Palesh, to serve as an Interim Fire Chief in May of 2007, until his permanent appointment in April of 2008. Hammon's appointment as Fire Chief was the first time Auburn went outside the Fire Department to hire a Chief. The selection of Hammon created friction with some firefighters and city residents who disagreed with the decision to hire from outside the department. Hammon's position was contingent on achieving a top three score on a qualifying civil service test. He ranked second on the list.

Chief Hammon implemented a Work Force Consolidation plan following the closure of the Frederick Street Fire Station on April 1, 2008, with only hours' notice to the firefighters and public. Discussion regarding the closing of the Frederick Street fire station was referred to as the City's best kept secret. The closure had the approval of the City Manager and was anticipated to decrease overtime, equipment and building utility costs. The building was initially leased for two years by TLC Emergency Medical Services. A failed sale to Helping Hands Transportation led to the former fire station being placed back on the market for sale via a sealed bid process. Upstate Paving successfully purchased the former Auburn Fire Department fire station, and home of Engine 2.

In June of 2011, Chief Hammon retired from the Auburn Fire Department after being offered a retirement job that he could not resist at Godfrey's Pond, a privately owned fish and game protective association and family campground in Genesee County, outside of Batavia.

Jeffrey Dygert

Jeffrey "Jeff" Dygert was no stranger to the life of a firefighter growing up. The son of Larry and Barbara Dygert, Jeff's father was a Syracuse Airport fireman for 35 years prior to his retirement, 27 of them as Assistant Chief. Jeff saw firsthand the schedule his father worked and knew that he could be called back to the station at a moment's notice. He would often go to the fire station to see his dad and helped around the area on occasion. Following high school, he contemplated career options and considered a position as State trooper, like his grandfather. Dygert ultimately decided that he wanted to become a third generation firefighter in his family, as his father and a grandfather before him had. He took the Civil Service test and was appointed to the Auburn Fire Department in 1994.

In January of 2000, firefighter Jeff Dygert responded to a structure fire on VanAnden Street. There was a report that residents may have been trapped in the home. Upon arrival by Fire Department crews, the smoke was observed to be heavy in the second floor of the two-apartment home. Fire officials coordinated incident operations and assignments were designated for each responding Company. While firefighters began their attack on the flames, others set up ladders on two sides of the building to provide a means of exit in the event that the initial entry point became disabled. Crews were making their way deeper into the second floor area with an attack line. Firefighters were notified that a female was somewhere in the structure. Firefighters completed a quick study of the structure layout and quickly developed a search plan prior to advancing into the building. Firefighter Jeff Dygert and Captain Terry Winslow made their way into the building to search for the female. A search of the kitchen did not result in location of a victim. Dygert then made his way to a bedroom door that was closed. He pulled the door open and discovered someone lying on the floor unconscious. Command was radioed to indicate a victim was located. They carried the female to other firefighters, who removed her from the building. Winslow and Dygert completed their search of the building and cleared the second floor with no further victims identified. The rescued woman was transported to Auburn Memorial Hospital and later to a Syracuse hospital and was eventually completely recovered. The fire raged on and crews battled the flames for almost three hours. The fire was primarily contained to the second floor. While all responding staff were credited for the handling of the incident and the saving of the female occupant, Firefighter Dygert and Captain Winslow were especially acknowledged for their bravery and heroism during the rescue.

Jeff Dygert became a nationally certified firefighting instructor and taught classes around the state. His passion for fire science, and dedication to a job he excelled at, earned him a promotion to Lieutenant in 2001. In 2006, he was promoted to Captain and continued to exhibit strong leadership skills; he became Assistant Chief in 2010. Jeff Dygert was promoted to Chief of the Auburn Fire Department in 2011. Chief Dygert has been a State Fire Instructor for the NYS Office of Fire Prevention and Control (OFPC) for more than 13 years. He is currently a member of a committee evaluating and updating the Fire Officer curriculum utilized by New York State.

When questioned regarding those who were most influential in his career, Chief Dygert listed Chief William D. Maywalt among them. Chief William D. Maywalt is identified as having been an extraordinary chief by many people we interviewed, and Chief Dygert was no exception. Maywalt was with the Auburn Fire Department for nearly 45 years, with more than 20 of those as Chief. He was a man who continuously moved the department forward. He remained engaged in fire service issues and was motivated throughout his time with the department. He wrote many newspaper and journal articles. Chief Maywalt experienced a reduction in his workforce and was forced to wrestle with equipment and budget challenges along the way. He had a resilience and ability to thrive during difficult times.

Chief Jeff Dygert was the 2015 recipient of the New York State Career Fire Chief of the Year Award, presented by the New York State Association of Fire Chiefs (NYSAFC). Dygert was selected for the award for demonstrating exemplary leadership, innovation, professional development, integrity, service to the public, and contributions to the fire service as a whole. Chief Dygert is a consummate teacher, and has demonstrated great interest in improving the fire service throughout New York State. Dygert serves as a New York State fire instructor with the New York State Office of Fire Prevention and Control (OFPC), delivering courses throughout New York State. Chief Dygert serves on the NYSAFC's Fire Education Committee and as an instructor for its Hands-On Training and Officer Training program, working to develop future fire service members and leaders in both career and volunteer fire departments statewide.

Chief Dygert has been surrounded by many dedicated, passionate and competent leaders in fire service throughout New York State, in fact, the country. He acknowledges and appreciates the opportunities he has had to be involved in a network of collaborative leaders. He has experienced both personal and professional growth through his exposure to many innovative ideas and people. He is humble in discussions regarding his role at the Auburn Fire Department, always pointing to the current and past members of the Auburn Fire Department, as well as other fire service personnel and experts throughout the state. The fact remains that Chief Dygert leads the Auburn firefighters. The successes that have been achieved within the department during his time at the helm are due, in large part, to his effective and skilled leadership abilities. His years of involvement training new recruits and officers have helped cultivate an efficient and skilled membership within the department.

Chief Dygert's dedication and true passion for the Auburn Fire Department have resulted in the trust and motivation of the Fire Department members. He faces challenges daily and has the ability to assess and take actions in support of the firefighters and the mission of the department. Dygert takes pride in the department and the achievements it has made. The Auburn Fire Department is a leading one in New York State; research and implementation of new and innovative tools, policies, equipment and techniques illustrate its progressive nature. The Auburn Fire Department continues to evolve and keep pace with current needs and trends in fire service.

When addressing a group of new firefighters in 2014, Chief Dygert advised them to honor the legacy established by the city's firefighters before them, stating "They created an outstanding organization, and it's our responsibility—your responsibility—to continue the tradition and excellence of service."

FIRE FORCE

*Top: Engine Co. 2; Scott DeJoy, Steve Parker, Sean Crehan
(Photo courtesy of Steve Parker)*

The first paid Fire Chief for the City of Auburn was Chief Edward J. Jewhurst. The first paid member of the City of Auburn Fire Department was Thomas Dougherty; he was both firefighter and driver. Permanent paid fire companies were formed in 1894, and Auburn became a paid department on January 1, 1894. At the onset, the paid department consisted of four companies and three volunteer companies. Among them were a chemical engine company, a truck company and a hose company. The Fire Department had thirty full-time men at the beginning of 1894. The modern department proved very effective and efficient. Between 1884 and 1894, the City of Auburn experienced 395 fires and an estimated loss of $411,795. Between 1894 and 1904, the city had 652 fires resulting in approximately $191,030 in losses.

The early Fire Companies contained a variety of fire force positions. Hose Companies had a Captain, Driver, Hosemen and Callmen. The larger Hose Companies had Foremen, as well as First and Second Assistants. The Chemical Engine Company also had an Engineer who was charged with operation of the chemical aspect of firefighting. The Hook and Ladder Company had a Tillerman, Ladderman and Batteryman in addition to the same positions employed in the Hose Companies. A tillerman is the rear driver of a tiller truck. A tiller truck has two drivers, with separate steering wheels for the front and rear wheels, which increases its maneuverability. A tillerman had to work in sync with the driver using distinctive signals. Few people possess the extraordinary skill necessary to perform this job efficiently. The batteryman was responsible for the good working condition of the battery room and the fire alarm telegraph system and supplies. Callmen were employed in a variety of occupations during the day and were required to report to their assigned fire company stations by 11pm and stayed until 6am the following morning. Callmen slept at the hose houses as extras and received free lodging in return for their service. Due to the nature of the responsibilities, a callman was usually a young, single man who did not have a family. The benefits of the position were a comfortable room and bed during their shift. The callmen generally had an advantage over others for paid position openings within the department. The beginning pay for a callman was not substantial and required that he have a job or career outside the Fire Department. In 1915, the annual stipend for a callman was only $100. The call force was later divided into two classes; Class A and Class B. Class A callmen were on a merit roll and were able to take the place of permanent men who were on leave or off duty. The callman position was officially abolished on July 1, 1930. "Extra" men continued to be identified, but they were required to sleep elsewhere.

In 1918, the Auburn Fire Department consisted of 48 permanent men and 18 callmen. Permanent men received 36 hours off each week and were assigned a fifteen day block of vacation each year with pay. The annual salary of a fireman was $1,000, which was increased to $1,200 in July of 1918.

Before the introduction of the platoon system, firefighters were on duty 24 hours a day. Family life, or any life outside the Fire Department, was almost non-existent for department members. The hours and schedule were taxing and were soon realized to be a hindrance. The two-platoon system had been adopted by many cities across the United States with good results. The firefighters appealed to the Auburn Common Council to adopt the two-platoon system. The continuous duty system was antiquated and proven to be inefficient in studies completed on the topic. The two-platoon system had strong backing by the firefighters, fraternal and social organization members, business owners and the general public. Many endorsements were received and filed with the Council. It was decided to bring the matter before the citizens of the City of Auburn via general election. The two-platoon system was put to vote in November of 1919, and was passed with 6,640 voting for the platoon system and only 1,565 against. The two-platoon system strengthened each fire company, covered medical absences and vacations and met the demands of the fire insurance underwriters. The logistics of staffing, budgeting and operations was worked out and the system began on July 12, 1920. The off shift was required to answer alarms coming from the business district, but not from residences. Men on the off shift were allowed to leave the city, but only by permission of the Chief. There were 30 men on each platoon and an Assistant Chief. All members of the department reported to and left quarters in uniform. The system rotated shifts and days for each platoon. On the first three days, the first platoon was on duty from 8am-6pm, while the second platoon worked the opposite shift, from 6pm-8am. On the fourth day the first platoon, instead of going off at 6pm, continued on duty until 8am the following day, thereby allowing the second platoon 24 hours off duty and changed the night shift to day shift, and so on. The second platoon would then be on duty each day 8am-6pm until the eighth day, when they would work 24 hours in order to allow the first platoon the same amount of time off and bring the shifts back to the start. The two-platoon system allowed one day off in every eight and each platoon was on duty the same length of time overall. This system had the men working 100 hours in eight days! Such hours facilitated fatigue and were obviously problematic. In 1946, the firefighter work week was reduced to 72 hours. Through the 50's and 60's further decreases were instituted, and in 1974, the 48-hour work week was established.

In the early days, each fire company had their own uniform. Most consisted of a cotton shirt, pantaloons and fatigue caps. Some fire companies had flannel or wool uniforms. In 1892, it was decided that the uniforms should be standardized and a double-breasted sack coat of dark blue cloth was chosen. They wore dark blue flannel shirts with black silk neckties. Their caps were dark blue cloth. In the summer of 1894, the Auburn Fire Department, being an organized, paid department, received new uniforms that were patterned after those worn by New York City firemen. They were dark navy blue. Officers wore white straw hats and the others wore brown hats. For a brief time in 1899 they were required to wear standing white collars and stiffly starched white shirts. For practical reasons, that style shirt was removed from service. Over the years the uniforms remained standardized but changed in material and style. At one point the firefighters were issued a rubber coat and helmet and were responsible to purchase their own boots. The rubber coats were little more than heavy rain coats, and many of the firefighters purchased their own denim "farmer" coats to wear under them. Khaki pants and chambray shirts were the standard daily uniform for a time as well. Known as "suntans", they lent themselves well to the work assignments and chores that had to be done around the stations. In 1974, firefighters voted to change and modernize their uniforms to an Eisenhower jacket with navy blue permanent press work pants and a light blue shirt. One change in the firefighter coats stemmed from a firefighter who was hit from behind by a car while rolling up hose following a call. It resulted in the department securing reflective tape on all the coats. The tape was initially adhesive in nature. It was later stitched on the coat, but ended up leaking at almost every stitch. In 1988, the uniform was changed to the "Blues" that people are familiar with today. They are made of a flame-retardant NOMEX material that protects better in a fire condition. Assistant Chief Patsy DiNonno compiled data and conducted research prior to recommending the uniform selection. They proved to be safe and comfortable.

The current Fire Department has four platoons; "A", "B", "C" and "D". The Fire Chief oversees all department operations. Each platoon has an Assistant Chief assigned. Each platoon has a Captain and Lieutenants assigned, in addition to the firefighters. Auburn firefighters work four-day shifts. The first two consecutive days are 10-hour shifts, 7:30am-5:30pm. The next two consecutive days are 14-hour shifts, 5:30pm-7:30am. The department currently consists of 73 Full Time Employees.

The Auburn Fire Department generally responds to more than 5,500 calls annually, and includes structure and other fires, medical emergencies, hazardous material and condition situations, mutual aid, as well as false alarms. Fire suppression operations are some of the least frequent, yet most dangerous, operations conducted.

Every member of the department is certified by New York State to conduct basic fire safety inspections. Two members are fully NYS-certified Code Enforcement Officers. The department has one full-time Fire Inspector, who is fully Codes Certified and is an experienced firefighter. Pre-fire plans are conducted on commercially occupied buildings throughout the city. Such plans improve the effectiveness of operations during a fire and aid in firefighter safety. The Fire Department has six active fire investigators. The Fire Investigators work to identify the cause of fires in structures, motor vehicles and, in rare cases, outside. When all natural or accidental causes have been ruled out or when arson is suspected, the Auburn Police Department Investigators are included to handle possible criminal aspects of an investigation.

In 2014, the City implemented a Vacant Building Registry Program. Each of the approximately 180 vacant structures is inspected and information is maintained on file at the fire station and has been entered into the Emergency Dispatch System. Hazardous structures are placarded and identified in the Emergency Dispatch System so that upon notification of a call at a placarded location, the dispatcher can provide responders information regarding the hazardous conditions.

The Auburn Fire Department-Cayuga County Hazardous Materials Team responds to all incidents where hazardous materials are involved, or believed to be involved. They respond to all hazardous material incidents in Cayuga County, including the City of Auburn, and are part of the Regional Hazardous Materials Consortium. The Hazardous Materials Team responds to hazardous material incidents to; assist the Incident Commander with identifying the material or substance involved, advise the Incident Commander of appropriate actions to take based on the known hazards of the material or substance involved, provide rescue/recovery services for victims in the contaminated area, and attempt to mitigate the situation. The Team has extensive specialized equipment used to identify the hazards, enter the contaminated area safely, mitigate the hazards, and decontaminate both victims and Team members. Team members train on a regular basis to handle hazardous material incidents that may occur. There are more than sixty Auburn Fire Department members assigned to the Hazardous Materials Team. Team members train on a regular basis to handle hazardous material incidents that may occur in our response area. Training includes: in house HAZMAT Team training, NYS Office of Fire Prevention and Control (OFPC) courses and training through the Department of Homeland Security and Emergency Services (DHSES).

The Fire Department has a Technical Rescue Team that provides the City of Auburn, Cayuga County and New York State (NYS) with rescue services. The specialized areas of rescue include; water rescue (flood, swift water, ice and Scuba), collapse, confined space, trench rescue, rope rescue, to name a few. The team has been deployed and traveled throughout NYS.

The Auburn Fire Department spends considerable time preventing fires through several education, inspection and mitigation programs. Age-appropriate fire safety education is provided to Auburn Enlarged School District students, K-6. Staff presents fire safety education to the elderly residents of local high rises and senior complexes. Fire safety training is also provided to local industry to help maintain a safe workplace and comply with industry regulations. Such interactions also help to improve familiarity with local operations. Fire extinguisher training is provided to City staff each year. The Auburn Fire Department has staff trained and certified to provide Juvenile Fire Play Intervention services in cooperation with social services.

In order to ensure proper operation during emergencies, the Fire Department works with the Water Department to check the flow and operation of every fire hydrant in the city. This is a significant part of the ISO rating.

The Auburn Fire Department proactively engages the public through their official web page and social media with updates on department actions and safety messages. Educating the public on a regular basis and providing department activity information has fostered public support. The City of Auburn Fire Department web page provides extensive information regarding the Fire Department. The Auburn Fire Department Facebook page is approaching 4,000 followers and has received much positive feedback.

Kneeling: Bob Flynn, Bill Reiley, Jim Monahan, Joe Flynn.
Standing L to R: Grover C. Simmons, Frank Hawelka, Harry Orman, Don O'Brien, Jim McCarthy, Dutch Soule, Paul Darrow, Harold Murdock

Top L to R: Tom Gard, Francis Ryan (driver), Robert Flynn, George Bannon

Bottom L to R: Robert Hoey, Robert Sloan, William Keogan, Jim Pullen, Lawrence Roberts, Richard DiSanto, Tom Gard, Robert Regets, Frank Fiore, William Jacobs, boy, Chief William Maywalt

Top: Jean "Flash" Garropy, Francis Ryan

Bottom L to R: Bob Regets, George Riley, Bob DeChick, Angelo Spinelli, Patsy LaGambino Ray Walawender, Manager of Radio Shack, Jake Barrett, Dominic Milillo

Top: **Bottom Row L to R:** Dick Walsh, Glen Adams Jr., William Keogan, Adam Spicer, Paul Oliver.
2nd Row L to R: J. Christopher Keogan, Robert Flynn, Miskell, Taylor, Luke Bergan, James Byrne, Charles Kierst, Green, Walton Krell, Gordon McCormick.
3rd Row L to R: Dominick Bellerdine, Paul Darrow, Francis Bunnell, Maywalt, Tim Pelton, John Baran, Charles Guzik, Robert DeChick, Robert Hoey, Patsy DiNonno, David Turner, Joseph Graney, George Bannon, Robert Chabau, Paul Giovanetti, Stanley Bilinski, Victor DelFavero, Max Coggeshell.
Top Row L to R: Lucian DeSocio, Joseph Costello, Harry Emlaw, John Hoey, Al Speck, Lattimore, Anthony Zalone, John Gill, William Maywalt, Hunter, Quill, David Walton, Angelo Ruta.

Bottom L to R (1904): ?, Theodore Hamilton, John Colbert, Augustus Hemrick, Frank Scollan, Earl Adams, Patrick Morrissey, George Platt, John Winsor, Ross Duck, ?, ?, ?, ?
(From the collection of the Cayuga Museum of History and Art)

Top: Auburn NY Firemen c. 1900-1902
L to R: George Platt, ?, ?, Frank Hughson, John Winsor, Lionel Morris, remaining unknown.
Driver is Patrick Morrissey.

Bottom: Auburn Fire Department Headquarters c. 1907
Front Row L to R: *Frank Wright, John Kreigelstein, James Walsh, Capt. Patrick Morrissey, Asst. Chief George Platt, Capt. And Drill Master Frank Hughson, Capt. Fred Washburn, James Dempsey, Louis Spaid, John Maywalt.*

Back Row L to R: *John Taylor, George Bishop, Richard Graham, Theodore Hamilton, Francis McCarty, Earl Adams, Lionel Morris, Dorr Gage, John Colbert, John Clark.*

(Both from the collection of the Cayuga Museum of History and Art)

APPARATUS

Top: 1954, Unloading the new Seagrave truck from a railroad car
Bottom: Photo courtesy of Bill Lee

Photo courtesy of Anita Luisi Colvin

The Auburn Fire Department apparatus has evolved from leather buckets, hand-drawn hose carriages, horse-drawn engines and wagons, steam engines, ladder trucks, chemical engines, to motorized apparatus. For each type of apparatus introduced to the department, the firefighters used training and experience to develop their expertise. Auburn firefighters have always embraced new technology.

An efficient fire department requires good personnel, facilities, training and equipment. The village of Auburn identified the need to have fire apparatus in May of 1815. The first fire engine was ordered in December of 1815.The engine was purchased in New York. Delivery was delayed initially due to an ice condition in Newburgh, New York. The boat that carried the fire engine was not able to pass through the ice that had formed on the water. The engine was subsequently transported by teams of horses and resulted in a 15-day trip, arriving in January of 1816. According to records, Gershom Phelps completed the delivery drive. One-hundred leather buckets were purchased along with the engine. The engine was a hand drawn, hand-operated mechanism. It was a "goose neck" style consisting of two handles, one on each side, for hand pumping water through the 'goose neck' elbow at the top of the case which was attached to a six-foot pipe and hose. The pipe would stream water about 50 feet. It also carried ladders and leather buckets. Nicknamed "the rattler" because of the sound it made en route, some humorously say that this was the firemen's first pet. It was housed in a building on the south side of Market Street.

Other early apparatus within the fire companies were hand hose carts and hand hose carriages. A 2-wheeled hand cart was often referred to as a "jumper" and averaged approximately 300 lbs. A 4-wheeled hand hose carriage was termed a "spider" and weighed a minimum of 500 lbs. depending on the model and furnishings. When first introduced, the carts and carriages had steel or wood wheels. The mechanisms varied, but the reels were usually controlled by cranks on the left and right side or had handles. They usually came equipped with friction brakes. This type of equipment was literally pulled to the fire by the men. In today's world it's difficult to imagine a fireman having to run to the fire company upon hearing the alarm sound, get the spider or jumper and run to the fire before being able to commence extinguishing it. Running with the machines in those days was even more difficult given the nature of the roads in the 1800s. Auburn was known for its mud covered lanes. One must imagine having to pull such a heavy piece of equipment over muddy, bumpy unpaved lanes and roads, sometimes for over a mile, in order to reach a fire. Slipping, slogging and sloshing on the road, the equipment and men faced quite a challenge just getting to a blaze. Since they were transported using only manpower in the beginning, the firemen had to be in good physical condition and have the endurance to be able to fight a fire once they arrived. But fight the fires they did, and our fire laddies worked diligently.

Many of the department's carriages were purchased from Wills & Horne and Co., a carriage manufacturer and painting business located at 17 and 19 Dill Street and later 81 Clark Street as well. Wills & Horne Co. were said to produce fine carriages. The company was owned by George F. Wills and John Horne. They were innovative and throughout the years improved their designs and products. They were one of the first in this area of the state to manufacture rubber tires, introduce a ball bearing axle and construct a Berlin carriage (valued at $1,000). They made six passenger Rockaways, four passenger sleighs, Phaetons of natural wood and the first beer truck ever in Auburn. Wills & Horne Co. provided spiders, hose carts, carriages, service wagons and exercise wagons to the Auburn Fire Department throughout the 1870s and 1880s. Some of the exercise wagons remained in use even into the early 1900s. They produced both functional and ornamental carriages for the fire companies.

Wills & Horne Co. often displayed the carriages in a third story window until they were delivered. Some carriages and carts were particularly ornate for exhibitions and parades. The Fire Department carriages and carts were very popular displays. Neptune Hose 1 had a spider that was painted vermillion red. The spokes of the wheels and other portions of the woodwork were striped with broad bands of gold and fine stripes of blue. The iron work on the pole, the hub bands and lamp stand were nickel plated and were mirror-like. The Protective Hose Company had a Wills & Horne spider that was painted china white with an eggshell gloss finish, striped with a half-inch gold line beaded with fine lines of medium blue. It was ornamented with silver work. The reel handles had an ebony finish, and the pick, crowbar and axe were finished in dark blue and gold, with the name of the company lettered in gold, along with the reel cover. Cayuga Hose Company also had a Wills & Horne spider. The spider was painted pure black and was striped with gold. It had fine lines in light blue. It was lettered in gold shaded in carmine and the tools, axe and other accessories were finished in black and gold. The iron work was nickel plated. The side and cross bars were lettered with the company name in gilt letters shaded with red. C. N. Ross Company had a spider painted vermillion red with all iron work painted. It was ornamented with broad gilt bands and fine lines of blue. The wrench box had the company name in gilt letters. The carriages and carts needed to be periodically repaired, repainted and the schemes sometimes changed.

In 1820, a second pumper engine was furnished by the State and kept in the lower story of the prison armory. The 1820 burning of the north wing of the Auburn prison led to this precaution on the part of the State. Leather hose was introduced at about the same time and had to be greased periodically in order to keep them pliable and easy to use. The engine was manned by civilian employees at the Prison but was also used for fires outside as well. In December of 1853, a Smith Fire Engine was ordered for the Neptune Engine Company No. 1. James Smith built hand engines in New York City from 1810 to about 1864. The engine ordered in 1853 was a piano-box engine, which superseded the goose neck engine. It was received in the spring of 1854, and was the first engine of its kind in the city. It was also a hand pumper engine, but it was larger and more modern than the goose-neck style. The Smith piano box engines were largely made of mahogany. The Smith engine continued until the adoption of the Holly Water system in the 1860s. Water for the hand-drawn engines was supplied via large water reservoirs in different sections of the city. The piano box engine became known as "Old No. 2" and was repainted in later years with the inscription, "1776. I'm ancient but never beaten. 1876."

In 1872, the department bought a Jones & Quick hand-drawn, four-wheel spider for $300. Jones & Quick was a carriage manufacturing company located on Dill Street in Auburn. The company was owned by William Jones and Charles Quick. It was later purchased by George F. Wills and became part of the Wills & Horne Co. carriage manufacturing business. In 1873, a hand-drawn spider was purchased for the Cayuga Patrol Company. In 1878, the D. M. Osborne & Co. plant acquired and installed a steam engine. The fire hose of the Auburn Fire Department was tested by subjecting it to a pressure of 200 lbs. from the steam engine; any hose that failed and could not stand up to the stream provided was removed from service and replaced. By 1880 Logan Hook & Ladder had a horse-drawn truck in service. In 1882, Active Hose Co. No. 7 received a new spider manufactured by Wills & Horne Co. In 1884, Cayuga Fire Patrol replaced their spider with a light, but strongly built, hand-drawn patrol wagon. Manufactured by Zimmer & Schwan in Rochester, NY, the new protective carriage was identified as Cayuga Fire Patrol No. 1 and cost $700. The wagon was painted red and black and had very elaborate nickel and silver finishings. It was equipped with two Babcock fire extinguishers, lanterns, leather buckets, axes, rubber blankets for covering the equipment and canvas bags to hold items removed from burning buildings. Fully loaded, the wagon weighed 1,000 lbs. In spite of its great size and weight, the men reported it was not difficult to pull. It arrived in time to be part of the 68th annual parade of the Fire Department.

The late 1880s and 1890s saw great strides made in the status of the apparatus of the department. The Logan Hook & Ladder Co. truck was aging and in need of replacement. By all accounts, everyone agreed that a new truck should be purchased. In September of 1884, the LaFrance Engine Company of Elmira, New York provisionally provided a new Hayes Hook and Ladder truck with a 65' aerial ladder. Casey LaFrance of LaFrance Engine Co. came to Auburn in person to announce and deliver the truck in time for the annual parade. Daniel Hayes designed the Hayes truck in 1868. Mr. Hayes was a former New York City fireman and Superintendent of Steamers for the San Francisco Fire Department (SFFD) and had a 14 year career there. Hayes understood the needs of the hook and ladder truck; to reach the upper levels of contemporary buildings in a stable and functional way without being too heavy. He conceived an idea for an extension ladder mounted on a wagon. He worked out of his home and completed construction of his first one in 1868. The Hayes aerial was considered by many to be the first successful aerial hook and ladder truck invented. The Hayes truck was developed to have an aerial ladder that could extend up to 85 feet (first class truck). Men could raise the ladder quickly using a crank. The aerial was mounted on a turntable so the ladder could be swung around to the desired location. Initially, a few fire companies had a Hayes truck, but there was some overall reluctance and apprehension to use them in actual service. The Hayes truck was unknown and employed a new mechanism. Many companies were leery due to an accident in New York City that cost several firefighters their lives during a demonstration of an aerial hook and ladder truck. In 1884, Hayes sold his patent to the New York-based LaFrance Company (later changed to American LaFrance). There were several designs and sizes of the Hayes trucks. Upon arrival, the Hayes truck was part of the annual parade and performed exhibition drills. One such exhibition occurred below the Genesee Street Bridge, when the truck was used to assist in raising a line of hose to the top of the Kraft building.

Also during September of 1884, the Fire Commissioners traveled to Seneca Falls to discuss the purchase of a new truck for the department. They returned with a proposed contract for a new truck for the Logan Hook & Ladder company from the Gleason & Bailey Manufacturing Company in Seneca Falls. Gleason & Bailey were well known for their high quality, efficient manufacturing of fire engines. Enter the controversy. Some individuals were in favor of the Gleason & Bailey hook and ladder truck made in Seneca Falls, while others favored the Hayes truck made in Elmira by the LaFrance Co. The Fire Commissioners had authority over the fire apparatus and the City Council had control over the City-owned buildings, of which the Market Street station was one. For almost two years the controversy over the virtue of each truck and the challenges of authority, primarily between the Fire Commissioners and the City Council of Aldermen, ensued.

By September 1884, the Hayes truck was already in Auburn and the Gleason & Bailey truck had a tentative contract to build a hook and ladder truck for the city. Reports indicate that the Logan firefighters were in favor of the Hayes truck. A petition was signed by firemen and citizens which requested the purchase of the Hayes truck by the City Council. Most of the Fire Commissioners were not in favor of the Hayes truck. In fact, they had the LaFrance Co. come to Auburn on two occasions to remove the truck. The LaFrance Co. agents left empty handed each time, having been persuaded to leave the truck in Auburn. The Fire Commissioners' reason for removal of the truck was due to the fact that the old Logan hook and ladder truck would be forced outdoors due to a lack of space in the firehouse. The Hayes truck was referred to as "Logan's White Elephant", something that could not be disposed of and whose cost (financially and logistically) was prohibitive to its usefulness. The City was facing a bit of a political struggle. The Hayes truck was put in the firehouse and the old hook and ladder truck was outside in the elements. The Fire Commissioners who were opposed to the Hayes truck, threatened to put it out into the gutter and replace the old hook and ladder into its quarters. Of course, that did not happen, but there was much controversy and speculation and drama surrounding the issue of the fire apparatus.

Fire Commissioners George Wilson and George Battams were against the purchase of the truck and did not see how the purchase could be made when there was not enough money and no means approved to borrow for the purchase. But money was not the only dispute between the two trucks. Some felt the truck didn't make sense for Auburn's building infrastructure, especially since it would be the only truck in use by the Hook and Ladder Company. It was acknowledged that raising and turning the aerial ladder with the turntable was beneficial. Throughout the dramatic evaluation and contemplation of the Hayes truck, Chief Jewhurst maintained a seemingly unbiased review. He was in favor of purchasing the Hayes truck. He had concerns regarding its heavy weight and reminded the City of the solutions that Oswego and Rochester had employed. They had two trucks, the lighter trucks were used for small or distant runs to fires and the heavy trucks were used for centrally located fires or very large fires. Chief Jewhurst suggested that if purchase of the truck was approved, the horses necessary for drawing the hook and ladder truck should be considered part of the apparatus and quartered as near as possible to the house. A man of advanced thinking, Chief Jewhurst pointed out that time saved was of prominent consideration when fighting fires. Any distance between the truck and horses would cost valuable time. Beyond that idea, he also volunteered to give up his own office space. With the wall between the Chief's office and the Logan truck room removed, the space could be utilized as a stable for the horses. He also suggested that a driver be appointed who was competent to man the hose tower and to be the keeper of the firemen's building. He further went on to suggest that any horses purchased would be able to be profitably employed during the day, in the immediate area of City Hall, and would still always be available in case of an alarm, day or night. He had proof of potential savings that he was able to cite from other municipalities that had implemented similar measures. Chief Jewhurst spent much time educating himself in personal exchanges with other fire companies and firemen, visits around the area and across the country, as well as reading the latest literature relative to his profession. He introduced innovative solutions that minimized expense and maximized manpower consistently. Fire Commissioner Battams thought the ladders of the Hayes truck were not long enough to meet the needs of the department, and that a suitable truck could be purchased for less money. He also indicated that if the Logan house held two trucks, he would have less of an objection.

Gross exaggerations of the benefits and shortcomings of the truck were slung between all parties who expressed an interest. Fire Commissioner Joseph Harrison Pearson was one of the few exceptions. He was outspoken in his support of the Hayes truck. In fact, he indicated that if a subscription in the amount of $1,000 could be raised through private funding, that he would secure retention of the truck in the city, utilizing his own money for the remainder of the purchase, if necessary. The total cost of the truck was $2,800, which meant Fire Commissioner Joseph Harrison Pearson was pledging $1,800 of his own money toward an investment he deemed worthy for the advantage of the city's firefighting apparatus. His security for the loan was the machine itself. He was confident that the city would come to appreciate and embrace the truck and repay the money in order to secure the purchase, in whole, of the truck. It was quite a statement and offer to make. Advocates of the Hayes truck pursued subscriptions privately and sold 4-$250 subscriptions to raise the necessary $1,000. Some of the subscribers were named as J. S. Dunning, Amasa J. Parker and Andrew W. Johnson. The exact number of individuals who contributed toward the subscriptions is not known, as several people could have pooled funds to enter into one subscription. With the funding in place, some wondered if the fire commissioners would endorse the purchase and accept the truck. Commissioner Battams expressed concern regarding the truck being the private property of the fire company and the company would retain full control of the truck and could refuse to run it in a fire if they became offended for any reason. He hoped the company would turn the truck over to the City to hold as its own personal property, thereby alleviating his concern over the control and housing of the truck. Chief Jewhurst addressed the issue raised by others regarding the ladders of the Hayes truck. He indicated that the argument was based on false propositions, since an extra ladder would be placed on the new truck, if purchased, and that it, along with those regularly supplied with the truck, along with splicing mechanisms, would result in a larger ladder than any of the current trucks were capable of. He was an advocate of the rotary ladder and felt it would be useful in getting to the upper stories of tall buildings and would allow four streams of water to be used on a fire simultaneously. The men working on the aerial ladder could be directed to various parts of the building instead of using ladders leaning against a building and limiting the scope of the extinguishing efforts. "Let reason prevail" he indicated.

The Hayes truck was used for the first time in actual service on March 26, 1885, at a fire affecting John Pimm's Clothing Store and other businesses located within the Shimer Building on Genesee Street. The Hayes truck was positioned in the front of the building along with the extension ladder from the old hook and ladder truck. It produced good results at the fire. Unfortunately, while pulling out of the company's house, it was not able to complete the turn, and the end of the truck crashed into one of the big front doors of the firehouse and resulted in considerable damage. Ironically, the Hayes truck provided fodder for both camps on its maiden voyage to a fire; it performed well on the scene but proved a little unwieldy on the move.

The Hayes truck and the old hook and ladder truck swapped places in and out of the firehouse and there was continued speculation regarding the longevity of the Hayes truck in the department. It was decided that a trial of the Hayes truck would take place in July of 1886, to test the concerns raised and/or prove the benefits of those expressed by others. The trial would include a run up East Hill on Genesee Street and would utilize Webster's horses for the event. The trial was conducted by the Hayes truck and it was concluded by the City Council that the truck was impractical for the city.

After much debate, deliberation, controversy, trials and political battles, the contract with Gleason & Bailey Co. of Seneca Falls was finalized and a new hook and ladder truck was ordered in July of 1886. While the truck was still being manufactured at the plant, representatives from the Auburn Fire Department visited the plant to see the progress of the truck at various stages of manufacture. The frame of the truck was 47 feet long and constructed of Oregon pine. The body was painted dark carmine red, and the ladders and under platform were painted light carmine red. The trimmings were done in gold-leaf with bright and cherry red accents. The ends of the top ride pieces of the frame projected several inches beyond the end cross pieces and eagles heads were carved on the projections. On the sides of the frame, in gold letters, was "A. F. D. 1". On the end of the truck was "Auburn, N Y". The length of each ladder was lettered "L. H & L". The truck was equipped with a Bangor extension ladder, also referred to as a "pole ladder". Major James M. Davis is credited with development of the original Bangor Ladder design after his return from the Civil War. Major Davis was Foreman of the Hook & Ladder Company in Bangor, Maine and patented an extension ladder design in 1875. He created the ladder to address a major downfall of ladders at the time; they failed under stress due to the wood beams sagging and breaking. Single ladders that were long enough to reach great heights were heavy and unruly. Major Davis is also credited with being the first person to develop an extension ladder with permanently attached tormentor poles that would fit flush to the ladder while stored on the truck. The poles swung out to assist in lifting the ladder and stabilized it once it place. General Joseph Smith, a Civil War Congressional Medal of Honor winner, saw the potential of the design and value of the ladder and purchased Major Davis' interest. He successfully developed the Bangor Extension Ladder Company. The truck built by Gleason & Bailey had eight Bangor extension ladders; 65', 50', 35', 30', 25', 18', 14' and 12'. The ladders were stacked on the truck, but were on rubber rollers, enabling the bottom ladder to be easily and quickly removed without contending with the others. The truck had four axes, two pick-axes, two crow-bars, one battering ram, one Detroit door opener (lever system design capable of delivering tremendous force), three pitch forks, two shovels, two brooms, patent wire cutters (for cutting telegraph and other obstructing wires), a large wire basket to hold clothing, a large wooden tool box, six nickel lanterns and two reflecting signal lamps. It had a driver's seat in the front and a steerman's seat in the rear. The sides of the truck had six-foot steps, on which up to a dozen firemen could ride. The surface bolts, handrails, holders and ladder hooks were polished nickel and added to its exquisite look. The axles were made of iron. It had Sarven wheels, four feet in diameter. The Sarven wheel was a much-celebrated invention by James Sarven of Columbia, Tennessee. The wooden hub interlocked the spokes and used metal collars and "thimble skeins" at the end of the axle. This provided strength and support to the hub and spokes. As long as the mechanism was lubricated, it lasted much longer than the wood-only styles. It also provided for a smooth ride. The company had three men build the fire truck exclusively. During one of the visits, a Gleason & Bailey representative indicated that as a result of others seeing the spectacular machine, they received additional orders for such a machine; one from Georgia, another from South Bend, Indiana and a third from New Jersey. The cost of the truck was $1,850 and it weighed 4,500 pounds. The truck was considered a masterpiece and certainly the showcase of the department. The mechanisms were top notch and it combined beauty and utility perfectly. It was a well-made truck, able to be drawn by hand or horses. Of course, many believed it would have taken more men than was practical to pull the two-ton engine by hand!

The Gleason & Bailey hook and ladder truck was received in November of 1886. As a result, four horses hauled the Hayes truck to the D. M. Osborne Co.'s storehouse on Seymour Street, where it was kept for a period of time. Not to say that was the end of life for the Hayes truck in Auburn, for the story does not end there. Eventually the City did see the benefit of the Hayes truck and repaid the expenses incurred by Joseph Harrison Pearson and the subscribers. During 1890, the Hayes truck was moved to primary service with the Hook & Ladder Company, and the Gleason & Bailey truck was placed on the reserve list. The Hayes truck continued to be used over the years. In November of 1891, the Hayes truck responded to an alarm from Box 46, located at the corners of Union and State Streets, for a trash fire on York Street. While traveling down State Street hill, the Hayes truck horses were running and as they neared York Street a carriage in the road did not respond to a warning issued by Driver Strong. In order to avoid a collision with the carriage, Strong turned to the right and the wheels of the truck skidded into a ditch about three feet deep. The horses kept running and dragged the truck for a distance. Lionel Morris was able to jump when the wheels first slid in the ditch and he escaped serious injury. Steersman (Tillerman) Platt was in a dangerous position and could have escaped injury if he bailed before the truck toppled over on its side, but he stayed at his post and attempted to bring the truck out of the ditch, along with Driver Strong. The truck traveled past York Street and was within a few feet of the Lehigh Valley Railroad crossing before it overturned. Platt and Strong received injuries but were not seriously hurt. While the Hayes truck was paralyzed, word was received that there was an alarm for a fire that originated at Salvatore Costa's Fruit Store located on Genesee Street. The Gleason & Bailey truck (at that point housed in the city's storehouse on Clark Street) responded to the alarm and although ladders were delayed in reaching the Genesee Street fire due to the Hayes truck incident, headway was made on the fire. The fire proved particularly difficult because the building had been segmented into many rooms. It took several men and most of the night to pull the Hayes truck upright. Captain Joseph Mullally, who started with the Auburn Fire Department in 1920 and was introduced to the Hayes truck toward the end of its lifecycle, described the hand-operated, 65' aerial ladder as "a daisy" (In the late 19th and early 20th Century, 'daisy' was a common slang term that meant 'best in class'). It took four men to raise it due to its heavy weight. The Hayes truck remained in service and was very useful. It even participated in the 1929 Auburn prison riot and fire to good advantage on the auto plate shop as well as the cloth shop and saved them from total destruction.

Hand-drawn engines were systematically discarded after the introduction of the Holly water works system. Hand pumper engines were replaced with coal stoker engines, steam generated engines and pumpers drawn by horses. Many of the companies that existed at the time were reorganized into hose companies as the horse-drawn era became more prevalent within the Fire Department. The Fire Commissioners traveled to Baltimore, Maryland to view and sign a contract for the purchase of Auburn's first chemical engine. A Charles T. Holloway chemical engine with two 50-gallon tanks and a 16' extension ladder was chosen. It arrived in the city by rail on May 29, 1890. It was put into service on June 10, 1890. Charles T. Holloway was a very influential man in the firefighting field during his time. He was the first Chief Engineer of the Baltimore City Fire Department in 1858. In 1872, he organized the Fire Insurance Salvage Corps of Baltimore. He later contracted with the Baltimore Fire Department to supply it with chemical engines that he built in his business. In 1881, Mr. Holloway organized the Baltimore County Fire Department. He held numerous patents in the firefighting and other fields, including chemical engines, fire extinguishers, electric lamps, stamping irons, velocipedes and more. After his death, the Holloway Chemical Engine Company was sold to American LaFrance Fire Engine Company who continued to manufacture the Holloway combination hose and chemical engine using the Holloway name. A chemical engine used water and carbonic acid gas to fight a fire. Carbonic acid gas is heavier than oxygen. The carbonic acid gas was forced with a comparatively small amount of water as a conveying agent to the fire. When the stream hit the flames, it displaced the oxygen in the area and the fire died out. The Holloway chemical engine purchased by Auburn had two 50-gallon polished copper tanks connected by a patented air vessel that attached to an automatic reel which allowed it to produce a steady stream by alternately using and charging the tanks. The Holloway chemical engine was said to be very attractive, strong, simple and durable. The frame was wrought iron and the tanks were bolted and braced. The acid chamber was outside the tank and was convenient. The acid holder was made of glass and remained viable for instantaneous operation when needed. It had a pressure gauge that indicated the amount of gas generated within the tanks and enabled the firemen to monitor how fast they were being emptied. The Holloway chemical engine was efficient and fast. It could be used without the delay of attaching to a hydrant and laying heavy hose. Extinguishing efforts could be focused and resulted in less collateral damage to buildings and contents.

In 1890, D. M. Osborne & Co. purchased a steam engine from the Silsby Manufacturing Company in Seneca Falls, NY for $5,000. Founded by Horace Silsby, Edward Mynderse and John Shoemaker in 1845, the Silsby Manufacturing Company, also called "Island Works" because it was located on a five-acre island in the Seneca River in Seneca Falls, started out manufacturing agricultural implements. Their first fire engine was built in 1856 and utilized a rotary design pump. The rotary pump used in the production of the Silsby steam engine was the design and patent of Birdsill Holly.

Birdsill Holly was born in Auburn, NY on August 8, 1822. He held many patents and developed a system to pump water under pressure directly into city mains without a reservoir. The "Holly System" was subsequently adopted by thousands of cities across the country. Holly's rotary pump design used in the steam engine was often criticized in its early stages, by those who preferred a piston or reciprocating system of engines and pumps. His early rotary pump design did have faults. However, he continued to improve and perfect the design, which resulted in a rotary motion that was considered by many to be superior to the piston motion, as it did away with the pump valves, which were vulnerable to malfunction and/or breakdown. The steam cylinder of the engine consisted of two rotary cams which worked together within an elliptical steam-tight case. Steam was admitted to the bottom of the case and forced the two teeth apart. It revolved the two cams in its movement and exhausted out the top of the stack and feed water heater. The construction of the rotary pump was the same as the cylinder, except it had three teeth. The water flow was large, direct and unobstructed in these engines; there were no valves in the pump. Therefore, debris such as mud, sawdust and sticks did not present a problem. The pump did not require priming and produced a steady flow without any irregular motion, uneven or pulsating pressure. The steam cylinder and pump were on one shaft so the action was direct and continuous with no loss of power between the cylinder and the pump. The fire engine could be used with low steam pressure and was stable and remained still while running. The rotary motion also reduced friction.

The Water Works Company in Auburn was privately owned for many years. Auburn's first water main pipes were installed in 1859, and were composed of wood. In 1864, a Holly pump was installed; it was the first pressure pump in Auburn. It was installed on a strip of land below the upper dam, between the race and the outlet. An air chamber extended to the opposite side of the outlet and was operated by water power. The pipes were made of light sheet iron and were covered inside and out with a patented cement manufactured in Auburn. Water mains were installed in Auburn in 1865, and the water was turned on at the pump house in December. Over the course of subsequent years, additional thousands of feet of water mains were laid. Within four years over 75,000 feet of mains were run. In 1892, the City of Auburn purchased the Water Works Company.

The D. M. Osborne & Company Silsby steam engine provided an attachment that heated the feed water supplied from a tank to a temperature of about 212 degrees Fahrenheit (boiling) and used the exhaust steam from the cylinder. The Silsby steam engine was built with a "crane neck" style. During the steam era of fire engines, Silsby built over 1,000 fire engines. On September 24, 1881, a Silsby Steam Engine was authenticated to have thrown a stream a distance of 364ft in Reading, PA. The Silbsy engine had nine major models throughout its history. The ninth model was the last major model change, although it had several variations. The ninth model was introduced in 1875, and included builder's numbers from approximately 500 to 3109. D. M. Osborne & Co. had a Silsby Steam Engine with builder number 956. It was the largest size that Silsby made at that time. The Silsby steam fire engine was named, the "D. M. Osborne". The last engine built by Silsby Manufacturing Co. was builder number 1015 for Jacksonville, IL in 1891. In 1900, the American Fire Engine Company combined with LaFrance, Rumsey, Gleason and Bailey, Holloway and others to form the International Fire Engine Company. The name was later changed to the American LaFrance Fire Engine Company. Silsby engines continued to be manufactured, but under the new company name.

D.M. Osborne's Silsby steam fire engine was gifted to the City of Auburn on August 2, 1900. It was turned over by Colonel E. D. Metcalf to Mayor Orlando Lewis. The official presentation document read, "To His Honor, the Mayor, and the Board of Aldermen of the City of Auburn: Gentlemen: The Manufacturers' Mutual Fire Insurance companies have criticized very severely the protection that this city affords against a general conflagration. They have criticized in the past the size of the mains of our water system and our dependence upon pumps when a large demand is made upon the city water supply service, and more especially that the city did not have a steam fire engine to depend upon in emergencies. The growth of our city and increase in manufacturing plants call for increased protection against fire, and with a desire to extend to all the manufacturers of the city and the owners of business and resident property every protection which we have enjoyed by reason of owning a steam fire engine, we hereby tender to the City of Auburn through your honorable body, as a free and good will offering, our steam fire engine No. 956, manufactured by the Silsby Manufacturing company, that the same may be placed in the hands of our efficient Fire Department to enable them to extend its usefulness to all alive. Yours very truly, D. M. Osborne & Co., By Edwin D. Metcalf, treasurer and general manager." As a result of the gift, the city not only increased its capabilities to fight fires and added to its inventory of apparatus, but insurance rate increases were eased as the city's fire rating improved.

Chief Jewhurst was very pleased with the addition of the Silsby to the department's list of apparatus. Prior to the Silsby, the department was dependent on the water main system for its supply of water. The water mains in the city were relatively new and had been challenging to the Fire Department at times. If the department was at a very large fire or a water main broke, they would be paralyzed. He was quoted as saying about the water mains, "They are alright for a small fire where but two or three streams of water are necessary, but supposing we should have a large conflagration in Genesee Street for instance, where eight or ten streams would be needed. I'll bet a new hat we couldn't throw a stream into the second story window." The generous gift of the Silsby from the D. M. Osborne & Co. was a much needed addition to the department. The city didn't have a proper house for the engine until 1901. It was housed on Market Street, on the property where the Hardenbergh house once stood. The Silsby was used in a demonstration of the new sprinkler system, the first in the city, which was installed in the Auburn Woolen Mill. It provided a 285 foot stream of water, which was considered quite good at the time.

The steam era had arrived for the Auburn Fire Department and they were able to add additional steam fire engines within the hose companies over the next several years. The primary equipment of the department was horse drawn, but there remained a number of spiders and carts and other hand drawn equipment in reserve, to be called upon when needed. In 1906, the department purchased a new Metropolitan steam fire engine from American LaFrance Fire Engine Co. in Elmira, NY for Engine Company No. 2 for $4,750. A team of horses was purchased for the engine at the same time. The Metropolitan was one of the final steam engines produced during that era and was considered to be an excellent machine. Auburn's Metropolitan steamer was Registration #3145. It was a second-class Metropolitan steam fire engine with a Fox boiler, 2 piston unit, 3HP, crane frame, with Archibald wheels. In 1924, it was no longer part of the department's active apparatus. It was purchased by the Auburn Water Works.

From 1894 until 1908, Chief Jewhurst used horses for his transportation. During the summer of 1907, the Chief's beloved horse, Dan, was removed from service due to his physical condition. Investigation into the practicality of purchasing an automobile to replace the horse showed that the expense involved in maintaining a horse and carriage, compared with that of an automobile, warranted the purchase. Chief Jewhurst traveled to the Cameron Automobile Company in Brockton, MA to look at and test an automobile for consideration and purchase.

Cameron Runabout, "The Flier"
Driver Jack Taylor, Chief Edward Jewhurst

At the conclusion of his visit he recommended the vehicle. Fire Commissioner J. F. Sperry placed the order in December of 1907, and obtained it for a price that was at a reduced rate for the city. It was placed into service in January 1908. Chief Jewhurst was one of a very limited number of fire chiefs in the country, and the third in New York State, to have an automobile of his own in which to go to fires. Auburn was leading the field. The 1908 Cameron Runabout, nicknamed "the flier" and "red devil", was a light-weight, 4-cylinder, 16 horse power automobile that was customized to be able to carry three passengers, a set of hand extinguishers, ropes, axes and other emergency equipment. It had an air-cooled engine and a patented rear axle transmission. The vehicle had three forward speeds and reverse and was direct drive on all forward speeds. It had 28" x 2 ½" wheels with combination ball and Babbitt bearings. The chassis was made of oak and the body was made of whitewood over an oak frame. The finish on the Chief's "flier" was enamel and flaming red in color with the interior trimmed in red leather. It was said to attract much attention without the use of a gong or a honk of the horn. The Cameron had a reputation around the department. It only failed to get to one fire in its history, but when it came to running the chief home and around on his trips of inspection, it never failed to balk. Its light weight and usual urgency in getting to a fire made it quite the sight to see on the move. The Cameron was traded to McClellan Stilwell in 1910, when the department replaced it with a Buick.

1910 Buick Model 16 Roadster, Driver Jack Taylor, Chief Edward Jewhurst

In June 1910 the Cameron Runabout was traded in as part of the purchase agreement for a 1910 Buick Model 16 Roadster from Stillwell & Whyte in Auburn, NY. Ironically, the Cameron "flier" that ran to fires for years was seriously damaged in a fire that took place while in for repairs at the Whyte Automobile Garage on December 16, 1910. The fire broke out in the garage when the wash pit ignited. The Cameron was positioned over the pit at the time of the flare-up, and it caught fire and spread to the surrounding woodwork and other equipment in the shop. The Fire Department was called. The fire was raging in the room and the garage was in the center of a number of buildings in close proximity on Dill Street. The fire was held back from spreading, however, the fire in the pit was not able to be extinguished and there was no means or accessibility to smother it. The men went to find sheet iron, snow, sand and other non-combustible material to cover the hole. Some reports had the poor Cameron vehicle as a total loss, however, it was later estimated that it had incurred about $300 worth of damage, which was still significant.

The Buick automobile was more powerful than the Cameron. It had 35 horsepower and was customized by the driver, John "Jack" Taylor, who removed the tonneau and arranged for a superstructure to be installed for Fire Department purposes. It had a 112" wheelbase and 34"x4" wheels. In July 1910, Chief Jewhurst took the Buick to Oswego to borrow some of their fire department relics for exhibition and display at an upcoming Central New York Fireman's Association Convention being held in Auburn. The Oswego newspaper reported the Buick, with John Taylor at the wheel as chauffeur, carried Chief Jewhurst from Auburn to Oswego in less than two hours. Impressive time during those years! A humorous newspaper story in 1915 indicated that the Buick was "in the hospital as a result of internal injuries which it received near the corner of North and Water streets" while responding to an alarm. The automobile was in route, driven by Jack Taylor, when he heard a loud grinding, crushing sound and the car stopped. The driver was not able to get the car moving again and it turned out that the gears were stripped. The Buick had a racy style, was dependable and always drew a crowd as it sped through the streets responding to alarms over the years. The Buick proved to be a reliable addition to the department and remained in service until 1920, when it was replaced with a Chalmers automobile.

The public historically loved to watch the horse-drawn apparatus pass by on their way to a fire. The sounds of the gongs, horns and bells commanded attention. The teams of horses running and pulling their charges and the sight of the various engines and carts and wagons made it impossible for folks to look away. However, the allure and awe was seemingly not tied to the horse-drawn apparatus of the responders, for when the Chief's car raced toward the scene, the flash of the brass fixtures, and the blur of red speeding by, captured their attention just as well. The excitement of witnessing bravery in action as city residents watched their firemen race toward flames was alluring regardless of the mode of transportation used. The department had already completed its transition from hand-drawn to horse-drawn apparatus. It was poised to begin the next phase; motorized apparatus. A new era was dawning for the Auburn Fire Department.

Knox Combination Truck, AFD Combination 4

   The first motorized fire-fighting apparatus was introduced to the Auburn Fire Department in 1911. This was cutting edge technology to introduce to the city and showed Auburn's progressive and forward-thinking manner. Outside of very large cities, such as New York City, it was rather rare to see automobiles and motorized apparatus in fire departments. Auburn was leading the way! Chief Edward J. Jewhurst and Fire Commissioner W. C. Burgess traveled to Springfield, MA to the Knox Automobile Company in July. A contract was signed for purchase of a new motor driven combination hose and chemical wagon to be housed within the quarters of Hose Company No. 4 due to its central location. The Knox Combination Truck was guaranteed to travel up to 40mph and had a wheel base of 145 inches and a tread of 60 inches. It had a 4-cylinder, 60 horsepower motor and a Holyoke box and Kelly dual block solid tires in the rear and single in front. It was furnished with heavy springs and a nut and screw steering gear. The car body was 8'5" long and 50" wide. It could carry twelve men, 1,000 feet of 2 ½" hose in the body of the cart and 200 feet of chemical hose in a wire basket, two combination extension ladders (18 and 12 feet long), one roof ladder, one crowbar, one door opener, two plaster hooks, two axes, one universal hook, one 40-gallon chemical tank set crosswise on the frame, two pony chemical holders (one on each side), storage boxes for extra soda bags, acid containers and small parts. There were also two 3-gallon hand extinguishers, two oil or electric side lamps and one oil or electric tail lamp, two gas searchlights, one prest-o-lite tank, electrically ignited, one hand horn and bulb and all necessary tools for work on the vehicle. The Knox truck was chain driven and low to the ground. It had a full complement of meters, speedometers, pressure meters, a cranking screw and clock. The car was painted a bright vermillion red and lettered on either side "Combination 4". It had many brass and metal trimmings. It was supplied with a No. 11 rotary gong under the driver's footboard. It was equipped with spark plugs made by the New York Mica & Manufacturing Company of Auburn, NY. When fully loaded and equipped with hose and other apparatus, the Knox truck weighed 5,000 lbs. The purchase price for the truck was $5,600. Prior to being shipped to Auburn, the Knox machine was exhibited at the Convention of Fire Chiefs in Milwaukee and the International Convention of Municipal Officials in Chicago. The truck attracted much attention and many compliments at both conventions. The truck was a new and modern device that not many fire departments owned. Syracuse, New York did not have its first motorized firefighting apparatus until after Auburn had motorized trucks implemented. During the manufacturing of the truck, Jack Taylor, Driver for Chief Jewhurst, went to the factory in order to be become familiar with the machine and its operation. The Knox truck shipped out of Chicago via freight car and was received in October 1911. The City was excited to see its new fire truck. Once it was unloaded off the train, it carried Chief Jewhurst, Fire Commissioner Burgess, former Fire Commissioner E. J. Moore, George H. Leonard (agent for the Knox Automobile Company) and representatives of the Advertiser and Citizen along the streets on an exhibition trip around the city. They traveled up State Street to Genesee Street to Hoffman Street and took East Genesee Street hill with ease, then back to City Hall, where it was then taken to Leonard's Garage for temporary housing. Members of the Fire Department and the public gathered around the fire engine to see the latest addition to Auburn's fine Fire Department. From the time it was received on October 3rd and officially installed on December 4th, the men of Hose Company No. 4 received extensive training on the truck's mechanisms and operations. Before it was officially installed, the truck was run through the streets and over the roads outside of town. All seven members of the hose company learned how to handle the truck. It was described as a miniature fire department on wheels and was the pride of the Auburn Fire Department. Hose Company No. 4's combination wagon and team of horses was transferred to Hose Company No. 6 in their newly built fire station at 184 State Street. The new Knox apparatus was housed in the Market Street station. The Knox performed well for the department. Auburn Fire Captain Frank B. Hughson told a gathering in Ithaca at the Cataract Hose Company No. 7's annual banquet that the Knox had traveled a mile and a tenth to a fire in 2 minutes, 51 seconds. It was also said to have traveled one and one-half miles to a fire on a bitter cold night and over a quarter of a mile of rough road in five minutes, ten seconds. The first horse-drawn apparatus to arrive on the same scene took ten minutes and 30 seconds, and the fire was already under control. Captain Hughson did caution against excessive speeding with the new fire truck. He indicated that it was not necessary to speed tons of apparatus down the streets at 35-40mph and recommended that it was far better to travel easily to ensure that the destination was reached. If some of the firemen or passersby were killed due to speeding through the city, they would always have something to think about at night. As excited as the firemen and citizens of Auburn were for their first motorized firefighting truck, the proof would be in the pudding. And boy was it! In the first three months of service the truck responded to 42 alarms and covered 62.6 miles. During times of heavy snowfall, the men practiced driving it about three times a week, anywhere from a half to three-quarters of a mile from headquarters, in connection with the 1 o'clock afternoon practice hitch. During these practice runs, the truck covered another 53 miles. The total distance traveled in the first three months was 115.6 miles. Upkeep for the three months was $17.73. Upkeep of a team of department horses for the same period was officially computed at $77. The automobile could be run for a year for what it was costing to keep a team of horses for four months. The 1911 Knox Combination Hose and Chemical Wagon was considered an overwhelming success and paved the way for continued transition from horse-drawn to motorized apparatus.

Knox Combination Truck, AFD Combination 3

So successful was the 1911 Knox Combination fire wagon, that in 1912, another Knox Combination Hose and Chemical Wagon were added to the department's rolls. The truck was almost identical to the first Knox automobile with the exception of some improvements noted over the first Knox. The new truck had a strengthened front axle and gear. This change was suggested by Auburn after Company 4's truck was damaged due to an accident. The Knox Company implemented the change and Company 4's truck received the same strengthened front axle and gear. Another improvement was made to the "jack gear", the gear upon which the main drive chain was run. Company 4's truck also had this improvement implemented on its truck. Hose Company No. 3 on Clark Street housed the second Knox combination hose and chemical wagon apparatus. The Clark Street firehouse had just been completed and was designed expressly for mechanized fire engines. The Knox truck remained in service until 1929, when it was replaced with a new combination hose and pumper motor truck.

Knox Combination Trucks, AFD Combination 3 & 4, 1910 Buick Model 16 Roadster

In December of 1915, a big, 6-cylinder American LaFrance Hook and Ladder truck was added to the department. It was the first hook and ladder truck purchased for the paid, permanent Fire Department. Specifications for the truck were provided to five companies; The Seagrave Motor Truck Company, The James Boyd and Bros. Company, American LaFrance Fire Apparatus Company, Whyte Motor Truck Company and The Service Motor Truck Company. American LaFrance got the contract. At a cost of approximately $5,500, it was considered a bargain for the benefits it provided the City of Auburn in its ability to perform. Chief Jewhurst indicated "It's one real joy of the department." The truck arrived in Auburn on a large, flat railroad car and remained at the LeHigh Valley railroad yard until a representative from American LaFrance in Elmira, NY could be on hand to oversee the installation of the truck. American LaFrance reported they had taken extra pains in manufacturing Auburn's truck. Given its proximity to the Elmira plant, Auburn was likely to be a place for potential buyers to see an example of their work. The truck was delivered in spite of a snow storm that covered Auburn with two feet of snow. The American LaFrance Company didn't shy away from delivery of the truck. In fact, they indicated that it would give them a chance to show what the truck could do and how it would handle under such conditions. The truck was successfully driven through the snow-covered and icy streets of Auburn and delivered to the Market Street station without incident.

The horse-drawn era was waning, and the benefits of the motorized apparatus were clear. However, there were stories shared over the years that illustrated some specific exceptions to the rule. Firefighter Frank Hawelka once recalled a day early in his career when he was assigned to Hose Co. No. 1. The department was not fully motorized. Frank Hawelka was assigned to a horse-drawn truck. An alarm came in and off they went! Of course, the motorized apparatus would have arrived first on the scene, were it not for the paving project that rendered Court Street impassable for the vehicle. They stopped and were forced to find an alternate route. Then along comes Frank Hawelka and his fire company in the horse-drawn wagon, able to pass through the construction area! They arrived at the fire first! Hawelka mused that it was certainly the last time that horses beat the motors!

In 1917, the men of Hose Company No. 5 illustrated the ingenuity of the firemen of the City of Auburn when they, themselves, converted an older Thomas touring car into a motorized piece of firefighting apparatus! The Fire Department had purchased a Thomas touring car in the years previous to the conversion. The car was not equipped to fight fires and had been placed in storage. The men of Hose Company 5 knew that the Fire Department would not be positioned to purchase additional motorized fire-fighting automobiles for some time due to the War that was underway and the resulting economic situation faced by the country. They had a vision for the car and saw that it could be modified into a new and functional automobile for their company. The firemen devised a plan to convert the touring car into a fire truck for their use. Once they had a plan in hand, they rolled up their sleeves and got to work! They worked on the car conversion in the Franklin Street station. The car had a six-cylinder motor which was found to be acceptable for their use. They built a box to fit the frame of the car and other necessary components to load it with equipment. As hardware was added and the structure modified, it began to look more and more like a fire truck. The men varnished the foot boards and put everything together as they had painstakingly planned. They even found brass guard rails to install on the truck. The only work completed outside the Fire Department was the painting of the truck. The men of Hose Company No. 5 in 1917 included; Captain Patrick F. Morrissey, Fred Hoyt, William J. Kehoe, William Maywalt, Wendall P. Linnenbach, Martin M. O'Neill, E. H. Arnold and F. J. Hawelka. The truck was unveiled August 31, 1917, when it was driven out of the Franklin Street station by Captain Patrick F. Morrissey and was admired by many of the firemen and other onlookers. Chief Jewhurst and Fire Marshal George Coneybear were said to have been "all smiles". The Thomas car had been converted to a combination hose and chemical truck. It was surely a great source of pride for the firemen of Hose Company No. 5, in fact, the entire Auburn Fire Department and the community as a whole. Such proactive work was consistent with the Fire Department's character and ingenuity. At the time of the Thomas touring car conversion, there were only three companies that remained with horse-drawn engines; Hose Companies 1, 2 and 6.

Edward J. Jewhurst, ever the progressive Fire Chief, saw the benefits of motorized fire apparatus first hand. It was faster and more efficient than its horse-drawn counterpart. It was also less expensive to maintain the motor equipment than it was to care for the horses within the department. Chief Jewhurst knew that he could not simply state that fact and have city officials accept his word. He developed a table that detailed the expenses related to maintaining the teams of horses and the motorized equipment. The difference was significant. Expenses for maintenance of the motor apparatus were much less than those of the horses necessary for the engines that were not motorized. In 1920, Mayor A. Percival Burkhart came out in public support of a completely motorized fire department and encouraged the City Council members to replace the remaining horse-drawn engines. Auburn's first City Manager, John P. Jaeckel, on more than one occasion, pointed with pride to Auburn's motorized Fire Department. In 1920, with only three remaining horse-drawn fire companies, Auburn spent approximately $30,000 to finish their transformation and became a completely motorized department. It was a pivotal time for the Fire Department and the City of Auburn. Another new era was beginning with the purchase of three fire engines.

In July of 1920, Auburn's City Manager, John P. Jaeckel, ordered two combination hose and chemical fire engines and one triple combination hose, chemical and pumper fire engine from the American LaFrance Company in Elmira, NY. The triple combination pumper was ordered for Hose Company No. 4 located on Franklin Street. The two combination engines were ordered for use by Hose Companies No. 1 and 6. Hose Company No. 2 received the nine-year-old motorized engine that was in use by Company 4 prior to receiving the new engine.

A comical story was reported in the newspaper that had Mayor Burkhart, City Manager Jaeckel and Chief Jewhurst traveling to Elmira in the Chief's Buick roadster to inspect the new fire equipment. The trip was rocky and rough and resulted in delays due to numerous tire changes. The tires on the Buick were "clincher" style. Clincher tires resembled a horseshoe in a cross section view, and the ends bent up to secure into the rim of the wheel. Tires were changed and/or repaired with the one-piece rim/wheel still on the car. A clincher tire was flexible and could be forced onto the rim. Mayor Burkhart was quoted as saying "We certainly had a rocky-road-to-Dublin trip. I can tell you. The old boat bowls along fairly well, but is far from being modern and comfortable and the clincher tires are a nightmare." It was said that the profanity used during the trip in the Chief's old Buick was shocking.

In November of 1920, the Auburn Fire Department had installed its new equipment and officially became a completely motorized department. It was the culmination of determined spirit, advocacy and leadership in Chief Jewhurst's career and the Auburn Fire Department's adaptability and experience. Jewhurst had seen the department grow from hand-drawn carts to horse-drawn wagons and engines to full motorization of the fire companies. Through the years the firemen had to learn a variety of ways to get their machines from the fire house to the flames; sheer manpower, horses and motorized vehicles. The skillset for each method varied greatly. Firefighters needed to possess the level of skill and bravery necessary to fight fires. They also had to be willing and able to learn how to hitch up horses quickly and run them in response to the alarms. They had to learn how to drive motorized vehicles, something most of us take for granted today, but which was a brand new venture in the early 1900s. It was a time when roads were still in their infancy and the technology of the traveler had advanced faster than the supporting infrastructures and the traffic rules. For the public, the awe and intrigue of the motorized fire engines held just as much appeal as their predecessors. The ringing of the bell, the sound of the alarms and the rush of the engines racing through the streets intent on reaching their destination was exciting.

Chief Jewhurst's Buick was replaced with a 1920 Chalmers vehicle in May of 1921. Ferguson & Helfer, located on Market Street, completed customizations to the automobile. It was painted red and had the seal of the City on each side.

In 1924, the City purchased two 750-Gallon American LaFrance triple combination (chemical, hose wagon and pumper) trucks, which were placed into service for Engines 2 and 3. The pumpers were purchased for $12,500 each.

In 1929, the City purchased three new fire trucks. In July a 1,000-gallon Mack combination hose and pumper truck was installed at Engine 4 at central headquarters. The old Knox truck was traded in as part of the purchase. The Mack truck was the first in the Fire Department to have pneumatic tires, as opposed to solid rubber tires. The Mack's first call to service was on July 17, 1929, and responded to a fire at the Romig Garage on Genesee Street.

The second truck purchased in 1929 was a Mack mechanical aerial hoist ladder truck. It was received in November and assigned to Truck 1 of the Hook & Ladder Company. The truck had an 85' reach and was tractor drawn, as were all aerials that were 85' or 100' through the 1930's. It had a six-cylinder, 150 horsepower motor and was equipped with pneumatic tires. It had an 85' double bank aerial hoist. The aerial hoist was powered through a Power Take-Off (PTO) on the tractor transmission. Power was transmitted to the hoist which was mounted on a trailer and through a vertical shaft. The shaft passed through the center line of both the fifth wheel and ladder turntable and was arranged so that any angle or lateral motion that resulted between the tractor and the trailer would have no negative impact on the operation of the hoist itself. The hoist was made of several components arranged in such a way as to allow them to be removed from the main assembly easily. The components included vertical drive units, clutch and horizontal shaft units, worm shaft unit, worm wheel and crankshaft unit, as well as a hand operating unit. They were encased in a metal housing and ran in oil at all times. The control column was mounted on the turntable, and the turntable operating hand wheel was mounted on top of the column. The hand wheel controlled the rotation of the turntable. The trailer frame of the truck was made of 8" channel construction and was heavily reinforced with channel-type crossmembers and adjustable truss rods to prevent sag and other distortions. The steering wheel provided a short turning radius and ensured easy handling. The bed ladder of the truck could be raised by power to any desired angle and held at that angle while the truck was moved or the turntable was revolving. This lessened the overall time necessary to place a ladder when conditions were particular difficult and in evolving situations. The 85' aerial ladder had two sections. The lower section (aka: bed ladder) was strongly trussed with steel and mounted on the turntable platform. The upper section (aka: fly ladder) could be hoisted by wire cable on a drum and secured in position with a safety lock. The truck came equipped with a 50' rapid-hoist "Bangor" extension ladder and stay poles, a 16' solid extension ladder, two 30' single ladders, a 25' single ladder, a 20' single ladder, a 15' single ladder, a 14' roof ladder with folding hooks, a 12' roof ladder with folding hooks and two 12' pompier scaling ladders. Up until the 1930s all aerial ladders were made of wood and were either spring-hoisted or utilized compressed air. The Mack truck purchased by the City had ladders constructed of thoroughly seasoned, select Oregon Fir which was free of knots. They were finished in natural wood and coated with varnish. The rungs of the ladders were made of hickory. The extension ladders had rope hoists and automatic safety locks. It was also fully loaded with the necessary equipment and apparatus pieces. The Mack mechanical aerial hoist ladder truck was favorably received by the Auburn Fire Department.

In December of 1929, a third Mack 1,000-gallon, triple combination truck was added to the list of apparatus within the department. The Mack truck was very similar to the one purchased in July of 1929. The purchase allowed the department to replace its Knox pumper truck. The purchase resulted from the loss of the Hose Company 6 pumper truck during the 1929 riot and fire at Auburn prison. The Mack Company loaned Auburn a pumper truck in August to use until the new pumper was secured.

After being in the department for 32 years, the two Mack 1,000-gallon pumpers were sold at auction at City Hall in May of 1961. Frank Barski purchased one for $175. Mr. Barski's truck was not in running condition at the time of purchase. He indicated a plan to use it at his milling business in Sennett to wash trucks. Theodore Trice bought the second one for $225. Mr. Trice, who was the proprietor of the Old Stuff Museum in Sennett, added his purchase to his display of antique fire equipment.

Fire Department procedures mandated the fire trucks had to be washed top to bottom, side to side, after every run. The firemen had to wash, detail and polish the trucks. The even had to crawl underneath the trucks and scrub them clean. Sometimes they would just finish cleaning a truck, when an alarm would come in and off they would go! They took pride in the apparatus. Cleaning the trucks over and over also served to reinforce a thorough knowledge of the truck layout and its components.

*1938 American LaFrance City Service Hook and Ladder Truck,
Auburn Fire Department Hook & Ladder No. 1*

In October of 1938, the city acquired a new American LaFrance city service hook and ladder truck. City service hook and ladder trucks were similar to their aerial counterparts, except they did not have the master aerial ladder. Instead, they carried ground ladders, hooks and other tools. City service trucks were used for areas and circumstances where an aerial ladder was not required. Generally speaking, city service trucks were run by hook and ladder companies. Auburn was no exception. The city service truck remained in the department for years. In June of 1948, it had a new, 12-cylinder engine installed at a cost of $2,696. This expense extended the life of the truck and proved to be an economical decision. The service truck started hard and was slower than some of its counterparts in the department. The truck had a long wheel base and it was tricky to drive around corners. As it aged, the truck became more temperamental. If the driver didn't watch the gauges

Mack Truck c. 1945 / L to R: Pete Mentillo, John Burger (Driver), Tom Gard, Richard Gunger.

and choke the engine at just the right time, as the truck was started, it would stall and was next to impossible to restart; oftentimes another truck would have to be used.

In 1945, the City contracted with the Mack Manufacturing Company for the purchase of two 1,000-gallon, triple combination pumper trucks at a cost of $10,250 each. The trucks were installed at Engines 3 and 6. Engines 3 and 6 retired their trucks upon installation of the new machines. Engine 3 had been previously operating with its 1924 American LaFrance 750-gallon pumper for more than 20 years. Engine 6, located at headquarters, had been utilizing a 350-gallon pumper truck. Chief James Doyle and Chief Mechanic George Reidy had recommended the purchase of the two new Mack pumpers due the aging condition and waning reliability of the existing apparatus.

In September of 1946, the two American LaFrance Fire Engines were sold at auction. The 350-gallon pumper was sold for $170. The 4-cylinder, combination hose and chemical pumper was sold for $100. The Cadillac squad car, which was purchased secondhand in 1933 for $100, sold at auction for $700. The squad car had been used to transfer hose and men to fires over the years. In 1948, as part of the Auburn Centennial celebration, the Auburn Fire Department displayed a nineteenth century, hand-drawn hose cart that belonged to the E. D. Clapp Hose Company. They also displayed Archie Goodwin's pony buggy used to respond to fires.

In 1953, the City Council approved the purchase of two Seagrave 1,000 gallon pumper trucks. The two new trucks replaced the two Mack pumper trucks purchased in 1929 as primary apparatus. The Mack trucks were held as reserve trucks. The new Seagrave engines were purchased for a total of approximately $34,000. A federal government grant was obtained as part of a Civil Defense program and provided $12,000 toward the purchase of both trucks. The City agreed to use the new vehicles in the event of a Civil Defense emergency in exchange for the grant money. The new truck, received in 1954, had a 12-cylinder motor and weighed between 9-10 tons fully loaded. It pumped 1,000 gallons of water a minute. The truck had two booster tanks which held 150 gallons each. The engine carried portable deluge guns capable of delivering all the water the pump could provide through one nozzle. The two new pumper engines were used on mutual aid calls as well. The Seagrave truck sustained pumper damage during the Osborne Street fire in September 1969. It was later traded in as part of a purchase for a replacement truck in late 1969.

In 1956, the City Council accepted a bid from the Peter Pirsch & Sons Co. in Kenosha, Wisconsin, for the purchase of a 100' tractor-drawn aerial ladder truck for $40,903. The purchase price included a $1,000 trade in allowance for the Mack 85' aerial truck purchased in 1929. The Pirsch family started building wagons in Kenosha, Wisconsin in the 1850's. The founder's son, Peter Pirsch, continued the company's innovations with his fire engine designs. Peter Pirsch was an inventor and held many patents, including door openers, hose shut-off valves and extension ladders. Peter Pirsch was cited by Congress for his smoke ejector machine which was credited with saving sixteen men trapped in a collapsed Chicago sanitary tunnel in April 1931. Pirsch & Sons were pioneers in the fire engine industry. Tractor-drawn aerial trucks were also known as tiller trucks. The 1956 Pirsch required two drivers with separate steering wheels for the front and rear wheels. One of the big advantages of the tiller truck was its maneuverability. The independent steering for the front and back wheels allowed the truck to make sharper turns, which was particularly useful for narrow streets. The truck was sold to the Village of Aurora in 1979 for $15,000. The truck was eventually decommissioned and sold to personal collector and Auburn firefighter, Kevin Donnelly. Several years later, arrangements were made with the new owner, and the Pirsch was driven by Frank DeJoy and Bob Hoey to a retired firefighter picnic. It was a great surprise to the firefighters and the topic of discussion much of the day! The Pirsch truck was also part of the 2012 Business Improvement District (BID) annual parade and was driven down Genesee Street. It was admired and remembered by many of those who gathered for the parade.

In 1965, a new $22,000 pumper truck was added to the department's apparatus list. The engine was an American LaFrance, Class A pumper and was housed at Engine 3 on Clark Street. It produced 150 lbs. of pressure on demand and carried 300 gallons of water. It had a 273 horsepower engine. That same year, a hydraulic aerial beam truck, also called a cherry picker, was purchased. Primarily used by the Auburn City Electrician, the truck was occasionally used by Fire Department personnel for rescue operations. The bucket could attain a height of 35' and proved versatile for any desired height within its specifications. A counterbalance was built into the truck to maintain equilibrium while the bucket and

arms could turn 240 degrees. The bucket was designed to carry one man, but could hold two when necessary. It was largely used for repairs of traffic lights, fire alarm telegraph system work in the city and other tasks that required the City Electrician to achieve heights the aerial beam truck could provide.

In 1969, the City contracted with the American LaFrance Co. of Elmira, New York for two, 1970 model, 1500 gallon per minute (gpm) pumpers for the Fire Department at a cost of $78,370. This purchase provided the department with two firsts; the first pumpers to have diesel engines and the first pumpers to have covered cabs. The 1953 Seagrave truck was traded in as part of the purchase deal. The transition to diesel was a bit challenging, because of the differing operating technique required. The diesel truck had a lot more torque. Diesel's advantage over gas for a fire engine is that it can carry more load with less strain on the engine. Diesel develops more horsepower lower on the speed curve than gas because of the increased torque. The '70 American LaFrance kept experiencing twisted driveshaft problems. The mechanic was able to fix it on site in the repair shop, but the issue recurred several times. The initial thought was that it was a driver issue. However, upon contacting American LaFrance after repeated incidents, it was discovered that the manufacturer had installed an incorrect driveshaft. The truck had the correct driveshaft installed and the issue resolved. The truck had a low cab and it was not uncommon for firefighters to hit their helmets against it while getting in for a call. In 2001, one of the American LaFrance pumpers (serial number 2287) was donated to the Poplar Ridge Fire Company.

A three-in-one combination truck was contracted by the City from Pierce Co. of Appleton, Wisconsin in 1978, for $217,811. Truck 2 was received in 1979. It was a rear-mount aerial ladder with a pump and a water way to the bucket, which could hold three people. The

bucket at the end of the ladder was equipped with a deluge gun as well as controls for maneuvering the ladder. LTI Aerial Service, a ladder tower company in Lancaster, Pennsylvania provided and installed the ladder on the chassis before Pierce Co. added the final pieces to the truck. The Pierce truck replaced the 1956 Pirsch aerial truck.

A new pumper was installed in the Auburn Fire Department in 1981. The City purchased a pumper, known as a "squirt", from the Pierce Co. of Appleton, Wisconsin for $155,600. The pumper differed from others in the department in that it had a water tower mounted under a ladder and had a power-driven nozzle at the end. The tower could be raised to any height of a house or small building. Rear controls powered the tower apparatus. Duplicate tower controls were also placed on the side of the pump panel.

A new, 25' Saulsbury/Chevrolet light rescue truck was installed within the Auburn Fire Department in the beginning of 1982. It was the beginning of the two-piece truck concept for the department and was also implemented during the infancy of the development of Emergency Medical Services (EMS) delivery by NYS certified Emergency Medical Technicians (EMTs). Truck R-1-1 carried Auburn's first "Jaws of Life", a hydraulic apparatus used to pry apart severely crushed vehicles in order to free people trapped inside. Firefighters received extensive classroom and practical training on use of the new truck's features, including the winch and "Jaws of Life". Much of the practical training took place over a ten day period at the Golden Arrow bus garage on Grant Avenue, where multi-car accidents were staged. The Auburn Fire Department demonstrated the "Jaws of Life" to the public at a simulated accident staged at Cayuga Community College as part of their "Think Before You Drive" campaign.

A 1985 Duplex/LTI 2000 Gallons Per Minute (GPM), 55' elevated waterway engine was purchased for $260,000 and originally assigned to Engine 3, followed by Engine 5 as a spare. It was retired with an estimated 120,000 miles. A 1989 Pierce Arrow 2000 gpm, top-mount pumper truck was purchased for $180,000 and assigned to Engine 2. It was retired with an estimated 130,000 miles. This truck was significant, as it was the first and only top-mount pump panel for the Auburn Fire Department. The top-mount pump panel allowed the operator to be more safely positioned, especially on narrow streets or in a high-traffic area, and provided a 360 degree view. A 1990 Seagrave, 110' aerial ladder truck was implemented in the department and was one of only 11 made. It still serves as a spare today.

A new 1995 Pierce International pumper was purchased for use as a dedicated reserve pumper. The 1500 gpm pumper was purchased for $109,000 and assigned as Engine 1. It was also traded in when the Pemfab rescue truck was purchased in 2011.

In October of 1999, the City of Auburn purchased a custom-built Pierce fire engine at a cost of $419,000. A committee compiled and completed a two-year study in advance of the purchase in order to determine the specifications and features that would be necessary on a new truck. The National Fire Protection Association's guidelines were instrumental in the selection of the new truck. The truck replaced Engine No. 4's 19-year-old fire truck. The Pierce engine provides 2000 gpm of water with a 55' elevated master stream and a 500 gallon water tank. It also has an on-board computer for vehicle maintenance. It remains in service as Engine 5.

A 1991 International-Sutphen mini-pumper was purchased in 2005 from the Syracuse Fire Department. It served as Mini 10 in Syracuse and was originally yellow. The Auburn Department of Public Works (DPW) painted it red for the department. It was placed in service as a rescue truck and also used to tow HAZMAT and special operations trailers. It was traded in when the 1989 Pemfab rescue truck was purchased in 2011. A 2001 Ford, 4-wheel drive truck with a 10,000 lb. tow capacity served as both a light rescue and HAZMAT truck for spill response.

A 2002 Smeal /Spartan, 2000 gpm Compressed Air Foam System (CAFS) pumper, equipped for drafting with a 500 gallon water tank and 30 gallon Class A foam tank was purchased for $430,000. It was originally assigned to Engine 3 and later became a spare, designated as Engine 1. A 2007 American LaFrance 100' tower truck was purchased for $750,000 and assigned at Truck 2. Two 2008 American LaFrance 1500 gpm pumpers were purchased for the Auburn Fire Department and assigned to Engines 2 and 3. They were equipped for drafting with 500 gallon water tanks and 30 gallon Class A foam tanks and injected Class A foam system on the hand lines.

A 2011 Kovatch Mobile Equipment Corp. (KME) 2000 gpm pumper with a 500 gallon water tank and 30 gallon Class A foam tank with a 55' elevated master stream was purchased for $600,000 and installed in the department as Engine 4. Also in 2011, a 1989 Pemfab rescue truck was purchased from Homewood, Illinois for $45,000. Rescue 1 increased the

Fire Department's ability to respond to a myriad of incidents. Included on the truck are an elevated light tower, 6-bottle 6000psi mobile cascade air system, 55kvw Power Take-Off (PTO) generator and increased communications with local and regional agencies.

Delivery of a new fire truck is scheduled for August of 2016, at which time the department will receive an E-One Typhoon, a 2000 gpm pumper, at a cost of $464,000. Assignment is slated for Engine 3. The engine will carry 750 gallons of water, a first for the Auburn Fire Department. All engines purchased after 1981 carried 500 gallons. With reductions in manpower, increased call volumes and an increased chance of one company operating alone for longer periods, it was determined the increased water tank would be very beneficial.

FIRE ALARMS

The first alarms to sound a fire rang from the First Presbyterian church bell in 1816. In 1821, the bell that was installed at the top of the Auburn Prison was also used to sound fire alarms as well as inmate escapes. In 1833, the First Methodist Church located on the corner of North Street and Water Street became the official fire alarm, and the church steeple bell was used in such service until 1837. Use of the church bell as the primary fire alarm ceased in 1837, when a new Town Hall was constructed at the current site of the fire and police station. A 500 lb. bell was installed in the Town Hall and took over primary responsibility for fire alarm service. Other, secondary bells, continued to assist in the fire alarm process. The First Methodist Church continued to toll the alarm as additional notice. In 1877, the D. M. Osborne Co. also had a bell that was used as a fire alarm. The D. M. Osborne bell was sold in 1903, when the factory was purchased by International Harvester. The ladies of St. Francis D'Assisi Church raised enough money to buy the 900 lb. bell. It remained at St. Francis until 1960, when the steeple was removed. The bell was acquired by Theodore Trice, who was a well-known collector of Auburn, New York memorabilia.

Before telephones, the telegraph system was used to sound alarms. A telegraph system was initially used in the mid-1860s and continued through 1870. The City of Auburn and the Water Works Company (which was privately owned) worked together to install a new telegraph alarm system infrastructure in 1872. The wiring system had a command post at the Water Works plant on Pulsifer Drive and another on South Street. After a number of years of use, the fire alarm system, which was made by the Automatic Fire Alarm Company of Ohio, was determined to be insufficient. In 1880, the City invited two companies to demonstrate their fire alarm telegraph systems as possible replacements; Gamewell Fire Alarm Company and Utica Fire Alarm Company. After a thorough review of the systems demonstrated and testimonials received from surrounding municipalities and fire companies in the state, the Gamewell Fire Alarm Company was selected. The contract was accepted in June of 1880 and included a large gong, an electro-mechanical large bell striker, six new medium automatic signal boxes, one 16-inch electro-mechanical engine house gong and alteration of nine street boxes already in use to work with the new Gamewell system. The total cost was $1,005. There were 70 keys initially ordered with the Gamewell system. The number of alarm boxes and keys was increased slightly by the time the system was finalized and installed. The work was to be completed by August of 1881. The City resolved to utilize the bell in the tower of the First Methodist Church and would have the bell striker perform there. In July of 1880, the old fire alarm boxes were removed from service and shipped to the Gamewell Fire Alarm Company in New York, where they underwent alteration. In the meantime, the contract with the Water Works Company expired and the Fire Commissioners took over management of the fire alarm system in January of 1881. George W. Wilson was appointed Superintendent of the Fire

Alarm Telegraph system. The alarm system was tested once a day to ensure the system was operational. The protocol was published for alarm sounding; the First Methodist Church bell first rang the alarm which was then followed by a general alarm and box number from the bell of D. M. Osborne Factory No. 1. In October of 1880, the following fire alarm box station locations and/or keyholders were published:

Box 3	Auburn Water Works Company, corner of Genesee and Exchange Streets. Sound alarm by telephone or call at office
Box 4	Office of J. Barber & Sons, and A. W. Stevens 7 Sons, Washington Street
Box 5	Residences of E. E. Cady, No. 108 North Street and Mrs. T. J. McMaster, No. 109 North Street
Box 6	Residences of William Byrne, No. 132 East Genesee Street and G. H. Meeker, No. 134 East Genesee Street
Box 7	Office Canoga Woolen Mill, Seventh Ward
Box 12	Office Auburn Manufacturing Co.
Box 13	Store of J. H. Pearson, No. 146 Wall Street and shop of William Brooker, No. 137 Wall Street
Box 14	Store of J. D. DeGroff, corner of Franklin Street and Grant Avenue, and residence of A. H. Clark, corner of Grant Avenue
Box 21	D. M. Osborne & Co.'s office, Factory No. 1, MacMaster Street
Box 23	Residences of Jacob Hoseman, No. 26 Frances Street and Thomas Jackson, No. 28 Frances Street
Box 24	Residences of T. P. Case, No. 196 Genesee Street and C. M. Howlett, No. 199 Genesee Street
Box 25	Office of D. M. Osborne & Co.'s office, Factory No. 2, corner of Genesee and Mechanic Streets
Box 31	Office of Auburn Woolen Works Company, Owasco Street

Box 32	Police office, City Hall
Box 41	State Prison, Central Hudson Freight office and residence of John Fischer, corner of State and Wall Streets
Box 42	Residence of J. G. Knapp, No. 74 South Street and B. F. Hall, corner of South and Elizabeth Streets
Box 43	Office of E. D. Clapp & Co., Genesee Street, corner of Division Street

Additional fire alarm boxes were added promptly and consistently to provide greater coverage and more efficient fire alarm activation and response for the citizens of Auburn.

A series of fire alarm boxes were located on street corners, telephone poles and buildings. Some were mounted on pedestals and others directly mounted on buildings or poles. Such technology was still relatively new in Auburn, and there were some amusing reports of people attempting to deposit their letters and other mail into the alarm boxes, mistaking them for U.S. Postal Service boxes. The boxes were connected via low voltage wiring. When an alarm box was activated, a signal traveled via wire from the alarm box through the overhead wire poles to headquarters. The poles in the city held fire alarm telegraph wire, telephone wire, electric light power, street railroad wires and numerous other signal wires for a variety of services. In spite of a city ordinance that regulated the stringing of wires on the poles, it was not uncommon to have reports of interference on the pole from wires crossing or being shifted during additional installations of service wires or due to high winds or heavy snow conditions. On those occasions when wires crossed or some other malfunction occurred in the telegraph wire, fire headquarters would receive a single alarm signal. Of course, at the sound of an alarm all firefighters immediately stopped whatever they were doing and waited to hear additional signals, which would provide the alarm location. The occasional single signal from the telegraph wire resulted in a phrase that every Auburn firefighter knows, "One blow, nobody goes."

At the onset, the public was not allowed to operate a fire alarm box directly to signal a fire. Specific individuals who lived in close proximity to the installed alarm boxes were issued a key to the alarm box. The keyholder would verify that there was a fire in the vicinity of the box to be pulled and would operate the box according to specific instructions. Depending on the type of box (weight-sector or spring-sector), when the lever was pulled down, it would either raise a weight that allowed gravity to motivate the clockwork mechanism when released or released a mainspring wound to sufficient tension to motivate the clockwork mechanism. When an alarm was triggered, a signal was tapped out onto the fire alarm telegraph wire. Each alarm box was assigned a specific number and when pulled, a code wheel containing teeth spun, causing the normally closed circuit to open for a momentary pulse. The pulses corresponded to the box number, alerting the Fire Department of the activated box alarm. The box number was transmitted four or more times. The multiple rounds of the box number transmission assured it was received properly at the fire station. A ticker tape device would record the incoming alarm sequence and fire fighters would match the sequence to the box number and neighborhood where it was installed. Once activated, someone had to wait at the box until firemen arrived so that they could be directed to the fire location.

In 1881, the keyholders included:

1	George Wilson (Supt. Fire Alarm Telegraph)	43	D. M. Osborne, 1
2	Robert Peat (Fire Commissioner)	44	Auburn Woolen Mill
3	George Battams (Fire Commissioner)	45	Police Office (City Hall)
4	Joseph Pearson (Fire Commissioner)	46	State Prison Gate
5	Edward J. Jewhurst (Chief Engineer)	47	Freight Office (N. Y.C. R.R.)
6	Thomas Spears (1st Asst. Engineer)	49	James G. Knapp
7	Thomas Heffernan (2nd Asst. Engineer)	50	George Underwood
8	Nelson B. Eldred (Supt. Auburn Water Works Co.)	51	E. D. Clapp (Manufacturing Co.)
9	H. B. Fay	52	Charles Rattigan (Bank Watchman)
10	Charles W. Jennings	53	Willard L. Bundy (Alderman 10th Ward)
11	James Parker	54	Benjamin R. Webster (Ald. 3rd Ward)
12	Joseph Cook (Police)	55	Allen McKain (Alderman 2nd Ward)
13	Michael Boyle (Police)	57	James Malone (Police)
14	S. L. Hughson (Police)	59	George Lightfoot (Police)
15	Patrick Graney (Police)	60	John Underwood (Supt. Poor)
16	Adolph Casper (Police)	61	Peter Anderson
17	William Reynolds	62	Eli Gallup
18	George Wilder	63	John D. Osterhoudt

19	Henry Crosbie (Chief Police)	64	J. Lee Bundy
20	Peter Callanan (Police)	65	Thomas R. Dean
21	Hugh Taylor (Police)	66	Edward C. Hall
22	Byron Dennison (Depot. Police)	67	Clarence Day
23	George Webber (Police)	68	John McGarr
24	Geoge Fullmer (Capt. Police)	69	Richard Russell
25	John D. Crayton	70	George E. Thompson
26	Office of J. Barber & Sons	71	Matthew Tobin (Police)
27	Office of Stevens & Sons	73	Peter Kelley
29	Z. M. Masters	74	D. M. Osborne (Store House, Seymour)
30	William Byrne	75	Clarence Hoose
31	George H. Hacker	75	J. L. Elliott
32	Office of Canoga Woolen Mills	77	Henry C. Allman
33	Office of Auburn Manufacturing Co.	78	James Hamilton
34	Store of J. H. Pearson	79	H. Coffran
35	William Brooker	80	D. O. Connor
36	John D. DeGroff	81	Jerry Quill
37	Abel H. Clark	82	George E. Barber
38	D. M. Osborne, 2	83	George Bryant
39	Adam Friend	84	S. C. R. R. Telegraph Office
40	Thomas Jackson	85	James Armstrong
41	Theodore P. Case	86	Dunning & Co.
42	Charles M. Howlett		

In the early years of the fire alarm telegraph system, Auburn had four different styles of alarm boxes. The first fire alarm boxes were vulnerable to interference if two or more boxes or other transmission on the same circuit were sent at the same time. Under those circumstances, a jumbled signal would be received at the fire station. To obviate this issue, the City began to install new boxes and replace existing boxes with a non-interfering style fire alarm box. Gamewell had improved upon its original design. The newer style fire alarm box was designed such that when a box was activated to signal an alarm, that box took

control of the circuit and disabled other boxes from transmitting. When the transmission was complete, the circuit was made available for other alarms.

Maintenance of the fire alarm telegraph system required periodic runs of new wires and relocation of poles. The city's original repeater was second-hand. The fire alarm telegraph was arranged with three circuits. In 1891, Circuit 1 entailed the Wheeler bell, a bell striker and 100 feet of wire; Circuit 2 contained 12 alarm signal boxes, 5 ½ miles of wire, 107 poles and mechanical and electrical gongs of varying sizes; Circuit 3 contained 19 alarm signal boxes, 9 ¼ miles of wire, 141 poles and mechanical and electrical gongs of varying sizes along with bells. A "modern" repeater and switchboard was added to the fire alarm telegraph system at a cost of $1,500 in 1899. In 1903, the City began the work of placing the telegraph wires underground. This type of fire alarm system proved to be very reliable.

During 1894, an increased number of false alarms were received. Since many of the firemen responded on foot with apparatus, a false alarm was particularly problematic. A long run in response to a false alarm not only rendered the responding apparatus unavailable in the event of a real fire elsewhere, but also exhausted the men needlessly. In September of 1894, the Board of Fire Commissioners requested the Auburn Common Council to have the city ordinances amended so as to make false fire alarms punishable. The request was approved, and the matter was referred to the Auburn Police Department for enforcement of the ordinance.

A fire company's response to a call depended on, among other things, a definitive location for the alarm. The telegraph system provided the exact location of the box turning in the alarm. During the late 19th century, telephones were largely unavailable to the masses and not highly populated within Auburn. The telegraph system did not rely on word of mouth or verbal references to areas in the City of Auburn that not everyone would quickly ascertain. It provided an objective location for a call that the firemen could quickly respond to. In the mid- to late-1800s and continuing into the 1940's, Auburn had a variety of communities (some of their inhabitants occasionally identified as 'gangs') within the city that were commonly referenced in conversations, reports and news stories of the day; Hackney, Stump City, The Swamp, New Guinea, Hog Hollow, the Quarry and the Bloody Fourth to name a few. Such informal references to locations within the city during times of fires would likely have resulted in increased response times, as the men would have had to first figure out where they were going. The telegraph system pinpointed an exact box location in the city. The community groups within Auburn were geographical in nature. New Guinea included the area surrounding Osborne and Elizabeth Streets. Hog Hollow was in the area of S. Division Street and along the Owasco outlet and bordering the LeHigh Valley Railroad tracks. It was so named because hogs were raised between the railroad and the outlet. The Swamp included the 9th Ward of the city. Stump City included the area around Paul and Lansing Streets. When houses were built in that section, the heavy woods were cleared away, but the stumps remained behind. Stump City later became known as Five Points. Hackney was in the west end of the city and included Wall and Aurelius Streets, among others. The Hackney boys had a reputation for being tough and indulged in vices such as gambling and drinking alcohol. They were also partial to fire and were said to be responsible for several significant fires in the city over the years. The Bloody Fourth included the 4th Ward of the city; the designation was made long before it transitioned years later to become known as a community of Polish residents. Laborers who lived in the Bloody Fourth area formed into bands and continuously rivaled each other. Not being barbaric, they barred the use of stones and knives. Instead they would fight with bare-knuckled fists. The streets were often covered in the crimson blood of the fighters; hence the name, Bloody Fourth.

For decades the groups in the city would celebrate "The Night Before", the eve of the Fourth of July. Each clan would try to outdo the others with bonfires, fireworks and hijinks that were usually taken too far and required the assistance of the Police and Fire Departments. Participants prepared for weeks for the event. The crowds were noisy and full of energy. The object of the night was to make a lot of noise; the louder, the better. Fireworks would be launched down streets and toward neighboring communities. The bonfires that were lit on these nights were huge. It was not uncommon to see a large bonfire built by the Stump Gang on the corner of Genesee and Market Streets, with the wood piled almost as high as the buildings themselves in the early 1900s. Participants would gather lumber for the fire for weeks in advance of July 3rd, sometimes stealing wood and barrels from around the city. The fire in this location occurred year after year and was observed to be blistering hot. It would sometimes crack the windows in nearby stores. Crowds of onlookers would gather to see the fire. It filled the audience with awe, but it was also a very dangerous situation that involved the Fire Department on numerous occasions. The area near Five Points always saw a massive bonfire. There was a fine line between celebration and danger. In those days, the tolerance for Independence Day activities was much greater. The Auburn Fire Department, itself, participated in some of the joviality of the July 3rd celebration. At headquarters there was a cannon that was said to have looked like a small howitzer. They would pack it full of black powder and set it off repeatedly through the night. The entire city could hear the boom from the fire station, and the houses in the vicinity of the fire station shook.

So many Auburnians are familiar with the bell that sits atop City Hall. Many people don't realize that the bell started in service in Auburn as a fire alarm bell. In 1881, the Auburn City Council decided that a larger and louder bell was necessary to sound fire alarms. The city was growing in population, number of buildings and overall size such that it required the city to be divided into fire districts and a bell installed that could be heard throughout the city. In January of 1881, at the request of the City Council, the Committee on Fire Department was formed and instructed to contact manufacturers to obtain information about a new fire alarm bell, which was to weight no less than 3,500 lbs. While discussions were underway to identify a new fire alarm bell, the City had wire run between the bell striker in the tower of the First Methodist Church with a mechanism in Alderman Willard Bundy's jewelry store. Beginning January 12, 1881, one stroke of the bell at 1pm daily would test the circuit of the alarm system and show that it was operational and also to give the correct time. One o'clock was selected as the test time of the circuit to avoid confusion with the many bells around the city that rang at noon. Any break in the current or the telegraph wire was detected and registered on the surface of a cylinder connected to the apparatus in Bundy's jewelry store. The mechanism that caused the bell to be struck was designed by Willard Bundy.

Willard L. Bundy was born on December 8, 1845, in Otsego, New York. His family moved to Auburn and he worked as a jeweler, establishing his jewelry store in 1868. Willard Bundy was a noted inventor, having held patents for many mechanical items. Among his patents were a key time recorder to mechanically record employees who clocked in and out of work, a card printing attachment for cash registers, improvements in napkin holders, improvements in sleeve buttons, and an electric station indicating apparatus. Together with his brother, Harlow, the Bundy Manufacturing Company was formed in 1889, in Binghamton, New York. It was their time recorder innovations that proved most valuable to the company. The concept of using a mechanical device to record the clock in and clock out activity of employees forever changed the workplace and remains a means in use today. Willard left the Bundy Manufacturing Company and moved his family to Syracuse, New York and formed the Bundy Time Recording Company. He died in January of 1907 in Syracuse, New York. Over the years the original Bundy Manufacturing Company was part of a group of mergers and acquisitions and eventually became part of International Business Machines (IBM). IBM consolidated the offices and removed the holding company structure and subsidiary names in the 1930s. Although he had left the original company, Willard L. Bundy was a founder of it and contributed significantly as an inventor. He played an undeniable role in the successes achieved by the Bundy Manufacturing Company.

City Council members decided that City Hall would be a good and central location for the bell once the tower was strengthened. The Committee on Fire Department reported to the City Council that four bell manufacturers were considered; per pound rates were identified:

Meneely & Co.	Troy, NY	29¢/lb.	Delivered in Troy
Buckeye Bell Co.	Cincinnati, OH	25¢/lb.	Delivered in Cincinnati
Jones & Co.	Troy, NY	25 ½¢/lb.	Delivered at Troy
Clinton H Meneely	Troy, NY	31¢/lb.	Delivered in Auburn

Meneely & Co. was considered a frontrunner, as they had already provided bells in Auburn at the First M. E. Church tower, E. D. Clapp Works, D. M. Osborne & Co. and on the house of C. N. Ross Hose 5 Fire Company. A sub-committee of three was appointed and provided the authority to purchase the bell for the fire alarm. Three bids were received after public notice was made. Jones & Co. was selected as the foundry to make the bell for the city for 25 ½¢ per pound. The bell would weigh 4,500 pounds and cost $1,147.50, with an additional $140 for mountings, $40 for hanging and $200 for dome complete. As part of the purchase price, an expert from Troy would come to Auburn to evaluate the installation site, order the necessary timbers and give direction regarding placement of the same. The bell founder would also furnish all the necessary tackle, blocks and pulleys and assume all risk during installation of the bell. It was felt that the services would be well worth the extra money. The resolution was unanimously adopted. Jones & Co., of Troy, New York, would cast the large fire alarm bell for the City of Auburn.

In choosing Jones & Co. to manufacture the fire alarm bell, Auburn had selected a company that already had ties to Auburn. In 1819, Andrew Meneely apprenticed under Julius Hanks. When his apprenticeship was complete, he went to work for Horatio Hanks in Auburn, New York. The company's business profited from the construction of the Erie Canal. In 1826, Horatio Hanks closed the shop in Auburn, New York and moved to Troy, where he opened a mathematical instrument company. Julius Hanks had opened a company in Troy by that time. Across the river, in Gibbonsville (renamed West Troy in 1836, and currently, Watervliet), Andrew Meneely, Julius' former apprentice, opened a competing business, Meneely & Company, in 1825. Andrew Meneely achieved a reputation for producing fine and beautiful bells. After Andrew's death in 1851, his sons, Edwin and George, took over the business, then known as "Andrew Meneely's Sons". Edwin and James Harvey Hitchcock broke off and formed a new, competing foundry with the backing of Eber Jones. James Hitchcock was the son of Andrew Meneely's older sister and had married the younger sister of Andrew's wife, Philena Hanks Meneely. Hitchcock was a foreman at Meneely's bell foundry at the time of Andrew's death. The business was initially known as Jones & Hitchcock and had constructed the Troy Bell Foundry. James Hitchcock retired from the business in 1857, and the company name was changed to "Jones & Co."

Jones & Co. operated the Troy Bell Foundry, a premier bell foundry, known for its rich history and vast experience. Their fire alarm bells had a reputation for clear, far-reaching and pleasing tones. Their first bell was produced on Christmas Day 1853 for the New York City Fire Department, and weighed 10,000 lbs. They owned the patent and had exclusive rights to a rotary yoke and round shank bell. The bell hung with the rotary shank which allowed the bell to be turned and the clapper to strike in a different place to prevent breakage. Other manufacturer's bells were hung so that the clapper would strike constantly in two places only on opposite sides of the bed, which led to the unit cracking and breaking over time. Jones & Co. won many awards for their bell designs and tones.

Hildreth's Patent Rotary Yoke and Round Shank Bell used with Jones & Co. bells only

Mr. Octavous Jones, of the Troy Bell Foundry, came to Auburn to inspect the bell location. He also conducted tests of the First Presbyterian and First Methodist church bells to ascertain their key. The fire alarm bell would be significantly larger than either of the two church bells,

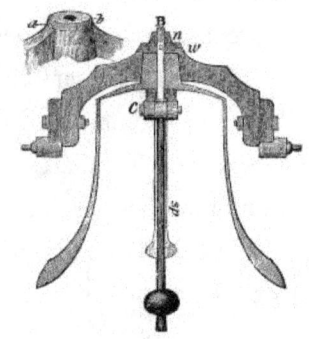

Greatly increased durability and provided a more full and perfect tone

however, the company wanted to ensure that they would be in a different key so that their peal would not be confused. The Troy & Co. bell would be in the key of 'C'. Auburn citizens were given the opportunity to provide appropriate metals to be incorporated into the bell as it was being cast. The bell would become a product of its "home" and would be forever embraced and tied to Auburn. While the bell was being cast, two Aldermen from Auburn traveled to Troy to inspect the quality of the metal and manufacturing of the fire alarm bell. The Aldermen returned satisfied with what they saw.

The bell was received in May and raised into the tower at City Hall. The tower had been strengthened and opened to allow the bell to be placed and the sound to be maximized. The striking equipment was transferred from the First Methodist Church to City Hall. Within days there were those who expressed disappointment, not in the bell itself, but in the sound that it provided. It was felt that the bell was not large enough to carry the alarm to the far reaches of the city. The City Council met and rejected the bell. Mr. Jones requested to address the City Council regarding the issue. On May 23, 1881, Mr. Jones spoke to the City Council and indicated that his company would take back the bell and recast it to provide a heavier and larger one at a rate of 26¢ per pound. He recommended the bell be hung higher and that a larger striker be used as well. The Common Council discussed several increased sizes for a new bell and finally decided the bell would weigh 6,000 pounds. The rejected fire alarm bell was removed from the tower and transported to Troy to be melted down and recast. A new tower for the bell would be built in place of the existing one and would be 25 feet higher, as suggested by Mr. Jones.

On May 25, 1881, another contract was signed with Jones & Co. for a new fire alarm bell to weigh no less than 6,000 pounds and made of pure bell metal (copper and tin). The price was 26¢ per pound, with an additional $60 hanging fee and $20 mounting fee. The new bell arrived and was hung in the tower of City Hall on June 17, 1881. The bell weighed just over 6,022 lbs. and was considered a fine and handsome bell.

The Wheeler Bell, City Hall, Auburn NY

The bell has raised letters that read on one side:

FIRE DEPARTMENT

AUBURN, N. Y.

1881

"THE WHEELER"

The other side reads:

THE JONES & COMPANY

TROY BELL FOUNDRY

TROY, N. Y.

1881

The bell was known as "The Wheeler" in honor of Mayor Cyrenus Wheeler, Jr. The Common Council paid $1,645.91, calculated by the price per pound of the bell plus the additional charges for services related to mounting and hanging. The bell striker was installed by the Gamewell Company and the whole weight of the striker equipment was estimated at two tons. It was connected to toll using electricity by a device using clockwork gear developed by Willard Bundy. The newspaper humorously indicated that the bell could strike back if it wanted to! When tolled, the bell was reported to have been heard some six miles away. The bell was used to sound fire alarms, alert residents of an escaped prisoner and notify of a lost child. Ten tolls of the bell were used to indicate a lost child. Continual, rapid tolling of the bell indicated an inmate had gone over the wall at the Auburn Prison.

Over the years, concern was raised about the strength of the tower. The original tower was built in 1836, and was reinforced and strengthened in 1881 to support the bell. Years of use and tolling of the Wheeler bell had perhaps

Cyrenus Wheeler Jr.
Mayor of Auburn
1881-1886, 1889-1890
(Courtesy of City of Auburn)

taken a toll on the tower as well. It was said that when the bell rang, it made City Hall creak and groan. Some were fearful the bell would come down or cause damage to the building. On July 23, 1901, the Wheeler bell struck at its usual 1pm and then had its wire connections cut and it was removed from service. Businessmen and the citizens of Auburn immediately called for the City to provide the necessary structure in order to put the bell back into service. The big Wheeler bell was already in the hearts of Auburnians and they spoke loud and clear. In 1902, the City Engineer drew up plans for a strengthened tower to sufficiently carry the Wheeler Bell. Work was completed on the roof and tower, including the flooring and supports, in 1903. The Wheeler bell was reinstalled and its powerful and far-reaching toll could be heard again!

The old City Hall and the original home of Col. John L. Hardenbergh (part of the adjoining fire headquarters) were razed in 1930 to build a new Police Department, city jail and Fire Department headquarters. City officials ensured that the old Hardenbergh residence (which had been used for a multitude of private and City purposes over the years) would be dismantled with care so that any possible hidden papers or other relics related to early Auburn would not be overlooked. The key to the Mayor's office in the old City Hall was presented to Leonard Searing, president of the Cayuga County Historical Society, to be kept as a historic relic. The Wheeler bell rang for the last time in the old City Hall on September 2, 1930, when Mayor Charles D. Osborne and City Manager John F. Donovan rang an alarm together from Box 37 at the corner of South Street and Chapman Avenue. The Wheeler bell was removed from the old City Hall on September 3, 1930. A large crowd gathered to watch and take photos as their faithful servant was lowered from its tower. The future of the Wheeler bell was not known at that time. What was known, was that this friend of Auburn would remain in the city and would have a place of prominence. "The Wheeler" found a new home in 1931, atop the new Memorial City Hall on South Street. It was retired from service as a fire alarm bell, but would continue to toll at 1pm and 8pm daily for years to test the fire alarm circuit and indicate the time. It also tolled for memorial occasions and lost children.

The Wheeler bell has witnessed and celebrated many positive events throughout its history. As news was received and confirmed Germany's surrender on November 11, 1918, which would end World War I, Fire Chief Edward J. Jewhurst and Captain Frank Hughson arranged to have the massive fire bell announce the news to the people of Auburn loudly and continuously! Of course, the fire alarm bell was just part of the city's celebration; it was joined by church bells, factory bells, shouts of joy, horns and whistles blew along with all other means of blasting their relief. The fire engines were driven around the city with sirens wailing in celebration! The Wheeler bell called out on the 11th hour, of the 11th day, of the 11th month in 1918, on Armistice Day, and on the anniversaries of that date for years as Auburn would pause to remember and reflect. On May 21, 1927, the Wheeler announced and celebrated the Lindbergh Trans-Atlantic solo flight from New York to Paris. Throughout the years, the Wheeler Bell has signaled the end of wars, celebrated events, welcomed dignitaries, added to 4th of July celebrations and rung excitement and attention to Auburn's revelries.

The Wheeler Bell remains installed in a tower on top of City Hall today. It has been a part of many alarm notifications, celebrations and mournings. With almost 135 years in service, it is an honored veteran of fire service within Auburn. Its callings have changed over the years, but the significance of the Wheeler bell has not. Citizens of Auburn pass the bell on a daily basis without a thought or perhaps they glance up at it as they pass City Hall. It is unassuming and humble in its perch, available even today to those who call upon it for duty. Those who hear the bell pause with a feeling of respect and honor. The strong, determined clang of the bell is felt within. It captures attention even today any time it is tolled. The Wheeler bell is tolled twelve times for funeral processions of veterans and city officials, recognizing and acknowledging their service. It is operated with a thick, yellow rope and tolled by human hands. The Wheeler bell has witnessed much from its location and has a connection and history within Auburn that can never be replaced.

With the advent of the telephone, fire alarm notification changed significantly. Citizens could now phone the operator to report a fire. Up until 1912, the New York Telephone Company switchboard operators in Auburn, affectionately known as the "Hello Girls", were responsible for answering fire alarm calls placed by telephone. With the installation of a new fire alarm telephone system, a monitor switchboard was installed at the quarters of Hose Company No. 4, which was the central office of the department and located at fire headquarters. When a fire alarm was called in by telephone, the telephone central office rang headquarters and the information regarding fire locations was received there. When an alarm was received, the operator immediately connected it to all companies so that information would be received simultaneously. The operator at headquarters consisted of firemen detailed in rotation to fulfill this duty.

In November of 1953, the City Council authorized City Manager, Alfred Turner, to purchase new equipment for the city fire alarm system from the Gamewell Company at a cost not to exceed $14,000. New equipment included a new automatic switchboard with six box and two alarm circuits, along with additional fire alarm boxes. In 1962, the City's replacement of 8,000 feet of underground cable, linking the fire alarm call boxes in downtown Auburn with the Fire Department headquarters, was completed. The Gamewell Company replaced the cable in the underground subways. While the Gamewell fire alarm boxes are no longer in service today, plenty of us remember them in a variety of locations throughout Auburn.

ANIMALS

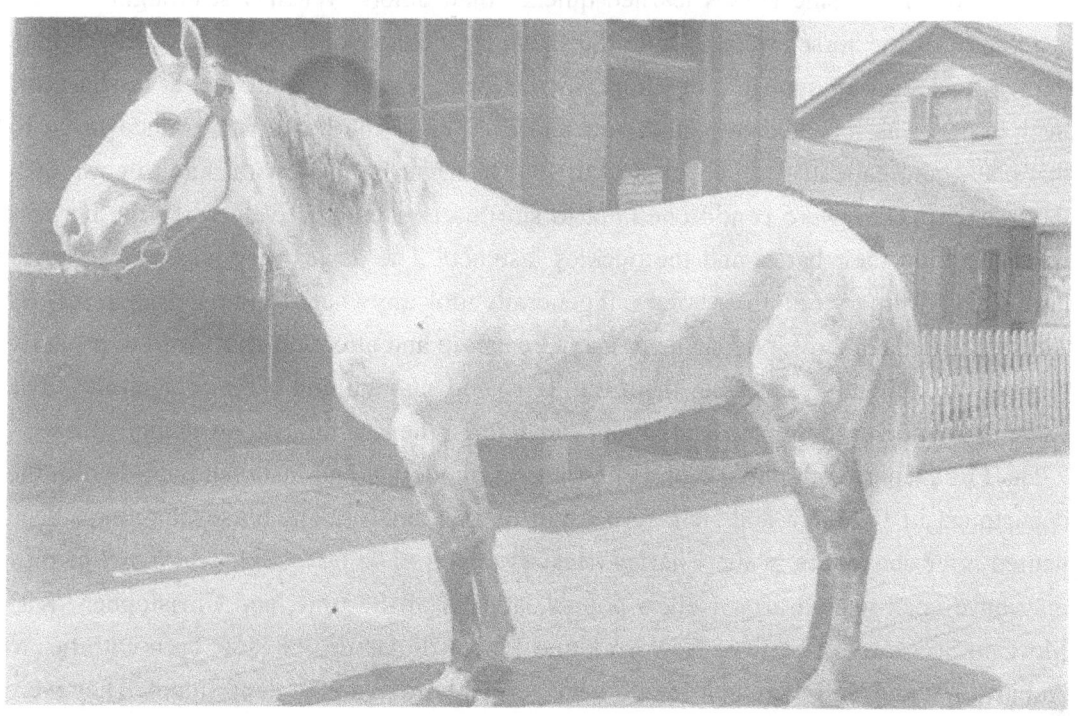

Trilby

When one thinks about an animal at a fire station, the vision of a Dalmatian immediately comes to mind. However, the first animals in the department, and those of greater service, were the horses that worked to pull the wagons and equipment to the scene of the many alarms they responded to over the years. The horses used by the department were trained to respond to loud alarms and bells, much commotion and were expected to run toward fire. They needed to quash their natural instinct to bolt or startle at sudden movements or unexpected noises. They had to have the ability to be trained to be in proximity of a fire and not respond negatively. The firefighters cared for and trained their Auburn Fire Department horses to do just that. They were, in many ways, partners with their human counterparts. The firemen relied on the equines' abilities to deliver the equipment and them safely to the scene. Chief Edward Jewhurst was particularly fond of horses. His father had trained horses for years and Edward had become quite familiar with the care and training of them. His skill with a horse and his natural affinity for the animal, proved valuable within the Fire Department. The successful use of a horse in fire service is not the result of one man; it is the culmination of hard work by many people. The horses were not simply beasts of burden. To those who fed them and trained them day in and day out, they became truly cared for. Chief Jewhurst kept meticulous records regarding the horses of the Auburn Fire Department. Without such records, many of their names and particular characteristics would have been lost.

Training the horses of the Auburn Fire Department was a process that involved varying amounts of time. Some horses learned quicker than others. When first brought to their headquarters, the horses were put into the stable for a couple of days in order to acclimate to their new surroundings. On the third day they were led out to stand under the harness. Such action was repeated over and over and eventually the horse was trained to go to that place automatically at the sound of the big Wheeler bell and with little to no human intervention. They were conditioned not to startle or react negatively when the harness was placed on their backs and the buckles fastened. The department was said to never have used a whip to train their horses. It generally took anywhere from ten days to several weeks to train a horse for department use. Great care and attention was given to properly feeding the animals, exercising them regularly and maintaining their good health. The value of the horses to the department depended upon their being in good shape.

The Fire Department purchased its first horses at auction and installed them within the department in 1890. Kit and Nell were a pair of black mares. The horses may have been named after characters in the Charles Dickens novel, *"The Old Curiosity Shop"* or they may have been named after Nell, a popular actress of the time, and Christopher "Kit" Morgan, Secretary of State of New York and Mayor of Auburn in 1860, both with ties to Auburn. Kit and Nell were considered very good additions to the department. They were initially assigned to Hose Co. 4 and later pulled the Chemical Company No. 1 apparatus. Jewhurst reflected that Kit was the idler animal of the two. Nell was a fine horse with many good traits. The fire station had a clock that struck every hour. When the clock sounded at 11am Nell was said to whinny until she had her oats. She seemed to know exactly when she was supposed to be fed and would continue until the men responded. She would not whinny at other hours of the day. Nell never missed a run to answer an alarm or a meal. The horses were trained to stomp a hoof when nature called. In her mature years, Kit developed rheumatism. The two horses worked hard for the department, and remained active for many years. Kit served the Fire Department for 11 years and Nell for 14.

In 1890, Roxy was introduced to the department. A gray mare who served with Hose Company No. 1 for 12 years, she was an efficient horse. In 1898, a handsome black horse was assigned to Hose Company No. 3. Dewey served for six years in the Fire Department. Fred and May, a pair of full brother and sister bays, provided service to Hose Company No. 3 until motorized apparatus was introduced to the company. Fred and May were big horses, strong and saucy. They were loved by the firemen. The two were reassigned to the Hook and Ladder Company and eventually became "extras". They were ultimately purchased by Alderman John Titus for his farm in Cayuga. Alderman Titus thought they would transition well to farm life and learn to enjoy the green fields and pastures there. As the horses were led away from the Hook and Ladder Company in April 1913, Driver Lionel Morris was said to have a lump in his throat. Captain Platt, who was particularly attached to Fred and May, admitted that he felt bad about seeing them go, "And don't you think they didn't hate to go either." Platt continued, "Old Fred knew that there was something up and that he was going away for good. You could tell that by the way he gave us a parting look when they led him down the street. He never used to look that way when he was going for new shoes or in another house. That horse knew that his firefighting days had gone."

The Hayes hook and ladder truck, purchased in 1885 from the LaFrance Manufacturing Company, was initially pulled by horses leased from a local livery. In 1892, the department purchased a pair of bay horses for $550. George and Dan pulled the hook and ladder truck. Dan pulled the hook and ladder truck for approximately one year before he died of colic. George was described as a nearly perfect horse in disposition and general makeup. Upon Dan's death, a new pair of horses was purchased for the Hook and Ladder Company, and George was used as an extra horse, filling in among the fire companies where needed. Jewhurst described George as a horse with good instincts. He was quoted as saying "If you put him in a 20 acre lot and left a harness at one end, when the gong struck he would have gone to it." Through the years George was a consistently healthy horse. George served 15 years for the department. The two replacement black horses purchased for the hook and ladder trucks, after Dan's death, were Nick and Pudge. They joined the department in

1902. They were considered very good horses and served with Hose Company No. 3 after their hook and ladder truck assignment. While on parade, Nick and Pudge seemed to know they were the center of attention and reacted very positively to the applause offered up as they strutted by. Nick died at Hose Company No. 3 after a bout of severe indigestion on December 26, 1914. At the end of his career, Pudge was sold to P. Corrigan on Throopsville Road, just outside the city.

Also in 1892, a second pair of horses was purchased for the Hook and Ladder Company; Rounce and Buck. Buck became a wind-broke horse. He had developed a chronic respiratory disease, similar in characteristics to chronic obstructive pulmonary disease. Rounce served the department for four years. He became sick and was housed in a box stall in another location away from the Fire Department. If someone was with him, Rounce was content, but when he was left alone he would whinny and thresh around. One night while left alone, Rounce broke through the gate and was later found running down Market Street, swaying side to side. He ran until he arrived at the Hook and Ladder Company's doors, and the men let him in. The proud fire horse ambled to his old stall and laid down, content in his familiar surroundings. He died two hours later.

The introduction of horses to pull the apparatus proved so useful, the department purchased a pair of white-gray horses for Hose Company No. 1 at a cost of $456 in 1894. The horses were said to be strong on short runs but would tend to want to quit on long runs. A pair of horses was acquired in Buffalo for Hose Company No. 3. The pair served four years in good service to the department. In April of 1899, the department purchased two dapple grays for Hose Company No. 2. Bob and Bill proved to be reliable and solid additions.

Chief Jewhurst's first horse was a gray mare named Trilby. Trilby was with Jewhurst for eight years. Some joked that Trilby would rather stand than move. Trilby was left untied many times without incident. She was generally a trustworthy and predictable horse. She did, however, break her record one day when she took off on a run toward headquarters while left untied. The chief was said to have commanded her to "whoa" in a tone that "would have made a fireman jump from a seven-story building", but Trilby kept going until she hit the brick pavement that existed on East Genesee Street at the time. She then slowed down and was brought under control, her only injury being her reputation. Trilby was transferred to the Chemical Company in place of Kit once she was retired. In 1901, Chief Jewhurst acquired a large sorrel horse that was purchased from Dr. Moses M. Frye for $200. The horse was a good driver and was said to be able to run at a fast clip. He then acquired a chestnut gelding. The gelding was a good trotter. However, while exercising one day he dislocated his hip joint and never fully recovered. He developed a rather mean disposition and would bite and fight his keepers. He was only in service for approximately

18 months. The gelding was replaced with a black horse named Dan, reminiscent of the original Dan purchased for the Hook and Ladder Company. Chief Jewhurst described Dan as an intelligent and fine appearing animal who was completely trustworthy. The chief had a narrow escape once with Dan while responding to a fire in the west end of Auburn. Jewhurst jumped into the buggy, picked up the lines and the horse started out as soon as the station doors were opened. Chief Jewhurst suddenly realized that neither of the lines was snapped in the bits, rendering them all but useless. Dan had a habit of following the Chemical Company. He must have heard the clang of the engine going through Garden Street, and he went down Garden as well. Jewhurst thought he could grab the harness and call Dan's attention, but as he leaned over, the buggy wheel hit a hole and threw the Chief between the side of the wagon and the rear wheel. Chief Jewhurst was wedged between the proverbial rock and a hard place. A precarious position for sure, the other man in the buggy was holding on to the chief, who was not able to get back into the wagon. Dan was soon looking to overtake the Chemical Company engine, and Jewhurst later admitted that he thought his time was up. However, Dan turned onto State Street in a long turn without upsetting the wagon, and a relieved Jewhurst was able to recover his position in the wagon. Still with no lines and the fire illuminating the sky in the west, the horse wanted to go to the fire. He wasn't running away from the fire, but was looking to respond to it. Edward Jewhurst had several occasions to retell this story, and he would often pull out the coat he was wearing that night to show the damage and effects of his wild ride. The department kept Dan for three years.

The City sent two men to Chicago to purchase five horses for the department. There were 2,000 horses sold at the auction in that location, only three of which were deemed worthy of purchase for fire department service. It was not easy to identify and acquire a horse with the necessary characteristics to be successful in responding to a fire. A horse that was predisposed for fire service made training and implementation smoother, but finding such an animal required patience and a good working knowledge of horses. Conversely, a horse that was well suited for fire service was not always a good choice for other purposes. Chief Jewhurst would often advise people regarding the risk of purchasing an old fire horse. They didn't forget the gong. A team of horses previously in service with Hose Company No. 1 was sold to a farmer on Franklin Street Road. While the farmer was in town one morning with the horses, the Syracuse trolley car came through and rang the gong as it passed. The horse started off at full speed, overturned the wagon, threw off the farmer and came directly to fire headquarters. He was looking to grab his gear and men and head off to the fire!

In 1905, the department purchased two roan horses, John and Otto, from a farmer in Owasco for $600. John and Otto were brothers, and the pair was wildly popular with the citizens of Auburn and were known for their quick hitch work, always beating the other teams. John and Otto were part of Hose Company No. 4 until they were transferred to the newly opened Hose Company No. 6 on State Street upon motorization of their previous assignment. They were described as enthusiastic horses. In January of 1912, it was noticed that "Old John" had difficulty breathing after a run to a fire. He appeared to have laryngitis and the muscles of his throat had become paralyzed. His illness continued, and no amount of care or attention by the veterinarian or firemen seemed to help. John was not able to eat. In March of 1912, "Old John" laid down in his stall and passed away. John was replaced with Spot, a calico horse who originated from Oklahoma, having been employed as a brewery wagon hauler. Spot lost his brewery wagon job when the Oklahoma area went rather "dry". He was taken to Kansas City where he was purchased by John M. Griffin for the Fire Department and brought back to Auburn. Spot was matched with another horse and the two were purchased by the Fire Department and assigned to Hose Company No. 3. Spot was well known for his striking spots and mottled hide of white, brown and gray. He attracted much attention as he ran through the streets of Auburn. Spot's mate broke down and had to leave fire service. Spot and Otto were teamed together, but Spot suffered injuries, developed pneumonia and died.

Sam and Jack were a team of grays that were purchased and assigned to Hose Company No. 3. Jack was a horse that made himself at home at the fire station, behaving and sounding very little. Sam was considered the more stylish of the two horses and was a good worker but he did not as readily accustom himself to varying circumstances. Edward Lyons, driver of the truck company wagon, fell victim to Sam when five nickel buttons from his overcoat were eaten. At approximately 1am on the evening of Sam's late night snack, he had freed himself from his halter strap and wandered around the first floor quarters. He must have come across Edward Lyon's overcoat and rather mischievously proceeded to nip off all the buttons. The firemen woke up when they heard the horse moving about the quarters. They found five buttons lying on the floor and assumed Sam ate the other five. Jack was said to eat like a pulp machine and took cat naps in order to respond rested when the alarm rang. He was always first in line when the bell rang to indicate exercise time. Jack had also discovered a way to reach over his stall partition and lift the catch with his lips. He was also seen attempting to work the lock on the door of the room where the feed was stored. The only opportunity Jack had to try to work the lock was at night when others had gone to bed. The firemen caught Jack after he had unfastened his strap and ventured quietly around the building, seemingly examining points of interest along the way. Captain Strong discovered Jack trying to get back into his stall with the stable broom in his mouth, but the horse held the broom crosswise in his teeth and his entrance into the stall was prevented and resulted in quite a noisy racket. Jack was described as being similar to a good natured dog. When he was tired of standing in his stall he would stretch his muscles just as a dog does, spreading his fore legs out in front of him and leaning back on his hind legs until his body almost touched the floor. He would yawn heartily. Jack was a wise horse who endeared himself to the firemen.

Around 1906, the department purchased Old Joe and Doll. Old Joe was a gray horse assigned to Hose Company No. 2 for 14 years. Old Joe was a big and faithful gelding and was loved by many through his years of service with that company. He was replaced by Rastus, a large sorrel horse with a white face. Rastus was acquired for the Fire Department by John M. Griffin. Rastus almost immediately showed his skill as a fire horse and was assigned to duty rather quickly. In his later years, Old Joe had 'spells' that were not able to be resolved and became increasingly more painful and frequent. The very difficult decision was made to put him out of his misery. Old Joe was brought to the Hazlitt yard on the west side of Auburn and led to the area where his life would be ended. Old Joe was reported to sniff and balk a bit as he approached, but continued to follow where he was being led. Veterinarian A. J. Tuxill ended Old Joe's suffering with a bullet from a Colt .45. The shell casing used was retained as part of the collection of the Fire Department and was kept in Chief Jewhurst's office as a reminder of the fine horse who had served so loyally over the years. Many citizens of the First Ward expressed grief and regret at the loss of their fine servant, Joe.

With the introduction of motorized apparatus, the Fire Department horses were gradually replaced with automobile engines. Fan and Bess were two such horses. The two black horses were small but strong and able. They often were called upon to respond to multiple fires in a row and completed each run as if it was their first of the day. They were fast and had much stamina. Originally assigned to Hose Company No. 1, Fan and Bess were retired from Hose Company No. 5 amidst a throng of firemen who gathered to send them off as they left their quarters in January of 1921. Fan and Bess were sold to J. W. Brinkerhoff in Niles for $100. They were provided comfortable bunks to spend the remainder of their days.

The last two horses to be replaced in the department were Patty and Babe. Originally purchased in 1912, and assigned to Hose Company No. 5 under the direction of Captain James Walsh, the pair was transferred to Hose Company No. 6 in 1920, upon motorization of Hose Company No. 5. Each horse had spent 13 years in fire service to Auburn and was retired to the Sunnycrest Sanitarium farm in Sennett. They were provided plenty of room to roam and graze. They were 18 years old at the time of their retirement in 1925. Their retirement signaled the end of an era. No more would the firefighters experience the sights, smells and sounds of equines within the department. The stories that were told of each horse's peculiarities would become memories repeated through the years and experienced firsthand no more. The citizens of Auburn would no longer hear the clattering of hoofs or the neighs and snorts of the horses as they bound through the streets, eager to deliver their apparatus to the fire. The regal sight of a team of fire horses standing proud with manes blowing in the wind would be relegated to parades and occasional exhibitions. In their final year, Nick and Pudge were not called on very often. They did, however, prove invaluable on those occasions when snow accumulated on the road during their last winter in service, making it impossible for the motorized equipment to pass through. Their time of usefulness had come to an end. The paved streets and concrete areas were hard on the horses' hooves. The horses were more expensive to maintain and were not as consistently reliable as the motorized vehicles. The wheels of progress were quite literally rolling past the old horse-drawn apparatus. The melancholy that some felt at the loss of the horse-drawn apparatus, which had become so much a part of the awe of the Auburn Fire Department, was soon replaced with the blur of red and roar of the engines as they raced through the streets. The fascination with fire department equipment continued regardless of the transport. The Auburn Fire Department continued to captivate those who saw them en route to a fire. The mode of transportation had changed, but the attraction and interest did not.

Horses were not the only animals associated with the Auburn Fire Department. There were several mascots and pets over the years. There are many dogs described within the Auburn Fire Department in the 1800s, although most not by name. Two of the earliest dogs that were identified by name were Strike and Veney, two dogs at Hose Company No. 3 on Clark Street. During a Cayuga Patrol business meeting in 1885, John Crosbie, brother of

Horses: Dan & Joe / Dogs: Veney & Strike
(Photo courtesy of Anita Luisi Colvin)

Henry Crosbie, Chief of the Auburn Police Department, introduced his famous dog, "Fly" and bragged of what a natural fireman the dog was. He said she would run from her dinner at the stroke of the alarm. Of course, the dog was immediately put to the test. A plate of food was brought in for Fly and one of the firemen rattled the fire gong while the rest of the men in the company rushed toward the door as if running to a fire. Fly ruined her supposed reputation by remaining at the plate of food and never responded. Those present at the meeting shared a laugh and poor Fly had lost all hope of ever becoming the department mascot.

In the 1880s and 1890s there were newspaper stories that identified the big proud dogs of a variety of fire companies, especially in parades. Sometimes the beloved horses were referred to as "fire dogs" and other times they were referring to actual canines. In 1898, the Auburn Fire Department was said to have had a Dalmatian as a pet at headquarters. The name of that canine mascot has been lost in the annals of time.

In 1926, the Fire Department had a mascot named Lindy. Named after Charles Lindbergh, Lindy was a beagle owned by Michael Burns, Hoseman for Company No. 1. Lindy was loved by the firemen. In 1927 Lindy wandered off and disappeared.

In 1933, "Pete" joined the department and quickly became a beloved fixture around headquarters in Franklin and Market Streets. Pete was a little black dog who became the department pet. He responded when the men whistled for him. A humorous story was told in 1936, when Pete was called for dinner with a whistle from one of the firefighters. The men had prepared him hamburger. Pete went over to the bowl, inspected his meal anxiously and then walked away from it. One of the men thought that Pete must have been ill. Chris McEvoy laughed and quipped "Why, he isn't sick. Don't you realize he doesn't eat meat on Friday?" The firemen shared a laugh at Pete's vegetarian habit that evening. Pete's big claim to fame resulted after he attended the circus in town. He spotted a full-grown elephant and attempted to bring the animal down by grabbing his tail. The elephant proceeded to swing poor Pete around through the air, but Pete hung on until the pachyderm's trainer was finally able to convince him that he had bitten into more than he could chew! The story was so amusing, that newspapers all around New York reported the story of Pete getting a mouthful! Pete had a reputation for answering all alarms with the men. However, he nearly missed a call on February 2, 1938, when an alarm came in for a fire at 185 State Street. Pete had just retired to his comfortable area in the workshop at headquarters and missed his ride. He did, however, manage to follow the trucks and ran behind them until he arrived at the scene shortly after the companies. The newspapers joked that Pete was in the "dog house", as he had missed two alarms earlier that same week. His actions that day likely restored his reputation. In August of 1938, Pete left his berth under the tool bench in the workshop and left the fire station. He did not return. Pete had never been gone more than 24 hours in his time with the department. A plea was made for the public to keep an eye out for Pete, the firemen's pal. He was wearing a leather collar that had his 1938 tag riveted on it. As far as is known, Pete never returned.

In 1955, a Dalmatian named "Pepper" filled the vacancy that had existed in the department for years. Pepper was the adopted pet and mascot of the Auburn Fire Department. Before becoming a firehouse dog, Pepper belonged to Patrolman John Sawran of the Auburn Police Department. Pepper was given to Richard Walsh after the dog had shown signs of liking mischief. He was provided a blanket in one corner of the firehouse and

Pepper

was introduced to department operations by riding in Chief Luke Bergan's car and in the alarm repair truck. His mischievous reputation was not seen at the firehouse. Chief Bergan reported that Pepper didn't even bat an eyelash when he heard his first alarm come into the station. In fact, pepper slept through that first alarm when he first reported for duty. The Dalmatian occasionally rode in open areas of the fire engine, atop the booster line tank, but he generally preferred the comfort of the Chief's car. Pepper was said to be the best fed dog in Auburn, with 50 firemen eager to contribute to his feeding schedule. Pepper continued to be a constant companion within the department until 1961. He was eight years old and had undergone removal of an abscess from his foot and later died of a blood clot in the brain on December 27, 1961. Pepper died exactly 25 years to the day after the Auburn Police Department's mascot dog died. "Pal", the German Shepherd belonging to the Police Department, died December 27, 1936, and is buried in front of the Police Station on North

Street. Auburn Policemen contributed to purchase a memorial for "Pal" that was placed at the site. Pepper, the fire dog, had been a favorite of visitors at headquarters and was popular in the local parades and fire prevention activities that occurred around Auburn. There are still those around today who remember Pepper fondly.

L to R: Birch O'Hora, Harold Short, Jim Monahan, Jake Barrett, Luke Bergan, Art Stephens

Top: Pepper

FIRES

March 1908, Telegram from Fair Haven, NY requesting assistance from Auburn Fire Department

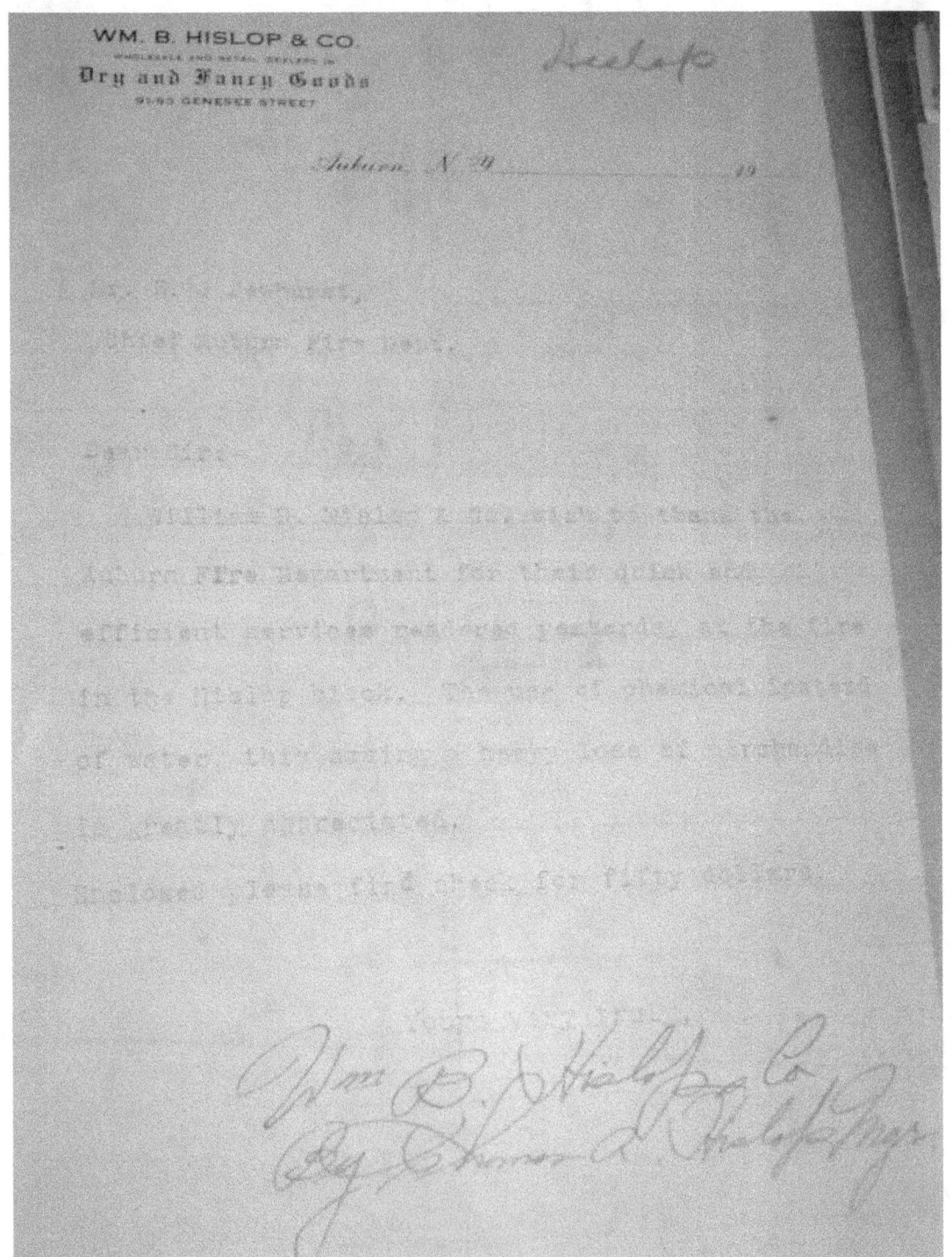

Letter from William B. Hislop & Co. following a fire in their location

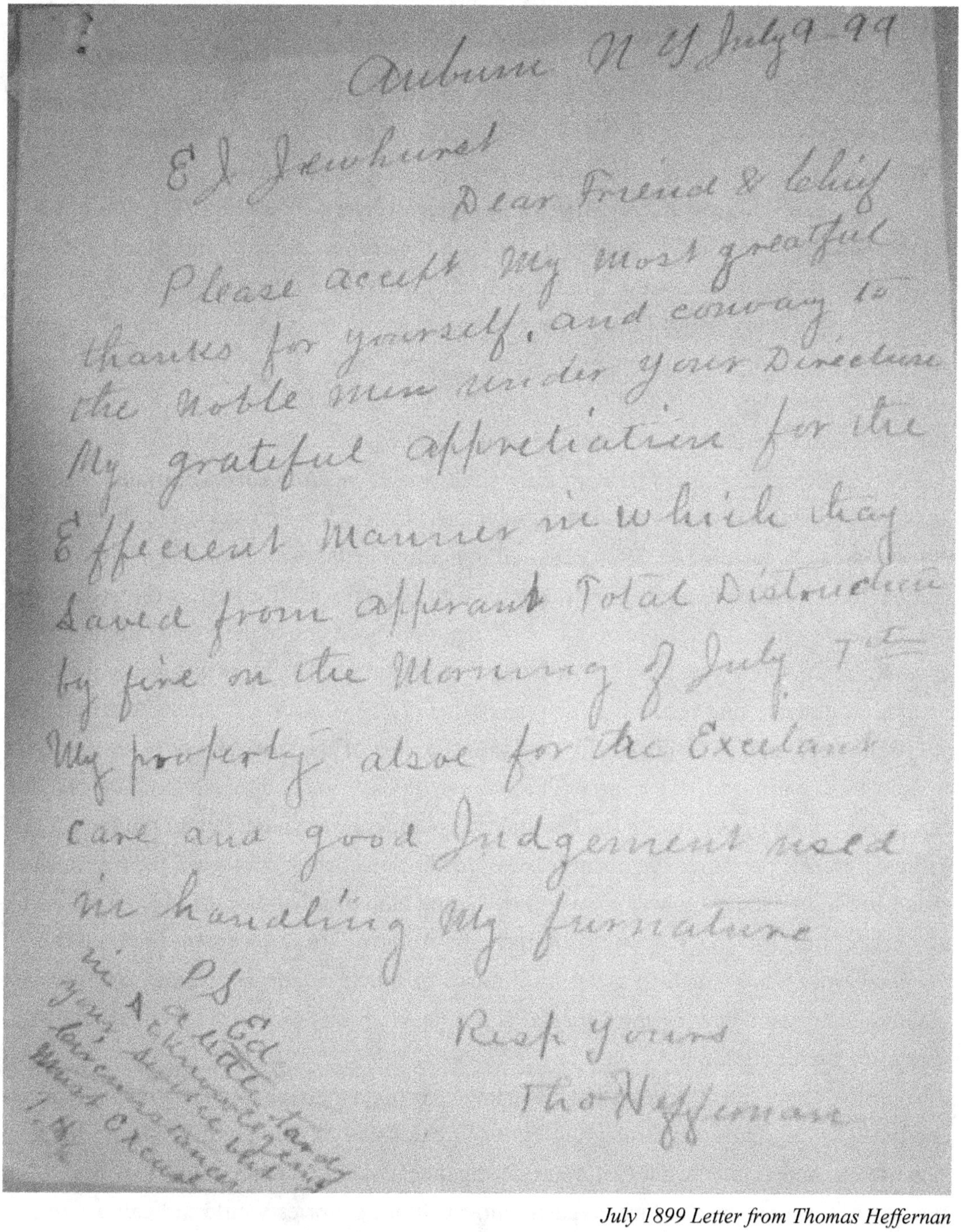

Auburn N.Y. July 9-99

E J Jewhurst

Dear Friend & Chief

Please accept My most greatful thanks for yourself, and convay to the Noble men under your Direction My grateful appretiation for the Effecient Manner in which they Saved from apperant Total Distruction by fire on the Morning of July 7th My property alsoe for the Excelant care and good Judgement used in handling My furniture

P.S.

Resp Yours
Tho Heffernan

July 1899 Letter from Thomas Heffernan

The fires experienced by Auburn have been recorded back to 1816. The meticulous records kept and maintained by personnel thru the years prove an invaluable piece of history within the Auburn Fire Department. Chief Jewhurst, in particular, created and maintained a detailed account of each and every alarm the department responded to during his decades as Fire Chief. He also gathered information and documented fires that occurred prior to his time with the department. He was able to identify fires back to 1816. Perusing the log reveals dates and locations, as well as the consequences and damages resulting from the fires. Unfortunately, the department's biggest successes were and are those that are not deemed newsworthy or particularly noteworthy to the public. The fire at E. S. Miner's Grocery Store on November 9, 1861, on the corner of North and Market Streets, was quickly extinguished by the Fire Department with little damage. The January 8, 1870, fire at the oil refinery on Monroe Street resulted in small losses due to the rapid response of the firemen. George Hamilton, of 58 Owasco Street, surely thought the Fire Department successful when they responded to an alarm at his house on February 25, 1870, and saved his home with only a small amount of damage. The Sartwell, Hough & Co. Shoe Factory that experienced a fire in 1871, with only slight losses ensured their continued business due to actions taken by the firefighters. Salvatore DeJoy's fire that started in the chimney of his home on December 11, 1920, resulted in negligible damage. The 1950 Thanksgiving fire that threatened a one-story building at 33 Wood Street was thwarted by the skilled Fire Department members. In September of 1945 the men faced one of their smokiest fires ever at the Rock Cut Quarry on North Street, near the city limits. The blaze was being fed by an oil and tar mixture that resulted in huge amounts of billowing black smoke and impaired the firefighters' ability to physically navigate the area of the fire. The only hydrant was located at the entrance to the quarry. The firemen quickly coupled together a total of 3,000 feet of large hose lines to reach the fire and two pumpers were hooked into the lines to get sufficient nozzle pressure. The foam mix hopper was used and smothered the fire in short order. In the 1970s, David Major was relieved (and embarrassed, because his Uncle Frank was part of the crew that responded) to have the Auburn Fire Department show up to free his head from being stuck in a railing. Stories of quick responses, blazes extinguished without extensive damages and successful rescue situations could be told over and over, year after year, even today.

Countless times over the years the department responded to and put out fires that threatened to become roaring infernos and result in extensive building and property damage. It is hard to appreciate "what could have happened" when what actually happened was a successful response by the Fire Department. Such news stories would indicate a fire had started and was quickly extinguished before extensive damage was done. Point of fact, they are wonderful stories. However, they do not generally draw the public interest as a whole. A fire department tends to be judged solely by losses; the greatest saves aren't extensively taken up by the "grapevine" or in news accounts. A fire that is contained and extinguished before it evolves into a large blaze and results in no loss of life is victory. Individually, those who have directly experienced the benefits of our Fire Department personnel know firsthand their value. Many proactive measures are taken by the Fire Department in preventing fires, through inspections of buildings, businesses and hydrants as well as fire prevention and education provided to the community in a variety of formats. Another aspect of the job is reactive in nature. A call is received indicating a fire is in progress or is suspected. The clock starts ticking on an incident before the department even receives the alarm. The countless letters received by the Auburn Fire Department over the years, expressing thanks for their swift actions and small losses, attest to their amazing efforts and service to the City of Auburn.

There have been many large and notable fires in the history of the Auburn Fire Department. Some that resulted in death. Some resulted in extensive and total losses. But even those have successes attached to them; lives saved, containment of a fire and preventing it from spreading to other buildings and ultimate suppression of an ongoing fire. Many of the large fires brought the community together to grieve and reflect. Through the years, as technology has grown, our access to media, photos and videos is immediate. We have all seen photos of our firefighters pulling lines, releasing streams of water, exhausted after hours spent working a fire with black soot surrounding their faces and a quiet reflection of the efforts that were made. The upcoming fire descriptions serve to illustrate the dedication, service and bravery of the Fire Department. These large events are part of Auburn's history and include loss of lives and significant property and building damages. For most Auburnians, we can remember or are somehow connected with each of these incidents and they are not always easy to recollect. However, the history of the Auburn Fire Department could never be complete without mention of the fires that tested the limits of its equipment and service.

December 21, 1816

Samuel Dill Saw and Cording Mill near the big dam

On December 21, 1816, the first recorded fire broke out in Auburn at the Samuel Dill Saw and Carding Mill (where Dunn & McCarthy Co. would later be). The fire was discovered at 11:45pm. The village was in the throes of a blizzard with temperatures below freezing. Shouts of "Fire!" and calls for help were rung throughout the village, but the response was less than adequate. Those that showed up to assist extinguishing the fire were quickly impacted by the icy conditions. It became clear that a more formalized system and apparatus were needed.

January 20, 1837

"The Great Fire of 1837"

In January of 1837, the nation was on the brink of the Financial Panic of 1837. During a precarious economic time, Auburn was hard hit with *"The Great Fire of 1837"*, which involved 14 stores on Genesee Street, (Nos. 73-101) and North Street, including everything from the ten cent store to the Carpenter Hat Store. At approximately 11:30pm the fire broke out in the Hyde, Watrous and Co. dry goods store. The weather worked against the Fire Department; temperatures were below zero and the snow was very deep. With over $100,000 in damages (the equivalent of more than $2,500,000 in today's dollars), the fire resulted in significant damages and the destruction of fourteen Auburn businesses.

The stores of Hyde, Watrous and Company, Norman Bennett's dry goods store, H. C. Pease's furniture store, Melbie Camp's dry goods, Crashy & Polkbun's dry goods store, Munger & Perry dry goods, J. S. Bartlett & Co. dry goods, T. M. Hunt's drug store, D. C. Stewart dry goods, Bemus & Leonard's restaurant, Carpenter Hat Store and the ten cent store were among those that sustained damage.

As a result of the Great Fire of 1837, the Fire Department and the citizens of Auburn saw firsthand evidence of the benefits of brick structures in the face of a fire. Two of the buildings involved in the fire were made of brick and sustained relatively minor smoke and water damage. The buildings constructed of wood did not hold up well to the flames that attacked them, while their brick counterparts fared much better. The Great Fire of 1837 resulted in many future businesses in Auburn to be constructed of brick and stone. It was a pivotal fire that influenced the construction material and design of future buildings in Auburn. While the immediate effects of the fire were devastating, the lessons learned regarding building materials against a fire had long term benefits that were priceless.

October 23, 1861
Foster Block

At approximately 3:15am on the early morning of October 23, 1861, a fire broke out in the area opposite the American Hotel in Auburn. The Foster Block (from Genesee Street to the corner of William Street) was a wooden tenement structure comprised of five stores and many residences on the upper floors. It was 3 ½ stories high. The entire block burned to the ground with a total loss of $17,500. The hand-operated engines struggled to reach the top stories of the Foster Block. Valuable time was used in positioning firemen in adjacent areas and treacherous locations to attack the flames. Some voiced that if the department had a steam engine in its apparatus inventory, the losses could have been smaller. Steam engines were believed to be able to shoot streams of water greater distances and firemen could have begun the attack from the ground while others positioned themselves at their assigned stations.

January 31, 1870
First Alarm for New Telegraph Fire Alarm

The first alarm that came in using the new telegraph fire alarm was on January 31, 1870, for a fire on the corner of Bradford and Howard Streets at the home of John O'Neill.

November 17, 1879
Auburn Prison Hame Shop Fire

At 6:45pm on the evening of November 17, 1879, Mr. Malloy, one of the night guards at the Auburn Prison yard, made his usual rounds. He saw a faint light in the lower area near the boiler room of the hame (carriage/horse harness hardware) shop. Thinking that the light was from a lantern of one of the foremen who must have remained late to repair machinery, he did not immediately respond. However, as he watched the area, he noticed that the light got brighter and brighter. Mr. Malloy ran to the building to investigate and found the shop to be engulfed in flames. He gave the alarm and prison officials responded with a prison fire hose cart. At the same time the convict fire brigade marched down to the yard and joined the fight. The flames soon proved to be moving too rapidly to be addressed by those present. Just before 8pm the alarm bell in the tower at D. M. Osborne & Co. sounded Box 14 at the prison gate. Auburn firemen responded quickly and were admitted within the walls of the prison. Upon arrival, the men saw a raging fire already well underway. The lower portion of the shop was wrapped in flames. Fire Chief Joseph

Morris quickly ascertained that any efforts to save the hame shop would be useless. He devised a plan in collaboration with his assistants, Edward Jewhurst and Thomas Spears, and a decision was made to save the adjacent buildings. Streams of water were set on the shoe shop, collar shop and hollow ware shop of Foxell, Jones & Co., as well as other buildings in proximity to the flames. The hame shop and collar shop were divided by a flight of wide stairs. Jewhurst was notified that at the top of the stairway was a wooden door that would be rapidly consumed by the fire, which would then be free to spread throughout the collar shop. Edward Jewhurst ordered a ladder and secured a line of hose. He broke in the windows in the area and directed firemen to keep a stream of water on the door. At one point, Warden William Moses and another prison official provided conflicting information about the door's existence and material. The firemen continued to hold a stream of water on the area. Later inspection would show the door to be made of wood, with one side charred almost to tinder. As the evening continued, the fire became so hot that panes of glass from the windows in the shoe shop melted. The Fire Department was able to keep the fire contained to the hame shop and extinguished flames that licked at the neighboring buildings. The hame shop was divided into a number of rooms with wood partitions, making the fire spread quickly and collecting anything and everything in its path. Additionally, the upper floor of the building held a quantity of combustible material used in the shop, such as turpentine. Three firemen from Hose Co. 6 were hurt by a falling roof. The fact that the collar shop was not totally annihilated was referred to as simply a miracle. It was through the persistent efforts of the fire laddies on the scene and their stubborn fight against the fire, that the battle was won. By midnight the fire was extinguished and the men returned to their quarters. Chief Morris kept a team of men at the prison all night to guard against the fire rekindling. The town was buzzing with talk of the big fire. It was said to have illuminated the entire northern sky and was reflected off the spires of the churches. People flocked in droves to the front of the prison and stood in the rain and mud watching the progress of the fire. The fire resulted in an estimated $36,000-$40,000 loss.

June 17, 1880
Osborne House Fire

Mrs. Gibbs, an employee at the Osborne House, was asleep in her third floor residence on the South Wing of the building, when she was awakened by smoke at about 3am on the morning of June 17, 1880. She jumped out of bed and, upon looking out the window, discovered that part of the building facing Green Street and attached to the Osborne House, was on fire. The flames had worked up the lower floor and were bursting out of the second floor windows. Mrs. Gibbs ran through the hall shouting "Fire!" at the top of her lungs to alert the other employees in the wing.

At the same time, Officer Taylor was patrolling his beat on State Street and was opposite the coal office of William D. Slee when he detected smoke. He ran down the street and as he approached the Osborne House, the night watchman came running out alerting to the fire. Officer Taylor ran into the office and sounded an alarm on the telephone. A prompt answer came from the central office. The officer waited two or three minutes, and he did not hear an alarm on the bell. So he signaled again. He received an immediate answer to the effect that the operator could not "get" the watchman at Osborne's factory. Five minutes had lapsed and the structure was burning out of control in a mass of flames. Officer Taylor ran to the prison and gave an alarm from Box 14, which was promptly answered by the bell.

The men, women and children in the hotel were running around, some dressed and others still in their nightclothes. They were packing trunks with valuables and trying to navigate their way out of the building. The delay in the signal alarm resulted in the hotel being engulfed in flames when the firemen arrived. The roof was already burning and flames were creeping toward the main building of the hotel. Upon seeing the state of the fire, Chief Joseph Morris focused on saving the hotel and directed the men to position their streams of water in the hotel.

Cleophas Corbett, of Letchworth Hose 2, Nicholas Kierst and Lewis Chadderdon, of Alert 6, began directing their streams of water on the hotel from the rear side of the structure. They had been at work a short time when suddenly there was a loud crash followed by a sickening cry. The east wall and roof had fallen in and brought with it the brick cornices and a portion of the upper wall. The collapse happened in the exact spot where the three men had been working the fire. The firemen who were working the flames from the adjoining roof looked down in the debris and saw the forms of the three men on the ground. Chief Morris, quickly flew down the ladder to the area where the men were and directed his mens' attention to the site of the collapse. Chadderdon had been farthest away when he was struck by falling brick, about 20 feet from the wall. Corbett was buried in debris up to his hips. Kierst was in the process of running when he was hit by falling bricks. Cleophas Corbett and Nicholas Kierst were found alive. Kierst was in shock but was able to walk with assistance and got as far as the stoop at Stover's office on State Street, a few doors south of the Osborne House. Dr. Henry Whitbeck attended to him and with the assistance of Dr. John Crayton, was able to make him comfortable. His injuries included a scalp wound on the back of his head, his back was badly contused and his left leg was severely bruised. Kierst was assisted to his home once he had been attended to.

Dr. Frank Hamlin was present and first attended to Chadderdon. Chadderdon had been removed to the Osborne House. Upon examination, he discovered a hole in his skull the size of a man's fist. The doctor knew he was beyond all human aid. Lewis Chadderdon survived an agonizing ten minutes before he succumbed to his injuries. His lifeless body was carried to Searls & Tallman Undertakers. Mrs. Chadderdon was bereft upon learning of her husband's death and her lamentations were gut-wrenching. Dr. Hamlin turned his attention to Corbett, who was in horrible pain. His left ankle had been jammed, both hands were cut in several places, and he had several scalp lacerations and multiple bruises. He was given medication for his pain and later assisted to his home.

Others were injured in the course of the fire as well. Alderman Frederick VanPatten fractured his right leg just above the ankle as he was on his way to the fire. A member of Active Hose Company 7, he was in a hurry to get to the blaze and caught his chin on a clothes line while running through a yard on Hulbert Street. He was knocked down with a resulting fracture. While directing a stream of water, S. Wright Milk, a member of Cayuga Hose 4, stepped back and fell through an open skylight 12-16 feet down into the hotel kitchen. A table broke his fall and he was in a stupor. He was picked up, carried into the office and attended to by Dr. Hamlin. Milk's lower limbs were partially paralyzed. His head was bathed in ice cold water and his legs and feet were rubbed vigorously to restore a sense of feeling to them. Milk was later assisted to his home on Green Street.

The flames continued to crawl and pick their way toward the main building of the hotel. The servants' quarters, kitchen and laundry were burning quickly. Water pressure was problematic at the beginning of the firefighters' attempts to extinguish the fire. There was not enough water pressure to be able to effectively force back the flames. The delay in the signal of the alarm, coupled with the delay in adequate water pressure significantly impacted the men's ability to turn the fire around. "Give us water!" the firemen shouted, "and we will fix the old thing." Within ten minutes the water pressure came with a vengeance and the men were able to suitably address the mass of flames. They bravely continued their fight, aware of their comrade's demise and their fellow brothers' injuries. Eight powerful streams of water were sent down on the fire. About two hours later the fire was reduced to a smoldering heap and was extinguished. The walls that remained standing were ready to topple at any moment, and Chief Morris ordered his "hooks" to work. The masonry blocks and bricks were brought down to the ground.

The lower portion of the burned building was a storehouse on Green Street occupied by James Stout. It was generally thought to be an incendiary fire due to the hour of the blaze and the fact that the building had not experienced a fire in the recent past. Some speculated that a fire brand had been thrown through a broken pane of glass in the lower floor. The damages to the kitchen, servant's quarters and laundry were costly and extensive. The storehouse was a total loss.

The fire that fateful morning of June 17, 1880, cost Lewis Chadderdon his life and proved the necessity for a reliable fire alarm system in Auburn. Valuable time was lost in attempts to notify and alert of the fire. The telephone was not useful, as it would require many calls to be made individually to the firemen around town. A reliable fire alarm bell could notify all of Auburn immediately of the fire and location with just the pull of a knob.

Lewis Chadderdon was, by trade, a carpenter. He was an active member of Alert Hose 6 and was acting as the superintendent of the Auburn Telephone Exchange. He was about 37 years old at the time of his death. He was married and had two sons. The family lived at 5 Bradford Street. Within a day of the fire, someone suggested that a public meeting take place to consider providing some means for the protection of firemen's families in case of accident or death. A collection was taken up to provide relief for Chadderdon's widow and children; $1,700 was raised in all by a large number of grateful and sympathetic Auburnians.

Lewis Chadderdon's funeral was attended by hundreds of people. His body was shown at the house of his sister on Walnut Street and was visited up to the hour of the funeral. Lying in a rosewood casket, Lewis Chadderdon was surrounded by floral tributes, engraved honors and other memorial items. The march to the church was long and well attended. A platoon of Auburn Police, Fire Commissioners, Fire Chief Morris and Assistants Jewhurst and Spears, Neptune Hose, Logan Hook & ladder, Letchworth Hose, Protective Hose, Cayuga Hose, C. N. Ross Hose, former Chief of Ithaca Fire Department, employees of the Western Union Telegraph and Telephone Exchange and Alert Hose 6. The hearse was followed by carriages of mourning family and friends. The newspaper reported that an estimated 5,000 people witnessed the ceremonies at St. Peter's Church and Fort Hill Cemetery that day. Reverend John Brainard, of St. Peter's Church, led the service. He reminded the citizens gathered how much was owed to the firemen of Auburn. He eloquently spoke of the firefighters heroism and fidelity, "who for the performance of their arduous tasks, make not their own selection of time or place, but in the dead hour of the night, in the darkness and in the storm, in the winter's cold and summer's heat, go earnestly and promptly forth to save the lives and property of Auburn."

March 26, 1884
St. James Hotel

During 1828 and 1829 Colonel John Sherwood built the American Hotel in Auburn, New York, to coincide with the stage lines that he operated through the area. Officially opened January 1, 1830, the American Hotel was a four-story building located on Genesee Street. Genesee Street was a main thoroughfare for travel, and stage traffic kept businesses and hotels in the area very busy. The hotel attracted many prestigious guests, including President Martin VanBuren in 1839, Daniel Webster, Millard Fillmore, Lt. General Scott,

Henry Clay and Louis Kossuth. It also served as the headquarters of General Hancock and his staff when an honor guard was provided over the remains of Secretary William Seward's wife in 1865. The hotel was owned and operated by several people over the years, and Anthony Shimer purchased the building around 1865. S. P. Chapman became landlord of the building and took over the American Hotel. The name of the hotel was changed to the St. James Hotel. Over the course of time, the property fell on hard times and a state of disrepair. Shimer took over operation of the St. James Hotel when Chapman relinquished it. The hotel suffered a fire in 1879. Following the fire, Mr. Shimer decided to breathe new life into the old building and plans were made to renovate and expand the hotel. The front was extended out toward the street and was outfitted with storefronts and additional hotel space designed in the rear of the building and on upper floors. Before construction was complete, the vacant St. James Hotel suffered another loss due to fire. It would be completely destroyed. It was significant and costly, as Mr. Shimer did not carry insurance on the building.

In the handwritten log maintain by Chief Edward Jewhurst over the years, there are several entries that stand out as unique and significant. Most of the log entries contain objective information regarding a fire. On March 26, 1884, the entry reads "March 26, 1884. St. James Hotel. 7,550' hose used. Bad one!" On the afternoon of Wednesday, March 26, 1884, the St. James was still undergoing a facelift. Construction was underway and the building had shavings, wood and equipment scattered throughout. The first floor of the building held lumber. The second floor held old lumber, tools and equipment. The third floor was a storage area for waste lumber. The upper floors also held furniture from the old hotel and other items that were being held in storage. There was a heavy rain coming down and the wind had kicked up a bit. There was a chill in the air. Mr. Shimer was working in the Opera House when he was told that the St. James was on fire.

At approximately 5:15pm fire was discovered in the rear of the third story of the building. The editor of the Auburn Advertiser saw the smoke from the St. James and alerted those in the area, and in the newspaper office, of the fire. An alarm was sent from Box 42 at the same time that Box 32 was pulled; the result was a mixed alarm notification to the Fire Department, but the smoke from the St. James was thick and black and there was no mistaking where the fire was located. Every company of the Fire Department responded to the scene. Protective Hose Company 3 arrived first and started laying hose on the west side of the building even before the loud fire bells had sounded. Fire was seen eating through the building. Bright orange and white flames were visible through the windows and great amounts of smoke poured out of every nook and cranny. The men of Cayuga Hose Company 4 were positioned on the rear rooftop of Mrs. Harriet Baker's property. They began to pour water on the flames, attacking it from strategic locations to minimize the damage and prevent it from spreading to adjacent structures. The rear roof area and slated walls of the mansard (four-sided hip roof) fell to the ground within fifteen minutes. The chimneys remained standing and had to be watched carefully in case they, too, were brought down. Cayuga Hose also had men stationed in the front of the building. Letchworth Hose Company 2 brought its equipment to the roof of the Opera House block and covered the front of the east wall as well. Due to the ongoing construction inside the St. James, the interior of the building was filled with flammable materials. The fire quickly moved and spread toward the front of the building on Genesee Street. It was becoming a huge conflagration. A very large crowd of people gathered to see the fire on Genesee and Clark Streets. The rain did not seem to deter them from their observation posts. Neptune Hose Company 1 was ordered to position themselves on the building of Charles Sheldon. Alert Hose Company was located in the rear of the hotel. The stage area of the Opera House next door, also owned by Shimer, caught fire but was able to be quickly extinguished by the firemen. Alert Hose and Cayuga Hose together saved the Opera House. Active Hose Company 7 also provided coverage in the rear of the building. The east wall of the St. James fell against the roof where Cayuga Hose Company 4 was working. An area within twenty feet of the men was scorched and parts of it crumbled and fell to the ground below. The men quickly sized up the situation and decided to hold their ground. They continued to stream water down on the fire and began to make headway by 6pm. They narrowly escaped injury.

The men of Protective Hose Company 3 were positioned on a roof across from Company 4. One of the chimneys collapsed and fell through the roof, leaving a large hole, through which Fireman George Moynan tumbled. He was shaken up but not seriously injured by his fall. The front section of the east wall fell at 8:30pm. The assembled crowd gasped and women shrieked as they watched the building come down in pieces. One young woman was quoted as screaming, "My God! My God! Just look at that! I'll bet a cent he's in there!" She was referring to Fireman Matthew Flynn, of Hose Company 4. He was feared to be buried under the falling wall. He was not seen by the men or the spectators initially. Flynn then limped out of the billowing smoke and embers with an injured foot. He and another fireman had been working the water pipe and reported having moved clear of the falling wall by mere inches as it toppled. Frank Adams, of Hose Company 3, was injured when he was struck by debris from the falling wall.

The men continued to attack the flames and consistent progress was made. The fire finally conceded to the water the men were pouring down upon it. In the aftermath, the west wall was deemed to be unsafe and the Hook and Ladder Company was ordered to pull it down. At 10:30pm the skeletal remains of the building were pushed over with pike poles. The stone wall came crashing down. By 11pm the fire was out and Cayuga Hose remained on the scene to watch the area for flare ups. The Logan Hook and Ladder Company provided great assistance to the hose companies. Chief Jewhurst was later complimented for working the fire in a very fine manner and was said to have remained very cool throughout the blaze. It was skillfully managed and extinguished by the Fire Department. Jewhurst was very pleased with the harmony that was seen among the fire companies.

The building loss sustained by Mr. Shimer was conservatively estimated at $20,000. Furniture and other hotel items in storage were valued at $8,000. Fifty suites of bedroom furniture and marble top tables were stored in the building. He was not insured. In fact, Shimer hadn't carried insurance for almost 25 years. The Opera House sustained slight damage that was confined to the stage area. Approximately $10,000 in stock damage was reported by McConnell & Anderson Dry Goods. Mrs. Harriet Baker's residence was in the process of constructing a business for VanLaer & Son. The loss was protected by insurance. Other stores in the area that were damaged by smoke, fire exposure and water included the C. R. Hemenway Confectionary store, W. D. Tuller fruit dealer and Joseph Neyhart Flour store.

A newspaper account of the performance of the firemen, indicated "Too much cannot be said in praise of the heart and well-disciplined manner in which the department worked, and if anyone has heretofore objected to that increase of $2,000 in the fund, this single night's experience with a really destructive fire, must have persuaded them that it was not uncalled for, because though none of the hose called into play was unserviceable, much of it showed, by leakage, that it was not first class and will presently need to be replaced."

The exact cause of the fire was not determined. It was theorized that the tinners' furnaces, lighting of a fire in the store, or a lit tobacco pipe or cigar could have started the blaze. Some felt it was spontaneous combustion of material stored in the building. There were no serious injuries reported and no lives lost. The firemen had worked efficiently and quickly against the fire.

January 9, 1894
9 Wadsworth Street

The first fire the Auburn Fire Department responded to as a permanent paid department was on January 9, 1894. An alarm was rung in from Box 13 for a fire located at 9 Wadsworth Street. The chemical truck of Hose Company No 1 responded to the home owned by Mrs. John Patty and occupied by George Bryan. The fire company used 25 feet of ladder, one chemical charge and 500 feet of hose on the blaze. They were on the scene for close to 1 ½ hours. Damages were estimated to be $273.50.

June 28, 1894
Auburn Prison Broom Shop

The firefighters had just returned from a call at Nye & Wait at about 7pm on June 28, 1894. They took off their boots and had started to wipe the grime and soot from their faces when an alarm was received from Box 41, the Auburn Prison gate. Off they went! There was dense, thick smoke rising from behind the prison south wall. Upon seeing it, the fire laddies knew that something serious was going on inside. The paid Fire Department members were met by the then-volunteer Alert Hose 6 at the gate. Together they laid hose in the street and entered through the big gate. They saw that the second floor of the prison broom shop was on fire. Smoke poured out the windows, and red and orange flames sprang up in the center of the shop. Streams of water were used on the blaze, but the structure and contents were feeding the flames. Within moments the structure, 250 feet long and 60 feet wide, was a mass of fire with flames bursting through the roof.

The prison apparatus, manned by a gang of convicts, attempted to extinguish the flames, but the water available from the hydrants within the prison proved to be inadequate and of little effect. The City Fire Department hooked up to hydrants outside the prison and made some progress against the blaze, but it continued to grow overall. Thirteen streams of water worked the fire. The flames that had compromised the roof were reaching far into the sky and thousands of city residents gathered on State Street to witness the scene. The bright glow from the flames inside lit up the sky and the fire was visible above the prison gate. The marble shop was threatened as the fire continued to spread. Firemen worked to keep the fire away from it on the south side of the building and succeeded in saving it. The broom shop continued to be consumed; the heat was intense and the fire was difficult to combat. The thirteen streams of water that were being used against the fire were taking a toll on water pressure. In order to maximize the firefighters' efforts, Chief Jewhurst ordered several streams of water shut off. The Ross Hose Fire Company had arrived at the prison and had already laid a line of hose. Jewhurst's order resulted in the Ross Hose Company not being able to turn on their hoses and a verbal exchange took place between Chief Jewhurst and members of Ross Hose. There had been a conflict between Chief Jewhurst and the volunteer companies at the Nye & Wait fire earlier that same day. The paid Fire Department was but 6 months in service and the volunteer companies that remained were, at times, somewhat dissatisfied with the authority that Chief Jewhurst had over them. Ultimately, there was agreement that they needed to work together. Two of the volunteer companies present worked to combat the broom shop fire. There was harmony of action between the paid and volunteer fire members.

The number of streams of water was reduced to eight and much better water pressure was observed. As they directed water on the flames, they heard the cracks and pops from the roof as a portion of it collapsed and a shower of sparks flew into the air. At the time of the fire, the broom shop contained almost 50 tons of broom corn, which resulted in the hot, intense fire. Broom corn is a tall plant that closely resembles a corn plant. Broom corn tops have fan-shaped blooms and the stalks were used to make brooms. It was clear that the broom shop would be a total loss and efforts were made to fight the flames that had spread to the wood working shop. The oil, paint and varnish in that area were highly flammable, and several thousand newly finished toilet seats had been stacked inside as they were being prepared for shipment. A fire wall separated the burning building from the general office, but it did not prove to be very effective and the flames ate through the nearby roof and onto the roof of the general office. Staff and convicts rushed to remove furniture and records from the area.

As the fire continued to burn strong, another alarm was received from the rolling mill of Charles W. Tuttle & Co. Assistant Chief Kinsella was dispatched to the mill, along with the Chemical Company and Hose Company No. 3. Sparks from the prison fire had lodged on the roof of the mill and had started a fire. The fire had just been put out when another alarm was received from Box 14 at the corner of Franklin and Lewis Streets. Assistant Chief Kinsella and his battalion of men responded to the Five Corners area as fast as the horses could travel and they were just in time to see thick smoke coming from the grocery store of Wilmot Carrington on Grant Avenue. The fire was in a back room of the store. The fire was extinguished very quickly. The fire companies returned to the prison.

The prison fire seemed to be surrounded and it appeared that damage would be contained to the broom and wood working shops. The supports on the south side wall were compromised and about 30 feet of it bulged out and concerned the firefighters working in the vicinity. They continued to attack the flames, when they heard creaking and cracking noises. They had just enough time to get out of the way when the wall collapsed down and crashed with a huge amount of dust and sparks around them. The firemen returned to the area and worked until the fire was ultimately extinguished. The firemen were covered in dust and soot and were exhausted. The signal from the big bell indicated the fire was out at about midnight. Chief Jewhurst and a team of men remained at the prison to extinguish hot spots that ignited periodically in the aftermath.

The fire was attributed to spontaneous combustion in the broom shop. There was no insurance on the loss, which was estimated to be $17,000. The building that burned that night was identified in the newspaper as the last of what was known as the original shop buildings. A portion of the burned building was to have been torn down within a short time. A new death chamber, dynamos and the rest of the death apparatus was to be placed in a new building at the east end of the shop which had burned.

July 7, 1899
131 Cottage Street

On the morning of Friday, July 7, 1899, Auburn Patrolman Edward Hodgson, who had started with the Police Department just the night previous, experienced his first emergency situation. While on Wall Street he noticed a glimmering reflection of what appeared to be flames in the dark sky. He ran to the corner of Seymour and Washington Streets and upon further investigation he found a fire in progress. He sounded an alarm from Box 53 at 3:09am. The house at 131 Cottage Street, owned by former Fire Commissioner Thomas Heffernan, and occupied by the family of Michael Kennedy, was on fire. The Kennedy family was away camping that week and was not home at the time of the blaze.

Upon arrival, the firemen found the rear of the residence to be covered in flames. They quickly worked to extinguish the fire. Augustus Hemrick of Hose Company 1 nearly lost his life in the fire that morning. He was standing at the top of a flight of stairs, streaming water down onto the flames in a nearby room. Captain Frank Hughson of the Chemical Company was beside him. They cleared the fire immediately in front of them and started to advance into the nearby room. The smoke was thick and the fire had worked on the floor beneath them, weakening it. As Firefighter Hemrick stepped into the room, the floor gave way and a large hole opened up. He threw himself backward in an attempt to avoid going through to the floor below, where a massive fire was still brewing and licking at the underside of the floor. As he fell back, Hemrick's head went through another hole where fire was reaching upward toward him. He grabbed nearby burning joists with both hands and was able to raise his head from the heat and smoke. As soon as Captain Hughson saw Hemrick fall, he dropped everything and went to his assistance. The charred and burning beams remained treacherous and the fire below continued to threaten and eat away at the floor they were on. Captain Hughson made his way to Hemrick and was able to lift him to safety and away from the room. Fire had ignited Hemrick's clothing, but was quickly extinguished. Both of Hemrick's hands were burned, one of them severely, from holding on to the joist. His head and face were scorched and blackened. Captain Hughson had a reputation for stopping runaway horses and rescuing people. Augustus Hemrick could certainly attest to his skill on that nearly fatal morning.

July 7, 1902

Avery Hotel, First Arson Attempt Recorded by Permanent Fire Department

In the middle of the night on July 7, 1902, Mr. Alexander, a representative of the Baker Cocoa Company and guest at the Avery Hotel on State Street, woke to find his room on the second floor filling with smoke. He rushed out of the room and cried "Fire!" Charles Coleman, the night watchman, heard the call and realized immediately the fire was in his hotel. He ran out of the hotel, saw Officer Boynton close by and asked him to turn in the call while he returned to wake up the guests. Officer Boynton sent in an alarm to the Fire Department from Box 62 near the corner of Water Street. Mr. Coleman made sure everyone was out of the building. The Fire Department responded quickly and found the store room of the hotel on fire in two places. The store room dimension was approximately 8' x 12' and was located on the second floor of the hotel, in the rear of the building, adjoining the kitchen. The fires were burning in opposite corners of the room. The room had two entrances, both of which were found locked when firefighters arrived. They were forced to break through in order to gain entry. While battling the blaze in the store room, the men were notified that Room 31 on the third floor, in the center of the building, also had a fire. Upon arrival, the mattress and bed stand were observed to be on fire. The Chemical Company utilized one of their hand extinguishers on the flames successfully. While walking through the third floor in response to Room 31, firefighters spotted another fire. A board had been pried up and removed near a door, leaving an opening about one foot square, which had been filled with old matting, paper and rags soaked in kerosene oil. The area was smoking heavily, but the firebugs efforts were halted by firemen. H. L. Downs, the night clerk, retired around midnight and slept in the room next to Room 31. He reported that he did not hear any suspicious noises and was asleep until the firemen arrived. The only individuals authorized to have keys to the store room were Mr. Shimer and the housekeeper, Mrs. Metcalf. The evidence of the incendiary nature of the fire was collected and handed over to Auburn Police. The rest of the house was searched extensively for other indications of fire, and none were identified. There were twelve guests in the hotel that night and eight staff; twenty people in all. The owner of the hotel, George Shimer, was on his way to Rochester the night of the fire and said that he could not think of anyone who would do such a thing. Damages were estimated to total $500. The Avery Hotel fire was the first official arson attempt recorded by the paid Fire Department. The arsonist was never found.

June 16, 1905

Columbian Rope Company

An alarm was called for a fire at the Columbian Rope Company at 9:30am on June 6, 1905. The fire started in Storehouse 'A' among bales of hemp and was discovered by an employee at the rope plant. The flames were already reaching several feet in the air upon discovery. The fire doors were closed to prevent a rapid spread of the flames to the adjoined storehouse. The automatic sprinklers activated and water began to spray down on the interior of the storehouse. The Columbian Rope Company fire company was called for and responded to the area. At the same time, an alarm was called in to the City Fire Department. All Auburn fire companies responded to the scene. Firefighters arrived to find the new rope plant burning rather strong in an area that housed bales of raw hemp. The plant was kept running for some time after the fire was discovered, but was shut down when the smoke trailed in and began to sicken the workers inside. The smoke and fumes created a noxious scene for the firefighters and shop workers. The smoke from the burning hemp took a toll on several of them. It burned their lungs and some sixty men strained and gasped as they worked to extinguish the flames. Some became sick. The roof was ventilated and the room was sprayed with water. A steady stream of men fought hard against the fire. As the smoke and clouds of gases were ingested, the men cycled out to receive medical attention.

Physicians were called to the scene to attend to those who were stricken during the battle against the fire. Those who were overcome by the fumes were attended to on adjoining rooftops, under trees and in lawns on West Genesee Street, as well as in rooms of the rope company. The area resembled a battlefield hospital. Dr. Conway was first on the scene and ran up to a rooftop and attended to six firemen who were overcome by smoke and fumes. Luckily, Joseph Doyle was in the area at the time of the fire. Doyle, who was a salesman for wholesaler P. T. Quigley, had his sample case with him, which he turned over to Dr. Conway. The sample case contained an assortment of liquors. Dr. Conway revived and restored the firemen and workmen when he administered hypodermic injections of whisky and brandy to those who were unable to take the standard drink! In those days, liquors were thought to be effective cardiac and respiratory stimulants when administered subcutaneously. Neighborhood women arrived at the scene with blankets, clothing and other items to minister to those in need. As soon as the men were revived, they returned to continue to fight the fire. Word traveled throughout the city that firefighters and workers were overcome and soon became rumors of death tolls and horrible injuries. Throngs of people flocked to the rope plant to see what was going on, and to see if the rumors were true. There was relief to discover that there were no deaths. The fire was extinguished after approximately two hours.

In the end, all recovered from their injuries quickly except for Acting Captain Augustus Hemrick, and callmen Louis Spaid and Earl Adams, who were confined to beds at Fire Department headquarters. Captain Morrissey was said to have felt ill; he took a bath on return to quarters and found that he had incurred a rather large and deep cut above his left knee. He received medical attention for the laceration. There was no theory brought forward as to the cause of the fire. Damages were estimated to be in the thousands.

March 27, 1906
Temple Court Fire Consumes Two Blocks

Genesee Street was a main thoroughfare in Auburn in 1906, and held many businesses within its blocks. The Temple Court building occupied 148-150 Genesee Street. The Columbus block was situated at 140-146 Genesee Street. Around 8pm on the evening of Tuesday, March 27, 1906, while cleaning the E. N. Ross Grocery Store, Henry Washington, smelled smoke. Upon further examination, Mr. Washington traced the odor to the basement. On arrival, he saw that flames were already underway. After a failed attempt to extinguish the fire himself, Henry telephoned the Fire Department headquarters. The Fire Department responded, initially minus Chief Engineer Jewhurst. Chief Jewhurst had sustained an injured on a runaway horse prior to the fire, but he arrived within ten minutes. During the course of evaluating the situation and getting his men into position, the chief suffered a severe fall and was taken home. Chief Engineer Platt took over command. E. N. Ross Grocery was located in Temple Court. Due to the delay in sounding the alarm and the brisk wind that night, the fire spread from the basement of Temple Court to the Columbus block, the next building adjoining it on the east.

Once the blaze took hold of the Columbus block, it began to climb through the partitions to the upper floors and the roof. The Columbus block structure was older than the Temple Court building and burned more rapidly. The firemen battled the fire at two locations, the original source in Temple Court and the area between the Columbus block and the Swift Block, at the corner of Genesee and William Streets. A firewall was established between the two blocks in hopes of stopping any further spread of the flames. There were eleven active streams of water being poured onto the buildings. In 1906, the city was still working with horse drawn equipment, pumpers and some steam engines. Eleven streams of water was a large number given the constraints the hydrants had displayed in these days. Just as headway was being made on the Columbus block, Temple Court suddenly burst forth with flames. As the flames reached out of the buildings and were visible in many areas, residents panicked and crowded the streets. Many attempted to enter threatened buildings to remove the contents. The result was a bit of melee as the firemen had to then contend with the public converging on the scene. The men continued to fight, giving it their all. After some time, they again made headway on the flames.

In 1906, assistance from other fire companies could be requested but oftentimes they were delayed in arriving due to the men traveling on horseback to the location while their apparatus was loaded on a train and traveled via rail. Decisions had to be made in advance of the need for assistance in order to factor in the travel time necessary. Fire and city officials had decided to call upon Syracuse and Geneva for assistance. Syracuse sent three companies, a steamer truck and a hose wagon with 3,000 feet of hose which arrived on the scene at 12:05am after thirty-five minutes of travel. Chief Ryan was in charge of the Syracuse companies responding. Geneva left at 12:30am and arrived in thirty minutes. They sent a steamer and a hose wagon with 1,000 feet of hose. Geneva crew included Chief John E. Murray and R. H. Gulvin, Foreman. There was a delay in the apparatus being unloaded at the rail station and the fire was under control upon their arrival. They provided relief and additional manpower to continue to rein in the devastating fire. John Gargan, of Auburn, made a thrilling stop of a runaway horse which threatened the lives of the spectators in the area that night.

During the course of the long battle, three firefighters were overcome by smoke, removed to the court house, treated, and then taken to their homes. A Hose No. 3 member was more severely overcome by smoke and was brought to the city hospital by ambulance for treatment. He recovered without further incident. In Columbus Hall, a meeting was being held for the Catholic Relief and Beneficiary Association (C. R. and B. A.). Most women present at the meeting were able to get out on their own. However, Mrs. C. M. Hubbard, secretary and Mrs. Leo, president, were both rescued and carried down the fire escapes by firemen on the scene. Work continued on the fire into the overnight hours before it was finally extinguished. The fire that swept through two blocks was stubborn, but the Auburn firemen proved stronger. They remained on the scene all day Wednesday, looking for embers that threatened to cause the building to re-ignite.

The fire had taken a toll on businesses in the two blocks, but had it not been for the firewall established between the Columbus and Swift blocks, it is likely that the fire would have spread farther. The two buildings that burned were owned by Col. E. D. Metcalf. The loss of the buildings was estimated at $75,000. The E. N. Ross grocery store suffered the second largest loss, next to Colonel Metcalf. The Ross safe had fallen through the floor in the fire and landed in the southwest corner of the basement in the building, where the offices were located. In the offices, valuable papers and contracts were found to be mostly intact, albeit scorched and wet. The Ross safe was removed to the American Tobacco Company and opened. The contents were found to be in good shape, with only the bottom of the safe being affected by water. Mr. Ross gathered his staff and moved to the Auburn

Public Market temporarily. The bakery portion of the store was not extensively damaged by the fire. They were able to get the bakery in condition to produce the entire line of Ross baked goods and sold them at the Auburn Public Market the following Saturday. The tailor and clothing dealer, Quick & Rust, lost $10,000 in stock. Miss H. Martin, a fancy goods dealer, fared better but still lost stock. Most of her goods were saved. W. R. Meaker, plumber, lost all his stock, valued at $5,000. Miss Mary E. Mahaney, milliner, lost her entire stock as well. The Swift block suffered only about $500 damage. The second floor of the Temple Court building held the offices of the John Hancock Life Insurance Company, Dr. G. W. Whitney, Attorney Charles T. Whelan, dressmakers Baltes & Breads, Attorneys Leonard & Treat, Patent Attorney Warren Brinkerhoff, Gallt Novelty Dress Goods Company and the Empire Music Academy. Attorney Whelan's desk fell through the floor to the Ross Grocery store and was consumed in the fire, but the safe remained in his office. The contents of the safe were found to be in good shape. The third floor of the Temple Court Building held club rooms of the Knights of Columbus, from which access could be had to the Columbus block. The entire third floor of the Columbus block was occupied by the Knights of Columbus lodge room. They lost some of the finest lodge furnishings in the state along with their lodge charter. Their monetary loss was estimated at $10,000. Their losses were large, but they declared they would "rise from the ashes" and be better than ever. The fourth floor of the Temple Court building was occupied by the Auburn Lodge, No. 47, B. P. O. Elks. Mr. Leonard, of Auburn, made a valiant attempt to save their charter, but he was driven back by the thick smoke. The loss sustained by the Elks Club was $5,000. The big elk head on the front of the building remained. The other firms, businesses and individuals were estimated to have lost $40,000 combined. The total loss resulting from the fire was estimated to be $175,000.

October 13, 1910

Monroe Avenue, Pest House and Hoboes' Haven

Who could have predicted the fire that occurred on October 13, 1910? Health Commissioner Frank N. Richards could have, and in fact, did. In 1881, it became necessary for the City of Auburn to consider construction of a pest house. A pest house was a location for people with serious infections, diseases and other contagious conditions to be treated. Those with smallpox, scarlet fever, typhoid and yellow fevers were cared for in the pest house. The City Hospital had received a gift of land upon which a pest house was proposed to be built at the expense of the city. In 1881, construction of a two-story frame dwelling, to serve as a pest house, was completed for $1,509.40 on the corner of N. Division Street and Monroe Avenue, near the city limits. The pest house was close to the railroad crossing and nearly opposite the Wildner brewery. The structure was described as pleasing to the eye, but not palatial. It was clean and comfortable. Over the years the pest house held patients who required an isolated area for their conditions. In 1902, Auburn experienced a smallpox outbreak, and an increased number of people were treated during that time. Following the 1902 smallpox outbreak, the pest house was used less frequently, and by 1910 had fallen into disrepair and had become a bit of an eye sore and a place for transients to gather. The pest house had become known as "Hoboes' Haven." Tramps from far and wide had passed around word that there was a shelter available off the rails in Auburn. The fact that the house had been a smallpox resort did not seem to faze those who made use of the premises. The newspaper reported, "The 'bos' have held their mixed-ale parties and bridge whist gatherings in the place unmolested. Occasionally, when some hen coop or farmyard in the vicinity has been raided, the police have been called in and in turn have raided the pest house and picked up a ding-dong wagon full of wanderers, temporarily loitering." After careful consideration, Commissioner Richards issued an edict that the pest house be razed. Upon hearing that the pest house would be razed, many in the area asked permission to tear down the old building for the lumber. It was felt that smallpox had been absorbed into the timbers and city officials did not want to take any chance on having the malady perpetuated. Commissioner Richards, Mayor Thomas O'Neill and City Attorney Whelan together made the decision to declare the pest house a public nuisance and called upon the Auburn Fire Department to burn the structure.

The event was publicized as an attraction. City residents were notified that the burn would occur at 3pm on October 13, 1910. The police patrol was to be on hand. Exterminators were to be present for any smallpox germs that tried to escape. The public was charged 25¢ admission, but no effort was made to collect the money. Upon hearing the decision to burn the pest house, the Fire Department expressed regret that the decision was made after the firemen's convention. The burn could have been a feature of the convention. On October 13th, nearly 2,000 spectators gathered around the pest house to witness the event. Auburn Patrolman Murray was present on his motorcycle and Police Commissioner Leonard with the Patrol Wagon. Division Street to the west and York Street to the north were lined with carriages and automobiles. The crowd was astounding. The newspaper account of the fire that day described the scene as such:

> Nearly 2,000 persons witnessed the funeral pyre of the Hoboes' Haven, the ancient inn of the wanderlust tribe and at one time in the Middle Ages, a pest home of the City of Auburn. Yesterday afternoon when, amid appropriate ceremonies, a detail of the Fire Department touched the torch to the venerable structure and then withdrew to a safe distance after seeing

that every fragment of combustible material went up in smoke. Everybody of importance in the city government was there. The ceremonies opened at 3 o'clock when Health Commissioner Richards, followed by a delegation of small boys, reached the portals of the old tavern. He entered alone and spent a few minutes in final communion with the spirits of the upstairs garret while the small boys examined the spirits that still gave amber hues to the bottom of many half-pint flasks that mutely testified to the revels of the past, bottles being found in profusion. When the Health Commissioner withdrew and nodded solemnly to Fire Commissioner Burgess, that gentleman took up his part in the observance. He also went through the building in the walls of which lurked many frightened smallpox germs who peeked suspiciously out of thousands of cracks and crannies at the strangers. When Commissioner Burgess came down he stood for a moment in the doorway, faced the crowd on the ramparts to the north and addressing Chief E. J. Jewhurst, solemnly repeated the mystic signal to go ahead. Then came Ladderman Edward J. Lyons of the Hook and Ladder Company bearing a five gallon can of sacred ointment and Fireman John A. Colbert of Hose 1 hefting the sacred axes and Fireman Joseph Anton of Hose 5 with the purifying pikepoles. With Captain F. B. Hughson of Hose 4 and Chief E. J. Jewhurst, they entered the building and spent some time in making necessary vents and scattering incense. At 3:24 o'clock they reappeared and Chief Jewhurst, like Dewey at Manila Bay, acknowledged the salute of his subordinate and gave the historic command: "You may fire when you are ready, Captain."

The torch was then applied and in a minute smoke was seen issuing from every part of the building. Great clouds of smoke traveled across the fields. The red fire roared within the walls of the house and heaved itself through the roof and windows to the sky, while the draft of the flames sucked up a great sheet of pale smoke from the burning roof over the eaves of the house like the rush of whitewater over the verge of a cataract. Already the smallpox germs had discovered the attempt upon their existence and were endeavoring to escape and from every crack in the clapboards their wicked eyes would be seen, causing multitude to fall back farther and farther from the pest house. But the axes and pikepoles of the firemen outside cowed them and they remained inside until it was too late to escape and after the fire was a mass of glowing ashes and the chimney had fallen, Commissioner Richards, who had been carefully watching for any possible escapes, announced that not a single "bug" reached safety.

The heat about the fire grew intense and the crowd of sightseers was driven slowly back as the flames increased in volume. The roof fell in, but did not make much noise. Only the rapid snap and crackle of the flames like the sound of very distant musketry, and the fluttering thud of falling timbers.

The fire was truly a magnificent spectacle and repaid all who made the long journey. It was estimated that nearly 2,000 persons were on hand, and they packed not only the knolls in the immediately vicinity of the place, but could be seen on the surrounding hills, railroad tracks and in automobiles and wagons on the roads nearby. Had the occurrence taken place at night, the crowd would probably have been larger and the spectacle more impressive.

The method of incendiarism was perfect and the experts who were disturbed in the old Fanning brewery several years ago could not have done a better job. While it is generally known that the Auburn Fire Department is most expert in putting out a fire, it was never demonstrated until yesterday that they are quite as skillful in the game of arson. In five minutes after the torch was applied by Jack Taylor, Igniter of the Benzine Ointment, the entire two-story structure with rear wing was one pillar of fire, and within the building the fascinating glow of the furnace heat was seen in its ever changing shades of red and gold.

Photographers took advantage of the opportunity and obtained several good pictures. The building proved to have been substantially constructed and it was 45 minutes before the siding had burned away and left the blazing outlines, these remaining a few minutes, after which the heavier framework leaned westward and then crashed into the ruin. The chimney alone remained firm, pouring out volumes of smoke like a man who was making up time for having long been deprived of tobacco. It was not until the mob of small boys in the vicinity had cleaned up all of the loose stones in the neighborhood fields and bombarded the crumbling base of the chimney, that it leaned and finally crashed to the ground. The performance was then formally declared over in the return of the firemen to headquarters and only the boys remained on the scene.

The old pest house was gone. The Auburn Fire Department completed the burn and the safety of the spectators gathered and the surrounding area was maintained.

December 5, 1910
Lincoln Flats Fire

Auburn had a few years in the early 1900s with no significant property loss due to fire. In 1908, there were no major fires in the city. The Mohican grocery store fire on November 24, 1909, proved to be the only large blaze that year. It looked like 1910 might also pass without large fire losses. The Auburn Draying Company had a fire on August 23, 1910. As 1910 drew to a close, fire struck the city hard. It was a frigid, cold night in December when firemen were called out to fight flames that had taken hold of another building. The Lincoln Flats occupied 28-30 Genesee Street in Auburn, near Osborne Street. It held two businesses and six residences. The Eastern Estate Tea Store, an agency of the Red Stamp Trading Company was housed there.

At just after 7:30pm on the evening of December 5, 1910, the staff of the Eastern Estate Tea Store were preparing for the usual Monday night customers when they were alerted by the smell of smoke coming from the cellar. Adelbert Hart, a clerk at the tea store, went to investigate and found a fire underway in a pile of debris and papers. He ran for a pail of water and threw it on the fire. The fire continued and started to spread rapidly, edging along the walls and making its way toward piles of furniture and cabinets and items used for trading stamp premiums. Mr. Hart called an immediate alarm. Box 25 was pulled at the corner of Genesee and Osborne Streets.

Chief Edward J. Jewhurst was sitting down to a lovely turkey dinner at the home of Henry F. Mott on Nelson Street. He had just received a nice portion of turkey when the alarm sounded. He sprang from his place at the table and rushed to the fire. The fire was roaring in the basement upon arrival of the Fire Department and plumes of smoke could be seen rolling out of the tea store and moving throughout the building.

At the first indications of trouble, the residents of the building were warned and most got out on their own right away. The top floor residence found Mrs. J. Dewitt Forman and Miss Minnie Bartholomew, another resident in the building who was visiting Mrs. Dewitt at the time of the fire, were unable to escape through the thick smoke that quickly filled the area. They ran to the windows and waved their hands frantically and yelled for help to the people in the street below. People in the street worried that the two would jump from the windows. Joseph Hickey, a brakeman on the Owasco River railway, along with Mrs. Forman's son, Claire, were familiar with the stairways in the interior of the building and went to the rear side. They were able to make their way upstairs to the top floor and assist both women down to the street.

The firemen attacked the fire strategically. Assistant Chief George Platt and Captain Frank Hughson led their crew of men to the front of the building on Genesee Street to launch their attack. Captains Strong, Washburn, Hemrick and Morrissey took their men to the rear of the building and to the neighboring rooftops to fight the fire from the top. The building was surrounded and the men had good vantage points and positions in place to make progress against the threatening flames. The fire in the basement was difficult for the men to fight, as they were compelled to go down into the sidewalk pits where the smoke was thick and suffocating and where leaking gas fumes were present. In spite of the laborious process of positioning to extinguish the cellar fire, the firefighters were able to bring it under control and had it practically extinguished within thirty minutes. Their attention then turned to the construction of the building. The structure did not have interior brick walls; instead, it was balloon construction; light wood partitions that would draw up the fire into the spaces between the studding like suction tubes and then spread to the upper floors. This type of construction was difficult because there was little indication of where the fire might be found and could be anywhere from the attic to the basement. They identified an airshaft on the east side of the building that had ventilation for the bathrooms, which they surmised would provide a vent for the fire and facilitate it rolling upward through that area. As it rolled through the floors upward it would ignite additional rooms in the building. Without the interior brick walls, the fire would cross over to the rooms on the west side of the building and continue to consume room after room. The flames were likely within the walls and spreading without being seen. It was a dangerous situation. This hidden enemy was skulking through the Lincoln Flats, making its way forward until a time when it would reveal itself in a showy and consuming way, attempting to maximize damage. The firefighters had to actively seek out their enemy. Knowing the likely path the fire would take, Chief Jewhurst personally trekked through the building and issued orders in the grimy, black smoke-filled rooms and identified the places where flames were likely present and instructed and positioned his men to be able to stop its appearance before it could continue along its path.

There were nine streams of water and two chemicals pummeling the blaze. Chief Jewhurst evaluated and weighed up the situation constantly. He saw that conditions had turned quickly, and it was no longer safe to have his men in the building. He ordered them out. The Chief called for the Hayes truck with its water tower arrangement of ladders to be brought toward the area between the Lincoln Flats and the Herron Hardware building to the West, and streams of water applied to prevent the fire from spreading into the hardware store building. He also ordered hose lines to spray the Olheiser block to the East. The Hayes truck's huge arm extended over the roof and a group of firemen were fighting the spread of the fire. The flames roared through the opening in the joists. The building was a tinder-like structure and it became apparent that little of the building would likely be saved. All of a sudden, at about 8:45pm, the fire burst through the skylight in the roof of the Lincoln Flats building at the top of the central hallway. The roof collapsed and a shower of sparks was sent skyward. The apartments became victims of the draft that the roof collapse provided to the flames. Until this time, the fire did not show columns of flames. Shortly after the roof collapse, the fire emerged visibly and could be seen from great distances away. The red glare lit up the sky and smoke pulsated upward in massive plumes. The Hayes truck continued to provide a barrier between the two buildings. The hardware store was filled with combustible and very flammable materials in large quantities. It was imperative that the flames not be allowed to reach them. It was now a question of saving the entire block of buildings on either side of the Lincoln Flats structure.

At about this time the International Harvester's private fire company was called. The whistle called for the volunteer fire company workforce of the International Harvester company, who manned their equipment and provided water from the rooftop of the Osborne Street corner. The stream ultimately proved ineffective, as it sent a continuous spray of water onto the firemen working on the front of the building on Genesee Street below. The water froze as it came down and covered the men and apparatus with ice. The International Harvester Company's fire apparatus was moved to an area where they assisted in preventing the fire from spreading toward the rear of the building.

Auburn Fire Commissioner William Burgess, Auburn Police Commissioner Edmund Leonard, Fire Marshal Coneybear, Auburn Police Department officers and patrolmen as well as Mayor Thomas O'Neill were on hand throughout the night, securing the scene and providing assistance to the firemen when necessary. Thousands crowded the area and police worked to keep them back from the fire and provided the firemen with plenty of room in which to work. The Eastern Tea Company had the Axton dining room at 24½ Genesee Street provide hot coffee and sandwiches to those who were displaced from their homes as well as those who had fought the fire.

The Auburn Fire Department fought without fail against the fire and was finally able to stop it in its tracks. They worked beyond exhaustion, suffering from the smoke, heat and fumes that clung to them. The long night ended with the Lincoln Flats building being all but lost completely, but the adjacent buildings were protected and encountered minimal, if any, damage. By just after 11pm the fire was brought under control and imminent danger had subsided. The entire department remained at the scene until almost 4am, when the fire bell sounded the signal to indicate that the fire was extinguished at last.

The total loss was estimated at nearly $50,000. The owners of the Lincoln Flats, P. M. Herron and William D. Ganey, suffered a $20,000 loss. The Eastern Estate Tea Co. lost $5,000 in stock and fixtures. Cuddy & Geherin (Coal Co.) lost $600 in fixtures. They occupied the opposite side of the ground floor. Rowe & Cronin dry goods store had $1,200 damage to stock due to water. The occupants of the residences were taken in temporarily by friends and family. Their losses were great and many got out with just the clothing on their backs. Those few that held insurance did not have enough to cover their losses. The second floor of the building had two residences. Oscar Herrling and his wife lost $1,400. Having just been married the previous August, they had recently returned from a trip west and just settled in their new residence together. Their loss included all of their beautiful wedding presents which had just the day prior to the fire been received from Great Falls, Montana. The crates and boxes of wedding gifts included cut glass, silver, and many other fine items. They had unpacked the wedding gifts and placed them around their home before the fire. While clearing debris and after the fire, Hoseman Claire VanDusen found a box containing a watch, diamond ring and necklace as well as an alligator skin pocketbook containing $10 and a box of valuable papers belonging to the Herrlings. They were overjoyed at getting the items back. The only other two items that were saved were a fur coat and a new derby which had left behind in Herrling's meat market on North Street. M. L. Fleischman had $2,000 in loss. The third floor of the building held two residences. Former Alderman and Fire Commissioner, Thomas Heffernan, lost much personal property from his home at Residence #3. His loss was estimated at $1,600. Minnie Bartholomew, who provided piano instruction in Residence #4, suffered a $1,600 loss. On the fourth floor, Mr. and Mrs. Michael Dunn, whose rooms were elaborately furnished, suffered a $1,800 loss in Residence #5. Among their losses was a $500 piano. Mr. and Mrs. Dewitt Forman and son, Claire, lost $2,200 in property from Residence #6. Mrs. Forman had lost a valuable diamond pin in the fire, which was later found in the burned out debris and returned to her.

The exact cause of the fire was not definitively identified. It was possibly caused by faulty wiring in an area that contained papers and flammable debris. The weather that evening worked against the firefighters with temperatures plunging to near zero. Ice became a disastrous bystander and adversely affected the ability to get water to the fire at times. Ice coated the apparatus, the men and the area such that every action required additional time and attention in order to proceed. Several firemen sustained injuries during the night. John "Jack" Taylor, driver for Chief Jewhurst, fell through the ground floor and into the cellar of the burning building and was overcome by smoke. He later returned and continued to fight the fire. Unfortunately, he was struck down again by a heavy piece of glass that fell from an upper window. His injuries were not serious. An International Harvester fire company responder suffered a fractured left leg after falling from an icy ladder. Michael O'Neill, Mayor O'Neill's son, received eight stitches after he was cut on the top and side of his head by a piece of falling glass.

Mr. P. M. Herron gave his highest commendation to Chief Jewhurst and the men of the Auburn Fire Department for the efficient manner in which they handled the blaze and prevented it from spreading to other properties. He offered his company's sincere appreciation and extended heartfelt thanks to the Auburn Fire Department. Many firefighters who were present at the Lincoln Flats fire would later describe it as the worst fire of their careers. The Lincoln Flats building was rebuilt by P. M. Herron and employed fire safety components and construction methods within the structure. The beautiful block of stores and apartments were once again made a handsome addition to the Genesee Street blocks.

August 13, 1912
19 Coon Street, Fireworks Explosion, Five Dead

The aftermath of the Coon Street explosion

For the Cheche family, the morning of August 13, 1912, started as any other. They gathered together for breakfast and likely spoke of their plans for the day. The Feast of the Assumption celebration was coming up on August 15th and the Italian Catholic community was excitedly anticipating the elaborate celebration that had been planned. Raffaele Cheche was the President of the Society of the Assumption and the Celebration Committee. He had been busily planning the annual event with other members of the St. Francis D'Assisi church. As in previous years, there would be food, music and fireworks. Italians from across the state had been invited to attend the celebration. Following breakfast, the Cheche family started their daily activities. Raffaele Cheche, a foreman for the track repairers of the Auburn & Syracuse Electric Railroad, left his home and went to work near the foot of the lake. Raffaele's son, Matthew, was employed at the Dunn & McCarthy shoe factory. He left the house and went to work following breakfast.

Cosimo Carmelengo was a manufacturer of fireworks from Fairview, New Jersey. He was married and had six children. He had been hired to provide a fireworks display for the upcoming feast celebration. He had arrived in Auburn the day prior to the explosion. The fireworks had been shipped from Little Ferry, New Jersey and had arrived via the American Express Company the day before the tragedy and were stored in the Cheche home. More than 400 pounds of firework material arrived in three boxes, one barrel and one iron pipe. They were said to be valued at $300. The explosives were placed in the front area of the cellar, where it was thought they would be most safe. Mr. Carmelengo had provided firework displays for several years for the event and made the pyrotechnic material in his New Jersey factory, Flammia & Carmelengo. Each year the explosives were stored in the Cheche home for a couple of days prior to the feast event. Mr. Carmelengo had more than thirty years' experience with fireworks manufacturing. On the morning of the catastrophe, Mr. Carmelengo went to the residence of Tony Oropallo, who lived about two hundred yards away on West Street. After his visit with Mr. Oropallo, Cosimo headed back to the Cheche home.

The 7am whistles were sounded around the city, signaling shift starts for employees at various factories and businesses. Many people in the community had already left for work and were not at home. Shortly after 7am, suddenly and without warning, Auburn was utterly rocked with a concussion and boom that reverberated so loudly that it was heard and felt for great distances. Three additional blasts were heard, but the first one was by far the heaviest and most destructive. Glass crashed and wood popped and tore as it was thrown in the explosion. The huge blast blew apart the two-story frame dwelling of the Cheche family home and threw timbers, rocks and other material high into the air. Several other adjacent houses were destroyed. Large timbers had been blasted into the neighboring houses, sticking out like gigantic arrows. One large foundation timber had been thrown across the street and through the wall of the Kennedy house and protruded the house for several feet. The family of Tony Vitale, at 22 Coon Street, miraculously escaped death when their home was almost demolished in the aftermath. Mrs. Vitale was home with her two-month old baby at the time. Timbers penetrated the house and flew through the windows, and one had been hurled through the house, landing against a bed with such force that it bent the brass rods. Windows were shattered in houses blocks from the site. Plaster and explosive dust were everywhere. Splintered wood and stones covered everything. Panic set in for those in the immediate area; worry and fear consumed everyone who heard the blast. Auburn Fire Department records indicate that the alarm was received at the station at 7:11am that morning. Fire Companies 1, 3, 4, 5, 6 and the Hook & Ladder responded to the scene at 19 Coon Street (Venice Street today). A number of residents in the area at the time of the explosion were cut by flying glass and falling wood and other material. The scene was apocalyptic. Screams and cries, crowds swarming to find their loved ones, a blast site and a number of casualties made the morning one of complete shock and mourning.

Hoseman Claire VanDusen of Hose Co. 3 was on his day off from the Fire Department. He was on his way home on Wall Street when he heard the explosion. VanDusen ran at top speed in the direction of the explosion. He met up with John Gleason and they made their way to Coon Street. The first sight that met their eyes was the crumpled form of a little girl lying in the street fifteen feet from the home. Emma Cheche, age 11, was examined and found to be alive, but barely clinging to life. VanDusen ran to the store on the corner of West and Coon Streets and instructed them to call for physicians and police. The call was immediately placed. Within a few minutes the patrol wagon arrived and took little Emma to the city hospital. Emma Cheche, who had suffered a fractured skull, many broken bones and other internal injuries, died at the hospital about two hours later.

Small explosions continued to go off in the area where the house once stood. Hose Company 3, under the direction of Captain James Walsh, was the first on the scene. Hose lines were run and the fires in and around the debris field were being extinguished. Smaller shell explosions continued around them. Captain Walsh and his men started to climb on the blazing wreck and there was one final explosion directly underneath them. The firemen doused the area to eliminate further fires and blasts. As the firemen found unexploded shells in the field, they watered them down. The firemen raised timbers to seek out bodies. They worked desperately in their search. Five people were in the home at the time of the explosion. All of them were killed by the tragic event. Four died instantly: Mary Cheche, age 45; Armando Cheche, age 9; Carmela Cheche, age 7; Cosimo Carmelengo, age 47. Hose Company No. 3's equipment was used on the scene.

Matthew Cheche was standing in the hall of the shoe factory when he heard the boom and felt the rattle and shake of the explosion. He and others rushed out of the factory and toward the direction of the blast. In the meantime, the loss of Mrs. Cheche and three of the Cheche children soon reached Raffaele Cheche. Some of the car men on the Owasco line of the trolley told the father of the horrific tragedy. He did not want to believe the news, but finally consented to go back to his home. Upon arrival he became prostrate with grief and tears flowed at the site of the area where his family and home were last seen. All that remained was a large pile of debris. Raffaele and Matthew were taken in by a neighbor, Saverio Colella, and surrounded by friends. They watched over Raffaele, fearful that he might attempt suicide.

Massive crowds ran to the scene and the street in the vicinity of the Cheche home.

Auburn Police Department Chief Bell, along with Sergeant Graney and Patrolmen O'Brien, Corcoran, Main and Titus held back the crowds and established a cordon around the area as firemen and others began clearing out debris and looking for the bodies of the poor family members which were scattered throughout the area. Little Armando was the first to be located. Mary Cheche was found in the area of the kitchen. She had been pinned down by a timber on top of which was the kitchen range. It was a tragic and devastating sight. Seven-year-old Carmela was found near the west wall of the basement. The Cheche family bodies were not in good shape, and were gathered by the firemen and removed with care. Mr. Carmelengo's body was found in the northwest corner of the area. He was found under many big timbers and a section of the roof, in a sitting position. Portions of his body were not present, having been blown away in the blast. The black smoke that covered his crushed skull rendered him almost unrecognizable. He was brought to the Meagher morgue and was positively identified later. The northwest area of the lot contained a large mass of wreckage. Mayor O'Neill had arrived on the scene and after conferring with Chief Jewhurst, a large detail of firemen and street department employees under the supervision of Superintendent Henry Ivison, went to work on the debris that had not yet been fully examined to see if there were additional victims. Although Mr. Cheche had indicated everyone who would have been present in his home, it was thought by officials that perhaps neighbors might have been in the area at the time of the explosion.

Along the foundation walls of the wrecked house, firemen found several cast iron pipes, such as were used by fireworks handlers. Fire Marshal Coneybear retained an unexploded bomb as evidence. In the hours and days that followed, many speculated on the cause of the explosion. Some suspected dynamite; others offered that there was trouble between the Catholic and Protestant Italians in the area. James Marino, a partner of Carmelengo, offered his own opinion as to the cause of the blast. He suspected that sparks from striking a nail head in the unpacking of one of the boxes set off the explosion. Mr. Carmelengo had packed the boxes himself and was experienced at such work. If they had not been packed adequately, they would likely have exploded while in the possession of the express company. Mr. Marino suspected that while opening the boxes a hammer struck a nail which created sparks and set off the event. An inquest was conducted by Coroner A. J. Forman to ascertain the cause of the explosion that resulted in the death of five people. Edward Brayer, Brayer Bros. contractors firm, testified that he had considerable experience in dealing with explosives and felt the Coon Street tragedy was caused by a high explosive. He did not believe that black powder would have wrecked the house in the manner that occurred. Raffaele Cheche testified that there was no friction between his family and others and that Carmelengo had been a close friend for many years. Cheche and Carmelengo had been neighbors in Italy. Mr. Cheche reported he was not aware that it was necessary to get permission to store the fireworks. He reported that he was sure there was no dynamite in the fireworks. Tony Oropallo reported that he had seen Mr. Carmelengo around 6:55am on the morning of the explosion. Mr. Carmelengo had entered Oropallo's store on West Street. While in the store, Carmelengo smoked an Italian cigar. After a brief exchange of greetings, Carmelengo left. Oropallo did not know where Cosimo went after he left his store. Fire Marshal Coneybear was examined by Coroner Forman as well. Coneybear indicated that it was necessary to get special permission to store fireworks, and he had not issued a permit to Cheche or Carmelengo. Michael Falcone of 59 West Street and Specioso Rainone of 12 Coon Street, both members of the Society of the Assumption, testified that they knew nothing of the cause of the explosion, had heard of no threatening letters to Cheche, Carmelengo or the Society. The Coroner found that the victims died from the effects of the explosion of high explosives that had been shipped to Auburn and stored as "fireworks" in the cellar of No. 19 Coon Street. The report indicated "that the cause of said explosion is not known to me." The report also indicated that the material shipped by Flammia & Carmelengo of Fairview, New Jersey was labeled "fireworks" and that such designation was in violation of the Interstate Commerce Commission regulations. Chemical analysis of the unexploded material collected by Coneybear at the scene was found to fall into the "high explosives" designation and should have been labeled as such. No one will ever know exactly what set off the Coon Street explosion. What is known is that two families were devastated by the events that unfolded in the explosion that collected the lives of innocent victims.

July 1913, Monarch Drug Fire

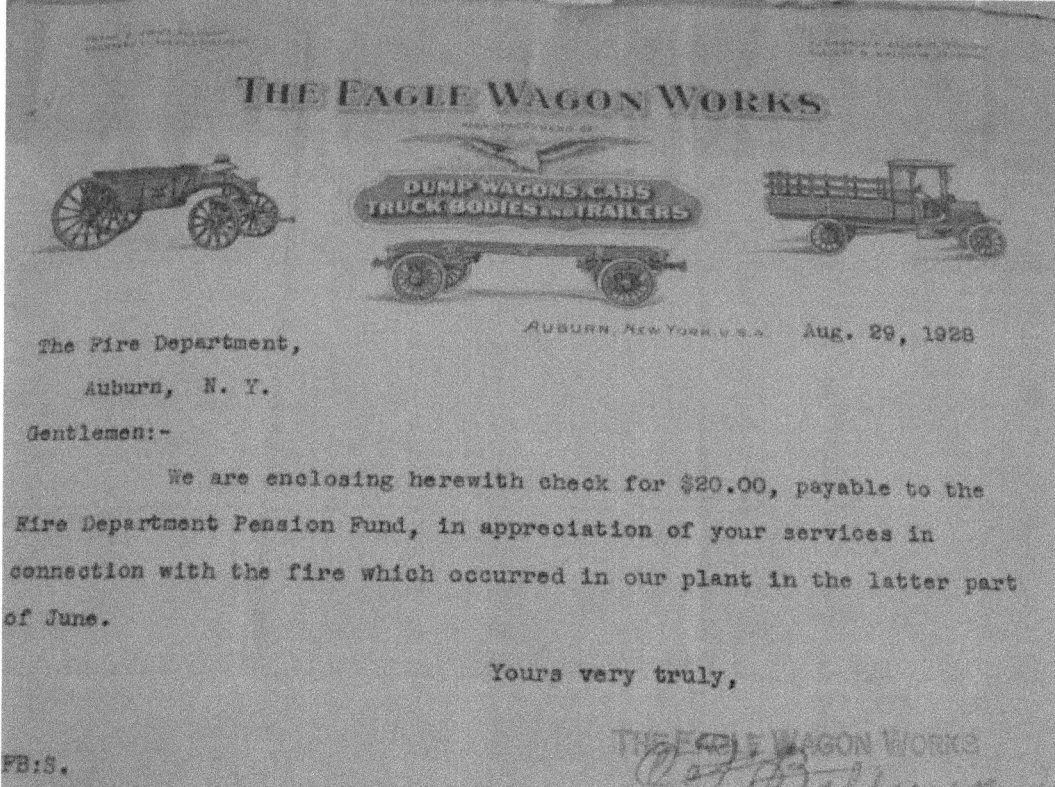

Top: July 1913, Monarch Drug Fire

STATE OF NEW YORK.

Office of the Agent and Warden of Auburn Prison.

Auburn, N.Y., March 30,1898.

To the Chief of the Auburn Fire Department.

Dear Sir:-- Please extend to the Auburn Fire Department my thanks for its zeal and efforts in extinguishing the fire in the Auburn Prison yesterday, and also my appreciation of its prompt and efficient service in that behalf.

Yours &c

[illegible]

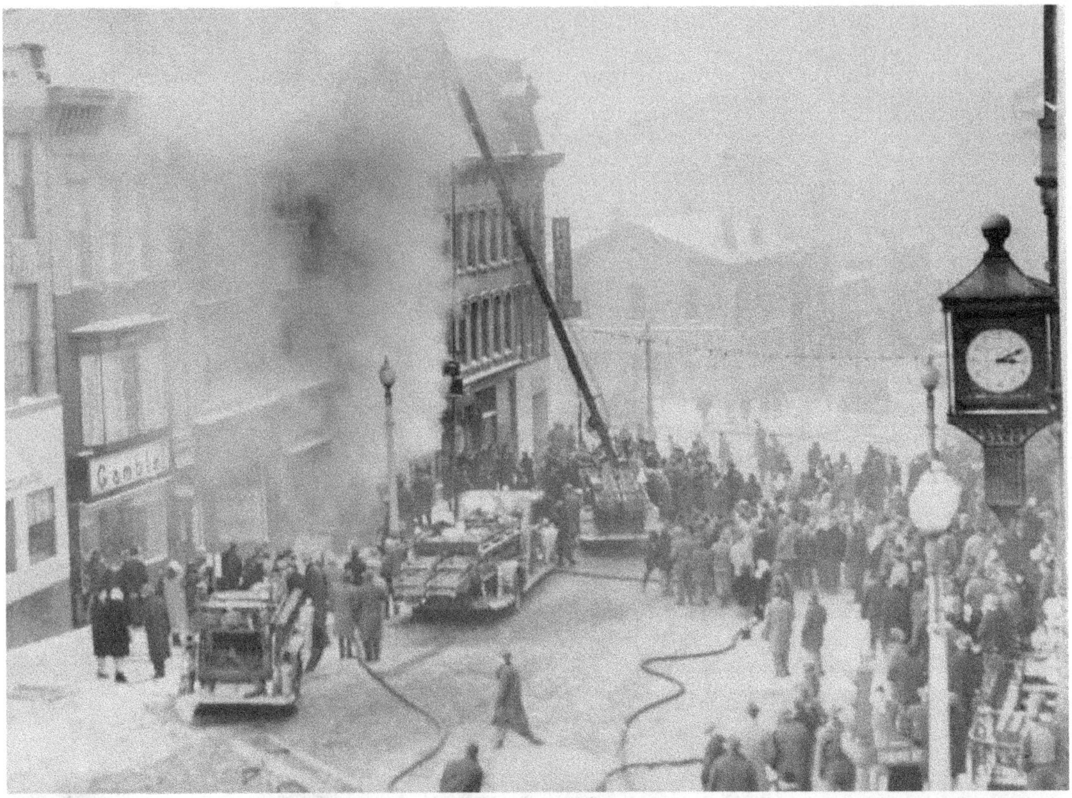

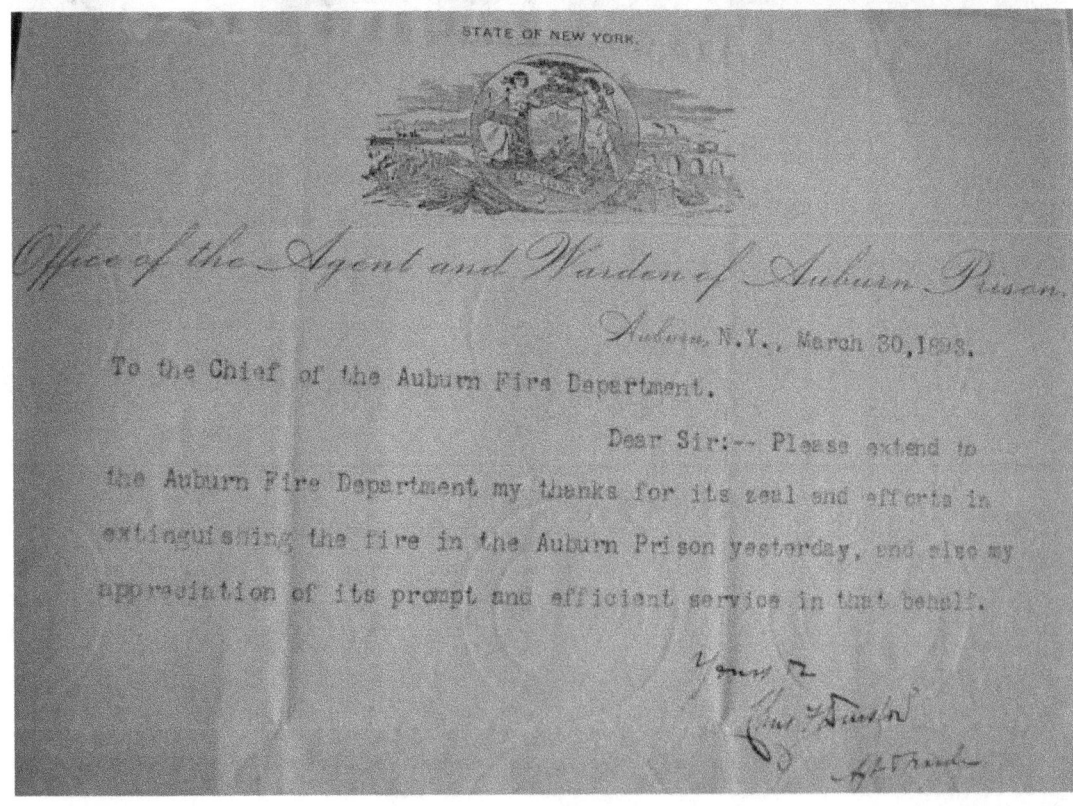

Top: Kalet's Fire

FIRES 205

Bottom: September 1907, International Harvester Fire

Top: *Osborne House fire*

Bottom: *From the collection of the Cayuga Museum of History and Art*

May 1, 1914

Wegman Piano Company Fire, $100,000 in Losses

The Wegman Piano Company was established in Ithaca, New York, in 1882, and moved to Auburn in 1887. It was initially located on Genesee Street in the rear of the Genesee rink. After a few years, demand for their pianos increased such that a new, larger location became necessary. The factory on Logan Street was chosen as the new location for the Wegman Piano Company. The location had previously been the Logan Silk Mill. Over the years the factory continued to grow in size and demand, and it became one of the largest and most comprehensive piano manufacturers in New York State. The instruments produced by the company were of the highest quality and much sought after. The 'L' shaped factory was three stories high and was of brick construction. It had 200 feet of frontage on Logan Street and the north wing which extended from the west end of the Logan Street frontage was 175 feet deep. There was another 100 foot long, one-story wing on the east end of the building.

On the night of May 1, 1914, Night Watchman Lewis Clifford had started his midnight round of the Wegman building and was on the third floor when his attention was drawn to a reflection of a fire on the floor below him. He instinctively knew that the reflection came from a blaze in the factory and raced down the stairs. At about the same time, Patrolman Charles McMaster was approaching the factory when he noticed the flames in the window on the second floor. He rushed across the street and pulled alarm Box 39. Gilbert Johnson, who lived across the street from the factory, was in bed on the second floor of his house when he saw a small flicker in the factory. When he first discovered it, the fire was very small and hardly a blaze. He quickly got dressed and made it to the street within three minutes and found the flames were already leaping high and licking their way out of the windows. His discovery was about the same time as Clifford and McMaster. The alarm came into the Auburn Fire Department at 12:19am. The fire companies responded quickly, but when the first of them reached the scene, the flames were already leaping from the second and third story windows. In all the excitement, Watchman Clifford had forgotten to pull the auxiliary box located in the front hall of the Wegman building. The auxiliary box alarm would have notified the Fire Department that the piano company was the exact location of the fire and all companies would have responded at once. In an incredibly short amount of time, Hose Companies 1, 2, 4, 5, 6 and the Hook & Ladder responded to the scene.

On arrival, Chief Edward Jewhurst quickly sized up the situation and ordered eight hose lines connected. The eight hose lines were directed on the fire; three on the Logan Street side, two at the rear and two on the west side of the factory. The ladders of the big Hook & Ladder truck were run up the west side of the building and an additional hose line was brought up. The firemen were directed to locations by Chief Jewhurst, and they quickly, and with great precision, took up their positions in various locations throughout the building. The fire was growing by leaps and bounds, burning molten hot and igniting everything in its path. Everything in the building was kiln dried and the varnished lumber burned with great voracity. The fire seemed to defy the streams of water that were being poured on it. Glass smashed and the flames roared and crackled, while the wood popped and other material gave way. The red and orange flames could be seen throughout the city as they reached out of the factory windows and snaked their way upward to the roof. The firemen inside the building continued to fight the flames in an effort to keep them in check and stop their advance. They stood bravely in their tasks, keeping an eye on the interior walls of the building, many of which were not strong. On the interior of the building was one brick partition that extended to the attic and formed a sort of fire wall for that area. Firefighters held the fire at bay and kept it from being introduced into that portion of the building. In other locations of the building, the story was much different. The hissing and spitting of the fire continued and the blaze broke through to the roof. Members of Hose Company No. 5 were stationed on the third floor when the blaze took hold of the roof. Chief Jewhurst quickly surveyed the situation and determined that the structure was compromised in that area. He ordered his men out. The last man had just exited through a window when the roof suddenly caved in with a giant crash. A gas pipe on the first floor had been severed and the escaping gas fueled the already raging fire. Hoseman Dayton Smith of Company No. 2 bravely made his way into the cellar to shut off the gas. A deluge of water was poured into the basement, and Smith waded in the water up to his armpits to the entrance of the gas main and successfully turned it off.

Throughout the night, the tight wires of the Wegman instruments gave way and a sort of musical cacophony of odd notes and cries from the piano keys was heard as the flames heated and consumed them. The piano strings became super-heated and they vibrated and reacted to the varying tensions that resulted. Here and there the notes from the pianos were heard clearly as the elegant machines voiced their despair.

As if the fire wasn't difficult enough to battle, the night was cold, and ice coated the ladders. Firemen had to use great caution. Chief Jewhurst declared it was the first time in his firefighting career that the firemen had been hindered by ice on May 1st! Captain Fred Washburn and two other firemen were working on the big Hayes ladder truck when part of a ladder became ignited. The flames were discovered by Hoseman Michael O'Neill, who extinguished them quickly.

The roof above the arcade that led from Logan Street north into the rear of the plant, in the crotch of the 'L' angle, collapsed. This facilitated the fire to quickly roll in waves, unobstructed, through the attic of the west wing and east along Logan Street. Varnishes and other flammable material exploded as the fire continued its sprint. At one point two groups of firemen working at the 'L' angle were, literally, steaming from the heat that beat down on them from the two walls. One group stood on the low roof of a building in the rear and threw a stream of water into the west wing while another group was on the ground shooting water into the upper windows of the rear of the Logan Street building. This was done in an attempt to keep the fire from working backward toward the east end of the building and also to supplement the work of the men on the roof to prevent fire from jumping over the fire wall and into the remaining part of the building. Logan Street had a six inch main, and the water pressure had fallen off on one or two streams at one point, due to the large demand from the multiple streams. In spite of the varied water pressure, it was generally good and provided plenty of water for the fight.

The Wegman Piano Company fire illustrated the advantages of fire walls in the construction of buildings. The one brick partition in the Logan Street Building created a barrier against the advance of the flames. If the building had utilized multiple sections with brick fire walls between, there was almost no question that the fire could have been confined to the place of origin. The worst feature of the building was the open attic which enabled the fire to roll across it in unrelenting waves, covering the building completely and quickly.

In four hours the fire was under control and the fear of it spreading to the lumber area in the back, or to the residences on either side, subsided. By 6am the fire was extinguished. At 8:30am the men returned to the station, but a detail of firemen was left to watch the ruins against flare-ups. A total of 3,850 feet of hose and 219 feet of ladders were used in the battle. The loss was estimated at approximately $100,000. Among the instruments that were lost were two famous Wegman pianos that had been manufactured for the 1893 World's Fair in Chicago. Each piano required an entire year to carve by hand. The carving alone on the instrument was worth $1,000. Each of the pianos was valued at $2,000. The company had $85,000 worth of insurance.

The fire came at a time when the Wegman Piano Company had just re-organized and consolidated with the Vough Piano Company of Waterloo. A large number of high class pianos and expensive equipment and machinery were destroyed by the fire and water. The fire was found to have started on the second floor, under a workman's bench on the south side of the factory at Logan Street, and a little to the east of the archway that ran through the building. All that remained of the large, heavy bench were the charred stems of its legs and the outline of the heavy top.

Within 36 hours of the fire, Wegman Piano Company General Manager, P. C. Sherman, announced that the company had finalized the acquisition of the property formerly occupied by the Birdsall Manufacturing Company, and owned by the Nelson Beardsley estate. The new property was located at the foot of McMaster Street. General Manager Sherman was quoted as saying, "We are not going to halt business any more than necessary. I have written our salesmen to go on with their trips and the fire will only mean the holding up of some of the orders a little longer than otherwise would have been. We anticipate no trouble from our customers under the circumstances." The accessibility of the Birdsall plant to the railroad was convenient. The Logan Street location was deemed by the Wegman family and Officers not to be a suitable location in the city for a factory, and it was abandoned. The company began salvaging what little could be saved from the Logan Street location and secured the purchase of the necessary equipment, machinery and parts from suppliers. They started business from the new location the following morning. The business conducted was of an administrative nature. The company was up and running within six to eight weeks and was manufacturing again. The company employed eighty-five people at the time of the blaze, most of them skilled craftsmen. No one lost their job as a result of the fire.

The day after the blaze the firemen spent a good deal of time pulling nails from the bottoms of their rubber boots. Luckily none of the men were injured by the rusted nails. Their clothing was soaked and their apparatus and bodies were covered in a mucky black coating of soot. The paper published a letter of appreciation from the Wegman Piano Company to the members of the Fire Department for their fine work in handling the disastrous fire.

The Wegman Piano Company seemed to flourish initially, but World War I, and a dwindling demand for the luxurious pianos, forced the company to declare bankruptcy in January of 1915. Wegman Piano Company attorney R. J. Burritt stated, "The recent fire and the stringent condition of the money market are responsible for the present situation." During the course of the bankruptcy proceedings, which began on February 26, 1915, the company bookkeeper testified that he was responsible to implement a new bookkeeping system, but he failed to do so because he "did not know the cost of making a piano." It became known that General Manager P. C. Sherman had been closely associated with two other failed companies. The company never emerged from bankruptcy. The Wegman property on Logan Street later became the home of the Warwick Furniture Manufacturing Company. In 1945, it was purchased by the Auburn Button Works.

February 18, 1918
H. R. Wait Company Fire

The business section of Auburn, containing the Traub and H. R. Wait Furniture stores on Genesee Street, was long regarded as problematic from a firefighting standpoint. The "Great Fire" of 1837 decimated 14 buildings in the very heart of the city and started in the area of the dry goods store of Norman Bennett and the Hyde, Watrous & Co., the site where the H. R. Wait Company stood in 1918. For years the Fire Department studied and

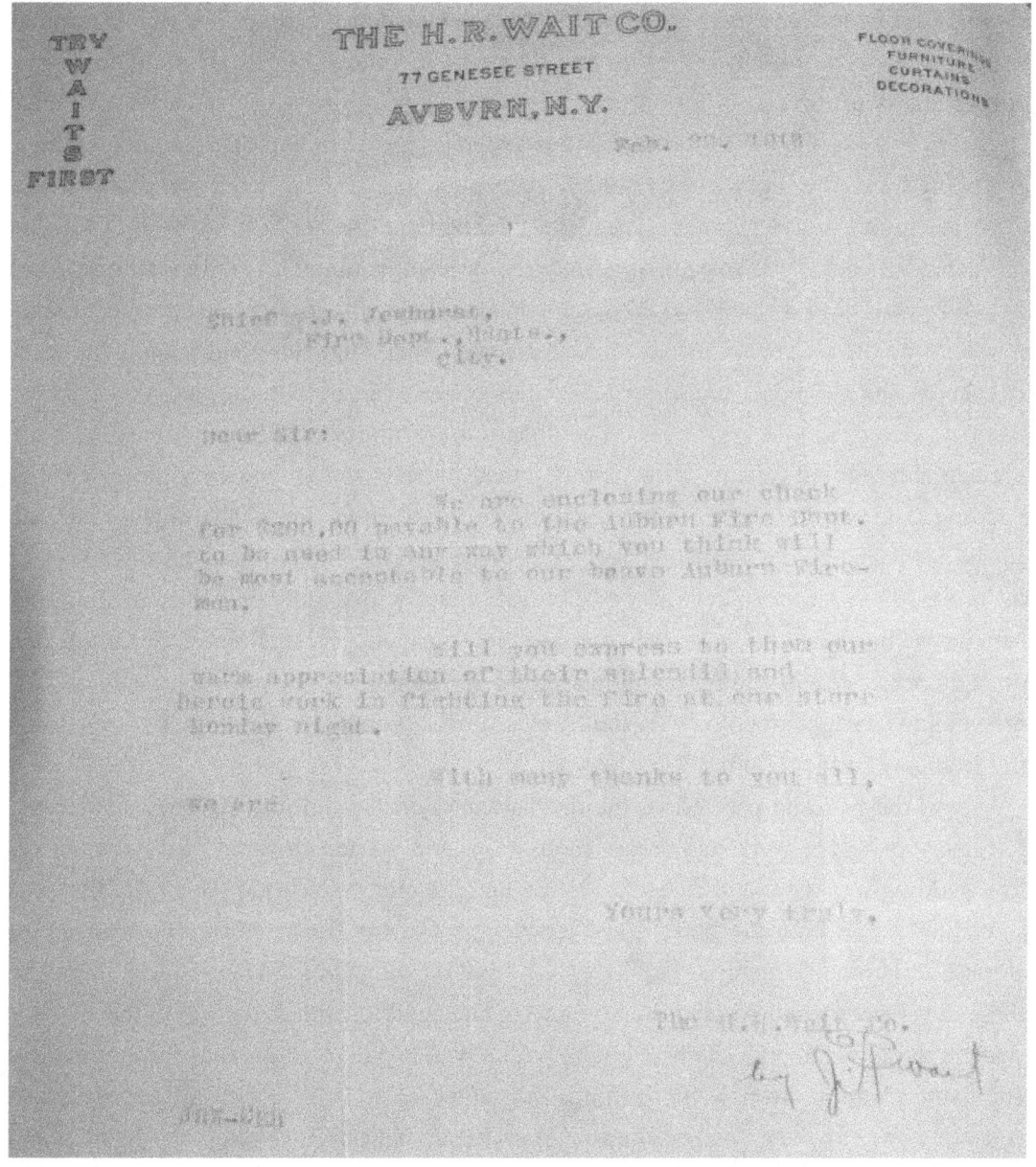

mapped out a plan of action for use in the event that a fire again broke out at one of these locations. The Wait Annex on the North side of Genesee Street and Traub Furniture store on the South side were considered to be especially dangerous due to their size, contents and location in the heart of the city. The buildings in that block had interconnecting basements which provided a perfect landscape for a fire to spread fast and furiously. With so many buildings close together, it was also very hard to get positioned with water and equipment. The plans developed by the Auburn Fire Department were tested on the night of February 18, 1918.

The employees of the H. R. Wait Furniture House went home at 6pm that night. The janitor, Bert Rusco, had just started his shift when he smelled smoke. The smoke seemed to be coming from the sub-cellar (ground floor of the Annex). Mr. Rusco went down and opened the door. Smoke billowed out and flames were already rolling inside. The Fire Department was called. The alarm was received at a time when half the force was off duty and home for dinner but the men quickly responded and arrived at the scene of the fire. Chief Jewhurst was on site and immediately recognized the seriousness of the fire. The sub-cellar was described as a "red hot cauldron of leaping flames". The firemen would not be able to enter the sub-cellar, so they chopped an opening in the door and sprayed streams of water into the area below. Meanwhile, Assistant Chief Augustus Hemrick and his team of firemen and callmen were scaling the sides of the Wait building to get good vantage points to cover the area with water. The department's largest ladders were used, and the firemen showed hair-raising skills as they raced up four stories and over the top of the building. The weather that February day was very cold, and the ladders quickly became coated with ice, making use of them even more treacherous. The impressive ladder work of the fire laddies seemed to defy all odds for successfully managing their ascent. Dragging heavy hose lines up with them, they reached their positions and then flowed water. At one point a cornice fell in and narrowly missed the firefighters. Men were positioned on Dill Street and Genesee Street to cover the front and back with water in an attempt to halt the fire from any further climb.

As was the fear and prediction, the fire launched up through the elevator shaft to the top floor where the work and repair shops were and started to spread across the area. The building was now sandwiched with fire, and the men were faced with a fire that was spreading across both the bottom and top floors. The top floor, with its open area and storage of flammable material facilitated the rapid movement of the flames. The flames in those areas were white hot, but the firefighters managed to confine the fire to the elevator shaft in the lower floors. The firefighters on the roof began to chop holes through the tin and flames shot up through the openings in grand display and the crowd below let out a collective gasp as they watched the roof start to sag beneath the weight of the men and show signs of imminent collapse.

The struggle continued and the men worked against overwhelming odds to rein in the blaze. The city's business district was threatened and the men knew they had to give it their all to prevent further disaster. The spectators who gathered did not soon forget the sights they saw that night. The flames were molten and spewing from the roof and bottom floor. The firemen showed their adept skill in completing the tasks that had been previously laid out in plans under the leadership of Chief Jewhurst.

The height of the fight was at around 10pm. The smoke was particularly difficult to work in on this fire. It didn't move the way that they expected; it hung in the air like stubborn storm clouds. A combination of large amounts of burning feathers, as well as large amounts burning oil and paint from the finishing room contributed to the horrible smoke condition. The men began to feel the effects of the thick, dark smoke. Chief Jewhurst directed his men to go through the Holmes & Dunnigan dry goods store on one side of the Wait building, and Egbert's clothing store on the other, in order to spray the adjoining walls down with water. Captain Frank Hughson of Hose Company No. 4 and a crew of firemen went to position a line of hose at a point atop the Annex via the Holmes & Dunnigan store. They carried the hose through the store and up into the burning building, every step becoming hotter and hotter, the smoke becoming impenetrable. Their lungs burned and their throats seemed to fry with the effects of the gases they were subjected to. The conditions finally took a toll on several of the firemen before they reached the top. It required almost superhuman strength and endurance to continue. Captain Hughson and William Kehoe of Hose Company No. 5 were the only two to reach the summit. After the hose was in place, William Kehoe was overcome by the smoke and noxious fumes that surrounded him, and Captain Hughson sent him back. Captain Hughson bravely remained at the top alone. For over 20 minutes he held his position, despite what was probably the worst condition that he or any fireman had been subjected to in the history of the department. Four firefighters were overcome by smoke on the climb up the stairs and required treatment at the hospital; Clarence Harkness (callman, Hose No. 3), Captain Bernard Rooney (Hose No. 5), Ray Otis (volunteer helper, Hose No. 5) and William Delaney (Hose No. 5). Each of them recovered. Chief Jewhurst, speaking of Hughson's valiant performance, said "He is a regular fire and smoke eater. Nothing is too hazardous for him to undertake and no one can do his work in a better and more efficient manner. Captain Hughson is one of the best firemen in the state." Captain Hughson definitely proved his resolve that night. The newspaper referred to "Hughson and His Little Band, Heroes of the Fire" in their headlines.

As luck would have it, nurse graduates of the Auburn City Hospital were present that night. Miss Eunice Nellis and Miss Irene Carris had been discussing the fire with Mr. Henry Keeler and Mr. George Nellis, Eunice's father, while they were standing in front of the Wait store. George Nellis was a lawyer with an office above the Egbert store next to the Wait building. Miss Nellis asked her father if it would be ok to go up to his offices. He consented, and a makeshift infirmary was setup with the two volunteer nurses attending to firefighters overcome by smoke and fire conditions. Firefighters were passed through the window to the office at times in order to get them out of danger and for the nurses to administer to them. About a dozen men were treated by the nurses. William Delaney was one of those who were brought to the nurses unconscious. When he was revived he insisted on going back to continue his fight against the fire. He was advised to go home, but he would have no part of it. He wanted to stay and endure the conditions to help end the blaze. Delaney was drawn in the selective draft and was waiting his chance to go to war; he didn't shy away from the poisonous gas conditions and looked at it as a training experience for what he would likely experience in the war. Back into the fire fight he went, and he continued his tasks that night. The prompt attention and aid that the two nurses provided that night proved invaluable to the men and their families and likely saved several of their lives.

The fire was stubborn and the men had to fight long and hard for almost six hours to force it to subside. Sometime after midnight the men were finally able to declare success. A team of men stayed at the site overnight and into the morning to watch for flare ups. Chief Jewhurst and other officials indicated that the city was lucky the night was not icy cold with sub-zero temperatures, as had been their experience earlier in the week. The wind was light and from the south that night, which worked in the men's favor as well. There were no combustible materials reported to have been stored in the sub-cellar, where the fire originated. Mr. H. R. Wait surmised that a cigar or cigarette was likely to have been carelessly tossed aside and started the blaze. The fire was well established by the time it was discovered. The H. R. Wait Company suffered an $85,000 loss, Egbert's $30,000 and Holmes & Dunnigan $10,000.The only item rescued from the blaze was the famous $5,000 Persian rug that had been on exhibition at the Wait Store for several months. When J. Reynolds Wait arrived on the scene of the fire he directed that the precious masterpiece be carried to a place of safety. The offices within the building escaped total destruction; being blackened with soot and soaked with water, the papers and books of the company escaped permanent damage. The photography studio of Ernsberger likely suffered a significant loss, given that photography material does not hold up well to heat conditions, let alone fire. But in 1918, such knowledge was not readily available. When interviewed after the fire, Mr. Ernsberger said he was prepared to lose all his stock and had been told previously by fire officials that if a fire ever started in the H. R. Wait Annex, that he might as well "hang up my flute" due to the basement connections between the two. Mr. Ernsberger indicated he had not had a chance to see the effects of smoke on photo stocks or supplies and did not know how it would affect them. He provided the following opinion on the efforts made by the Fire Department:

> "You should have seen those firemen work, though. I stood at my window and watched them chopping holes in the roof over there in smoke so blinding that they were lost from view entirely at times. When a hole was cut through, the flames would shoot up from the raging furnace below, but those fellows would get a nozzle stuck through it and fight back the flames. All the time that these fellows were working up there the roof was gradually settling under their feet, and it looked as though any minute the whole thing, firemen and all, would go down together. It was the best fight that an Auburn fire force ever put up, in my opinion."

Each of the businesses had insurance that covered most of their losses. The other merchants, businesses and residents of Genesee Street and the surrounding area were saved thanks to the strategic and precise work of the Fire Department. Their heroic work stopped a blaze that started in a dangerous area and threatened the business heart of the city.

November 2, 1921
Two-Mile House

Two-Mile House was a popular spot located at the north end of Owasco Lake, on White Bridge Road. It was a two-story, wooden building with large sweeping verandas. It operated as a hotel, tavern and gathering place. Many laughs and stories were shared among those who visited or stayed overnight at the house. The two-mile house was built in 1850 by Charles Peet after the Auburn-Moravia Plank Road was completed. Ownership of the Two-Mile House changed hands over the years, but it remained a hotel and tavern. Many old timers would recollect their times at the resort back in the day when a wooden bridge would be swung over the outlet to allow entrance to the Island. Hunters, fishermen and travelers would gather to relax and tell their tales. In the days of Prohibition, Two-Mile House had a bit of a reputation as a speakeasy. It became a place rather prone to vice. Cocking-mains (rooster or game fowl fighting for sport and betting) took place between birds from New York and adjoining states until it was discovered and shut down by New York State (NYS) Troopers. In July of 1921, the house was raided and a large quantity of "home brew" was seized by NYS Troopers. Three hundred, forty-nine bottles of liquid and one hundred forty gallons of bulk liquid were removed from the premises and suspected to be alcohol.

On the early morning of November 2, 1921, William Nugent, a tenant on the east side and facing the outlet, spotted the fire burning on the outside of Two-Mile House on the outlet side. The water level in the outlet was low and the water in the creek was down about a foot. Consequently, Owasco firemen had a difficult time trying to save the property. An appeal for aid was called to the Auburn Fire Department, and at about 1:30am, Hose Company 4 was sent to the scene by Chief Jewhurst. The ground in the area was very soft and the heavy pumper got stuck to the west of the burning structure. Hose Company No. 1 was sent for and pulled the pumper to the State road. The pumper went to White Bridge and secured enough water from the outlet to operate against the fire. The fire companies worked together to battle the fierce fire. A barn and several cottages lined the outlet to the east and west and south; they were protected against the fire by the streams of water poured on the adjoining structures and the Two-Mile House itself. The flames from the house lit up the sky, and it became apparent that the house was destroyed. In spite of the cooperative efforts of Owasco and Auburn, Two-Mile House was not able to be saved; however, the buildings which were perilously close, were rescued from potential demise.

April 30, 1922
Cayuga County Courthouse, Genesee Street

The Cayuga County Courthouse was built in 1836, and replaced the original wood frame courthouse of 1809 on the same site. It was the design of John I. Hagaman in the Greek Revival style and employed a massive Greek Doric order. The large dome was originally intended to support a statue of "Justice", but the plan was not realized due to the Panic of 1837. The portico was to be adorned with statues of "Liberty" and "Temperance", but it became necessary to abandon those plans as well due to financial restrictions. The courthouse design incorporated limestone and featured six fluted columns. The architect, John I. Hagaman, was an important local architect, who designed a number of prominent public and private buildings and residences in and around Auburn, including the Second Presbyterian church, the Courthouse and Town Hall. He started as a carpenter's apprentice, became an expert in architectural drawing and design, and then instructed others in the art for many years. The Courthouse has been an important landmark in downtown Auburn since its initial construction in 1836. It is not only architecturally significant as an example of two trends in classical architecture, but also a reminder of Cayuga County's long and varied history. The Courthouse saw many important events within its confines over the years, including William Seward's 1846 insanity defense in People vs. Freeman. The iconic landmark in the City of Auburn was tested and nearly brought to its knees on the morning of Sunday, April 30, 1922.

Gilbert Johnson, janitor of the county buildings, was busy cleaning the courtroom on the second floor, getting it ready for the May Term of Supreme Court that was to open Monday, May 1st. During the course of his work, he detected smoke and went to the rear of the building. He opened the stairway door and was faced with a wall of flames that rushed toward him. Mr. Johnson ran to the Sheriff's office and turned in an alarm to the Fire Department, which was received at 12:22pm. The churches in the area were just concluding services and the parishioners were filing into the streets of the downtown area. As fast as the Fire Department's response was, the attic and dome were already blazing when they arrived. The smoke was dense and poured out of the building in great puffs of big black clouds. All available apparatus was brought to the scene of the fire. Firemen launched an exterior and interior attack on the blaze, but the construction of the building led to its ultimate demise. First Assistant Chief Frank Hughson was on the roof with a group of his men. The attic had many beams of dry lumber with a wide opening to the big wooden dome and tall cupola. The fire was burning from the inside and the streams of water poured on the dome from the outside did little good. Hughson saw that the roof had become compromised and was no longer safe. He ordered his men off. The fire suddenly broke through the dome on all sides and it crumbled and fell into the middle of the courthouse, providing one of the most spectacular sights ever seen in the city. The massive crowd that had gathered around let out gasps, while others held their breaths and prayed, as they watched the Auburn landmark uncrowned. At the time of the dome collapse, Chief Jewhurst had been directing the fight from inside the courtroom on the second floor. He saw the fire break through to the outside and the dome start to weaken and show signs of its imminent demise. He quickly directed his men to the far ends of the courtroom. There, they watched the massive structure give way and fall, landing in the middle of the courtroom in a shower of cinders, sparks and debris. The floor shuddered and shook and flames shot high up in the air. People in the street stood back as the structure came down. The firemen inside the courtroom could not initially see the extent of the collapse or the status of their other brothers in the room. The massive structure had just fallen into the very room they occupied. The cupola, which looked rather small from the street, loomed large as it lay in the courtroom, charred and broken. The timbers were falling around them and the dome was going up in flames before their eyes. Without missing a beat the firefighters jumped on the burning mass with their hoses and sent streams of water over the burning pile. The wind sent the burning debris to the south and caught several roofs on Court Street on fire. Men were detailed to the area to douse them. They were able to extinguish the fire after almost two hours. Chief Jewhurst and First Assistant Chief Frank Hughson were later credited for their good judgment and keeping their men safe while quickly working the fire. The Fire Department stayed at the courthouse until late in the afternoon. Once the fire had been doused, they strategically lifted beams and debris looking for creeping fire. From the outside the courthouse looked to be in good shape with the exception of the dome and cupola missing. The inside was a different story. There were charred and exposed timbers and the second floor courtroom was fully exposed to the sky. The first floor was not touched by the fire. There was water damage resulting from extinguishing the blaze. Judges Woodin and Rich had libraries in the courthouse that had extensive water damage. The Surrogate's Office records were undamaged, as they were in a fire-proof room, and the papers were in metal cases. District Attorney Benn Kenyon had his minutes and presentations for the upcoming Grand Jury; he was able to rush in and rescue them along with other valuable papers. Luckily there were no records or valuable furnishings kept in the second floor courtroom. The floor and wall of the courtroom held up well to the structures that plummeted down on them. The first floor held up as well; other than water damage, the only other issue was the metal ceiling tiles that fell from accumulated water in Judge Woodin's office. Auburnians were grateful that the walls and façade of the building were preserved and not lost in the fire. After a review of the fire and the scene that was left, Chief Jewhurst thought the fire had started in a closet in the rear of the second floor. It did not start on the first floor, as it had just broken through the top of the stairway when it was discovered by Mr. Johnson. The department had known that if fire ever visited the courthouse attic, it would be a very difficult fight due to the wood construction and many very dry beams open to the dome and the cupola.

An American flag that hung at the back of the judge's bench was seen through the window by James Wright of the American Legion, W. Mynderse Rice Post. He expressed a desire to retain the flag for the Post. Joseph Flynn, Hoseman for Company 6 and ex-serviceman, volunteered to save the flag for that purpose, which he did.

The courthouse was reconstructed as a three-story building, with the third floor and plain gabled roof replacing the dome. The fire-damaged Greek revival structure was rebuilt in the Neo-classical Revival style, typical of the early twentieth century popularity of classical architecture for government buildings. This makes the courthouse architecturally significant as reflective of two trends in architecture from two distinct historical periods.

April 24, 1928
Exchange Street Block

Auburn Police Officer Steve Doyle was walking his beat overnight when he spotted a reflection of fire in a third story window in the Pearson Block on Exchange Street. He ran to Box 32 on the corner of Genesee and Exchange Street and rang in the alarm at 2:43am. The firemen sprang from their beds at the sound of the alarm and were on the scene in no time. Upon arrival, flames were seen throughout the third floor of the building. Thick smoke filled the air and the firefighters quickly began their battle against the fire. Chief Fred Washburn and the Assistant Chiefs directed the men to varying vantage points and an avalanche of water was poured on the flames. Ten minutes into their attack, a huge roar was heard and flames burst through the roof and shot up more than 20 feet in the air. Firefighters who were positioned on the adjoining roofs could feel the intense heat and their faces became scorched and blackened by their proximity to the flames and the thick smoke that was present. Their eyes burned and a black, grimy coating soon covered them. Other firefighters had been directed inside the building. They bravely battled their way to the second story through the smoke that choked the stairway and corridor. They battered down the door to the Probation Officer's headquarters. The flames immediately leapt out at them and circled around as they held streams of water on the fiery arms that continued to try to hem them in. The fire successfully ignited some of the firemen's clothes and they proceeded to go down the hallway and out into the street, where they were extinguished. They ran right back into the blaze to continue their work.

Every piece of apparatus was on the scene, even the old Hayes truck, which was horse drawn and on the reserve list since the advent of motorized trucks. All men working the shift, including callmen, were on the scene. The flames continued to rise and Chief Washburn called for all members of the off platoon to respond. To their credit, every single man responded to the call for assistance. With full devotion to their public duty, each and every firefighter was prepared to face the raging fire. Such dedication has been characteristic of the Auburn Fire Department for generations. Water was sprayed on the fire and the men continued to push back the flames for hours. The flames were brought under control by 4am, and by 5am, they extinguished some remaining sparks and smoldering piles that had reignited.

The blaze was found to have started in the lounge room of the Roman Athletic Club on the third floor of the building, over the Water Department offices on Exchange Street. The caretaker and house manager, Orlando Cimildoro, stated that when he left the club rooms shortly after midnight, everything was okay. He looked around, as was his habit, for lighted cigarette stubs, but did not find any. Based on his investigation and review of the scene, Chief Washburn indicated that he believed the fire had started from a cigarette butt that had been overlooked. Damage to the G. A. R. Hall was not extensive and property was able

Smith & Pearson fire

to be salvaged from the building, including dishes and valuable pictures. The Water Department and Probation Office on the second floor were partially destroyed. There was smoke and water damage throughout both the second and third floors. George C. Pearson, President of the Smith & Pearson Company, spoke, "I wish to state that I firmly believe Auburn has one of the best Fire Departments in this state. Fire Chief Washburn and his men are to be commended for the quick put-out of the fire, in the face of tremendous odds."

Smith & Pearson, Inc.
Hardware
AUBURN, N. Y.

June 12/28

Mr. Fred Washburn,
Chief, Auburn Fire Dept.,
Auburn, N.Y.

Dear Chief:

    We enclose our check for $75.00 for use in your Pension Fund.

    We wish to take this opportunity to thank you and every man in your department for the loyal service rendered in fighting the fire we had in our Exchange Street property recently- you may well take pride in your organization. Your quick response and fast stop in the early hours of the morning saved our block for us.

Very truly yours,
SMITH & PEARSON, Inc.,

Vice-President.

July 28, 1929
Auburn Prison Riot and Fire

In July of 1929, the Auburn Prison had 1,768 inmates in a facility with a cell capacity of 1,285. Longer sentences and fewer early releases resulted in overcrowded conditions. With longer sentences and not much hope of parole, the inmates had little to lose by rioting. Shortly after noon on July 28, 1929, the hottest day of that year, an inmate gained access to the guardroom in the Administration building on the pretext that he had a lunch bag for an officer. When the steel door to the guardroom was opened, the inmate sprayed acid in the officer's face. Other inmates who had been hiding nearby rushed in and overpowered officers in the area and took over the arsenal where they obtained weapons. Rifles, pistols and shotguns were grabbed by the inmates. Four prisoners escaped over the wall and two were killed. Four guards were wounded by gunshots during the outbreak. The complete story of the prison riot of July 1929 would consume hundreds of pages describing the brave law enforcement efforts as well as those of city officials and the population in general. The actions of the Auburn Fire Department and their efforts during the riot are described here, with full acknowledgment that there were many concurrent efforts undertaken by countless others that day.

The riot spread through the prison population. Once the guards had secured the perimeter, the inmates' aim turned toward massive rioting since their hopes for escape had diminished. Multiple buildings and prison shops were set on fire. The prison siren was wailing and a fire alarm was turned in to the Auburn Fire Department. Clouds of billowing, dense smoke filled the air, providing a screen from which some attempted to go over the walls. The fires that accompanied the smoke proved to be too much for them and they turned back and raged through the yards, destroying and smashing everything in their path. The first fire company to arrive on the scene was Hose Company No. 6 under the direction of Caption Patrick Morrissey. They arrived at the North Gate and were cautioned not to enter by the inmate custodians at the gate. Morrissey gave the order and the men proceeded to enter the gate. Once inside, they saw multiple buildings on fire and the riot fully engaged. Bullets were flying everywhere! The first ten minutes after their entry in the gate was the most treacherous. As soon as the truck was inside the gate the convicts started firing at them. The men were forced to evacuate the truck or be killed by the armed prisoners. As they were moving through the prison, they saw groups of inmates carrying torches and setting off fires in the buildings and other locations. The firemen worked their way to the hoses that had been hooked up to hydrants and began to work on fires in one wing and the foundry. Upon turning on the water, electricity must have followed the stream down to the nozzle and gave the firemen a severe jolt. It was thought that the inmates had managed to wire the top of the wall of one of the buildings to affect such a zap. Hose lines were secured and started flowing water on the flames, when suddenly they slowed and the water supply stopped. The men discovered that the convicts had severed the hose lines with axes and other means of cutting tools. Captain Morrissey ordered the inmates to stop and was answered with a volley of bullets. He was hit with a bullet in the middle finger of his right hand and his scalp was hit with another. The convicts yelled to Morrissey to get out of the way, as they did not want to bump off a "nervy old-timer". The cut hose lines became useless, and the men had to try to re-engage the hydrants with new hose lines. The men had bricks and other debris hurled at them by the rioters in an effort to stop them from extinguishing the blazes. A company of firefighters on the roof of one of the prison shops felt the increasing heat on the surface and climbed down just in time to see the roof cave in within a few minutes of their descent. It was later reported that the inmate ringleaders had ordered the firemen on the roof to be shot, but a convict, whose brother was a fireman, had made the decision to spare them.

Meanwhile, the Fire Department's Hook & Ladder truck was used to batter through the walls when the gates became jammed at the height of the incident. Bullets were zinging by them in a fury of buzzes. They concentrated on the job at hand. So much so, that George Reidy, Ladderman with the Hook & Ladder Company, did not realize he had been hit until he had returned to the station much later. He discovered he was bleeding from his back and was sent to the hospital. Doctors found that Reidy had been shot in the shoulder blade, and the bullet was lodged in his body. Fearing that the situation at the prison would escalate and spread to a larger portion of the city outside the prison walls, the Auburn Fire Department sent to Syracuse, Geneva, Port Byron, Skaneateles and Elbridge for assistance. Two companies from Syracuse and motor pumper rigs from Skaneateles, Port Byron, Waterloo, Geneva and other municipalities provided assistance. The pumpers and engines provided thousands of gallons of water and the additional firemen were very helpful. Chief Washburn later expressed his gratitude and indicated that the aid provided by the other companies was invaluable. It was shortly after midnight before the fires were under control.

For more than five hours the battle continued. Sirens, bullets, screams and a cacophony of chaos surrounded everyone. Troopers, Prison Guards, Police and the NYS National Guard were fighting the uprise and trying to quash the rioting inmates' actions. Sorely outnumbered, law enforcement personnel stood brave and strong against the prisoners. A heavy pall of smoke hung over the prison, flames shot up from a variety of locations. Copper John stood over the riot stoically, while behind him the walls were fire-charred and blackened from the prison shop fires. Six buildings were destroyed. The Fire Department lost the pumper truck of Hose Company No. 6, 1,200 feet of hose and many articles that were stolen from the trucks in the melee. Lieutenant George Searing of Hose Company

No. 5 suffered injuries to his back, a compound fracture of his left arm, a bad scalp wound and a lacerated ear, as well as other cuts across his face and head. Michael Walsh, Hose Company No. 6, suffered five broken ribs and a broken wrist. Searing and Walsh fell from a 30-foot wall in the north side of the prison yard while fighting a fire there. They were hospitalized due to their injuries. Charles Lavey, Callman with Hose Company No. 5, was shot in the leg and taken to Mercy Hospital. Chief Fred Washburn was quoted after the riot as saying "Every man of the firefighting companies and each of those who assisted in the battle at the prison Sunday and yesterday is a real hero."

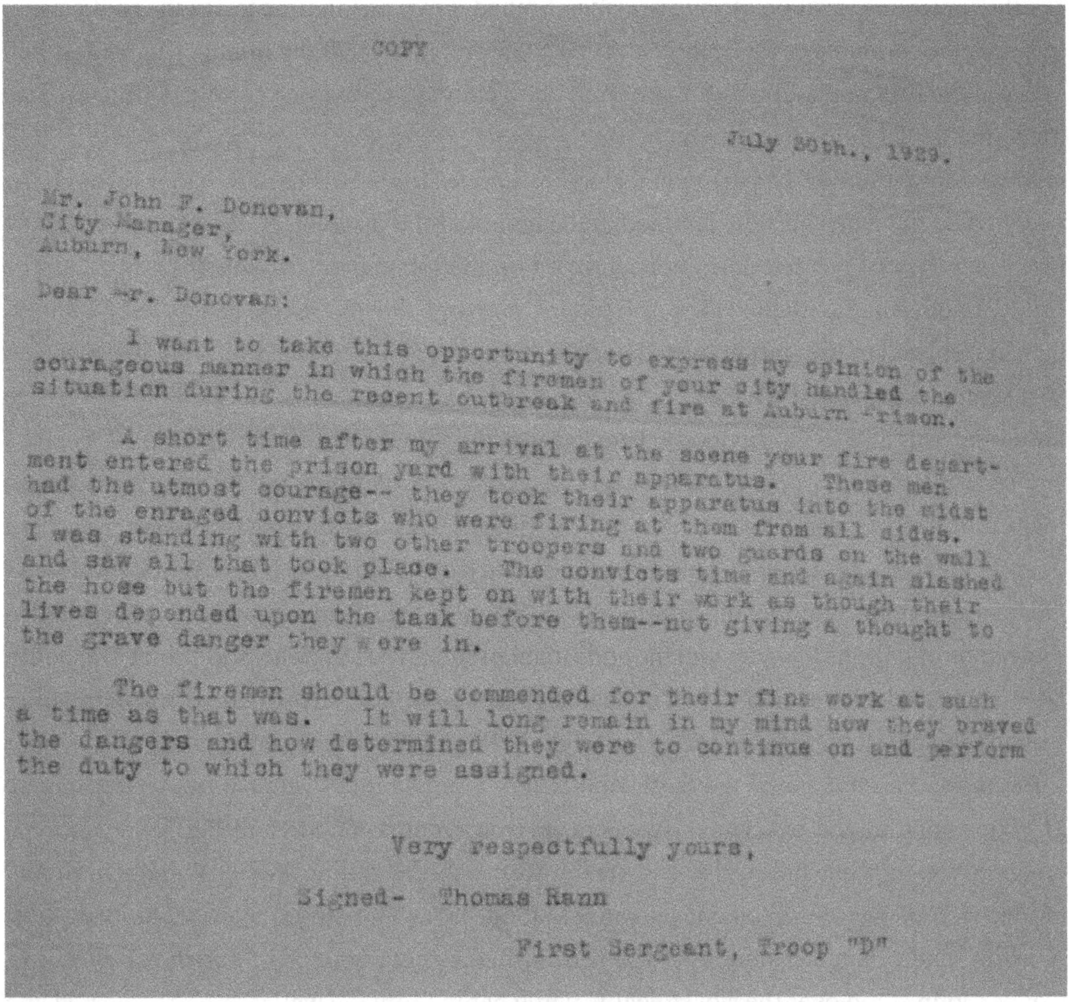

COPY

July 30th., 1929.

Mr. John F. Donovan,
City Manager,
Auburn, New York.

Dear Mr. Donovan:

I want to take this opportunity to express my opinion of the courageous manner in which the firemen of your city handled the situation during the recent outbreak and fire at Auburn Prison.

A short time after my arrival at the scene your fire department entered the prison yard with their apparatus. These men had the utmost courage-- they took their apparatus into the midst of the enraged convicts who were firing at them from all sides. I was standing with two other troopers and two guards on the wall and saw all that took place. The convicts time and again slashed the hose but the firemen kept on with their work as though their lives depended upon the task before them--not giving a thought to the grave danger they were in.

The firemen should be commended for their fine work at such a time as that was. It will long remain in my mind how they braved the dangers and how determined they were to continue on and perform the duty to which they were assigned.

Very respectfully yours,

Signed- Thomas Rann

First Sergeant, Troop "D"

December 21, 1931

Hislop Store, Lt. Irving Dwyer of Engine 3 Killed

On December 21, 1931, Auburn suffered a serious and deadly fire in the same location as that of the *"Great Fire of 1837."* The fire in 1837 had shown the benefits of brick construction and firewalls in buildings. The building was rebuilt and brought back to life using brick construction, which played a key role in battling the fire in 1931. The Hislop and Richman Blocks were about to be struck again by a deadly blow.

The William B. Hislop and Company department store had been in business in Auburn since 1881 and was celebrating their 50th year in the city, when it was hit with a devastating fire. It was Christmas week and shoppers were bustling around downtown picking up items for friends and family. Hislop's was running a holiday sale; Dorothy Perkins toilet water $1.00, fabric gloves $1.00, wool scarves $1.25, a diamond cut crystal choker on a chain 89¢, men's faultless no-belt pajamas $1.69, men's dress shirts 85¢, Old Spice toilet water $1.00, misses' silk striped bloomers 22¢ a pair, dolls 50¢ - $5.95, boudoir slippers $1.00 and many more items. Hislop's was the largest department store in Auburn. Tinsel and pine tree swags were hung everywhere. Crepe paper decorations and other holiday garlands and ribbon were displayed all around the store. Holiday shopping was in full swing.

On December 21, 1931, there were over 100 employees working in the Hislop's store, waiting on shoppers and wrapping packages with ribbons and bows. Women and children were strolling throughout the store, browsing for gifts and enjoying the festive nature of the store. Christmas music was playing and everyone was in jovial spirits. Men milled about the store shopping as well. Shortly after noon, a fire was discovered in the basement of the store, toward the rear of the building in a rubbish bin. Billy Hislop was in a different area of the basement of the store at the time of the fire. He was rescued by his father, Thomas A. Hislop, who ran into the basement and carried the boy to safety through the dense smoke. The fire spread quickly due to the flammable materials and the holiday decorations that were strung throughout the store. An employee of the Citizen Advertiser spotted the fire at the rear of the Hislop's store and an alarm was rung. The Fire Department responded quickly. As soon as the alarm was received for the Hislop block, Chief Washburn immediately ordered all men on both platoons to report for duty. The fire had already spread toward adjacent buildings. Efforts to check the blaze were futile, as it had already reached the cafeteria section of the store, midway between Dill and Genesee Streets. Every fireman in the city, from both the night and day shifts, reported to the blaze. At the start of the fire, Hislop's clerks had no time to grab their coats, street clothes or personal items. Auburn Police Officer William Flynn, who was in the area at the time the fire was discovered, worked to alert everyone in the building and had found and roused two men who were found asleep in the upper floors. The fire was moving so quickly that they had to run from the store immediately. The Auburn Police officers quickly called for ropes and wooden barricades from the Auburn Street Department and worked to clear Genesee Street from the location of the fire to State Street. News of the fire spread quickly and spectators and reporters from surrounding cities showed up. The police efforts to keep the area of Genesee Street clear for those who were fighting the fire continued for hours. Within thirty minutes the four-story Hislop block was boiling with flames that rolled through the interior. The display drew crowds to the area to see the source of the billowing smoke that could be seen for large distances. Several times spectators pushed their way past the lines established and were in danger from falling bricks and glass. Columns of flames blew out of the buildings and police worked hard to keep the spectators back and away from the danger zone.

The flames quickly consumed businesses, fire shot out of windows and the blaze continued to course through the Hislop Block. It was apparent that the Hislop's department store, Jacob Wackenhut's clothing store on the second floor along with the American Window Cleaning Company, the offices of George McCarthy, Joseph Purdy and the Creditors Service Company would be a total loss. The WMBO radio station on the fourth floor was also among the victims in the Hislop Block. The fire set its sights on the Richman Block as its next victim, and the raging inferno remained stubborn in its determination to spread. The Richman Brothers store, the Phayre photography studio and Howard Gladke's offices were soon threatened. Mr. and Mrs. Herbert Phayre had remained in their photography studio over the Richman store hoping to save their expensive equipment and photographs. Patrolmen Joseph Fogarty and William Flynn worked their way through the stifling smoke to reach the couple and led them through the dense, inky air into the street below. Another couple was discovered in the rear of the building and firemen rescued them and led them through the thick, choking smoke to Genesee Street. Miss Jessie Rea, an assistant bookkeeper for Hislop's department store, was trapped in her office on the second floor. She was unable to escape through the building. She managed to work her way through the smoke filled room and broke a window. She leaned out the broken window and screamed for help. Firemen quickly extended a ladder to the window and rescued her from the burning building. An announcer from the fourth floor WMBO radio station was also rescued by firemen and carried down a ladder.

The Citizen Advertiser building was threatened by the flames. The building was adjacent to the Hislop store and smoke crept into their offices. The walls became scorched and the heat was oppressing. The editors and reporters of the newspaper continued to cover the story from various locations around the blocks, some within the Citizen Advertiser building itself. Newspaper staff were busily trying to continue their jobs of getting news to the people. Several of the Citizen Advertiser staff were positioned with eyes on the progress of the blaze in case it became necessary for them to completely abandon the building. The stories were documented and the type was set up, with the heat from the fire on their backs. Fortunately, in the end, the fire had not breached the newspaper building, but caused substantial damage due to ancillary effects. Editors and publishers from the Syracuse Post Standard and Rome Sentinel were among the newspapers that offered their services and equipment to the Citizen Advertiser.

The fire was centered between Genesee and Dill Streets and the buildings were affected quickly and burned with determination. As early as one o'clock, the buildings started surrendering and walls began to collapse. Each wall that fell resulted in a rash of sparks and flames, and the loud boom of the falling structures as they hit the ground was frightening. The sound of falling bricks and shattering glass was all around. There was an explosion that ripped out windows and sent flames everywhere. The gas boilers in the building had blown up. By that time the firemen had managed to vent the roof and continued their attempts to bring the mighty beast under control. Ten minutes after the boiler explosion, the walls on the west side of the building collapsed. Some of the walls fell into the building and other fell outward. One of the firemen who had been directing streams of water from that location was forced to crowd into an alcove to avoid the falling debris. The roof in the rear portion of the building collapsed, as the walls that it depended on finally submitted. Within a few minutes the walls on the east side of the building began to give way and fell over as well. As the flames roared upward they were carried by the north wind and soon threatened the older buildings located in the rear area of Genesee Street, known as the "jungle" due to its reputation as one of the city's worst fire trap sections. Thousands of tons of water from dozens of hose lines were being poured on the flames from a variety of locations and vantage points around the blaze, which seethed with intent. At 1:45pm the roof on the east side of the building collapsed. The ground rumbled and the air was filled with disastrous sounds. The firemen continued to face the blaze and worked to prevent damage to other buildings in the two blocks.

At the height of the fire, Chief Washburn was directing firemen from the alleyway between the Hislop Block and the Citizen Advertiser building, when he narrowly escaped serious injury from a cluster of falling bricks that missed him by just three feet. After evaluation of the incident with Chief Washburn, Mayor Charles D. Osborne requested aid from the Syracuse Fire Department. There was concern that the falling walls could potentially take out Auburn's apparatus and/or sever hose lines, which could effectively provide the fire free reign on the city. The Syracuse Fire Department arrived during the 2 o'clock hour under the direction of Chief Edward Gieselman. New York State Troopers assisted by clearing traffic along their route so that they could have the right of way. Their pumper provided streams of water through the windows on the top floor of the Hislop Block. As word of the blaze was received in Moravia, a contingent of firemen from that municipality reported for service to Chief Washburn. The men were assigned to various Auburn fire companies and provided valuable service.

The firemen continued to fight without hesitation and attacked the blaze amid falling glass and bricks, thick smoke and constant danger from the fire that was hurling debris and flames at them from all angles. Walls of water were aimed at the blocks to stop the progression of the flames. The roof of the Richman building, which faced Genesee Street, west of Hislop's, succumbed and caved in. The collapsing roof carried intervening floors with it, some clear through to the cellar. By 2:30pm firemen had made headway on the west side of the Hislop Block and had drowned the flames in that area. Every foot of regular and reserve hose the Auburn Fire Department owned was used on the flames. Some 10,000 feet of hose line was utilized and forty streams of water attacked the fire. Arthur Adams, Water Board Superintendent, reported that over three million gallons of water had been pumped through late afternoon on the day of the fire. The Kresge Company 5 and 10 cent store had substantial protection from the blaze due to a thick firewall that had been constructed when they took possession of their building on the block. Their cellar flooded with water and their stock was affected. The firewall prevented the flames from spreading east, which could have resulted in substantially more damages within the business section of Auburn.

Two firefighters were seriously injured during the course of fighting the fire that day. Bernard Shoots, of Hose Company No. 6, sustained lacerations to his head when he was hit by falling bricks. John Mohan, of Hose Company No. 4 and former President of the State Association of Firemen, injured his back and suffered a broken leg from falling debris.

From the collection of the Cayuga Museum of History and Art

The wreckage struck and pinned him down. Both men were removed from the scene and transported to Mercy Hospital for treatment.

At close to 3pm, as the smoke was clearing in the alley on the west side of the Hislop building, Captain Bernard Rooney spotted a small bit of uniform showing amid the debris. Rooney made his way over to the uniform piece. He cleared away some bricks and timber and made the horrifying discovery that Lieutenant Irving Dwyer of Hose Company No. 3 was buried under a staggering pile of debris! Dwyer was covered by rubble under the west rear wall of the building that had toppled during the blaze. Shouts were made to alert others to the horrible discovery. Chief Washburn directed the rescue efforts. The men pulled bricks and mortar with their bare hands as fast as they could, throwing debris aside and clawing their way to uncover their fallen brother from the wreckage. He was pulled free and rushed to the hospital, but it was too late. He had been crushed in the blaze and died from his injuries. He was pronounced dead at 3:30pm at the hospital. He suffered a depressed fracture of his skull, multiple leg fractures and other injuries associated with the wall falling on him. He was thirty-eight years old.

Dwyer was appointed as a firefighter on July 12, 1920, at the age of 26. He was promoted to Lieutenant on December 17, 1926. Irving Dwyer was married and the father of five children. His wife, Juliette, had been one of those present watching the blaze, fearful for her husband and his fellow firefighters. Rev. Donald Cleary, assistant pastor of Holy Family Church, was at the hospital and notified Mrs. Dwyer of her husband's death. She became overcome with grief and had to be assisted home by friends. Lt. Dwyer's death cast a pall over the entire city.

Many individuals volunteered to assist during the fire and helped in the fight. Dr. Percy Bryan (an optometrist who was a callman with the Auburn Fire Department during his high school years), Melvin Titus (whose brother, Marion, was a member of the Auburn Fire Department) and Gerald Fitzgerald (a rodman at Memorial City Hall) were just a few of those who provided service. Once the blaze was relegated to a smoldering mass of debris and smoking cinders, firemen remained on the scene overnight to keep an eye on the ruins and continued to put streams of water on flare-ups and areas that were particularly perilous. Linemen from the Empire Gas & Electric Company provided floodlights. There were several flames that ignited over the course of the following 24 hours, particularly in the area where the fire began. Auburn firefighters continued to water them down, subjected to alternating rain and snow in the process. Chief Fred Washburn and Assistant Chief Clarence Whiting remained on the scene for almost 48 hours straight, standing watch and looking for reignited embers. The firefighters ensured that the fire did not start again and cause more destruction.

Lieutenant Dwyer's funeral was held on Christmas Eve day 1931. Attended by his fellow Auburn firefighters, city officials and Auburn Police Department officers, there were also throngs of other firemen from neighboring areas. Almost 100 vehicles were in the funeral cortege which made its way from Holy Family Church to St. Joseph's Cemetery, pausing in front of Memorial City Hall for The Wheeler bell to toll its sad cadence for the fallen firefighter. The floral tributes were so numerous, it took three vehicles to transport them. The procession was led by a detail of police commanded by Captain David Sawyer. The night shift from the Auburn Fire Department marched in the procession, with Assistant Chief Clarence Whiting in charge. A delegation of twenty prison guards also marched. Those riding in the procession included Chief Fred Washburn, Former Chief Edward Jewhurst, former Assistant Chief Augustus Hemrick, Fire Chief George Allen of Fulton (along with a delegation), Fire Chief Monte Lass of Oswego (along with a delegation), Fire Chief Joseph McKeon of Seneca Falls (along with a delegation). A delegation of firemen from Syracuse was also in the procession. Lt. Dwyer's family was prominent in the procession, along with his friends outside the Fire Department. The day platoon of Auburn firemen stood at attention as the cortege passed by the new fire and police stations, honoring their brother who had lost his life during the course of his job and provided the ultimate sacrifice. It was a solemn and final goodbye to one of their own.

Damage from the fire was estimated to be more than $500,000. Thomas A. Hislop reported that he was insured. His losses were conservatively estimated to be $400,000. The Hislop's records and book accounts were charred and partially destroyed in the blaze and they were forced to rely on the honesty of individuals regarding their accounts. The safe of Hislop's was found in the cellar of the building, where it had landed after falling through when the floor supports gave way. The doors remained secured and the contents were anticipated to be intact. Mr. Hislop opened the safe in the presence of employees and newspaper reporters and found the contents to be in excellent condition. The safe had stood up to the intense heat, smoke and water. Insurance papers were among the valuable documents contained within the safe. A second, smaller safe was also located in the basement. The combination dial and handle were broken off. A chisel was used to open the safe. Richman Brothers clothing store losses totaled $20,000. Jacob Wackenhut suffered significant loss due to a shipment of clothing valued at $1,600 which had just been received at his store. The Wackenhut losses totaled about $6,000. Since the fire occurred during the height of the holiday season, a large number of people found themselves suddenly unemployed. The WMBO radio station was a total loss, but they were able to scramble with great effort to establish a place to be on the air by the following night. Shoppers who had purchased gifts and requested Hislop's to hold them until Christmas were forced to quickly scramble for replacements.

The dedication of the new Public Safety Building on North and Market Streets, which housed both the Auburn Fire and Police Departments, had been scheduled for the day of the fire. It was obviously called off. Among the speakers who were to be present for the dedication was William Rapp, Director of Public Safety for the City of Syracuse, and Major John Warner, head of the New York State Police. Mayor Osborne stated "These men have dedicated these buildings by giving their lives in the fulfillment of duty and our sadness at the news makes it seem to me desirable that we call off the formal ceremonies we had planned." The building was opened for inspection by the public.

Thomas Hislop declared that the Hislop and Richman blocks would be rebuilt and that Hislop's department store would be back. The Auburn architecture firm of Hillger & Beardsley was selected to be in charge of the new store design and plans. The General Contractor for the project was Ludke Brothers Harrington Company, of Auburn. Although bids showed that a considerable sum of money could be saved by awarding the construction contract to outfits outside of Auburn, Mr. Thomas Hislop stuck with his plan to provide work to Auburn contractors and workmen. He was quoted as saying; "with faith in Auburn and the surrounding community, and with faith in Auburn contractors and Auburn labor" he would make Hislop's bigger and better. The new building was fully equipped with sprinklers, and all exits were approved by the New York State Labor Department. Heavy foundations supported a frame of reinforced concrete to the first floor, above which steel girders and trusses spanned more than 50 feet. The roof was constructed of pre-cast gypsum. A girder across the street front and above the mezzanine floor was 46 feet long, the largest of its kind. A modern heating and electrical system was installed that eliminated radiators throughout the store. Terrazzo floors were chosen for safety reasons and ease in cleaning. Strength, dependability and architectural beauty were apparent in the construction of the building. The interior wood trim and doors were made of American walnut, birch and lacewood. The storefront was made entirely of Onondaga Litholite, a manufactured stone which was selected for its textures and colors. In spite of the adverse economic conditions of the 1930s, Hislop's was back in business in Auburn by November 1932, less than one year after the fire.

August 17, 1932

Masonic Building, 2nd Presbyterian Church, South Street Cady Building

On August 17, 1932, Auburn's landscape was forever changed when fire took hold of the 102 year-old Second Presbyterian Church and the Masonic Temple building on South Street. The Masonic Temple building was nine stories high and was the tallest structure in Auburn at that time. The Masonic building was 20 years old and was a stately structure. Located on what was known as the "Cady" block, owner Frank Cady sold the building to the Masonic organization. The fire originated in the church building spire from an undetermined source. At approximately 3:45pm smoke was observed billowing out of the roof of the Second Presbyterian Church. Auburn City Comptroller, Robert Swart, was in his father's office on the second floor of the temple building when the fire broke out. The office filled up quickly with smoke and Mr. Swart groped and stumbled around the office and eventually found his way to the front stairway and worked his way safely to the street below. A fire alarm was rung and Chief Washburn and his men responded. Immediately upon seeing the location of the fire and the potential for significant damage throughout the downtown area, a general alarm was called in for all available men and apparatus to respond to the scene.

The church building had been vacated years previous and was owned by the Schine Enterprises, Inc. The old church building provided ample flammable construction material that was very dry and aged to tinder. The fire spread quickly. The Masonic Temple building housed attorneys, insurance agents, opticians and other offices. A call was sent for aid to Syracuse, Geneva, Seneca Falls and Moravia. They arrived on the scene and provided additional assistance. The firemen worked quickly against the flames, but within 20 minutes the spire on the church creaked and crackled and finally buckled under the pressure of its weakened state resulting from the flames that were ravaging it. The steeple fell toward the road below, directly in front of the church with a crash that broke the steeple into pieces and sent sparks and embers up into the air. By that time, the roof and the top floors of the Masonic building were on fire. The Fire Department's aerial ladder was raised and a stream of water was directed through the windows of the Masonic building as well as into the church structure. The wind was strong and coming from the south that day. Embers and burning debris were carried north and threatened to spark additional fires in the area. The gas station adjacent to the church building, owned by Frank Hendrick, was threatened for a time due to its proximity to the blaze and the highly volatile material it housed. A steady stream of water was used to prevent the fire from claiming another building. The firemen stood strong against the fire and by 5pm it was under control, and immediate

danger to the surrounding area was diminished.

Damages were estimated to be in the neighborhood of $400,000. The top three floors of the Masonic building were a total loss. The remainder of the building suffered varying degrees of smoke, fire and water damage. The WMBO radio station was the victim of a fire for the second time in one year; having been burned out in the Hislop Building fire of 1931. The eighth floor of the Masonic building was occupied by the American Mutual Liability Company and Dr. Harry Bull. The Auburn Credit Bureau was also located on the eighth floor and was a victim of the blaze. The office of insurance agent Earl Hamilton was on the sixth floor. The fifth floor was occupied by attorney offices and a small Masonic lodge room. The fourth floor held the grand and elaborate rooms of the Masonic temple proper and had expensive robes and regalia of the chapter. The third floor was occupied by the Masonic temple proper as well. The second floor held the Masonic ballroom and the offices of Fred Swartz (optician), David Wills (insurance agent), Dr. Murray Bond (dentist) and William Long (insurance agent). The offices of A. J. Wright & Co. (brokers) and the Auburn Dollar Dry Cleaning and Dyeing establishment were located on the ground floor.

The heat generated from the blaze melted the soft wax tips on the sprinkler systems of nearby buildings and water poured through them; the Auburn Savings Bank building and the Swaby block among them. Embers reached to a number of awnings in the area and burned them. The firemen were able to hold the fire to the two buildings and saved much of the Masonic building structure.

The Masonic Temple was rebuilt as a three-story building and was completed in 1934, and was dedicated on February 26th. The renovated and restored building contained two lodge rooms, a ballroom, dining room, kitchen, office and social rooms on the second and third floors. Businesses occupied the ground level.

Top: *November 1936 Letter from Theodore W. Case*
Bottom: *1953 Fire at Cayuga Cordage*

Top Left: 1937 Genesee Street

Bottom Left: Fire in Angelo's Pizza building; Rescuing women from upper apartments. Far Left: Walton Krell, Percy Bryant. Far Right: Paul Darrow, Chief Luke Bergan

Right: 1954 Fire scene

1965 Fire scene

Bottom: 1954 Firefighters at work

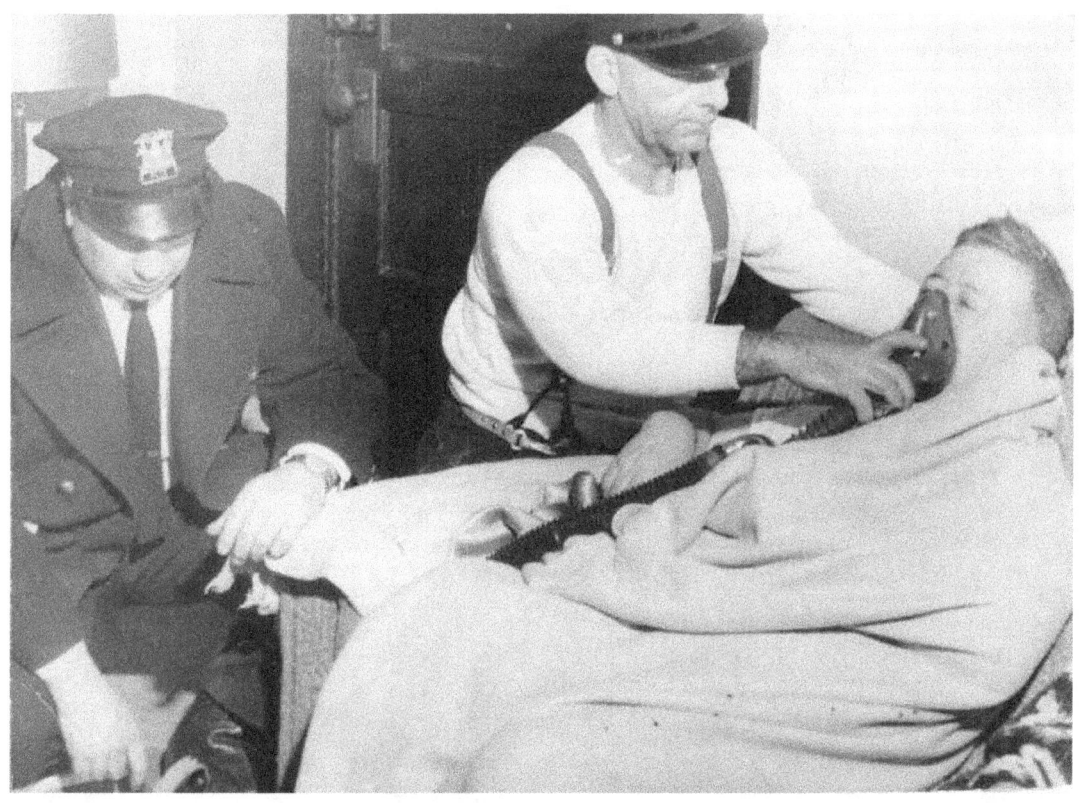

Top: 1962, Auburn Police Officer Emmi, Firefighter Walton Krell

Bottom: Fire scene with Auburn Prison tower in foreground

Singer Fire

U. S. NAVAL TRAINING STATION
SAMPSON, NEW YORK

November 17, 1942

Chief of Fire Department
Auburn, New York

Dear Sir:

    It is a pleasure to extend to you and the members of your department our thanks for the valuable assistance rendered this U. S. Naval Training Station last Friday evening when you responded to our request for additional fire-fighting equipment.

    Your efforts are appreciated and we want you to feel, as we do, that you have done the Navy a fine service.

Sincerely yours,

H. A. BADT,
Captain, U. S. Navy,
Commandant.

Top: 1968 Fire scene

September 9, 1933

L.V.R.R. Roundhouse

Early on the morning of September 9, 1933, a fire was discovered simultaneously by three people in the vicinity of the Lehigh Valley Railroad (LVRR) roundhouse in Auburn. At approximately 5:30am flames were seen coming through the windows and roof of the building. Auburn Patrolman Raymond Donovan was walking his beat and had just crossed the tracks when he saw smoke and heard an explosive sound. Flames shot out of the roundhouse building. Night watchman Hayes Wescott had just walked out of the building when he heard the same explosion. Thomas Walsh, a train dispatcher, heard the explosion and saw the flames. All three called in an alarm to fire headquarters. The roundhouse, located on Clark Street, was used for servicing locomotives. The roundhouse was built as a large, semicircular structure that utilized a turntable to facilitate access to the building by locomotives. Mr. Wescott ran to an engine that was in the freight yard. Officer Donovan had previously been employed as a brakeman with the Lehigh Railroad. He and Mr. Wescott began moving the locomotives away from the burning building. They jumped into a yard engine and drove up the side of the building, hooked onto freight cars and pulled them to safety.

The Auburn Fire Department night shift arrived on the scene. The fire was well underway at the time of discovery and was now becoming completely engulfed. Upon seeing the extent of the fire, Chief Washburn immediately called for all day shift firemen and all firemen on vacation to report to the fire. The additional firemen responded quickly. They attacked the burning building with water from multiple angles. Fourteen hose lines and thousands of gallons of water were poured on the roundhouse. Locomotive whistles could be heard as the battle against the blaze continued. The smoke rose from the massive flames in dark, black plumes. The smoke masks the firemen used were helpful but they still suffered burns and were covered with the sooty grime of the fire. The roof crashed into the building with a mighty roar and embers and flames shot as high as one hundred feet in the air. There were seven locomotive engines inside the building and the threat of explosions seemed imminent. There was fear that the boilers in the stately behemoths would let loose with a huge blast. Firemen concentrated efforts to prevent any such eruption. Their bravery in attacking the blaze, in the face of certain death if the boilers exploded, was a testament to their dedication to service and their professional abilities. The Lehigh Valley station and residences nearby were threatened by burning embers carried in the air. As the valves melted off the equipment in the roundhouse, small pops could be heard. One particular locomotive whistle shrieked in shrill protest for nearly 30 minutes. The intense heat and the increasing temperature of the boilers caused steam to escape through the safety valves and the whistles. The constant cry of the locomotive steam whistles called many spectators to the scene of the fire.

The fire was brought under control within two and one-half hours. The roundhouse suffered almost total loss. The brick walls remained standing. Much of the roof had collapsed. The seven locomotives inside were significantly damaged by the flames. Damages to the building were estimated at $30,000. The cabs of the seven locomotives were a total loss and there were other fire, heat and smoke damages caused to them. Fire Chief Washburn believed the fire was the result of a spark from a backdraft of one of the locomotives that had been run into the roundhouse late the previous day.

January 12, 1946
Polish Falcons

1946 Polish Home Fire (Photo courtesy of William Brahney)

A wedding breakfast had been served at the restaurant of the Polish Falcons on Pulaski Street on the morning of Saturday, January 12, 1946. The group concluded their celebration and left. At about 10:45am, fire was discovered and an alarm to the Auburn Fire Department was sent. The fire was believed to have started on the second floor in the area of the gymnasium and quickly spread. Six Auburn Fire Department companies responded to the alarm. Smoke poured out of the structure and was thick. The two-story building was composed of concrete frame and brick construction. The fire was made worse by a strong west wind that fanned the flames. Firefighters hooked up to hydrants, ran hose lines and started to go after the blaze. The fire roared through the gym area and moved toward the front of the building and the offices, library and caretaker's residence. It was reported that several people were trapped inside the building. Firemen worked through the interior of the burning structure. They found the individuals and rescued them from the building. Adam Leja, Auburn City Treasurer and Secretary of the Falcon nest, had been in his office on the second floor. He was rescued from the building via a ladder by firefighters. Work continued to push back the fire. Flames rolled down in a massive ball of fire into the restaurant, bar and bowling alleys. As firemen attacked the flames, part of the gym caved in and debris fell through to the floor below. Four firemen were working in the restaurant portion of the building when the timbers and debris from the gym fell down into their area. They nearly became trapped, but all were able to maneuver quickly to safety. The concussion of the collapse, and the resulting embers and sparks that flew around them, stunned them briefly. The additional smoke that was generated from the collapse required them to clear their eyes in order to continue with their hose lines. They fought for over two hours to bring the fire under control. Just after 2pm Chief Doyle indicated that fire was out. No one was seriously hurt in the blaze.

Fire Chief Doyle surmised that the fire resulted from defective wiring that ignited scenery on the stage of the main auditorium and gym. The flames quickly grew and spread in both directions and flowed toward the front main offices, the bar and restaurant. The damage to the Polish Falcons was considerable. Initial estimates were placed between $65,000-$75,000. Social events, dances, basketball games, etc. had to be rescheduled or moved to other venues. Bowling equipment was destroyed and valuable papers in the office were burned. It was reported that about $26,000 in negotiable papers, $200 in cash, as well as membership papers had been in the safe that was buried in debris from the roof collapsing. The west wall of the main building and gymnasium was all that remained. The cause was officially determined to be a short circuit in the wiring on the second floor.

The Polish Falcons were formed in Auburn in 1906, and the initial membership included 20 men. The local unit was Nest 74, as designated by the national Headquarters of the Polish Falcons of America. The Falcon Society was determined to take on the challenge of rebuilding. Following the fire, plans were made to rebuild the Polish Falcons Hall. The members supported the efforts with their time, money and service. The new building was completed, and in January of 1951, a two-day event took place to celebrate the opening of the new Polish Falcons Hall. The new building included 16 bowling alleys, a circular bar, offices, a large dining room and space for an auditorium and/or gymnasium.

June 24, 1950
Close & Brady Restaurant

The Close & Brady restaurant was an Auburn fixture for years, but it was not originally located in Auburn. Close & Brady was established in Syracuse, New York in 1924. The original building was moved to Auburn by horse and wagon during the depression and brought to the location at Clark Street and Aurelius Avenue. Auburn loved Close & Brady, and business was good. A dining room was added in 1932, and it underwent several renovations over the years. Advertising as "It's inexpensive at Close & Brady's" and "The Best Food....Always," the restaurant was popular with the blue collar crowd, families and other gatherings. The restaurant's owner collected keys, and before long, there were more than 15,000 keys on display in the bar and dining room. The keys were from all around the world, old and new. The display was quite a conversation piece. The collection had some rare and antique keys with stories of prisons, churches, wine cellars, airplanes, railroad cars, etc. Residents enjoyed viewing the collection and sometimes contributed to it. The 'keyhole' restaurant had a close-knit staff who worked for years at the restaurant. They knew their customers by name and oftentimes what their 'usuals' were.

The Close & Brady restaurant at 211 Clark Street suffered a huge loss on the night of June 24, 1950. It was a Saturday night; the last guests left, and the restaurant closed at 8:30pm. The last employee left the restaurant at 9:40pm. At 10:05pm flames were discovered shooting through the roof on the back side of the building. The Auburn Fire Department was called and crews were on the scene quickly. Ladders were raised and hose lines were run. Firemen attacked the flames from both the front and rear of the building. The dense smoke was billowing out of the structure, making it difficult for firefighters. The fire had taken over the main dining room and spread through a wing that housed the lunch counter. The heat from the blaze was intense and the black smoke was choking the firefighters. They worked to put out the fire, which had spread quickly throughout the restaurant. Sections of the ceilings came down and rafters and joists were charred. Firefighters continued to attack the flames, and the building was extinguished by 1:45am Sunday morning. The main dining room, storage room and bar room suffered the most damage. The fire rekindled several times and crews remained on the scene to extinguish the flames that reappeared.

The loss was estimated at $60,000. It was one of the worst blazes the city had seen in a number of years. It came at the tail end of Fire Chief James Doyle's career with the department and a day after Bernard Rooney was named as the appointed Acting Fire Chief due to Doyle's vacation prior to his retirement.

Close & Brady was restored and renovated and re-opened for business. It continued to be a popular location for years. Another fire would strike the establishment in later years and prove to be too much; Auburn ultimately lost one of its classic restaurants.

September 8, 1959
H. J. Gardner Auto Body and Paint Shop

H. J. Gardner Auto Body and Paint Shop Fire

Tuesday, September 8, 1959, was a hot one! At 91°, it was nearly a record-setting day in Auburn. It was just after Labor Day and folks were settling back into their normal daily routines at work. Mr. Gardner, owner of the H. J. Gardner Auto Body and Paint Shop on Lincoln Street, returned from vacation that afternoon to find that his shop had suffered a severe fire. Around 2:50pm, an employee at the shop was using an electric torch to cut a bumper bolt on a 1957 Cadillac. The gas tank on the vehicle became compromised and gasoline poured out onto the floor. It was presumed that a spark from the torch must have ignited the gas fumes. The employee heard a noise, and when he looked underneath the car, he saw flames covering the floor and creeping fast, covering an ever-increasing area. There were three people working in the shop that afternoon. They attempted to use foamite extinguishers on the flames but failed to put out the fire.

The Fire Department was called to the scene at 3pm. On arrival, they saw flames had already consumed the partitioned car rack shop at the east side of the building. There were twelve cars in the shop at the time of the fire, and the three employees were able to remove seven before the flames had become too much for them. The rapidly spreading fire and highly volatile substances in the area were particularly concerning to firemen. It was a hazardous fire due to the nature of the business that inhabited the building. There were two 55-gallon drums filled with paint thinner, one of which had started to buckle. Firemen directed water on the drums throughout the blaze in order to keep them cool and prevent an explosion. Their work to prevent the drums from exploding and likely claiming lives, illustrated their courage and resolve. All firemen on duty were brought to the scene and off-duty firefighters reported to headquarters to cover the city in the event there were simultaneous alarms. The flames burned hot and fierce and were seen crawling along the interior brick walls of the building. The flames that traveled across the walls were fueled by years of buildup of flammable materials that had settled on the interior of the building. The smoke generated from the shop was thick and black, suffocating the firemen as they worked to attack the flames. Firefighters chopped holes in the two dormers facing Lincoln Street and streamed water into the burning structure. The roof was also ventilated to direct water into the building. The heat from the unusually high temperatures that day and the thick, noxious smoke, took a toll on some of the firemen, who became weakened and were forced to exit the structure. They were treated with oxygen and returned to continue to fight the fire. The fire was out within a couple of hours, but department members remained on the scene until 10pm that night to watch for and extinguish hot spots that cropped up.

It was theorized that lacquer dust from the paint spray may have been responsible for the fast spread of the fire throughout the building, especially along the brick walls. Gardner Auto Body suffered an estimated $35,000 in damages. Five cars were damaged, including a 1959 Pontiac with 500 miles on it.

March 30, 1960

18 South Street, Gasoline Station Explosion, Five Fatalies

Auburn was hit with a staggering blow that left death and destruction in its wake on the evening of March 30, 1960. What seemed like a routine call ended up as one of the worst disasters in Auburn's history. As every firefighter knows, there is no such thing as a routine call. Every emergency to which they are called has the potential for catastrophe. At the end of that night, five men were killed; three of them firefighters.

Movie goers had settled in to watch "Suddenly Last Summer" at the Auburn Theater on South Street. Some folks attended a basketball game at Central High School to see the playoff championship game for the winter program of the City recreation league. Families had finished their dinners and were watching television or playing games. There was no indication that this Wednesday evening would be different from any other; but it would be. At the fire station, the firefighters talked about the next day's opening of trout season and some were in the basement readying their fishing gear.

Mr. Walter Ockenfels operated the gas station located at 18 South Street. Mr. Robert Connor was the proprietor of R. J. Connor Oil Company and distributor for California Oil Company. Connor leased the Chevron service station and sublet it to Walter Ockenfels. On that fateful night in March, Walter Ockenfels phoned Robert Connor and reported that there was a deposit of water and a mixture he believed to be gasoline under the building. Connor sent John Bell to the South Street station to check on the situation. John Bell worked for Mr. Connor and was experienced in pump installations and was in Connor's office at the time of the telephone call. John Bell confirmed that gasoline fumes were present.

At 7:29pm Mr. Robert Connor telephoned headquarters and informed of gasoline fumes in the Chevron station located at 18 South Street. He requested the Auburn Fire Department to investigate. Engine Four was detailed to respond to the call at the Chevron station, at the northeast corner of Lincoln and South Streets, at 7:30pm. The four men responding were Lieutenant Alfred "Spuds" Murphy, Firefighter John Searing, Firefighter Anthony Contrera and Firefighter Sidney "Sid" Burridge. Lt. Murphy had assumed duty that night to allow a fellow officer to attend a meeting. Another firefighter might have been present that night, but he had been assigned to another detail. The service station operator, Walter Ockenfels, and John Bell, an attendant, were also present at the time of the call.

Upon arrival, the firemen found three to four inches of gasoline covering the cellar floor. John Bell showed the firemen where he believed the gasoline fumes were coming from in the cellar. The only way to get into the basement under the building was through a hole in the floor. Lt. Murphy phoned headquarters at approximately 7:45pm indicating that the gas fumes were very strong in the building. It was decided to flush the gasoline away. The firefighters had to lower themselves through the hole in order to get to the cellar. A large 2 ½" hose line was hooked up to a hydrant in front of MacKay's service station at Richardson Square. John Searing moved the fire truck up to the monument at Richardson Square and positioned it across South Street to divert northbound traffic from coming into the area. Searing then went back into the building along with Contrera, Murphy, Ockenfels and Bell. A gas-water mixture on the cellar floor had accumulated. The cellar drain was about six inches off the floor level and the amount of water needed to flush the area required the use of the large hose line. Gas had leaked from a 3,000 gallon tank into an old grease pit which had been covered over when a new station had been built, and the old pit had not been removed. Lt. Murphy, who was in the gas station, sent Sid Burridge back to the fire truck to get a hose strap at 7:52pm. Burridge was on his way to the truck and was about 20 feet from the station when the unthinkable happened. With a WHOOSH, immediately followed by a horrific KABOOM! the gas station exploded with an incredible force that obliterated the station completely! The report was louder than any cannon and there was a tremendous concussion! The ground trembled and buildings all around were rocked on their foundations. The firefighters at the station felt the headquarters building shake, and they were immediately alert to the gravity of the situation. The booming sound from the detonation was apocalyptic. The blast knocked pedestrians in the area off their feet. Flames shot high into the air. Windows were sucked from their frames by the vacuum created by the explosion, and glass shattered all around. Burridge was knocked to the ground and his helmet thrown into the air. He was hit with debris flying at him from all directions. All that remained was a debris filled pit where the station used to be. The 30'x40' cement block station was gone. In the blink of an eye, three men of Engine Four were lost, along with two others. Debris from the blast was thrown all around South, Lincoln and Exchange Streets, just steps away from City Hall. Burridge picked himself up and rushed back to the truck and radioed to headquarters for help and told them to send an ambulance. Back at headquarters, the men had heard and felt the explosion, and Engine Company #1 and the Truck Company were already en route. A general alarm was called and ambulances were also called to the scene. Sid Burridge ran back to where the station once stood. Flames made it impossible to get near the wreckage. In spite of the wall of fire, he attempted to get to his brothers-in-arms. His efforts were not successful and Burridge received facial burns in the process. Earlier in the evening, firefighter James Gillooly had been detailed to the Auburn Theater for fire watch; it was common for a junior firefighter to receive these types of assignments. The explosion shook the theater and Gillooly ordered everyone out. He emerged from the building to find the gas station on the same block had exploded. He immediately reported to the scene and commenced his firefighting duties.

By 8:05pm almost every firefighter in the city was on the scene. Assistant Chief William Maywalt was in charge of the firemen at the scene. Chief Bergan was immediately apprised of the situation. Foamite fire foam was used to combat the blaze. Foamite was a fire-smothering, fire-extinguishing agent that covered burning objects with a blanket of white foam that suffocated the fire by shutting off the supply of air. It is similar in characteristic to that of Class A or B foam used today. It coated and clung to surfaces and floated on inflammable liquids. It put out destructive oil and other petroleum-type fires in seconds and minutes, not hours. Re-ignition was prevented because the foamite clung and stayed on surfaces. Firemen were extinguishing the blaze with foamite in order to stabilize the area enough to allow other firemen to continue to dig furiously with their hands to try to clear debris and

find the victims. Twice they were forced away due to a leaking gas main near where the bodies were buried. Walter Ockenfels was pulled free first. He was alive but in critical condition. He died within minutes. Ockenfels' son stood by the rubble during the rescue attempt. An extra supply of foamite was brought to the scene from the Seneca Ordnance Depot in Romulus. A crowd of more than 6,000 swarmed the area and were controlled by Auburn Police officers, Cayuga County Sheriff deputies and NYS Police. Civil Defense auxiliary policemen were also detailed to the scene to assist. A natural gas line was compromised by the explosion and continuously shot a flame into the air during the time the men were digging the victims out.

Firemen worked for nearly two hours to recover the bodies of the remaining four. The continued flames in varied locations due to the gas throughout the area made their work even more difficult. Gas lines continued to flame up all around. Line crews placed floodlights on poles to help the firemen see. John Bell was located and recovered from the wreckage in the basement. Captain Bud Maywalt was in the basement along with other Engine Company 2 men. They had a 2 ½" line on a small area of fire in the basement. There was a lot of rubble that had fallen into the pit. The firefighters could see Lt. Murphy in the basement pinned by debris to the wall, but they could not initially get to him, because the natural gas line coming into the basement was broken off at the shutoff and was blowing gas, which was on fire and shooting flames almost 20 feet across the wreckage. "Spuds" was below the flaming gas. The gas company had a difficult time getting to and shutting off the gas at the street. With the gas shut off, Lt. John "Butch" Delaney, Captain Paul Darrow and Captain Bud Maywalt were finally able to reach him. They freed him from the debris that covered him, wrapped him in a tarp and gently removed him from the area and handed him up to firefighters on the ground level. Work resumed on the flames that continued to shoot out here and there. The men spotted what they thought might be a boot partially sticking out from the pile of debris a distance away from them. Assistant Chief Maywalt had the men direct the hose line toward the boot in order for him to locate it as he made his way over. He got to the location and found the boot. He reached out and grabbed it, to find that it was another fallen brother whose body was pinned against a radiator. Captain Bernie Searing (George Searing, Jr.), John Searing's cousin, crawled over the wreckage to get to the area. Together he and Captain Maywalt worked to try to uncover their fallen comrade. They were able to free an arm from the debris and Captain Searing recognized his cousin's watch. They called for the Truck Company's chain and hook in order to remove the radiator to free John's body. Firefighter Anthony Contrera was the last man found at the explosion. He was located under a pile of debris on the sidewalk of Lincoln Street. He was found lying face down. A priest bravely approached Contrera, whose face was badly damaged, and administered last rites. The scene and the devastation left behind caused the priest to be physically sick, but he continued to administer to those in need. Reverend Ralph Philbrook, the department's Protestant chaplain, reported that he was in the pulpit of his church on Seminary Street at the time of the explosion; he stated "It rocked the pulpit." He rushed to the scene to assist in whatever way he could. Reverend Richard Nangle, the department's Catholic chaplain also reported to the scene. Together Reverends Nangle and Philbrook pushed aside debris and rubble in order to administer last rites to the men that night. The Reverends John Nacca and Raymond Wahl were also present administering last rites to the victims. The tragic scene was too much too bear. Exhausted and covered in white foam, the men knelt and stood in the area leveled by the blast that resulted in the death of their friends, more to the point, their brothers. The firemen wept.

Fire Chief Luke Bergan and City Manager, George Train were now faced with the difficult task of notifying the families of the victims. Together they went to inform them of the fallen men in person. Train stated, "It was terrible. What could you say?" They assured the families that the whole city felt as they did, in deep sympathy with them in their sadness.

The aftermath of the explosion was horrific. Steel beams laid in a twisted mass 25 feet away on Lincoln Street. The doors of the Auburn Theater were blown open. A woman who lived in an apartment building on Lincoln Street, adjoining the gas station to the east,

suffered a heart attack following the explosion. Another occupant in the same apartment building suffered a concussion and the effects of shock. Both were treated at Auburn Memorial Hospital for their injuries. Several people were injured after the explosion, while on the scene. Captain James Gillooly sustained injuries to his forearm and had first degree burns on his face. Fireman William Griffin injured his foot when he stepped on a nail. Police Detective Carmen Bertonica punctured his right foot. Assistant Fire Department Electrician Charles Conboy also punctured his right foot. The Salvation Army of Syracuse rushed to the scene, escorted by Onondaga County Sheriff Deputies, and provided sandwiches and coffee to the exhausted rescue workers. The Red Cross set up a canteen in the lobby of the Auburn Theater and served to those who were working at the scene.

Exhausted, devastated and in shock, the firemen returned to headquarters hours later. The white foam used to battle the blaze still clung to them, covering them from head to toe. The pall that hung over them was unfathomable. The loss of life is never easy; when it is one of your own, the pain hits you like no other. The disaster would always be remembered by those who survived, and the tragedy of the lives lost that night was woven into the history of Auburn forever.

Fire Chief Luke Bergan surmised that a spark from a compressor motor probably ignited the fumes from the gas that leaked into the pit area of the building attached to the station. Official reports confirmed that an electric compressor likely came on unexpectedly and detonated the vapors. The firemen thought the electricity had been turned off.

Gas fumes were later detected in the Auburn Theater and a beauty parlor in the area. A precautionary evacuation was conducted. An apartment building on Lincoln Street that housed twelve people and an office building on South Street were evacuated and closed. The two-block area was roped off and police continued a 24-hour guard at the scene during the cleanup and excavation following the explosion. Two concrete blocks were found embedded in the roof of the Auburn Theater. A mechanic's creeper, parts of car generators and fragments of concrete almost two feet long were found scattered on top of the Theater roof as well. Traffic on South Street from Genesee to Exchange Street and on part of Lincoln Street was blocked off. The following day workmen began to remove the rubble. An eerie silence surrounded them as they completed their work. Debris and gas-soaked soil was removed from the area. Gravel was brought in to fill the voids. As work to identify and remove storage tanks began, firemen filled them with water to force any gasoline to the surface and then emptied the tanks. Nine storage tanks were ultimately identified in the area and removed. The 3,000 gallon tank that was suspected of having leaked was taken to Syracuse for testing by the California Oil Company.

The American flag in Richardson Square was flown at half-mast, in mourning for those who lost their lives in the explosion. The Auburn City Council ordered a week-long state of mourning in a resolution:

> "Whereas, on Wednesday evening, March 30, 1960, a most tragic explosion took place in our city taking the lives of three gallant city firemen, Lt. Alfred Murphy, Anthony Contrera and John Searing, who were faithfully and diligently and conscientiously performing their duties to protect the citizenry of auburn and,
>
> Whereas, this council feels that these men, in so performing their duties, were upholding the finest traditions of their department and,
>
> Whereas, this council in behalf of and for all of the citizens wishes to acknowledge and take public notice of the heroic work performed by these men who in the discharge of their duties gave their lives.
>
> Now, therefore, be it resolved, that we, the citizens of Auburn, who have been the fortunate recipients of the services rendered by these men record with deepest sorrow the passing of these faithful servants of our city; these men who by the very nature of their positions constantly braved hazards and dangers that Auburn might be free from fire and destruction,

and it is further,

Resolved, that in honor of these men this council declare a state of mourning for one week and directs that the flag in front of Memorial City Hall be flown at half-mast during that period, and, it is further,

Resolved, that this council does extend its deepest sympathy to the families of these men who gave their lives, and, it is further,

Resolved, that as a mark of our deep respect to the memory of these honored dead this resolution be spread upon the minutes of this meeting and a copy thereof be forwarded to the members of the families of these heroic men, as our humble tender of condolence for their irreparable loss."

No roll call was taken, because the resolution was sponsored by the Council as a whole, instead of by a single councilman.

The Auburn City Council, in a resolution, requested City Manager George F. Train to express official appreciation to all those who had helped during the explosion. Letters were sent to many who were identified as assisting the Fire Department and City of Auburn on that fateful evening, including:

Cayuga County Red Cross	The Salvation Army	Civil Defense Workers
NYS Troopers	Auburn Police Chief	Head of Water Department
Head of Park and Sewer Dept.	Sheriff Willard Wilcox	Sgt. Hugh T. Mahar, NYS Police
Arthur E. Stephen, Civil Defense	William E. Bouley, Contractor	Ralph Webster, Vol. Fireman
Mrs. David Moore, Red Cross	Dr. Percy Bryan, Vol. Fireman	Dennis J. Harrington, Contractor
Francis Cunningham, Contractor	Joseph Pettigrass, Contractor	Ralph L. Schooley, Contractor
Capt. Leland E. Waldron, Salvation Army	Cayuga County Volunteer Fire Departments	

Auburn has always been a strong community. In troubled times, Auburnians rally around those in need. This disaster proved no different. A variety of collections were taken up for the families of the victims. Firemen's Associations from around New York State also took up collections and sent them to the benefit fund for the families. Individuals and businesses contributed to relief funds. Benefits and other charitable endeavors were pursued to assist the families of those lost in the explosion.

Auburn radio station, WAUB, started a firemen's benevolent trusteeship, and aimed to collect $5,000. The goal was to provide $1,000 for each fireman's family and have $2,000 left in the trusteeship for future needs. Donations were accepted at the radio station, as well as at various other businesses in Auburn. The Auburn Civil Defense Auxiliary Police raised more than $1,100 in donations for the families of the fallen firemen. The money was raised through the selling of boutonnieres, made possible by the clergymen in the city, who permitted the sale in front of their churches. The flowers were donated by the Auburn Florist Association and the boutonnieres were made up at a group meeting of multiple Auburn florists. Funds raised from the boutonnieres were turned over to the Firemen's Benevolent Trusteeship fund. The Firemen's Benevolent Trusteeship fund exceeded their initial goals, and $9,168.80 was provided to the widows of the firemen killed. The firemen's widows exhibited true kindness and generosity and turned over $1,000 to each of the widows of Walter Ockenfels and John Bell.

The Auburn City Council voted unanimously to give each of the firemen's widows $5,000. The payment was made due to the fact that there was no municipal provision for a lump sum death benefit which would supplement the NYS retirement pension and Social Security benefits to the surviving widows and children. A similar action was taken by the council after the Hislop fire in 1931.

The Auburn Fire Department received many Western Union telegrams from all around expressing their sympathy: Yates County firemen; Fire Commissioners from Chicago, Illinois; Albany Division of Safety; American LaFrance President, Dan Ellis; Olean Fire Department; Scipio Center Fire Department and the National Board of Fire Underwriters, to name just a few. Many letters were also received from throughout New York State and various parts of the country. The loss of the firefighters was felt by many and the expressions of sympathy that were sent were numerous and in many forms.

Lt. Alfred H. Murphy was 51 years old at the time of his death. He was born in Seneca Falls, New York on October 29, 1908. He became a firefighter in July of 1938, at the age of 31. He was promoted to Lieutenant in 1958, at the age of 49. Lt. Alfred "Spuds" Murphy loved sports. He was a pitcher for Bob Davis' Auburn semi-professional baseball club. He was known for his blazing fastball and baffling curveball. He was also an outstanding bowler. It was said that Spuds would discuss or argue about any sporting event or record, and he was usually right. Baseball was always close to his heart. A particular incident was recalled where he had worked half the night at a fire, got off duty at 7:30am and drove to

New York City with his friend, Steve Tarby, to see a World Series game on his day off. He was reported to be a happy-go-lucky, devil-may-care man and frequently was heard saying "Okay, kid" in conversations. During his days as the Chief's driver, "Spuds" was said to have wheeled the car through traffic like his own pants were afire. Alfred "Spuds" Murphy married Irene Brunner Murphy and together they had two daughters and a son.

Firefighter John F. Searing was 27 at the time of his death. He was born February 22, 1933, in Auburn, New York. He became a firefighter in July of 1957 at the age of 24. Contrera and Searing were appointed as firefighters on the same day. John Searing was a Korean War Veteran, having served in the Navy. He played in the Firemen and Policemen Softball games to benefit the Babe Ruth League and was a good ball player for the Fire Eaters. John Searing left behind his wife, Elizabeth Smith Searing, a daughter and son.

Firefighter Anthony T. Contrera was born on July 20, 1924, in Auburn, New York. He graduated from Central High School in 1941, the first graduating class of the new high school. He married Josephine Vitale Contrera. Anthony Contrera was a veteran of World War II, having served in the Army Corps of Engineers. He landed on Normandy Beach on D-Day. He became a firefighter at the age of 32, in July of 1957. Contrera and Searing were appointed as firefighters on the same day.

John H. Bell was 50 at the time of his death. Born in Reynoldsville, New York, he had lived in Auburn for many years. He operated the Bell Trucking Co. and was in the heating service repair business. He worked for R. J. Connor Oil Company, distributor of California Oil, as a truck driver and as an attendant at a gas station on Seminary Street. The husband of Anna Slywka Bell, together they had two daughters and five sons.

Walter Ockenfels was 64 years old at the time of his death. He was married to Mabel Knight Ockenfels. Together they had two sons. A native of Auburn, New York, he was the proprietor of the Genesee Street garage prior to becoming proprietor of the old Hendrick's station at the corner of Lincoln and South Streets.

Services were held for the victims on Saturday, April 2, 1960. City officials attended the services of the three firemen who were killed in the explosion. The Wheeler Bell at Memorial City Hall tolled in memory of the deceased firemen in the morning, and for John Bell, World War II Veteran, in the afternoon. The processions passed Memorial City Hall, just over 100 feet away from the scene of the explosion. The firefighters received full Fire Department honors. Fire Chief Luke Bergan collapsed during services at St. Alphonsus Church while attending Lt. Murphy's services. He was taken by ambulance to Mercy Hospital, where he was admitted. Sid Burridge was also taken from St. Alphonsus church to the hospital during Lt. Murphy's services. Mayor Maurice Schwartz, Corporation Counsel George Shamon and Councilman Thomas Brogan attended the church services for Murphy. A delegation from the Auburn Council of Knights of Columbus also attended.

The firemen were led by Captain Ralph Quill, Charles Hardy, Leonard Bochenek, George Bannon, James Gillooly, Reynolds VanScoyk, Thomas Burke, Stanley Bilinski, John O'Hora and Paul McGinn. Ramond Donovan served as honor guard at the church and cemetery. Honorary bearers included Stephen Tarby, Andrew Lepak, William Bouley, Dr. Russell Nolan, William Duffy, Peter Pettigrass, Charles Scrubbs, Edward Murphy, John Kudla and Floyd Germano. Bearers at services for John Searing included Captain Ralph Hoyt, Lt. John Delaney, Paul Kierst, Jean Garropy, John Schlegel and Harry Mullen. Honorary bearers included Mayor Maurice Schwartz, Corporation Counsel George Shamon, City Manager George Train, City Councilman Harry Oropallo, Fire Chief Luke Bergan, Assistant Chief William Maywalt, Reynolds VanScoyk and Sid Burridge. Searing had an honor guard of firefighters and police officers. Active bearers at the services for Anthony Contrera included Assistant Fire Chief Peter Mentillo, Firemen Charles Conboy, Nicholas Aversa, James Gillooly Jr., Bernard Simmons and Edward Bilinski. Honorary bearers included Chief Luke Bergan, Captain Ralph Quill, Captain Andrew Guter, Firefighters Lucian DeSocio, Francis Fiore, Michael Carbonaro, Glenn Adams Jr., Angelo Spinelli, Francis Bunnell and Nicholas Luisi. Also included in the list were Auburn Police Department Chief John Costello, Captain Joseph Conboy, Patrolmen Daniel DeMaio, Joseph DeMaio, Joseph Frabrize, Carl Nicandri, Dominic DeSocio. City officials served as honorary bearers as well and included Mayor Maurice Schwartz, City Manager George Train, Councilman Harry Oropallo, Corporation Counsel George Shamon. Officials and members of the Oswego, Fulton and Syracuse Fire Departments and several volunteer departments, as well as New York State Policemen were honorary bearers. At the funeral home, members of the Auburn Fire and Police Departments paid respects in a group.

The Auburn Permanent Firemen's Association (PFA) passed a "last alarm" resolution conveying sympathy to the families of the three firemen killed in the explosion. Reynolds VanScoyk, PFA President, expressed the association's thanks to all organizations and individuals who worked at the scene of the disaster. The resolution read:

> "Whereas God, in His infinite wisdom, has removed from our midst a beloved member in whose death the association has lost a sincere and loyal and revered friend, the community a valued and respected citizen, and the family a kind and devoted member and
>
> Whereas we shall miss his pleasant companionship and good fellowship, his wise counsel and his loyalty to the best interests of the organization and to his fellow men, and desiring to perpetuate his memory and to convey to the family of each of the following brothers:

Lieutenant Alfred H. Murphy

Fireman Anthony T. Contrera

Fireman John F. Searing

our sincere sympathy in their bereavement, be it

Resolved that a copy of this resolution be spread on the minutes of the meeting of the Auburn Permanent Firemen's Association, a copy be sent to the bereaved family and a copy be sent to The Citizen-Advertiser for publication."

In May of 1960, three trees were planted in memory of the three fallen firefighters. The project was sponsored by the Auburn Kiwanis Club in cooperation with the City. A ceremony was held in front of the parking lot on Exchange Street, opposite Memorial City Hall. The trees were planted by Mayor Maurice Schwartz, City Manager Train and Fire Chief Luke Bergan as a living memorial to the three firefighters. In October of 1960, a plaque was placed near the scene of the explosion, on the entrance post of the City parking lot. The bronze plaque was 10" square with a black background and called attention to the three trees planted in memory of the firemen between the parking lot and the sidewalk. The inscription read, "MEMORIAL TREES, PLANTED HERE BY THE AUBURN KIWANIS CLUB AND THE CITY OF AUBURN, IN MEMORY OF AUBURN FIREMEN, LT. ALFRED H. MURPHY, ANTHONY CONTRERA, JOHN F. SEARING, KILLED IN LINE OF DUTY, MARCH 30, 1960." The three red maple trees and the plaque were later moved beside City Hall in the same area as the monuments honoring the soldiers and sailors from Cayuga County who served in the Civil War to the south of City Hall.

Soon after, the City passed a number of laws to prevent the situation from occurring again. In August of 1960, the City Council passed a resolution governing the installation of storage tanks for flammable liquids. The resolution added amendments which required that permits must be secured from the Council by resolution or ordinance for the construction or installation of storage containers for gasoline or a similar substance. The new amendments classified flammable liquids, regulated the storage of flammable liquids inside buildings and regulated the construction of special storage rooms within buildings. City officials oversaw the removal of old storage tanks and inspected the installation of new ones.

The tragic event of March 30, 1960, prompted Bonnie Lee Walters to submit a legislative bill to a YMCA Hi-Y Youth and Government Conference in Albany in 1963. The daughter of Mr. and Mrs. Lionel Walters of Melrose Road, Bonnie submitted a bill which would require annual inspection of underground gasoline storage tanks with a capacity of over 100 gallons. Bonnie's bill was selected for submission from over 400 presented.

Sid Burridge was never the same after that fateful night. He would leave the Fire Department for a few months to work at Green Haven Prison in Stormville, NY as a Corrections Officer. He returned to the Fire Department and worked for another 21 years before his retirement in 1983.

In a recent newspaper article, Irene Murphy, the wife of Alfred Murphy, spoke of that tragic day with great difficulty. Although she was 94 at the time of her newspaper interview, she remembered that night very clearly and, not surprisingly, indicated she would never forget. She had recently returned to her job at Mercy Hospital after an absence, and was attending a dinner party thrown by her friends to celebrate her return. The dinner was at Darhes Manor Restaurant on Grant Ave. She was sitting at a table enjoying an evening with friends, when the waiter hurried to their table and asked if they had heard about an explosion that had rocked downtown. Mrs. Murphy sensed something may have gone bad for her husband, "Spuds", who was working that evening. She called the fire station but they couldn't tell her anything. Mrs. Murphy had a friend drive her down to the scene. Police were holding back the crowd, but she inched forward, hoping to see her husband busily working on the flames. She went from the scene of the horrible explosion to the hospital, hoping to get information. She waited at the Emergency Room and watched two covered bodies taken past her on stretchers. She still did not have any idea that her husband was lost in the blast. She phoned home. Her father, who was living with the couple and their three children at the time, said "Irene, come home." She knew then that her worst fears had come true. "I knew something had happened....but I never thought of (my husband) being killed." But her 51-year-old husband was one of the three firefighters killed in the explosion that evening. Mrs. Murphy was 44 at the time of her husband's death. She supported their children working in an office at Auburn Memorial Hospital. She never remarried.

Butch Delaney also vividly recalled that horrible night. He was a Lieutenant with Engine Company Co. 3. "The building was completely demolished. We knew there were three of our guys in there. We tried to rescue them, but we knew they were deceased. It was terrible." One of Delaney's tasks that night was to shut off the valve on one of the gas tanks. The firefighters doused him with water while he turned the valve with a pipe wrench, just in case there was another explosion. The service station was gone, debris littered a two-block area downtown and there was no hope for those who were caught in the explosion. "It's something I'll never forget, that's for sure."

Memory of the fire also remains with Mayor Michael Quill. He was helping his father, a career Auburn Firefighter, fix the boiler at their home at the time of the blast. As soon as his father learned of the explosion, he raced to the scene. Mike Quill was 11 years old. "The big thing that sticks in my mind still, to this day, is how quickly life can change." Michael Quill followed in his father's footsteps and served over 32 years with the Fire Department, 11 of them as Fire Chief.

When talking with the men who were firefighters at the time of the explosion and who were present at the scene that night, a long pause and shake of the head is seen, usually followed by a physical slump and heavy sigh. The same words are used over and over to describe that night; tragic, scary, unbelievable, devastating. It is difficult for some to talk about, as it brings them back to that fatal night when an unanticipated series of events led to the death of so many.

September 7, 1960
Drake Oil Co. Inc. and Endicott Johnson Shoe Co.

The expertise of a department is tested during any fire call. The organization and skill of fire personnel in the face of concurrent alarms requires even greater planning and execution to ensure each emergency is addressed, and the remainder of the city remains protected against further calls. Such was the case when Auburn experienced several simultaneous events on the afternoon of Wednesday, September 7, 1960. Firemen were called to the Drake Oil Co. Inc. building at W. Park Avenue at 12:12pm, where nearly 17,000 gallons of gasoline had spilled into the parking and loading lots of the company. A tractor trailer had brushed against and snapped off a three-inch pipe leading from a 24,000 gallon tank to the ground. Not being able to predict the course of the emergency incident, but knowing the potential of the situation, it was decided to call for mutual aid while they were on the scene at Drake Oil.

In order to ensure coverage of the city in the event of additional calls, volunteer fire companies from Fleming, Aurelius, Sennett and Owasco were called to provide mutual aid in stand-by positions at the three Auburn Fire stations. Owasco was on standby at the Owasco Street fire station, Aurelius was on standby at the Clark Street fire station and Sennett and Fleming were at headquarters on standby. The benefits of the Mutual Aid plan were soon realized when at 3pm the Owasco Fire Company was called from its standby position on Owasco Street, to the corner of Bradford and Owasco Streets to extinguish a telephone pole fire. At 4:36pm the Aurelius Fire Company was called to an automobile fire on the corner of State and Seymour Streets.

As they approached W. Park Avenue, the Auburn firefighters did not initially see any smoke or flames, but upon arrival at Drake Oil Co., the smell of gasoline fumes was very strong. They arrived and saw a gasoline tanker with flames around it. At one point, gasoline poured out at approximately 200 gallons per minute. It gathered all around the area and also ran down the hill. Immediately recognizing the danger of the situation and the potential for a blast that would claim more life and property than was imaginable, the men swiftly worked to ensure public safety, contain the incident and extinguish the flames. Their actions illustrated true service in the face of danger. The area immediately surrounding the tanker was notified of the event and evacuated. They needed to ensure that there was no source of ignition introduced to the area; someone smoking, starting a vehicle or any activity that resulted in a spark, would wreak havoc and likely cause an explosion that would wipe out everyone and everything in the immediate area and beyond. Upon initially seeing the tanker and flames, firefighters shut down the fire truck as they approached and coasted the apparatus near the scene. It had been less than six months since the gasoline station explosion killed three firemen, and the firefighters were certainly sensitive to the volatility of this type of situation. One of the firefighters made his way over to the tanker. When he reached for the door handle, he was electrified and thrown up in the air and away from the truck. The tanker had become electrically charged during the course of the event unfolding. An employee had been working under the tanker to fix a pump. He had been using a trouble light. When the bottom of the pump was removed, gasoline poured down onto him and hit the light, which in turn burned components of the light. The wires from the electric light quite literally became welded to the driveshaft of the truck. The truck became even more dangerous now that it was electrically charged. Electric and gas line services had been shut off. The firemen ran lines and worked to extinguish the flames and flush the area. The man who had been working on the tanker was taken by ambulance to the hospital. Foamite and sand were used on the spill location. They had handled a very tricky situation, avoided further disaster and succeeded in putting the fire out. The men breathed a deep sigh of relief. As if the event at W. Park Avenue wasn't treacherous enough, the firefighters would not be able to rest on their laurels.

As firefighters were addressing the gasoline spill, a call came in at 4:37pm for a fire at the Endicott-Johnson Shoe Co. on Genesee Street. Auburn Fire Department Engines 1, 2, 3 and 4 along with the Hook and Ladder Company responded to Endicott-Johnson directly from Drake Oil Co. One Auburn Fire crew remained at Drake Oil to stand watch and cover hot spots. Fleming responded to Endicott-Johnson from headquarters and Aurelius responded to the scene from Clark Street, as did Owasco from their Owasco Street location. Given the number of calls being experienced that day and the need to protect the remainder of the city, three additional mutual aid trucks were called for. Equipment from Skaneateles and Throop moved into headquarters and another Aurelius unit moved into the Clark Street fire station.

The fire at Endicott-Johnson had started in a rubbish pile in a back room of the basement. As the firefighters made their way through the building, the situation evolved into an even more aggressive beast. The flames were rolling toward the door in great waves. One of the firefighters was pulled away from the charging flames just in time. The fire took hold and continued to work on the shoe factory. The smoke and flames that resulted were thick and firemen were forced back a few times as they continued to work their way toward the source of the fire. Smoke ejectors were brought in. The men, wearing air masks, skillfully navigated the store in the billowing smoke and arrived at the area they believe to be above the fire. The firefighters identified the source of the fire and chopped a hole through the floor of the shoe store. Once opened, flames sprung up through the hole, and the men were able to pour water into the basement using a large 2 ½" hose line. The fire resulted in damaged floor joists and loss of inventory. Damages to the store's stock on the first floor were small. Some smoke rose through to the second and third floors of the building, but for the most part were not impacted.

The Auburn Fire Department illustrated its ability to implement a plan of action for multiple simultaneous alarms in the city. Firefighters who responded to the alarms that day recall how delicate the situations were. They acknowledge 'what could have happened' and are very humble about their actions that day, which likely saved many lives and much property.

July 9, 1968
Emerson Park, Circus Tent Collapse

The residents of the city were enjoying their summer and looking forward to the Clyde Beatty-Cole Bros. Circus coming to town July 9, 1968. The circus was the world's largest under-canvas show and made an appearance in Auburn every year at Emerson Park. There would be two shows that day, 2pm and 8pm. The circus had 150 performers from 14 different countries. There were over 600 people that worked for and traveled with the circus from town to town. There was a large array of wild animals as well. The circus had elephants, lions, tigers and a 5-ton hippopotamus highlighting the event. "Big Sid" was a favorite elephant with the crowd. In 1968, the show would include many stars under the big top. The Vienna-born Illusionist, Ferry Forst, along with his wife, Lillian, and daughter, Yutta, would perform one of their best illusions. Ferry would shoot his daughter out of a cannon and into a box suspended high above the crowd. When the cannon was fired, the box would fall to the floor and Lillian Forst would go over and reveal that Yutta was in the box! The Flying Gaonas made their debut at the Clyde Beatty-Cole Bros. Circus in 1962. They amazed audiences with their somersaulting and aerial feats on the trapeze and dazzled crowds with their act. The Franconia Family, daring bare-back riders from Italy, would perform. The very glamorous Miss Prisk would be on the high trapeze. The clowns, jugglers and daredevils would entertain the crowd during the night. There would be plenty of peanuts, popcorn and cotton candy. It was sure to be a great night for the circus!

The Clyde Beatty-Cole Circus at Emerson Park was set up, people were pouring in and the performers were ready to dazzle the audience. The 300-foot tent was large and beckoning to those who wanted to hear the circus music, listen to the ringmaster and see the performers. Let the show begin! The 2pm show was a success and there was much laughter and fun times for the audience. The performers wowed the crowds. One of the Flying Gaonas did a triple somersault but failed to make it to his colleague on the other trapeze, and fell into the safety net. The world's smallest woman, a sword swallower and a snake charmer were all part of the side show features. The lions and tigers, under the direction of Captain Hoover, performed in the center ring. The afternoon show ended and the crowd dispersed.

The 8pm show was ready to provide its audience with another great night at the circus. With an audience of 1,683, the show got underway. It had started to rain at about the time the show started. Things were progressing fine. The elephants had completed their portion of the show. The acrobats were next up. The weather had turned during the course of the circus show, and the wind had kicked up. The acrobats would not perform that evening.

Thunder, lightning and a heavy downpour of rain hit the circus. The wind coming off Owasco Lake was strong and the winds were reported to be gusting upwards of 40 mph. At about 9:20pm, a large gust of wind lifted the canvas and the aluminum tent poles started to sway side to side. Rain poured in through the top of the tent and down the center pole. The three main support poles lifted off the ground and swung around crazily between the grandstand area and the exit. Some of the circus workers grasped the poles to try to hold them in place, but they had too much momentum and the wind continued its intensity. The workers were whipped around a bit and were forced to let go. The gusts and rain continued to attack the tent, and the poles eventually toppled over. With the poles no longer in place, the tent instantly collapsed down to the ground, catching 1,400 of the 2,000 spectators and performers within the mass of canvas and other debris. As the tent came down people screamed, but there was no time to get out. The lights on one side of the big top blew out and threw those trapped inside into darkness. Three hundred people remained safely in an area that did not collapse and another three hundred were sitting where the tent was pulled away from them by the wind. No one could say for certain what portion of the tent collapsed first, but it was felt that the south end was the first to uproot as the stakes pulled out of the ground. Poles hit audience members as they fell to the ground. Spectators and performers attempted to assist each other. Aerial ladders, wires, cables and steel structures came tumbling down with the collapse of the canvas tent. The shouts and cries from the men, women and children trapped in the tent were terrifying. The rain continued to pound the canvas and the crowd that was trying to get out of the tent. Thunder and lightning continued to light up the sky and add to the chaos with its booming bursts. The Weather Bureau would later report that the fierce electrical storm had dumped 2.98 inches of water in about two hours. Power lines were swinging and broke loose. Electricity was lost to about 600 homes in the area. There was much cloud to ground lightning and torrential rain. A 75-mile wide swath of thunderstorms had pummeled the Central New York area.

The newly developed Emergency Plan of the Auburn Fire Department would be used for the first time July 9, 1968. Dispatcher Walter Davis took a call from the Owasco Fire Department at 9:33pm and within three minutes an engine company and a hook and ladder company were at the scene. The call back system was used for the first time to bring off duty firefighters directly to the scene of the emergency instead of reporting to the fire station and then moving out as a group from there. Within five minutes of the initial apparatus and on-duty firefighters arriving on the scene, there were 35 firefighters present. Within fifteen minutes of the first call, they were at a full strength of 45 firemen. An emergency communications system was also utilized for the first time and performed well. A special radio band with a range of approximately three miles was used to maintain contact with the Auburn firefighters and the volunteer units in the area. This system was used due to the congested nature of the regular channels during an emergency and the resulting difficulty in transmitting and understanding messages. There were a number of area fire companies from around the county that responded to the emergency.

People trapped inside were frantically trying to crawl to loved ones and find children in the heavy folds of canvas. Their movements were slowed by the pressure of the canvas and the circus equipment and big top components in their way. As word spread of the debacle, people swarmed to Emerson Park to check the status of their children and families and friends in the area. The shouts of names were continuous. County and City law enforcement officials helped to keep the crowd in check. Rescuers lifted the tent canvas around the edges to free people from its clutch. In some places the canvas was cut to release people. Some managed to crawl under the bleachers as the tent collapsed; others did not have time to move at all and were flattened to the ground by the falling tent. The rescue workers crawled under the canvas in the ankle-deep water that had accumulated and looked for people trapped under the tent. On their hands and knees, firemen looked for children in the twisted canvas and wires and other debris. They sifted through the mass looking for anyone who remained in the tent. Search lights were brought in to assist in locating people. People were drenched and cold and shaken. The emergency workers, law enforcement personnel and hospital staff worked together like a well-oiled machine. They averted panic and provided effective actions in response to the pandemonium that ensued. Their long hours of disaster planning and training were illustrated in the quick and efficient responses they provided. The animals that had already completed their performance were not in the tent at the time of the collapse. Had they been inside when everything came down, the results would certainly have been different.

Green Shutters restaurant was used for individuals removed from the circus tent, in order for them to be preliminarily evaluated. Minor injuries were attended to by nurses in the area who volunteered along with waitresses from the restaurant. Emergency aid centers were established at the Owasco Stockade Indian Village, the 4-H pavilion, and at Green Shutters. It became clear that locating the hundreds of lost children who had become separated from their families in the melee was paramount. The Indian Village and the 4-H pavilion were identified as areas for lost children to be brought and for those who were looking for them to check. The hospitals quickly got ready to receive and treat those that were being transported to their facilities. For the first time in its history, Auburn Memorial Hospital initiated its disaster recovery plan. The hospital had run full practice drills for their disaster plan twice a year for seven years prior to that evening. The emergency room called in doctors, nurses, aides, student nurses, orderlies and many other hospital employees from home. Patients were being transported to the hospital via all kinds of transportation methods. Families flocked to the hospital to see if their loved ones were brought in. Volunteers from the Hospital Auxiliary were on hand to guide individuals toward the dining room on the second floor, which had been set up as a waiting area. There were varying reports of the number of people seen at Auburn Memorial and Mercy hospitals. By sheer luck, no one was killed in the tent collapse or the aftermath of the incident. Almost 250 people were transported to the hospitals; about 99 were treated and 24 were admitted. There were sprains and bruises and some lacerations sustained by the victims. The most serious injuries consisted of broken bones, concussions and shock.

The force of the storm did not only impact the area of the circus. The Auburn Fire and Police Departments were deluged with concurrent emergency calls from all parts of the city. In fact, emergency service teams throughout the county were experiencing similar volumes of calls. Auburn Mayor Paul Lattimore ordered all non-essential traffic off the streets during the storm. There was flooding in the streets, power lines were down and trees and limbs were littered all around. Wires were down at the Bargain Center on Grant Avenue, Westside Plaza, Easterly Avenue and VanAnden Street. A tree fell across Swift Street. The Fire Department was called to Franklin Street in response to flooding conditions. Manhole covers were coming loose and popping up on several streets. Civil Defense staff worked to address traffic situations and other emergency response tasks. Police Chief John Costello called in twenty-five additional men. Approximately 2,100 customers in the city were reported to be without electricity. A 12,000-volt circuit was knocked out and impacted much of the west end of the city. In addition to the response at Emerson Park for the circus tent collapse, the Auburn Fire Department answered 25 other calls, most of which resulted from the intensity of the storm. Three fires, downed electrical wires and many flooding conditions were addressed.

Workers spent the night cleaning the area and salvaging what could be saved. The elephants were brought out to assist in lifting the large tent poles and other debris in the area. The circus workers lived up to the adage "The show must go on!" and ordered another canvas so that they would have it for their show later in the week in Niagara Falls. Damage was estimated at more than $40,000.

Inspectors from the Bureau of Factories and Mercantile Establishments, a Division of Industrial Safety Services, checked the circus tents before and during the afternoon performance. They checked for proper exits, made sure "no smoking" laws were enforced, checked for fire extinguishers and looked at the canvas to be sure it was fireproof. The inspectors also made sure the tent poles were properly in installed and in place. As a precaution, the tent had been triple staked before the show due to the potential weather conditions. There were no violations identified as a result of the inspections prior to the tent collapse. The investigation immediately following the event revealed no violations either. The weather was determined to have been beyond anything that could have been anticipated. The fact that no lives were lost was amazing. A variety of responding entities initiated disaster plans and was judged to be very successful. The responders, victims of the collapse and the people of Auburn came together and worked collaboratively toward the goal of saving lives, providing help to those in need and maintaining order. To this day, people still talk about the tent collapse and share their memories of that night when the circus came to town.

September 13, 1969
Osborne Street Fire

At approximately 8:30pm on the evening of September 13, 1969, an alarm was made to the Auburn Fire Department for a fire on Osborne Street in one of the buildings that housed the former Auburn Wood Products building. The building was owned by the City of Auburn and had been abandoned and boarded up. Upon arrival, the firefighters found that the flames were well underway and already consuming the third floor of the old building. It was moving fast. The area was long regarded as a particularly dangerous one for a fire to break out due to the congested nature and age of the buildings. The fire spread quickly and flames were soaring upwards of 150 feet and were reported to be visible for miles. A reporter traveling to the scene from Syracuse indicated he could see the sky glow from the flames as he exited the New York State Thruway at Weedsport. The four-alarm fire required swift thinking and prompt actions on the part of the firefighters. All available Auburn firefighters were called to the scene. Eight volunteer companies from around the county, and two from outside the county, also responded to assist with the unruly inferno threatening the heart of the city. The logistics of fighting a fire in this location proved challenging. The flames roared through the buildings and they became teetering masses of brick that threatened everyone and everything around them. As is the case with any very large fire, throngs of spectators gathered in the area to see the scene. By some reports, 2,000 people lined the streets to watch the headline-making fire. The crowds that had assembled at the fire hampered efforts to extinguish the flames, and they were moved away by Auburn Police Department and Civil Defense personnel. Mayor Paul Lattimore called it a "fire of catastrophic proportions." A State of Emergency was declared by Mayor Lattimore and all residents were ordered off the streets. There were fears of possible explosions due to the existence of a diesel storage tank and two underground gas tanks in the area. The diesel tank ruptured and fed the blaze, making the firefighters' work even more treacherous, but it did not explode. Power lines and telephone lines burned and there was a loss of power in the area. The five-story building of the Columbian Rope warehouse was consumed and the walls eventually tumbled down and collapsed. Red hot bricks were falling everywhere.

The fire covered a large area, and the wall of flames seemed insurmountable at times. The large, old buildings fed the blaze a steady supply of fuel to facilitate its ongoing movement through the area. Firefighters instituted an attack operation to protect the surrounding scene and make headway against the thriving flames.

Firefighters worked for more than four hours to halt the fire and extinguish the flames. In the end, three buildings were destroyed in the blaze; the old D. M. Osborne Works (later the International Harvester Company), the Auburn Transit Co. bus garage and a Columbian Rope Co. storage warehouse. The warehouses of the Logan Paper Company and Flickinger Grocery, both located in the same building adjacent to the fire, suffered some smoke and fire damage and had heavy water damage. The Fire Department's Engine 1 suffered damage from the intense heat that penetrated parts of the truck and melted the lights on it as well. Nearby homes and other buildings were protected against fire exposure and the flames were contained to the three buildings. The area of the fire was part of the SLOG project (South, Lincoln, Osborne and Genesee) and was up for demolition within a year as part of urban renewal initiatives that the city hoped would attract redevelopers to the area.

1971

Residential Gas Fire, Mother's Bakery, Mohican Bakery, Luke Williams & Son Lumber, First Presbyterian Church

Auburn had a number of significant fires in 1971 that resulted in the loss of lives and caused significant financial losses. Firefighters were called to Mother's Bakery, 165 State Street, at 6:10am on the morning of February 27, 1971. The fire started in the basement of the three-story brick bakery building. Both off duty shifts were called in at 6:26am. The owner of the building was Jim Kliss. The bakery was operated by Kliss' son, James, and his daughter-in-law. James and his wife were out making deliveries at the time of the fire. The building was not occupied. The upper stories were used as a storage area for Martin's Furniture Store of Fairmount. Martin Kliss, owner of Martin's Furniture Store, carried no insurance against the estimated $2,000-$3,000 damage. Firemen worked to bring the blaze under control. A 2-story vacant building on the corner of VanAnden Street was threatened by the fire. A large portion of one of the floors gave way, with firefighters making it out just in time. Three Auburn firefighters were injured in the fire when part of the north wall of the bakery collapsed on them at about 7:30am. Assistant Chief Francis Maywalt, Lieutenant Bernard Simmons and Fireman Frank DeJoy were taken to Mercy Hospital and were in the Intensive Care Unit for observation. All three suffered from smoke inhalation, but none were burned in the incident. Total damages of the fire were estimated at $85,000.

On April 7, 1971, a three-alarm fire roared for nearly two hours in the early morning as firefighters fought to put it out. Luke Williams & Son Lumber Co. on Greet Street sustained an estimated $120,000 in damages resulting from the fire. Unfortunately, the department's response to a false alarm resulted in delay of their arrival on the scene at Luke Williams. Fire alarm Box 417 was pulled at 12:10am at Auburn High School. Engine Co. 2, Engine Co. 4 and Truck Company 1, along with the Chief's car, responded to the scene. Engine Co. 3 went to headquarters to stand by in case of another call. Upon arrival at the high school, there was no sign of fire. The Chief ordered the men to search throughout the school. While everyone was at the school, the Chief's driver received a call over the radio that there was a reported fire at Luke Williams & Son Lumber Yard on Green Street. The Chief's driver had to go into the school to locate the Chief (portable radios were not in the fire service at this time) and advise him of the fire. The Chief ordered all personnel to return to their vehicles. The process took some time because personnel were scattered throughout the high school. The school's P.A. System had to be used to inform personnel, and no one could respond until all had been accounted for. Once underway, the men saw flames and smoke in the sky as they approached Green Street. The Chief immediately ordered a third alarm at 12:30am. Firemen arrived at the lumber yard and found it engulfed in flames. The display rooms, offices and mill workshop were completely involved upon arrival. The fire had broken through the roof and flames were already soaring 20-30 feet into the air. The fire was believed to have started in the center section of the lumber yard. The firefighters were faced with many obstacles during the fire. There were 8-10 wooden buildings in the area, including the Auburn Lumber Company warehouse adjacent to Luke Williams and the O. H. Greene Lumber Co. on Hulbert Street. The New York State Electric and Gas (NYSEG) Co. had a power substation adjacent to the fire. Had the fire spread to the substation, the results would have been catastrophic. There were threats on all sides of the fire that was already well underway. The firemen battled the flames from multiple angles and protected the area from the looming threats around them. The temperatures were in the mid-20s overnight and icing of the equipment hampered efforts to extinguish the blaze. Three volunteer fire companies were put on standby to give mutual aid if needed; Owasco, Sennett and Aurelius were ready to roll. After nearly two hours of work, Auburn firemen were able to bring the fire under control. Two firemen were injured in the fire; Lt. Lucian DeSocio sustained a knee injury and Fireman Frank Calarco had a puncture wound to his hand. Both were treated at Auburn Memorial Hospital. The losses sustained that night at the lumberyard might not have been as significant had it not been for the earlier false alarm at the high school.

At 9pm on the evening of September 2, 1971, a fire broke out in an Auburn residence housing a family of four. The husband had been painting a car outside his home and came inside to clean up. He used gasoline to clean his hands. He heard a noise behind him. Thinking his daughter might be tampering with the gasoline, he whirled around and knocked over the gas can in the process. The gas splattered across their gas stove, and the pilot light ignited the gasoline. The area was instantaneously covered in flames. The fire immediately spread to the husband's hands and chest. Hearing the commotion, the man's wife ran into the kitchen and attempted to smother the fire on her husband. The intensity of the fire was growing and the wife ran to the upstairs bedroom where their 18-month old son was sleeping. In the meantime, the husband scooped up his three-year-old daughter and ran her outside to safety. An alarm was called to the Fire Department at 9:24pm. Engines Two, Four and Truck Company 1 were dispatched to the scene under the command of Assistant Chief Ralph Quill. Additional assistance was requested from Engine Three. The house was fully engulfed on arrival and smoke billowed out of the building. The wife managed to get to her son, but the fire prevented her from exiting using the stairway. Firefighters later theorized that she became confused and disoriented in the smoke and flames and ran toward a back bedroom with her son in her arms. Smoke poured out of the house and made it difficult to see. The heat generated by the fire was intense. The husband had to be physically restrained from re-entering the home to attempt to rescue his wife and son. His hands were burned black and charred from the fire. Firefighters fought the smoke and flames to make their way through the house and upstairs to find the two remaining family members. The wife and son were found in a back attic-type bedroom within a few feet of a window. Firefighters immediately started mouth-to-mouth resuscitation and continued their efforts until they were out of the building. Their efforts to revive them failed. The wife and her eighteen-month-old son were transported to Auburn Memorial Hospital. Both were pronounced dead on arrival.

Auburn Police Patrolman Robert Walker was completing his rounds during the overnight hours of December 10, 1971, when he discovered a fire at the Mohican Bakery on Genesee Street just after 2am. He had passed the rear of the building about five minutes prior to spotting the smoke. He had been on his way to City Hall to turn off the Christmas lights, when he looked back and saw the smoke coming from the bakery building. He identified the source of the smoke and turned in the alarm at 2:08am. The Fire Department arrived on the scene within minutes. The heavy smoke poured out of the upper portion of the bakery building roof and flames could be seen inside. A second and third alarm was called at 2:14am. The firemen battled the blaze using all available equipment in the department, including two new ones that were put to the test for the first time. The building was covered by firefighters in the front, rear and one side of the building. Additionally, aerial ladders threw 1,500 gallons of water a minute on the flames. The fire was believed to have started in the basement or first floor of the bakery and then spread upward through the elevator shaft to the second floor and completely engulfed the area. By 2:30am flames were breaking through the roof and extended 50 feet into the air. Assistant Chief George Bannon opened a rear door to the elevator shaft and described the sound to be like a jet plane. Flames came roaring out with such intensity that the firemen were initially driven back. They pushed forward on the flames and attacked the blaze with every available hose line. The firemen poured approximately one million gallons of water on the blaze. The pockets of flames were stubborn and the heavy smoke hindered their ability to see and navigate the area. The building had false ceilings and a false front on the outside, which hampered the firemen from getting to the heart of the fire. The roof of the building collapsed just after 2:30am. There were no firemen on the roof at the time of the collapse. After almost four hours the fire was brought under control. The interior of the Mohican building was gutted. The cause of the fire was a 50-gallon drum of volatile liquid stored in the basement.

A three-alarm fire was fought at the First Presbyterian Church on Franklin Street on December 18, 1971. The fire started at about 7:10pm and heavily damaged the social room on the first floor and a boiler room below. The blaze continued for two hours while firefighters fought to bring it under control. There were heavy smoke conditions. The firefighters fought aggressively to attack the flames. Chief Maywalt called the efforts of the men one of the best 'saves' he had ever seen. The firemen went into the building and were able to stop the fire before it claimed the entire building.

June 21-30, 1972
Tropical Storm Agnes - Flood Emergency

Many residents of Auburn remember the Flood of 1972. We have photographs of the high water levels in various locations in and around the City of Auburn and the subsequent damages that were caused. Water was everywhere, and we recall the precarious situation that faced the city and surrounding areas during those days in June when the rising water level of Owasco Lake and the Outlet threatened even more damage. Hurricane Agnes developed on June 15 and was upgraded to a Hurricane on June 18. Agnes headed northward and made landfall near Panama City, Florida on June 19. After moving inland she weakened to a tropical depression. Agnes re-strengthened traveling over North Carolina and reached Tropical Storm status on June 21 and moved into the Atlantic Ocean, where it picked up additional moisture and then took a northwest turn and headed toward New York. Life is timing.

The first control structure for Owasco Lake was a dam built by the state of New York, which enabled the use of the lake as a water feeder for the Erie Canal. In 1886, the City of Auburn began managing lake levels. The lift gates were initially constructed of wood.

They were rebuilt as steel gates in 1954. The taintor (radial) gates were built in 1967. In 1969, the City acquired complete control of the operation of the State Dam. At that time, it was still necessary to maintain satisfactory flows for the small businesses that obtained hydropower from the outlet.

The information presented here is, in large part, compiled from a summary prepared by City Manager Bruce Clifford, Senior Civil Engineer William Catto and Water Superintendent John Poole. The City of Auburn, as part of its Urban Renewal Project, was continuing work on the Genesee Street bridge abutment on May 23, 1972, which required the City to regulate the water being discharged from the State Dam. In support of the project the flood gates were opened one per day. By June 7, 1972, three flood gates were fully opened. Water continued to be discharged over the State Dam until June 21, 1972. The lake elevation that day was 709.45 feet. In the days leading up to June 21, the city had received moderate to heavy rains and the decision was made to open all flood gates at 3pm on Wednesday, June 21. At 5am on Thursday, June 22, it was observed that the west bank of the Mill Street Dam was beginning to wash out. All flood gates and the tainter gate were closed because of the severe washing condition that could have resulted in severe flooding in the outlet below that point if the dam failed. At approximately 9am the west bank of the Mill Street Dam had washed out and there was a reduction in pond elevation behind the dam. The flood gates at the State Dam were opened one at a time in half-hour intervals until all flood gates were wide open by 11:30am. The tainter gate was manually opened, twenty turns per hour until 2pm when it had reached its maximum manual opening. At about 3pm the William E. Bouley Company crane removed logs from the outlet at Bowen Products. At approximately 5:15pm the east bank of the State Dam was observed to be washing out and measures were taken to secure it with sand bags and fill material. The City Manager and Chairman of the County Legislature declared a State of Emergency at approximately 6:15pm due to the increased water flows at the State Dam and the possible failure of the same. Additional sand bags were placed on the west bank of the State Dam and on the bullnose of the pier to restrain the flow in the outlet from overflowing the banks. The tainter gate was raised to a higher position by 2am on Friday, June 23. The rain continued to come down and the storm was unrelenting. Since 1912, the average flow in the Owasco River outlet was 289 cfs (cubic feet per second); the flow on June 23, 1972, reached 3,250 cfs, the maximum discharge recorded. The flashboards on the dam behind Procino & Rossi were removed to reduce flooding in the Washington Street area and increase the discharge capacity of the outlet at this location. As a result of the tainter gate being raised, Washington Street did flood, and by 9am, had flowed across Washington Street and into the parking lot of Dunn & McCarthy and back into the outlet. At about Noon on Friday, June 23, Dunn & MCarthy called in a fire alarm when their generator had caught fire and they were no longer able to generate electricity. New York State Electric & Gas (NYSEG) was requested to cut the wires to enable the turbine to free-wheel. However, the reduced rate of flow in the raceway and additional flows discharging over the State Dam from the increased elevation of Owasco Lake caused flooding in the West Street area. Sand bags were placed in hopes of retaining the flood waters to the Dunn & McCarthy parking lot. At 11pm the parking lot was encased with sand bags and pumping was started from the lower area on West Street into the parking lot.

The Auburn Fire Department furnished their 1961 American-LaFrance 1,000 gallon pumper at the Upper Pumping Station to assist in pumping back waters from the sump wells at the station. Sand bags were placed at the Canoga Street bridge to keep the flood water within the Outlet banks. It was later determined the water would not be able to be retained within the banks of the Outlet and the water was directed down Bradley Street and diverted back to the outlet. The rain finally subsided on Saturday, June 24th, but the lake level continued to rise. Sand bag dikes were reinforced, and a crane positioned at the Genesee Street bridge continued to remove debris carried down the Outlet. At 10am sand bags were placed on the access road to the Upper Pumping Station, as southern winds on Owasco Lake had increased the lake level to 712.50 ft., making the road almost impassable. The water level threatened the pump house and it was feared that it would be overcome and rendered inoperable for furnishing water to the city. At 3pm efforts were concentrated at the Upper Pumping Station, and the access road was reinforced with crushed stone. City workers, County workers and private contractors worked together to try to hold back the flood waters. The situation continued to evolve and quick-thinking and constant actions were taken to mitigate the flood water damage and the pressures the infrastructures were taking on. The Skaneateles amphibious duck was requested and brought in to assist and stand by in case the area needed to be completely abandoned. So precarious was the situation, that Civil Defense was called in to supply food and water and cots to the Upper Pumping Station in the event that the workers ended up isolated for a period of days. Work continued through the night.

Sunday, June 25, 1972, saw the lake elevation crest at 716.88 feet. At 1pm a crane operator observed that a stone block had been washed out of the east face of the stone pier supporting the tainter gate. Shortly thereafter, movement was noted of an upper stone block slipping into the cavity and causing increased water leakage through the masonry joints of the pier wall. The situation was becoming increasingly disastrous, with a possibility of significantly greater danger to come. Water Supervisor Poole called the U.S. Corps of Army Engineers to inform them of the condition and received recommendations from Colonel Moore. City, County and private contractors continued to work together to haul rip-rap and large stones to the State Dam for placement along the east wall of the pier. At 2:30pm, a meeting was held at the Auburn Police Department with the Auburn Police Chief, Auburn Fire Chief and City Officials. Evacuation procedures were drawn up for implementation in the event that the Dam failed. Failure of the Dam would result in the elevation of the Outlet rising some 50 feet. The flooding would directly affect approximately 15,000 residents in the city. All firemen, policemen and city public works employees were called to duty. Evacuation notice announcements were made on radio and television stations. Civil Defense Headquarters was mobilized in the basement of the Cayuga County Office Building. All incoming traffic was stopped at the city limits. Residents living in the evacuated area were ordered to leave immediately and directed toward one of the five evacuation centers. The Auburn Fire Department and NYSEG shut off all electrical and gas services in the evacuation area. The Auburn Fire Department Headquarters was also evacuated. Fire trucks were removed to the Nelson Street Garage and at the First Methodist Church parking lot on South Street. Mr. Joseph Foley of the U. S. Corps of Engineers arrived at the State Dam at 3:30pm and evaluated the damages and condition of the Dam and east pier. After a two-hour review, Mr. Foley concluded that the Dam structure containing the five flood gates would support the pressures created by the flow in the Outlet, but the pier containing the tainter gate could fail, which would cause flooding in the lower area of the Outlet from water passing through the 18-foot opening. He thought the cresting elevation of the Outlet could be decreased from 50 feet to 20 feet in height if a failure occurred and notice given. A supporting beam was fabricated by Water Department personnel and placed between the two piers supporting the tainter gate to reduce further horizontal movement of the east pier wall. With the flooding elevation reduced, the evacuation area was subsequently reduced to approximately 5,000 residents and businesses. The revised evacuation plans were prepared and distributed. Announcements were made. Monitoring of the State Dam continued throughout the night. Evaluations were performed. Measurements were taken. It had become somewhat of a waiting game.

By Monday morning, June 26th, the situation had remained stable. The evacuation area was opened and residents were advised to remain in constant contact with radio stations for possible evacuation orders. The Genesee Street bridge was opened to two-way traffic at 10:00am, as water had receded in the Outlet and the deck was no longer in danger of flooding. The estimated damages as a result of the flood emergency in the City of Auburn were $12,996,500. By Monday morning the lake elevation level was reduced to 711.90. Monitoring of the State Dam continued on Monday. There were additional cracks, movement and leakage that were observed in the stone blocks at the interior of the pier at the east side of the tainter gate. In the afternoon, the Lake Avenue Bridge piers were observed to be exposed and erosion was detected. Over the course of the next few days monitoring continued and actions were taken to maintain the stabilization of the structures and the subsequent receding of the flood waters. On Friday, June 30, 1972, at 11am, the City Manager and Chairman of the Cayuga County Legislature declared an end to the State of Emergency.

Tropical Storm Agnes was the maximum known flood in the watershed. Due to the irregular path of the storm through the central Finger Lakes, the flooding that resulted varied across nearby areas. Structural repairs of the masonry walls at the tainter gate were required as a result of the event. The Mill Street Dam downstream of the State Dam remained intact during the event, but the west abutment was washed out and the bluff experienced severe erosion.

An "Appreciation Day" was organized by the County legislature and held in August to honor and recognize the many area organizations, agencies and individuals who helped during the flood emergency. Twenty-seven certificates were presented in sincere gratitude of the efforts devoted to help the flood disaster area of Cayuga County from June 21-June 30, 1972. The Auburn Fire Department was among the organizations that were acknowledged that day for their hard work and dedication to public safety.

Tropical Storm Agnes resulted in the worst flood damage in the history of New York State at that time. Flooding began in Westchester County on June 19 and was followed by widespread flooding in the Southern Tier and Finger Lakes regions. The floods caused by Agnes resulted in 24 deaths in New York State and the evacuation of 100,000 NYS residents. The National Weather Service recorded measurements of rainfall in Cayuga County of 6-8 inches during the storm. Cayuga County was among the counties issued a Federal Emergency Management Agency (FEMA) Disaster Declaration.

May 12, 1973
Genesee Street, Patrick LaGambino Killed in Line of Duty

Firefighters execute the tasks of their job knowing that their lives are on the line. They understand and accept that the very nature of the job puts them at risk. Responding to others' emergencies on a daily basis is among their job duties. When called upon, they face flames with unflinching courage. When a fellow firefighter is struck down in the course of doing their job, their firefighter brothers and sisters are faced with the loss of life as well as their own mortality. Not since the March 30, 1960, explosion of the Chevron gas station on South Street, had the Auburn Fire Department experienced the loss of one of their own in the line of duty. On May 12, 1973, Patrick J. LaGambino's name would be added to the list of those who were killed in the line of duty. To make matters worse, his fellow firefighters were forced to witness firsthand one of their brothers struggle and ultimately succumb to the flames that night.

The alarm came in at 2:28am for a fire at 201½ Genesee Street. Engine Companies 4 and 3 along with Truck 1 responded to the scene. The building was a three-story, multiple family apartment house located on the corner of Genesee and Washington Streets. At least twelve people were reported to be living in the apartment house. All residents were safely evacuated, but firefighters did not have that information reliably upon their arrival. Firefighters worked to battle the flames. The fire had started in the boiler room in the basement of the building and spread quickly through the partitions to the upper floors. The boiler

room was close to the gas line and the firemen discovered that there was also a gas leak in the basement where the meter had been burned off. Without the ability to shut the gas off, firefighters faced a situation that became extremely dangerous and difficult. The gas line break fed the fire and repeatedly flared up as firefighters worked to knock it down. Meanwhile, another fire broke out in the city. An alarm was received from Box 135 at the YMCA on William Street for a curtain fire on the fourth floor of the building. Engine Co. 2 responded to the call and extinguished the blaze. The Genesee Street fire had grown worse and there was thick smoke billowing from the cornices of the house, an indication that the fire had worked its way up to the third story. Assistant Chief Ralph Quill ordered a second alarm at 3:27am and Engine Co. 2 responded. A third alarm was ordered at 3:58am which brought an additional engine and another hook and ladder truck.

Chief William Maywalt and Assistant Chief Ralph Quill were in charge of operations. Four firemen went inside the house to make sure there was no one inside and to ventilate it on the top floor; Lt. John Schlegel and Firefighters Patrick "Patsy" LaGambino, Raymond Walawender and Donald Alger. Schlegel and LaGambino had entered the building together and walked up to the third floor. They knew that Alger and Walawender were also on the same floor. The room on the top floor was filled with a thick black smoke. It was burning strong and fast. The flames forced the group toward the front of the house. The smoke was so thick that a hand light held up directly in front of one of the firefighter's face mask could not be seen. It became clear that they had to get out of that area of the house. A "flash-over" condition ensued, whereby the entire room suddenly became super-heated and completely involved in fire. The low ceilings, combustible materials and small rooms on the top floor provided conditions that facilitated the flash-over. The smoke was thick and impenetrable. The firemen became disoriented in the smoke and fire in the small rooms and hallways of the floor. Patsy LaGambino became separated from the group, but he was heard to say "I got a window." John Schlegel remembered that there was an outer room with a window that led to the fire escape. Stretching his hands out in front of him, unable to see, he worked his way along to a window. Lt. Schlegel could hear furniture being knocked over and a window break; at first, he assumed it was Patsy breaking through a different window. Once Lt. Schlegel found the window, he returned to find the other firefighters. He reported he "literally was just walking back in and reaching for any one of them, hoping to bump into them, but you couldn't see a thing." He bumped into one of them, grabbed him and brought him to the window. He then went back to find another and repeated the same actions. Walawender and Alger were the firefighters Schlegel had directed to the window and out via a fire escape ladder onto a porch roof. Walawender and Alger continued climbing down another ladder to the ground and Schlegel started to climb back up to find LaGambino, who was still in the building. LaGambino likely became confused and disoriented in the smoke and flames, but he did manage to locate a window. He appeared through a third floor window, farther away from the exit route the others had managed to find. Standing on the porch roof, Schlegel spotted him. The firemen below also saw Patsy in the window. Assistant Chief Ralph Quill, who had gone inside the building immediately headed for the area outside when he heard about LaGambino being trapped. The large window was separated by a partition down the middle; the result was a smaller portion of the window on each side. LaGambino was wearing his air-pak and was unable to get through either side of the window with the air-pak on. The available width of the window was too narrow to allow the firefighter through with full gear and his air-pak. Patsy screamed for help while the men frantically tried to reach him with help. A ladder was raised but was found to be too short. The men saw the struggle LaGambino was having. He was yelling "Get a ladder! Get a ladder! I'm trapped!" One firefighter yelled "Christ, Patsy, jump!" Patsy yelled, "I can't get the damn air-pak off! Christ, get me a ladder!" Firemen were positioned on the roof of the porch below and were just one story beneath him, unable to get to LaGambino. As the fire progressed, the flames forced them back. Close enough to see the anguish on his face and his struggle to get through the window, the firemen below continued to try everything to reach him. They were so close and yet so far. Patsy was unable to cut away his air-pak and could not escape through the window. Nothing was working. Patsy continued to plead for assistance. The flames were right behind Patsy, leaping up and moving forward. His clothes caught fire and his haunting screams continued. Don Alger had jumped in the aerial ladder truck and drove it across the lawn, and the firefighters extended the ladder to the window where LaGambino had been just moments before. But Patsy had disappeared back inside the fire. He was likely going to try to get out another way, but it was too late. It was just too late.

The men watched Patsy, helpless to save him, as the horrifying event unfolded before their eyes. The aerial truck arrived and the ladder was raised. The ladders were not in place in advance of LaGambino being trapped because they had been trying to work their way toward the fire from inside the building and had not yet been working it from outside. The third floor room was completely engulfed in flames. Once the men were able to enter the burning room, they were surrounded by flames. They had a 1 ½" attack line and fought to get into the room where LaGambino's body was found. He was located in the middle of the room. Patsy's body was brought out the window and carried down a ladder from the third floor. The devastated men realized what had just happened and collectively shrunk and felt the blow that the department had just been dealt. Lt. Schlegel collapsed to the ground, saying "We tried. God, we tried. We just couldn't get to him." One cannot imagine how a firefighter can continue the task of extinguishing a fire after the experience they had just encountered, but the job required that they finish. The residents of an adjacent house were evacuated as the heat and flames threatened the structure. Water was poured onto the fire that claimed one of their own. The roof was gone, flames having consumed it. The fire was all but out by 7am that morning.

Ray Walawender suffered a deep cut in his arm and underwent surgery to repair it at Auburn Memorial Hospital. Captain Bernard Searing was treated at Mercy Hospital for smoke inhalation he encountered while on the top of the aerial ladder trying to find LaGambino. Lt. Schlegel was treated at Auburn Memorial Hospital for arm and elbow injuries. Back at headquarters later that day, hardly a word was spoken. Boots and coats were lying on the floor. The firefighters sat in utter shock at the loss of Patrick LaGambino. When words were finally spoken, they centered around Patsy. The men spoke of LaGambino, still in disbelief that he was gone. Flags were flown at half-mast in Auburn in honor of Patrick LaGambino.

Patrick J. LaGambino was born in Auburn, NY September 9, 1931. He was a Marine veteran of the Korean War. He was married to Shirley (Robbins) LaGambino and together they had a son, John P. and a daughter, Theresa A. LaGambino. He was 41 at the time of his death. The family lived on Westwood Drive in Auburn. He became a firefighter in December of 1961, and had completed more than 11 years of service with the Auburn Fire Department. His funeral was held on May 15, 1973. He was buried with full military and Fire Department honors. Representatives from all over the state were present for the services. A 500-member honor guard was present for Patsy LaGambino. Firefighter LaGambino was borne on an Auburn Fire Department engine driven by Fireman Michael Harmon. Active bearers included Captain Charles Zambito, Leonard Bochenek, Charles Barrette, George Riley, Angelo Ruta and Robert Conner. The pumper truck carried LaGambino's casket from the Farrell Funeral Home on South Street to St. Mary's Church on Clark Street. Following services at the church, the flag-covered casket was carried atop the fire engine past Memorial City Hall. The Wheeler Bell tolled for Patrick J. LaGambino with the traditional 12 strikes for deceased veterans. It was also symbolic of his almost twelve years with the Auburn Fire Department. He was buried at St. Joseph' Cemetery.

Lt. Schlegel's actions that fateful day saved the lives of two firefighters, and yet he considered it as the day of his most haunting failure. In a newspaper interview in 1995, 22 years later, Schlegel remembered every moment of that day as if it were yesterday. He said he could still hear Patsy screaming to him "Don't leave me here, John. Don't leave me." Schlegel had tried desperately to save all three lives that night. He was nominated for and won the New York State Firefighter of the Year Award, but he did not initially accept it, citing that he had failed that night and wasn't deserving of it. He was urged to accept the award and reluctantly he did, stating "I don't really deserve this, but I accept it for the others who do." John Schlegel served 37 years with the Auburn Fire Department before his retirement as a Captain in 1994.

For those who were present the day that Patrick J. LaGambino died, it is a day that is forever etched into their memories. No loss of life is acceptable, but the loss of Patsy hit particularly hard. People on the ground below had to watch him struggle at that third floor window, the firemen unable to get to him. His retreat back into the room, never to be seen again did not seem possible, and yet it was. He was gone; but like the others before him, he is remembered and honored at annual memorial masses, anniversaries and in conversations among those who knew him. Even today, firefighters drive by the location of the fire, look up and remember their brother, Pat LaGambino.

September 13, 1973
Cayuga Museum Fire

The Cayuga Museum building was constructed as a family mansion in 1836, by John Seymour. Financial difficulties compelled him to sell the property. It was purchased by Erastus Case and ownership remained with various family members until Theodore Case built the larger Case Mansion on South Street. The Cayuga Museum of History and Art was opened in 1936. The museum displayed and accumulated many artifacts and historical items through the years. In the fall of 1973, the building was in need of exterior renovation. The brick facing was restored and the columns scraped and made ready to be refinished.

The upper portion of the building was in the process of being sandblasted and cleaned. A contractor and a crew of men had been working on the top of the building for almost eight weeks. Blow torches were used to remove paint from the façade on the front of the building. The contractor on the ground noticed a fire at the top of the building. He climbed the scaffold with intentions of putting the fire out, but quickly realized it was too much for him to handle. He descended and ran into the museum to alert those inside of the fire so they could evacuate. The fire started on the west side of the building in the attic area.

The fire alarm came in at 3:59pm from Box 24, across the street from the museum. Engines 3 and 4, along with Truck 1 were on the scene quickly. Seeing the smoke billowing out of the attic, Chief William Maywalt immediately ordered a second alarm. Engine 2 and additional firefighters arrived. The smoke could be seen from fire headquarters on Market Street. The fire was spreading through the attic area and was compromising the roof. The smoke continued to pour out at the men. Access to the attic was via a narrow winding stairway which could only fit one man at a time. The space was tight for a firefighter to navigate wearing full gear and carrying hose line. At 4:32pm, Chief Maywalt ordered a third alarm, which brought an additional engine and ladder truck to the museum blaze, along with all available firefighters. Assistant Chief George Bannon fought inside the museum with close to 30 men. A huge crowd gathered during the course of the fire; estimates put the number at 3,000. Auburn Police controlled the crowd and kept them back. Traffic was diverted from Genesee to Clark Street. Professor Walter Long, Curator of the museum, was on site during the blaze and lamented the sure loss of artifacts and collection items that would result. Long had spent many years of his life dedicated to collecting and preserving the items in the museum. Firefighters worked to cover artifacts and other valuables on the first and second floors, as well as fighting the fire inside. Almost all the tarpaulins in the Fire Department were used to try to protect items. The rest of the firemen were assigned to areas outside and around the building, as well as upstairs and into the attic to pour water on the blaze. Many of the men inside the building suffered from heat and smoke exposure while trying to protect the museum's precious objects. Jake Barrette and Chester Wiseman were two of the men working the outside of the building, streaming water to the attic window. Work continued and it was estimated that over 700,000 gallons of water were used to extinguish the fire during the nearly three-hour battle. Over 5,500 feet of hose lines were used to save the structure. The firemen were able to stop the fire before it consumed the entire interior on multiple floors. The roof was severely damaged as a result of the fire and the attic and its contents were just about gutted. The fire was declared to be under control at 6:30pm. As the men were picking up hose lines and clearing the area, they could not help but look across the street at the area where they had lost Patrick "Patsy" LaGambino just four months before. A crew remained at the museum all night to watch for and put out a number of hot spots that flared up.

While there were a number of items that were lost in the fire, an overwhelming amount of the museum's collections were not at all burned in the fire. There was water damage, as could be expected when a fire is in the attic, as gravity carries the water down. The firemen were commended for stopping the fire from consuming the entire building and protecting a large number of irreplaceable items in the process. The cause of the fire was determined to be workmen in the area using gas blow torches with liquid propane gas to remove paint from the exterior of the building, in the northwest corner. The fire started in the cornice of the building. The fire had a bit of a start before it was noticed. The community and a variety of historical societies immediately offered assistance in the cleanup, restoration and preservation efforts that were needed. The NYS Historian, Louis Tucker, reached out to offer any assistance needed, especially technical expertise in the processes to be used on water and smoke-damaged items. No time was wasted in finding temporary storage for items from the museum, and work immediately commenced on saving items. As usual, Auburn came together as a community during a time of crisis, and people contributed their knowledge, money and manpower toward the project.

October 10, 1974
Rondina Inc. Furniture Store Warehouse

The old Burtis Auditorium building on Water Street, then used as a furniture warehouse, would be reduced to a memory in 1974. The three-story brick building of the Rondina Furniture Store warehouse and several other businesses would be devastated by fire on the early morning hours of October 10, 1974. Auburn Police Officer Thomas Weed patrolled the area of the Rondina warehouse around 4:15am, during his routine patrol, and found no signs of trouble or fire. Auburn Police Officer John Malone smelled smoke in the area of Garden Street around 4:40am. Officer Leo Tortorici was detailed to investigate the source and discovered smoke filling the warehouse building. The first alarm came in at 4:42am and Engines 3 and 4 as well as Truck 2 responded to the scene with Assistant Chief Ralph Quill heading the firefighting operations. Thick black smoke was pouring out of the front of the building. A quick assessment of the situation resulted in Quill calling a second alarm at 4:57am and Engine 2 responded to the scene. Flames began breaking through the roof and boarded up windows. The thick smoke poured out of the front of the building and then turned to flames as the building on Water Street became engulfed. Fire apparatus had to be moved back toward State and Dill Streets. The heat from the warehouse caused a high temperature condition at the Rondina Store across the street. Windows became compromised and began to pop and shatter into pieces on the ground. Firefighters streamed water on the Rondina storefront to protect the building from further damage. The intense heat peeled paint away from the Rondina store and was blistering. The water helped to mitigate further damage. At 5:01am a third alarm was called. The fire had spread rapidly and within minutes had made its way through from the back of the building to the front and over to adjoining buildings. The two-story Fabric Center building was now in flames as well.

A fourth alarm was called at 5:10am. Every piece of Auburn Fire Department equipment and all manpower were being used to battle the blaze. A call was also made for mutual aid assistance from volunteer fire companies in the area; Owasco responded with two pumpers, Aurelius with two pumpers, Sennett with one pumper, Skaneateles with one aerial ladder truck and an emergency truck, Throop with one pumper, Weedsport with one pumper, Port Byron with one pumper and Jordan with one aerial ladder truck. Three other companies provided standby services for Auburn from their own stations. Fleming One moved to the Owasco One fire station and Fleming Two moved to Fleming One fire station. A massive assault of the flames took place.

There was concern about possible explosions from fuel tanks located behind the buildings. Crews worked to protect that area from flames and heat. The flames from the warehouse shot 100 feet in the air and could be seen for miles. Smoke flowed and chugged all around the buildings. The Fraternal Order of Eagles No. 96 and Onondaga Coach Corp., located on the ground floor of the warehouse building, were also under attack from the fire. Officers Leo Tortorici and Michael Vitale had earlier jumped into and moved buses to safety at a parking lot on Dill Street. In order to prevent the fire from spreading to the H. R. Wait warehouse adjacent to the Rondina warehouse, firemen poured a blanket of water on the building and roof of the Wait property. The flames continued to burn hot and strong in the Rondina warehouse building, and the walls began to buckle under the stress of the heat and flames. Bricks came falling down around the scene and smashed to the ground and burned white hot. Multiple small explosions were heard during the battle. The heat was so intense at the scene that two windshields on the ladder truck cracked and the directional signals blew out. A hose line sprayed the engine in order to prevent further damage. A west wind worked against the firemen as it facilitated the flames to jump from building to building. They worked diligently to thwart further spread of the fire.

By dawn the flames in the Rondina warehouse building were largely under control but the blaze in the Fabric Center continued and efforts were concentrated on that area for over an hour before they were able to quash the flames. The Rondina warehouse was a total loss, with only a group of twisted beams and portions of walls standing here and there. Charred wood and debris laid in a mass at the sight of the former Burtis Auditorium. Firemen continued to spray the area against hot spots. More than 150 firefighters had worked against the fire for hours. Estimates of the total damage sustained were approximately $750,000.

No lives were lost in the fire. The Rondina warehouse lost upholstered furniture, rolls of rugs, furniture and their administrative offices and laboratories of the Rondina Research and Development Corp. They also lost a new delivery truck that had been parked inside the building. The Fabric Center was gutted and destroyed. The Rondina Store and showroom across the street suffered mild to moderate damage. During the fire, Police Officer Thomas Weed assisted William Rondina to move an experimental car from the research area of the building before flames consumed it. The experimental car was used to demonstrate a new method of recapturing heat and increasing gas mileage with a new device. The car and device were saved and were estimated to be worth $60,000. Onondaga Coach bus depot suffered extensive damage. With the buses intact, they resumed service from the former gas station on the corner of Water and State Streets.

An investigation of the fire concluded that the blaze started in the rear of the building, adjacent to the boiler area. The area was used to house the delivery truck and functioned as a repair shop. There was no indication of a suspicious origin.

June 25, 1975
Taurus Chemical Company Fire

A three-alarm fire always presents great challenges to the firefighters who battle against it. The size of the blaze and the potential for it to spread and consume additional property is always a concern. Every fire has unique characteristics and this one was no exception. The nature and hazard of a fire involving chemicals is a particularly volatile and distinctive beast. This one would push the men to utter exhaustion and fight them with steady resolve.

The fire started in the warehouse of the Taurus Chemical Company on the corner of Canoga and Bradley Streets and was spotted simultaneously by both an Auburn Police officer and Edward Hockeborn, night shift foreman at the factory. Grafton Robinson, an employee at the factory, had been checking a vacuum gauge when the lights went out, and the room glowed red from the reflection of flames. He ran to the back of the building and alerted others to the fire. As he and the others in the area ran out, the roof was already falling and dropping to the ground in pieces behind them. The call to the Fire Department was received at 7:25pm on the evening of June 25, 1975. The flames were reported to have traveled from the front area of the plant, just behind the offices, up through the ceiling insulation. One worker indicated, "Sections of the insulation just began dropping in large chunks onto the plastics stored in bags." Engines 3 and 4 along with Truck 1 responded first to the scene. They could see the smoke as soon as they left the fire house. The whole structure was covered by flames. Upon seeing the nature of the blaze, Assistant Chief John Delaney requested that second and third alarms be called. Engine 2 responded to the

Jack Meehan, Buddy West, Tom Ward

scene. Additional firemen called in for the third alarm had to battle traffic to get to the site; word spread quickly and people were flocking to the fire in curiosity. Fire Chief William Maywalt arrived on the scene after the third alarm and immediately took charge of operations. The fire generated flames that could be seen for miles.

The smoke from the blaze was particularly thick and oddly colored. It rose hundreds of feet into the air. It filled the sky with ominous columns of inky smoke and curls and plumes of brown and yellow. The color and characteristics of the smoke were noted to be different than anything the firemen had experienced before. It was reported to be seen 15 miles away. Taurus Chemical President, Warren L. Vanderpool, indicated the unique-looking smoke was caused by the burning of barrels containing certain chemicals made with synthetic rubber. Vanderpool was at home when the fire broke out. He looked out his window and told newspaper reporters "I saw the color of that smoke and said to my foreman it could only be caused by a certain chemical made with synthetic rubber." Just after he spotted the smoke, he received a phone call informing him of the blaze. William Bisgrove, the plant manager, was at Vanderpool's home at the time of the blaze. They both rushed to the scene.

Firemen attacked the fire from all four sides of the building. Chemicals stored in large 55-gallon drums began expanding, sounding off and popping. They groaned and struggled to hold their contents. Unable to withstand the heat and flames any longer, the flammable liquids and other contents of the drums started to go off like cannons. The explosions of the compromised drums filled the evening with rounds of explosive resonance. It was feared that a larger tank on the northwest side of the building might cause an explosion, but thankfully it did not. There were so many hose lines used against the inferno that water pressure became an issue temporarily. Additional hose lines were run to hydrants on Frazee and Bradley Streets, and the pressure was restored. Spectators stood watching the fire. Onlookers continued to crowd the area and Police were called to assist in moving them back to safety. Traffic was blocked off. The main building was hosed down to protect it from becoming compromised. The fire was resisting extinguishing efforts. Two hours into the battle, the flames from the fire still rose above the walls of the building. The firestorm was persistent, but the firefighters pressed on and continued to douse the flames with thousands of gallons of water. They were determined to bring the inferno under control. The fire did not want to yield to the firefighters' efforts and continued to grow and spread and generated clouds of black and other colors of smoke that filled the sky and darkened the area. The harsh and acrid odors, searing heat and towering flames continued. The curiosity of onlookers turned to concern for their safety, as the odors and smoke began to infiltrate the area, and the crowds began to leave the scene of the fire.

As the blaze raged onward, the smell of chemicals became increasingly evident in the air. The flames began attacking drums of PVC (Polyvinyl Chloride) used for plastic pipes, and the thick, black smoke continued to billow up in great plumes. There was concern regarding the safety of the fumes. Newspaper reporters described the smoke as a "cumulous cloud machine"; such was the continuous nature of the coal black, brown and yellow smoke. Just before midnight, Chief Maywalt requested that residents on Canoga Street leave the area. The evacuation area was increased hours later. The fumes started spreading over a larger part of the city. Smoke was spotted as far away as Geneva and Aurora. The fumes were stated to be non-toxic, but were an irritant. Telephone calls poured into the Police and Fire Departments from concerned citizens. People heard orders to evacuate areas and panic began to set in. The evacuation included a ten block area surrounding the fire. George Underwood III, Director of the Office of Disaster Preparedness was at the scene and arranged to open the County Office Building to those who could not find housing. Thirty-five people took advantage of that availability. They were provided coffee and sleeping arrangements. The Salvation Army opened its facilities and took in twenty people. West Middle School was prepared to open, but was not required.

At 1:30am the smoke and fumes became so heavy that oxygen masks were requested for those on the scene. Police sent 14 masks, which were immediately put to use. The fumes seemed to permeate everything. Lieutenant William Jacobs approached Warren Vanderpool and indicated that the firefighters were picking up the smell of chlorine. Yellow smoke was seen below the clouds of black smoke. Vanderpool advised Lt. Jacobs to have the firefighters use respirators. Respirators were already in use by that time. Police ensured the crowds were removed from the immediate area. An estimated 200 onlookers had to be constantly reprimanded for moving too close to the conflagration. During the overnight hours the cooler air descended and the heavy mist and fumes fell closer to the ground. Firemen had been on the scene for hours and were exhausted, but they continued to pour water on the flames. Throughout the night the battle against the blaze continued, and by morning it was reduced to a smoldering mass, with only a charred shell of the office remaining. The Quonset hut type structure that held the main portion of the plastics was gone. A section of wall and supports was all that was spared. A crane was brought in to help remove debris. The firefighters stayed at the scene long into the evening of Thursday, June 26th.

Firefighter Michael Quill was injured when he lost his footing on an aerial ladder. He was taken to Auburn Memorial Hospital, treated and released. Captain Richard Walsh suffered from smoke inhalation and abdominal pain while attempting to clear an area to allow access by additional hose lines. He was taken to Mercy Hospital and admitted for treatment. Chief Maywalt suffered from smoke inhalation and was later taken to Auburn Memorial Hospital. Warren Vanderpool indicated that while the company was insured, he had lost all of his business records, inventory and financial records, as the flames engulfed and consumed the entire factory and office areas. The area had 55-gallon drums lying all around. Following the blaze, it was observed that much of the chrome finish on the fire apparatus was damaged as a result of a substance in the chemical fumes. Upon closer examination, several areas on the trucks were showing signs of paint damage and rust forming. Several police officers on the scene that night reported the "blue" finish on their service revolvers had come off. There were several reports of the paint on vehicles having melted away in spots.

Edward Hockeborn, the night shift foreman, was of the opinion that the fire could have started in a mixer in the mix room that ran off steam and gas with an electric motor. He also indicated that one of the barrels made a noise at about 4pm on the day of the fire and sounded like it contracted or expanded, which was an unusual event in the factory. In light of the events that played out, he thought maybe the barrel had become warm. William Bisgrove, Plant Manager, indicated that vinyl and polyvinyl chloride were stored in the plant. He stated the substances were not dangerous in the state they were in and that there was no danger if the chemicals were mixed with air. Bisgrove stated he was concerned about the almost 300,000 pounds of Acrylonitrile butadiene styrene (ABS) that was stored in one of the burning buildings. The material was volatile and could re-heat after the cooling effect of the water stopped.

On Saturday, June 28th, firemen were called back to the Taurus Chemical Company site when the area rekindled and ignited. Assistant Chief Ralph Quill responded with the men of Engine 2. The hot spots were doused. They planned to have the City move the material with a bulldozer so that they could douse any additional hot spots that remained.

The Taurus Chemical Company was incorporated in 1963, and began functioning as a business selling liquid plastics in 1966, at its original location at 9 Logan Street. It moved to the corner of Canoga and Bradley Streets, the location of the former Auburn Foundry, in 1968. Taurus Chemical was a producer of liquid plastics. The plant was expanded in 1973 with the addition of a 100' x 150' aluminum building. Their product line was diversified to include powdered plastics to its manufacturing program. The company employed 24 people at the time of the fire. After the 1975 fire, the Taurus Chemical plant moved to Frazee Street, to the concern and disappointment of the residents in the area who feared for their safety. The factory was not active after 1980, and the City foreclosed on the property in August of 1986. Residents in the area were concerned regarding the large amounts of chemicals in the factories in the area and urged city officials to ensure the progress of cleanup efforts for the abandoned buildings and the surrounding areas.

Because of the potential risk posed to human health and/or the environment due to contamination by one or more hazardous wastes, Taurus Chemical was investigated by the Environmental Protection Agency (EPA). A preliminary assessment and site inspection was conducted. The site was removed from the inventory of Superfund sites and archived in the No Further Remedial Action Planned (NFRAP) database. The archive status indicates that to the best of the EPA's knowledge, Superfund completed its assessment of the site and determined that no further steps would be taken to list that site on the National Priorities List (NPL). The 1975 fire destroyed the building on the site located at Canoga and Bradley Streets. At the time, it housed plastic resins and PVC. It was suspected that PCDD (polychlorinated dibenzo-p-dioxin) and PCDF (polychlorinated dibenzofuran) were formed during the fire. The presence of the compounds was unconfirmed according to the database report. The site was vacant for years. Sampling and investigations performed in 1985 and 1986 indicated that the details of the investigations were not available. Some excavation reportedly occurred and the materials were taken off-site. Given that contamination was not confirmed and neither of the suspect contaminants is water soluble and would not easily migrate off-site, Taurus Chemical was not considered to represent a significant threat to the environmental integrity of the property. It was confirmed that approximately 230,000 lbs. of plastics and PVC (polyvinyl chloride) were destroyed in the 1975 fire.

Almost 50 firemen were at the scene of the Taurus Chemical blaze; many developed cancer in subsequent years, and seven died within 15 years (six of them under the age of 60). There is no proven direct correlation between the fumes present at the fire and the deaths of the firefighters, but many venture to say that the fire and toxic nature of the fumes contributed to their premature deaths.

Bottom: 1991 Fire scene

Auburn Fire Department - Seneca Falls Fire

Top: Hoffmann Fire

Bottom: Fire Scene; Fire Scene; Max Coggeshell, Paul Darrow, Paul Tripicano, Paul Giovanetti

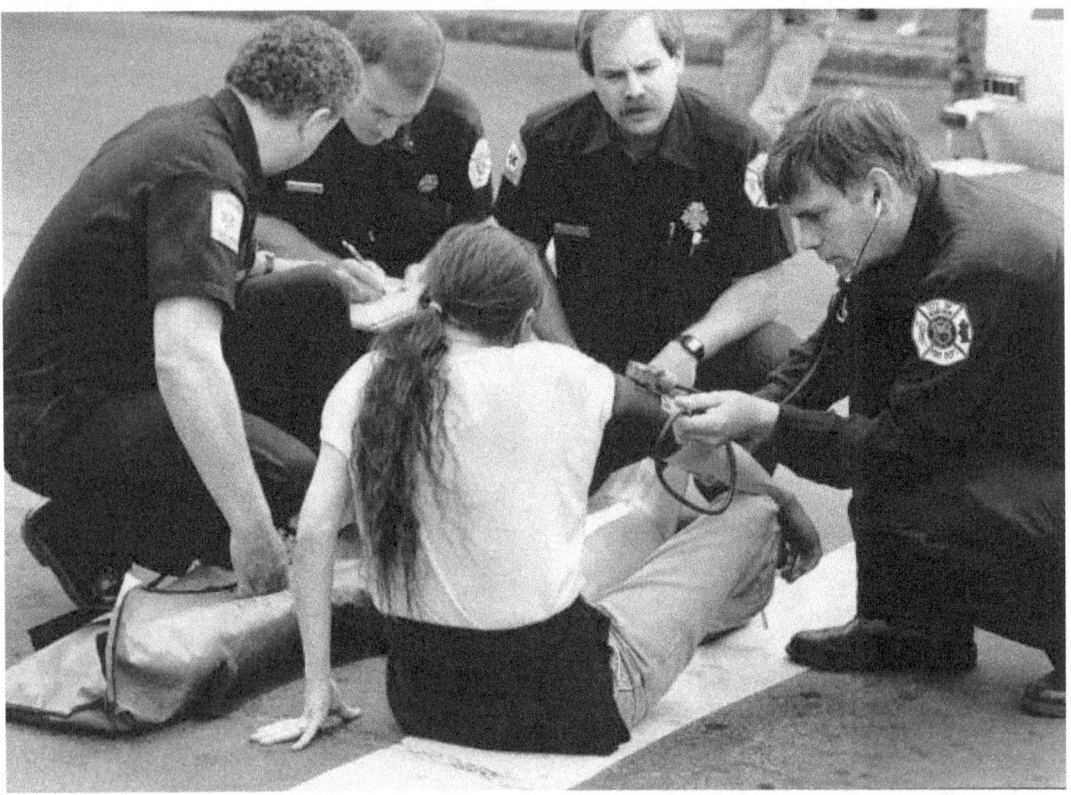

Bottom: Bill Weller, Dan Curry, Dave Radley, Ron Sroka

May 17, 1984
National Hotel Fire

On the night of Thursday, May 17, 1984, a call was received at the Cayuga County Fire Control dispatch center. The caller identified that the former National Hotel building was on fire, "It's on fire and it's really going!" The fire alarm came in at 11:18pm and Auburn Fire Department response was swift to the scene. The 179-year-old National Hotel building was a fixture in the downtown area. Just hours before the blaze, the site had been identified and plans were being finalized to renovate the building into a job training center for veterans. Upon arrival to the scene, flames were seen coming through the roof and the interior had fire throughout the second floor and was spreading fast. A second and third alarm were called due to the extent of the already-visible flames and the congested nature of the adjacent structures. East Genesee Street quickly became crowded with onlookers; everyone anxious to see the fate of the 1805 National Hotel building.

Forty-five Firefighters were on the scene. They attacked the blaze from varying vantage points to effect maximum exposure protection to the buildings on each side and to extinguish the fire. Firefighters found that the fire had worked its way into the attic of an adjacent building. They crawled into the attic to fight the flames that had spread to the area. Their quick actions in identifying and extinguishing the flames in the attic were critical to preventing what could have been an even larger and more devastating fire. The smoke was particularly thick and black due to the construction materials dating back more than a century. The heat generated from the fire was intense. Firefighters entered buildings on each side and led four families to safety from their apartments. The four-story red brick building was seething with flames and pillars of orange and red lit up the nighttime sky. Water was directed on the hotel by firefighters positioned on adjacent rooftops. The department's aerial ladder was used in the attack as well.

By 1:30am the fire was brought under control, and by 2:30am, it was out. Chief Maywalt credited his department members for doing a good job before it spread, and indicated it likely would have spread in both directions had it not been held in check. The roof and varying portions of the building had collapsed, leaving essentially a shell of a building remaining. The stability of the structure was evaluated and found to be unsafe. The front of the building had stress cracks and was susceptible to collapse. A crane was brought in to bring down what was left of the historic National Hotel. The fire was labeled suspicious by City fire investigators. Captain John Meehan and members of the Cause and Origin Team determined the fire had started on the west side of the second floor of a two-story addition on the back side of the former National Hotel building.

November 14, 1987

Ames

The fire that destroyed the Ames department store in Auburn on November 14, 1987, was the result of arson and caused nearly $3 million dollars in damages. Ames was an anchor store at the Auburn Plaza on Grant Avenue. No one was injured in the blaze, but the 64,000 square-foot store was leveled. A string of 17 suspected arson attempts of Ames chain stores occurred in New York and Pennsylvania beginning in November of 1987; Auburn Fire Captain John Meehan headed the multi-agency task force in the fire investigation. The Auburn Ames fire was discovered at 6pm on the night of November 14, 1987. The fire, later identified to have started in the curtain department, resulted in a large three-alarm fire that destroyed the building. The store did not have a sprinkler system. The building had been constructed during a time when sprinkler systems were not mandated and Ames did not install a system upon their occupancy in 1983, following the closing of the Barkers department store. Store employees attempted to put out the fire with hand-held extinguishers to no avail. Eight to ten employees and more than twenty-five customers were in the store at the time the fire was discovered. Everyone escaped without injury. Dozens of Auburn firefighters battled the blaze for more than two hours, working to extinguish the raging fire at Ames and to protect the adjacent stores. There were reports of the ammunition stock within the Ames sporting goods department exploding. The windows blew out of the building during the blaze, showering the front of the structure with glass and sparks. The flames were immense. Firefighters positioned on the roof felt it begin to rock and move. They repositioned and continued to attack the fire. Eventually, the roof and walls of Ames collapsed during the course of the fire.

Pick-a-Flick video store was saved by the skillful work of firefighters and a firewall that separated the two. The store had some water damage and ceiling panels that were damaged, but fared well overall in the incident. Central Tractor Farm and Family Center had nearly four feet of water in a basement storage area and some smoke damage, but was otherwise intact. Ames was rebuilt and remained in business until 2002, when it closed its doors after declaring bankruptcy.

March 15, 1991
Five Points Fire

The idea of someone setting a fire intentionally in a building is disturbing. Arson results in potential risk of harm to occupants, firefighters and onlookers. A fire on March 15, 1991, was investigated and officially determined to be just that; arson. The fire destroyed five local businesses, damaged others and left occupants of apartments without a place to live. It also claimed a stretch of long-standing structures in the city and the rich history that they held. The alarm was received by the Auburn Fire Department at 11:28pm on that Friday night in March of 1991, when someone driving by eyed flames in the back of the buildings. Fire personnel responded to the scene quickly. The area was being consumed by flames which could be seen large distances away from the historic Five Points location in Auburn, on Franklin and Lewis Streets. The flames quickly ate through the 100-year-old structures and reached high into the air. Smoke was pouring out of the buildings and flames took hold of an ever-increasing area. The upper stories of the buildings quickly became of greater concern, as there were initial reports of possible occupants within the apartments. Luckily, all were found to be accounted for. The four-alarm fire had all available firefighters at the scene, pouring water on the blaze and they worked to prevent the flames from spreading. Volunteer fire departments from around Cayuga County were brought in for standby services at the Auburn fire stations. As the firefighters battled the flames, windows cracked and exploded and glass tumbled down on them. The businesses directly impacted by the blaze included Legends Restaurant, Preston's Florist, Seal's Camera Center, Billy Martin's

Baseball Card Shop and Sunbrite Cleaners. The surrounding area was evacuated in order to secure the scene. Sparks and embers were all around and the heat was blistering.

Approximately ninety minutes into the fire, the upper story of the Legends building collapsed and sent bricks and debris crashing down. Within moments, another crash was heard, and sparks disbursed, as yet another layer crumbled. The top two stories of the building that housed Legends Restaurant were gone. The Legends Restaurant and Coffee Shop was filled with precious and irreplaceable memorabilia and photographs. Mary Ann Lattimore referred to Legends when she was quoted as saying, "It was a piece of everybody in Auburn." Ormie King and Bill Martin had opened Legends in 1988, a dream the two had since childhood. The collection of Auburn memorabilia was large and many Auburnians were featured in the photos and relics and had also contributed to the Legends collection. Sunbrite Cleaners was a family-owned business that opened in 1955. Bill Martin, a retired firefighter, also lost priceless pictures, portraits and baseball cards that were in his baseball card shop. Mayko Radio Specialists also suffered damage in the fire. Firefighters continued to stream water on the flames and protected the surrounding area from fire exposure. By 5am Saturday morning the fire was under control and work continued to extinguish hot spots. One firefighter sustained minor injuries. There were no other reported injuries.

City fire officials and a New York State Arson Bureau Investigator combed through the remains. An incendiary sniffing dog was brought in and identified a number of areas where flammable liquid remained. The fire was determined to have started on the second floor of 44 Lewis Street, above Legends Restaurant. It was ruled to be arson. Over the years there has been much speculation regarding the true origin of the fire; some believe it was accidentally started, while others believe it was arson.

October 28, 1993

H. R. Wait Co. Building

On the morning of October 28, 1993, the Auburn Fire Department was called to the former H. R. Wait Co. building. Fire Chief Frank Calarco had just finished getting his morning coffee at the Downtown Deli and was on his way out when he spotted a friend who looked worried and said that there was a fire. Upon walking out of the deli, Chief Calarco observed smoke billowing from the former H. R. Wait Co. building. It was Chief Calarco who called in the alarm to the Fire Department.

The four-story, 39,000-square-foot building had no electrical power or gas connected. The City had purchased the building earlier that year with an eye toward renovating it into a retail and residential complex. Firefighters responded quickly to the scene and worked on the fire from above using two aerial ladders, while others were positioned on adjacent rooftops and on the ground. The location of the fire downtown presented challenges due to the congested nature and age of the buildings in the area. They poured water down onto the building. The flames quickly spread to the second floor and were seen on the Genesee and Dill Street sides. Firefighters worked the front and rear of the fire. The firewalls within the building held and contained the flames to the former furniture company building. As the blaze raged within, the walls of the building became unstable and the threat of collapse seemed imminent. The smoke was thick and black and continuously poured out of the building. The flames made their way through the first and second floor and continued to attack the former furniture company location. It took firefighters just over 1½ hours to extinguish the flames.

Although there were no utility services in place within the building, there were reports of evidence of people inhabiting the building. Some speculated that the fire may have resulted from homeless people who may have been in the building. The loss of the historic H. R. Wait Co. building forever changed the downtown façade. Following the fire, the walls of the building were toppled in order to secure the location. The building remnants were completely removed in May of 1997. Lattimore Hall, a Cayuga Community College student housing facility was built on the site and opened in March of 1998.

December 19, 1993

Dunn & McCarthy

The Dunn and McCarthy Shoe factory's roots in Auburn dated back to 1866, when Dunn, Salmon & Co. manufactured shoes using convict labor in the Auburn Prison. In 1891, John Dunn Jr. and Charles McCarthy (Great-Grandfather of William Emerson) became partners and established the Dunn & McCarthy Company. The company manufactured women's shoes after the Auburn Prison contract system for utilizing prison labor for manufacturing was abolished by the State. The company site on Washington Street was previously used as a hame factory (manufacturing carriage/horse harness hardware), woolen mill, vinegar company and carpet factory. Dunn & McCarthy remodeled older buildings on the site and built additional buildings. The buildings were three and four stories high, some as long as 350 feet. The buildings were common mill-type construction. At its height, Dunn & McCarthy employed 2,000 people and made quality shoes that were in high demand. They were a leader in the shoe manufacturing industry. The company survived until 1990, when it was forced to shut its doors forever in Auburn after declaring bankruptcy. When the doors were closed in March of 1990, Dunn & McCarthy employed 250 people. The property was sold to a Charlottesville, Virginia company in 1991. The buildings comprised a large tract of land, extending from West Street to Washington Street to the Owasco River and Venice Street. The company was situated alongside railroad tracks and straddled the Owasco River with a raceway situated between two of its buildings. The old Dunn & McCarthy Company site would be the site of one of Auburn's largest and most spectacular fires on the evening of December 19, 1993.

At approximately 6:30pm the Auburn Fire Department was called to the former Dunn & McCarthy building complex on Washington Street. Three engine companies, one aerial ladder truck and a chief's car responded to the initial call. Heavy, black smoke was seen coming from the center building. Closer evaluation determined that the source of the fire was in the basement area of the building. The immediate assessment of the fire at the Dunn & McCarthy complex was identified as requiring additional alarms. A second alarm was immediately called and a third alarm followed on its heels. At the time of the first alarm, some off-duty firemen were already at headquarters for an EMT class. A second alarm unit was called to respond to a possible fire at Curtis Place. Upon arrival, it was determined to be smoke from the Dunn & McCarthy fire. Those present at headquarters assisted in making phone calls to all other off-duty Auburn Fire Department personnel. Auburn Fire Department officers, Cayuga County Director of Emergency Services and the Cayuga County Fire and EMS Coordinators worked together to notify and assign all responding mutual aid equipment into Auburn fire stations and the fire scene itself. Notifications were made to the City Manager, Water Treatment Plant, Auburn Memorial Hospital, Auburn Correctional Facility, Salvation Army, Red Cross, New York State Electric & Gas (NYSEG) and NY Telephone Company. Throughout the course of this event, eleven additional alarms were answered within the City of Auburn by the Mutual Aid fire companies. Inspection documents and Hazardous Material files were reviewed for information on potential issues in the area of the fire. By 7:30pm a fourth alarm had been called. The weather conditions and fierce nature of the fire resulted in a fifth alarm called within minutes.

The smoke from the fire could be seen for miles. The 5-alarm fire affected the three Dunn & McCarthy buildings on the West side and Mack Studios, Auburn Wire, Rood Utilities and others on the East side of Washington Street. Firefighters worked to aggressively attack the fires in the middle building of the Dunn & McCarthy complex. The fire was intense and spreading fast. The middle Dunn & McCarthy building had access limitations; the Owasco River ran on the south side and left only the north side as a means for extinguishing. Bolt cutters were used to get through a locked gate on the north side. Flames could already be seen in the center of the basement area and efforts were made to send attack lines of water into the basement windows at the flames that were visible to the firefighters. The situation continued to be assessed and it was discovered that the flames had, in fact, already fully involved the basement and were also affecting the south building of the complex as well. Fire from the middle building had blown over a wood crossover structure to the south building. Fire took hold and spread quickly within the south building. Flames had quickly covered the south building and were blowing out toward the Mack building. A defensive strategy was set up to protect the surrounding buildings. An aerial water tower was used to protect businesses on the other East side of Washington Street. A master-stream was placed in service to protect the Dunn & McCarthy building to the north. Engines were located on Venice Street at the northwest part of the complex to protect residential property in that area. In spite of efforts to protect the Dunn & McCarthy north building, it became involved with fire within 30 minutes. The flames covered a large area of land. As word spread throughout the city, onlookers flocked to see the immense walls of flames. Vertically and horizontally the fire was immense. The spectacular fire threatened many surrounding residences as well as the area immediately adjacent to the Auburn Correctional Facility.

As the fire continued to rise up and consume an ever-increasing area, concern for the Auburn Correctional Facility mounted. Prison guards in the towers became fire spotters and communicated to officials as they observed embers and fires landing on the rooftops of area buildings. Personnel in the prison hosed down the rooftops of the prison. The Auburn Prison fire trucks were activated for duty within the prison and were staged within the walls, poised to protect the institution. Communication between Auburn Fire Department and Auburn Correctional Facility officials was maintained. There was no loss of power to the facility.

The location of the fire was a nightmare for firefighters. The Owasco River flowed between two of the Dunn & McCarthy buildings and access was severely limited to the buildings that housed Rood Utilities, Auburn Wire and Mack Studios. The brisk West wind worked against them in preventing the spread of the fire across Washington Street. The intensity of the fire itself limited the available options for placement of equipment and staff. The railroad tracks ran parallel to the site. As if those impediments weren't enough, the area also had 37,000 volt power lines just north of the railroad tracks and running to the old power station at the Dunn & McCarthy complex. Each and every obstacle had to be considered when developing an ongoing and evolving plan of attack for this incident. As the flames continued to surge forward, each step the Fire Department took had to be quickly evaluated and reactions made in a safe and effective manner. Throughout the blaze that night, water availability and pressure plagued the scene. The methods and means used to battle the blaze were dependent on sufficient water supply; when the water supply for equipment in use was lacking, a backup means had to be implemented. A variety of nozzles, guns, hose lines, pumpers, portable ponds, hydrants and the Owasco River were utilized.

A fire engine had been stationed in front of the driveway and next to Mack Studio. The heat from the flames was so intense that the lens in the rear of the engine started to melt. The firefighters were severely impacted by the heat and flames, in spite of their being equipped in full turn-out gear. Embers and sparks were showering down on the firefighters and apparatus. It was no longer safe to remain in that location. The truck had to be moved or it would be lost in the flames. So intense was the heat, that one firefighter received blisters to the back of his legs in the process of lowering the tower of the engine in order to move the truck from its location. The fire engine was ultimately moved to the rear of the Mack building and the tower set up to protect businesses in the vicinity, including Auburn Wire, Auburn Leathercraft, Coffee Host and JLI Laboratories. Water was sprayed on the buildings in order to protect them from fire exposure. Firefighters were positioned on the roof of Auburn Wire as well as the JLI and Coffee Host building with hand lines in order to put out hot spots on the roof and provide additional water to the Mack building. The outside of the Leathercraft building was covered by the water tower on one of the fire engines. The Auburn Wire and the Mack buildings were almost abutted to each other. Firefighters were positioned inside Auburn Wire, at the rear, in order to prevent further spreading. A defense line was set up inside Auburn Wire, adjacent to the Mack building. Inside Auburn Wire, ceilings were pulled down and water poured in the area of the two adjacent buildings.

There was concern regarding a large, 2,500-gallon nitrogen tank on the scene. Calls had been made from headquarters to chemical experts and Auburn Wire Company representatives to determine the hazardous material potential at the location. Firefighters shut off the tank and positioned a hose line on it. Water supply continued to plague the firefighters, with a loss in pressure noted. A volunteer company pumper had mechanical difficulties and was forced to shut down. Headway made in battling the blaze was quickly affected by the loss in water supply and pressure. The water tower was temporarily shut down in order to continue effective use of the hand lines. The shutdown provided an increase in pressure for the hand lines. An urgent radio call was made to provide more water. The rear of the complex and the fire engine situated there were vulnerable. It was a precarious, but necessary, position for them to be in if they were to have any effect on the fire's rampage. The water situation resolved and another pumper was brought in to replace the failed pumper, and the water supply was sufficient to supply the tower on the fire engine once again.

Concurrent operations at the Dunn & McCarthy complex resulted in intense radiant heat and engines were forced to relocate to Rood Utilities to protect the building. The Rood building was able to be protected from exposure on the north side of the building. The back of Rood Utilities had limited access to the west side due to the Dunn & McCarthy buildings burning and collapsing, and there was almost no access to the south side due to the Owasco River and Mack Studios burning. The north and east sides, as well as the roof, were accessible and efforts were concentrated in those areas. Firemen entered Rood Utilities three times in an attempt to save the building. The windows and eaves of Rood Utilities caught fire. The heat radiating from Mack Studios was fierce and intense and was involving Rood Utilities with fire quickly. Water supply was an issue and extinguishing the flames and protecting the interior firefighters became too risky to continue. Fire officials could not continue to keep the firefighters inside the Rood Utilities building. Auburn Firefighters battling the flames around the Mack Building and Rood Utilities showed great resilience in their ability to hold their positions with walls coming down around them, smoke and embers and sparks flying everywhere, with intense heat and flames bearing down on them. All efforts and available resources were used to protect the building from the outside, but Rood Utilities ultimately was destroyed by fire spreading from the Mack Studios building fire.

Auburn Police Department officers were requested to videotape the scene as it unfolded. Fire officials requested copies and/or viewing of footage and photos taken by onlookers. A suspected incendiary device was recovered from the scene and detonated; officials indicated it was not a bomb. Local and State Fire officials investigated the fire, completing a door-to-door canvass of the neighborhood, collecting photos and videos taken of the fire and probing the origin of the fire. The city's water and sewer facilities chief indicated that firefighters used approximately three million gallons of water on the blaze, not counting water drafted from the Owasco outlet. Firefighters remained at the scene for three days. Seventeen pumpers, nine tankers and two trucks were involved in the attack. Many fire companies from surrounding areas responded to the blaze, including; Aurelius, Camillus, Cayuga, Elbridge, Fleming 1 and 2, Jordan, Long Hill, Marcellus, Montezuma, New Hope, Owasco, Port Byron, Scipio, Sempronius, Sennett, Skaneateles, Throop, Union Springs, Weedsport, West Niles.

Many people can still remember the scene, the news reports, videos and photos of the massive fire. In the end, the Dunn & McCarthy building complex was completely lost, along with Rood utilities and the Mack Studios building. Other businesses suffered varying degrees of loss and damage. The damage from the blaze was estimated at $8 million. No lives were lost as a result of the fire that night.

June 14, 1999
Masonic Temple Building

Auburn's Masonic Temple building is no stranger to fire. In 1932, a serious blaze destroyed five floors of the building and the Second Presbyterian Church next door (current home of the Schine Theater). The building, located in the heart of the downtown district, has seen businesses and organizations come and go over the years, as it has been a fixture in the city for decades. On June 14, 1999, the building would again be damaged by fire.

Sean McLeod, owner of the New York Institute of Dance and Education and the Kaleidoscope Dance Studio, on the third floor of the Masonic building, was ending his night. The dancers had been rehearsing for an upcoming performance at the end of the week and had gone home for the evening. McLeod was on his way out with his business manager, when he detected an odor and sounds reminiscent of a fire he had experienced at age eight. Instantly aware of a likely fire, McLeod alerted the Auburn Fire Department, even before he saw smoke or fire. His prompt actions probably saved the building from total destruction.

The Auburn Fire Department was called just before 10:30pm and responded quickly to the location with fourteen firefighters. An additional 30 off-duty firefighters were called in on second and third alarms. The streets immediately adjacent to the fire were closed to traffic. Many historic buildings line the area of South Street on which the Masonic Temple building resides. The Schine Theater, Swaby's Kangaroo Court and the Phoenix Building faced potential damage from fire exposure. The first floor of the Masonic building housed Byrn's Trophy and Sports and Dream Weaver Tattooing. The second floor was vacant but in the process of renovation for a future occupant. Upon arrival, firefighters found the structure involved in flames. A crew was assigned to the roof of the building in order to launch an exterior attack. Ladder trucks were used to get water on the third floor and roof of the building. The flames broke through the roof and the burning orange columns of fire and thick smoke poured out. Another crew provided an interior attack. Once inside, the firefighters worked their way to the third floor of the building and found a fury of flames. The fire was working inside the walls of the building, which had been constructed years ago with plaster and a wire mesh material in order to provide fire protection. The walls afforded some fire exposure protection, but also made them difficult to pull apart during the blaze. The Fire Department worked to extinguish the flames for over two and a half hours.

In the end they successfully quashed the blaze and prevented the fire from spreading to neighboring structures. During the course of the large fire, the roof of the Masonic building gave way and buckled. The third floor of the building suffered extensive damage as the ceiling had also collapsed. Fire Investigators concluded that the fire was accidental in nature, caused by an electrical short. The blaze originated in a crawl space between the ceiling of the third floor and the roof on the northwest side of the building. The flames then spread south along the exterior of the building. Early detection and notification, construction of the building itself and the skill and expertise of the responding firefighters resulted in the successful extinguishing of the fire. Firefighter actions also eliminated the threat faced by nearby historic buildings from fire exposure and spreading of flames.

March 29, 2001
Evans Street Home

This particular fire was referenced by more than one firefighter we interviewed, as one of their most memorable calls. It was not a fire as visually awe-inspiring as the Dunn & McCarthy fire, or as newsworthy as others in history; but the events that day could easily have proven fatal and must be noted here, as they are significant for what could have been.

During the overnight hours of March 29, 2001, Auburn Fire Department "D" Platoon received an alarm for an Evans Street home. Four college students occupied the two-story home and one of the occupants went upstairs to go to bed when he discovered black smoke coming from the bedroom. The other occupants of the home were alerted and the Fire Department was called. Within moments flames could be seen in the room. The all-too-familiar cause was an unattended candle.

As the first engine company arrived, the fire was blowing out from the second floor windows in the rear of the house. The Engine Company entered the home through the front door and advanced an attack line to the bedroom on the second floor to extinguish what seemed like a typical fire. As other crews arrived, they prepared to battle as trained. The second engine caught a hydrant to establish a water supply and was starting to pull a second line to back up the crews inside. The third engine was the Rapid Intervention Team (RIT). They set up outside with equipment in case there was trouble. The function of the RIT team is to stand by at the scene of structure fires with specialized equipment to ensure that firefighters operating in hazardous environments will have assistance should they become trapped, lost or incapacitated in some way. Truck Company prepared to ventilate, placed ladders and set up a fan.

The fire continued to roar and the flames were hot and strong, yet the building showed no signs of instability. Unknown to the crews fighting the fire at the time, the home had a previous fire in the same area; the attic and roof were already severely weakened. Just ten minutes after crews had arrived, and with no warning signs, the roof of the 4800 sq. ft. home became unstable and collapsed in a split second. It was surreal, and another example of how atypical every fire has the potential to be. The status of all firefighters inside and out was not immediately known, and for several moments, fire officials waited to receive word as to whether everyone got out and was safe.

In the initial moments following the crash, three firefighters were not seen and their disposition was not known. They were known to have been in the house, on the second floor, during the collapse. In those seconds following the collapse, the world stood still. Firefighters in the area held their breaths and were aghast at the possibility that they had just lost lives in the collapse. What must have seemed like an endless amount of time passed, when out of the smoke walked the three, previously unaccounted for, firefighters. One of the firefighters working the fire that night described it akin to a scene from the Bible, Daniel 3:23-27, in which Shadrach, Meshach and Abednego ultimately walked out of a fiery furnace completely intact. The three firefighters were unhurt and walked through the thick, dense smoke to join the others. There was a deep sigh of relief from everyone. Operations quickly changed from an interior attack to a defensive exterior attack and work continued to extinguish the blaze. Within several hours they had it completely out. There were no reported injuries in the fire. The structure was deemed unsafe and was immediately razed to protect the public.

February 24, 2014
Tinkers

On the morning of February 24, 2014, the Tinkers Guild bar and restaurant on Franklin Street would succumb to fire. That Monday morning started like any other in Central New York. People were traveling to work, appointments and running errands around town. The smoke that trailed out of Tinkers initially was either not noticed or did not alarm those passing by. Perhaps those that may have seen the beginning signs thought it had already been called into the Fire Department. Perhaps the building structure kept its flames hidden until they forced their way through. The Fire Department was called to Tinkers at 9:38am. The fire was already well underway.

There was concern voiced by onlookers regarding the availability of water due to the water main replacement project that was occurring on Franklin Street. However, a 10-inch main was available for use while the 30-inch main was being replaced. As with all projects involving water mains, the Fire Department had made plans in advance for any fire in the area affecting the water main replacement. In addition to the 10-inch water main, water tanker trucks could be called in from area municipalities to supply water. The water main work did not impede the department's ability to put the fire out.

Upon arrival, firefighters saw smoke and flames coming from every side of the large, three-story building. They entered the structure to extinguish the blaze but discovered that the fire had advanced to a level where it was no longer safe for an interior attack. The cold weather, snow in the air and wind conditions that included 30mph gusts, worked against the Fire Department in their attempts to contain and extinguish the legendary bar.

News of the fire spread almost as quickly as the fire itself and within minutes there were videos and photos posted to social media sites and other online forums. People recalled their happy times and memories made at Tinkers, expressed great sadness at the fire which was consuming an establishment held in the hearts of many Auburnians, and expressed hopes for the firefighters' safety in battling the blaze and in the ability of the owners to bring Tinkers back.

The flames grew and the building had fire extending out and reaching toward the power lines. Once NYSEG de-energized the power lines, the Auburn Fire Department was able to maintain a steady water supply on Tinkers. The building was old and of wood-frame, balloon construction. Balloon framing is a style of building that uses long, vertical 2" x 4"s for the exterior walls. The long wood studs extend uninterrupted, from the foundation all the way up to the roof. A huge drawback for this type of construction is the fire hazard potential. In the event of a fire, wall cavities extending from the foundation to the roof structure can be an open path for it to spread quickly.

The Auburn landmark was going up in flames and the surrounding areas were in jeopardy. The 3-alarm fire required: a well-coordinated operation that utilized firefighters and an exterior plan of attack against the flames that were raging through Tinkers, a plan to reduce the fire spreading to nearby areas by exposure, and protection of those who flocked to the area to see the scene. Tinkers was ultimately a total loss due to the head start that the fire had before it was discovered, but no lives were lost and there were no reported injuries resulting from the morning blaze.

The infamous Tinkers Ram sign was salvaged from the debris at the owner's request. When the fire was out, the shell of the building was all that remained. The portions of the building that remained were perilously teetering without much stability. The decision was made Monday afternoon to tear down the remaining structure in order to make the site safe and eliminate undue risk associated with leaving the unstable structure standing. Crews were brought in to bring down what was left. Auburn had lost a business that many felt an emotional connection to, but Tinkers would eventually return. Tinkers was rebuilt and opened in February of 2015. It has resumed its spot in the hearts of many. While the business looks vastly different than the original structure, the familiar Tinkers Ram sign hangs to greet all those who enter and serves as a reminder to long-time patrons of the memories made at Tinkers in the past.

CHARITABLE AND COMMUNITY-ORIENTED ACTIVITIES

Top: Packing food for needy,
L to R: Andy Guter, Jake Barrett, Dick Walsh, John Burger, George McCarthy & Pepper
Bottom: Bagging coal at the Police garage during World War II

The Auburn Fire Department members are involved in many community-based events and charitable organizations. To attempt to name them all would be futile, for their giving nature goes beyond anything that can be captured comprehensively.

For more than 60 years the Auburn Fire Department has raised funds for the Muscular Dystrophy Association (MDA). In the early 1950s, the International Association of Fire Fighters (IAFF) became one of several important sponsors and long-standing allies of MDA. Firefighters were part of the grassroots of the organization's donation collection efforts. They participated in nationwide door-to-door campaigns, and ran "fill the boot" drives to collect money for MDA. Firemen worked on their own time to collect for MDA. Spare fire engines were made available to the firefighters for their collection routes. They stopped only at houses with porch lights on, which indicated a contribution was available. They sounded the sirens and rang the bells on the fire trucks along the way. The Auburn Fire Fighters Association had a primary role in the local MDA telethon phone banks for more than 25 years. Firefighters Pat DiNonno, Paul Giovanetti and Bob DeChick served as Chairmen of the local MDA Committee. The MDA held a special place in the hearts of the firefighters and they donated much of their own time to the cause. During the Labor Day telethons, Auburn firefighters were among those who volunteered their time answering phones and taking pledges. Support of MDA was truly a task undertaken by every member of the Auburn Fire Department; each member playing an active role and contributing to the cause. Auburn Firefighter, Henry "Buddy" West, represented the Auburn Fire Department at one of the MDA National Telethons in Las Vegas, Nevada and was able to meet and present a check directly to the show's founder and host, Jerry Lewis.

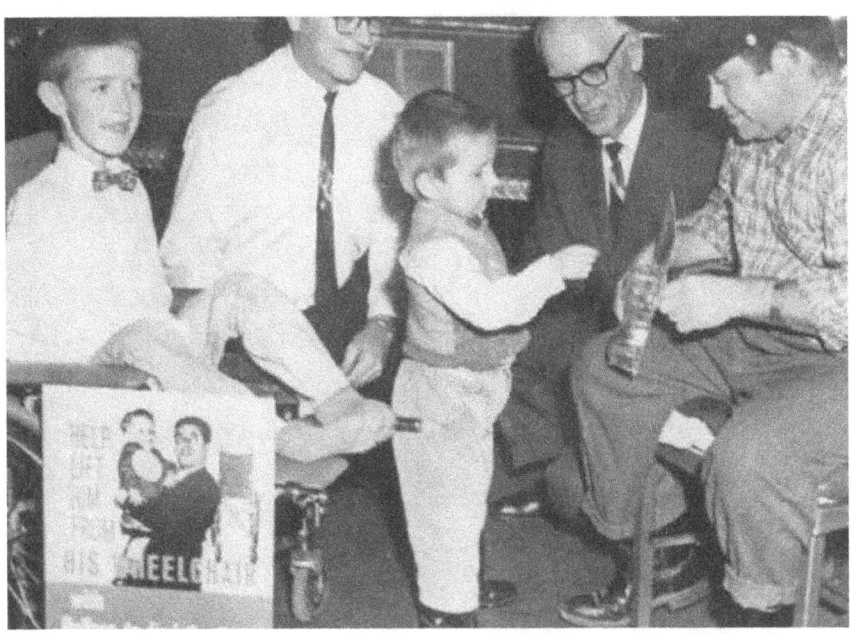

In 1977, the first Sports Weekend event was held to benefit MDA. William "Billy" Martin, Bernard "Bernie" Simmons and Henry "Buddy" West were instrumental in the creation and development of the annual Sports Weekend events held each year to raise money for MDA. The first Home Run Derby was held at Casey Park, and participants tried to hit a softball over a snow fence 225 feet away. The Auburn Linemen's Association joined the Fire Fighters in 1978. The event became an all-day affair and included raffles and a variety of games. The Home Run Derby would later move to Falcon Park and Miller Brewing Company and other associations and companies joined the Auburn Fire Fighters over the following years. The firefighters were directly and actively involved in support of the Sports Weekend events, volunteering their time and skills. Sports Weekend included softball tournaments, home run derbies, bike races, bocce, volleyball, horseshoes and many other sports competitions. They arranged to have well-known sports stars present at the events. The benefit softball games were wildly popular and attended by many. Some of the match-ups included the City vs. County workers, Ancient Order of Hibernians (A.O.H.)

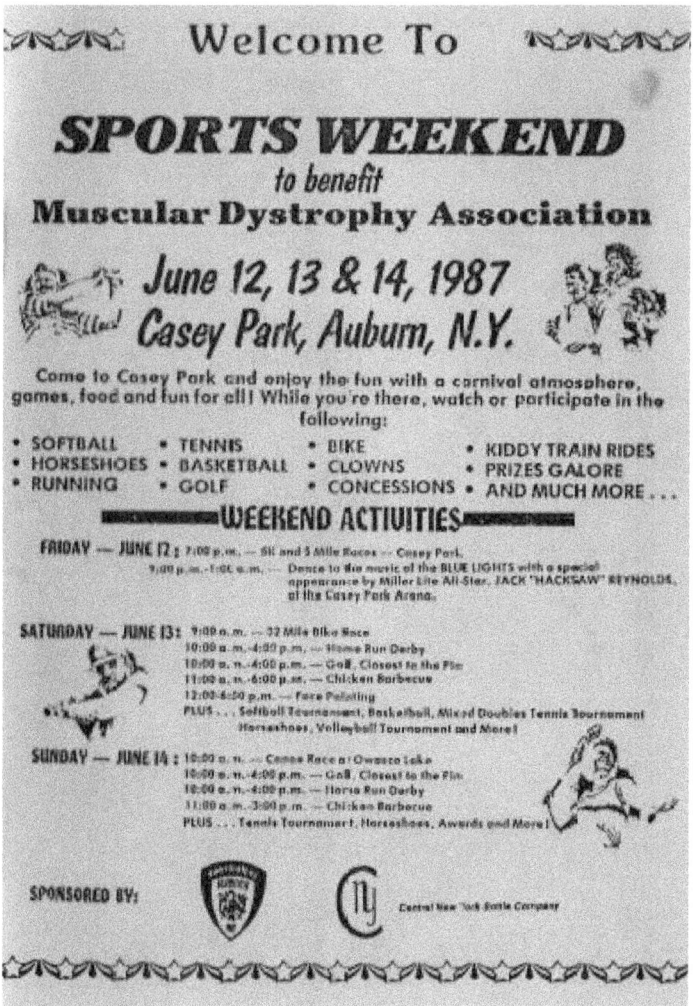

vs. Knights of Columbus (K of C), Goblet vs. Curley's, etc. Popular musicians and bands played at the event over the years as well. The all-in-fun rivalries were enjoyed by the players, and spectators always had a good time. Throughout the years, Bill Martin continued to be the driving force for the MDA Sports Weekends and Home Run Derby events. He and his committee members, along with a host of sponsors, made the Sports Weekends a rousing success. By 1991, the Sports Weekends alone had raised close to $100,000 for MDA.

Assistant Fire Chief Pat DiNonno served as a member of the Executive Committee of the Central-Northern Chapter of the Muscular Dystrophy Association, as well as the local Labor Day Telethon Committee. His involvement with MDA began while he was in still in high school and his dedication and support of MDA continues even today. The IAFF membership passed a resolution to support MDA's fight against muscular dystrophy until treatments and cures are found. To this day, IAFF continues its tradition as the No. 1 fundraising organization for MDA.

Beginning in 1944, and continuing for decades, the Auburn Fire Department held an annual "Firemen's Ball" to raise money for the vast array of charity work that the department was involved in. The Ball began as a Halloween event and was later held to open the

Photo courtesy of Anita Luisi Colvin

fall and winter social season in October or November. The first Firemen's Ball in 1944 was attended by more than 200 people. The gala event was open to the public and the firefighters would go about town selling tickets to the event, which were generally $1 each in later years. Area merchants also sold tickets to the event. Firefighters were on the rolls of the Ball Committees and worked to ensure the event maximized attendance and guaranteed a quality dance. The Firemen's Balls were enthusiastically supported and very popular in town. Everyone looked forward to the annual event. The Ball was held at the Osborne Hotel and the Auburn Inn. Balloons, paper hats, noise makers, lights and merriment ensured a good time was had by all in attendance. Over the years, music was provided by such greats as the Joe Cappiello Orchestra and the Soft Tones, the Bob Poyk Trio, "Dutch" Connors and His Orchestra, Hal Baker and His Orchestra, the Sox Tiffault Orchestra, Joe Manzone (Auburn's King of Swing) and His 11-Piece Orchestra, Peter Manzone (Joseph Manzone's son), Herbie LaHood and the Prison City Five/Firemen Five, Jane Tenity, Bill Bates, Joe Camardo's Orchestra, the Cayugans and the Blue Lights. Hundreds of people would attend the Firemen's Ball year after year and great memories were made, as the Auburn Fire Department raised funds to support their charitable activities.

The Auburn Fire Department has also been an active supporter of the American Heart Association, holding pasta dinners, annual chicken barbeques and other events in support of the group. The Auburn Fire Department was also a checkpoint in the American Heart Association's 200-mile bike-a-thon in 1975.The firefighters' "Pink Outside the Box" campaign has raised money for the Carol M. Baldwin Breast Cancer Research Fund of Central New York. The Auburn Fire Department's St. Baldrick's Foundation team includes firefighters, their families and friends annually, and is a top fundraising team for childhood cancer research. The Auburn Fire Department also raised funds for the 'Big Brother Fund'.

For years the firefighters made annual presentations of gifts to the residents of the County Home. They collected and purchased small gifts for the elderly in need; things such as

Photo courtesy of William Martin

candy, oranges, nuts, socks, gloves and small gifts. In the 1930s and 1940s, they collected donated toys that were in need of repair. They worked on them and fixed them to "like new" condition and distributed them to children in the community. Firefighters spearheaded the toy campaign, but many community members and businesses supported the annual event. The Meaker Co. store, Herbert Bros., Rondinas, Sears Roebuck, Hislop's, Auburn Tobacco Co., the Liberty Store, Knox & Knox and many more, either contributed toys, materials, packing boxes or services to restoring toys so that they could be given to the children. Firemen worked tirelessly on their own time to make it a success. In 1939 alone, there were more than 4,650 toys collected, repaired and distributed to more than 300 families! Over the years, thousands and thousands of Auburn children had their holiday season made special through the efforts of the firefighters, and the community at large.

During the Halloween season, the Auburn Fire Department had area children stop by the fire stations and sign Halloween Good Behavior Pledges. They are actively involved in Fire Prevention Week activities, area school educational programs, essay contests and much more. The Auburn Fire Department is comprised of a large group of giving individuals who act, both alone and in formalized groups, in support of a variety of charitable organizations and causes in the community.

FIREFIGHTER STORIES

Top: Asst. Chief Scott DeJoy
Bottom: Engine 2: Dick Walsh, Frank DeJoy, Buddy West

Top: Standing: Paul Darrow, Gil Cullen;
Sitting L to R: Frank Hawelka, Capt. Ed Lyons, Lt. Michael Mansfield
Bottom: 1958; Adam Spicer, Paul Darrow, Pepper, Dick Walsh

Top: Foreman, Hose Company 4
Bottom: Bill Lee, Tim Pelton, Ed Bilinski, Francis Dean

The Auburn Fire Department is one team made up of many unique individuals. Each one has their own story. Through the years there have been many firefighters who came with notable stories or who created memories and sparked conversations during their service years within the department. It is difficult to separate the "average" firefighter from the field, for their bravery and courage in the face of fire certainly merits each one a place in this book. Time and space do not allow us to write about every firefighter and we were forced to narrow the field. It was not an easy task, as the stories that are out there are numerous. What follows are those that stand out for a variety of reasons. We hope that these recollections spark other memories in the community and cause remembrance of those who came before us and of those currently in the Auburn Fire Department.

Clarence Q. Day: Proposer, 1872 Firemen's Convention

Only known photo of Clarence Day

While there is no formally documented confirmation of the individual who originally proposed the event in Auburn that led to the founding of the Firemen's Association of the State of New York (FASNY), many newspapers of the day reported Clarence Q. Day as being that individual. Whether it is fact or not will likely never be proven definitively, but suffice it to say, there were a large number of local people who accepted Day as the man who proposed the initial gathering in Auburn.

Clarence Q. Day was born in 1849. At the age of 16, Clarence secured a position as a torch boy for the old Hook & Ladder Company while he was still in school. Day was a schoolmate of Eddie Jewhurst, being just a few years older than he. As a torch boy, Clarence was able to run out of school any time the alarm sounded. Clarence Day was a good athlete and a particularly good baseball player. As a fireman, he distinguished himself with the Hook & Ladder Company as being one of the most daring and efficient men in the volunteer service. In 1869, Clarence Day suffered an accident and shortly thereafter incurred a severe bout of scarlet fever that destroyed his ability to continue work as a fireman. He was left paralyzed and confined to a wheelchair. He left the Fire Department and was not pensioned. In subsequent years, it was debated that Mr. Day had been injured on the job and that his disability should have resulted in receipt of a pension.

In April of 1870, Clarence received one of Smith's patented invalid chairs from Silas L. Bradley, Esq. The invalid chair allowed him to move around more easily and was much appreciated by Mr. Day.

In 1874, Chief Engineer George Battams was honored with a gathering and presentation

Clarence Q. Day, 1879 Exempt Fireman Certificate signed by Mayor D. M. Osborne and Secretary S. L. Paddock

of gifts at the conclusion of his service with the Fire Department. He received a silver water set with ice pitcher, goblets, salver and slop bowl, artistically engraved by Herbert D. Clough. A testimonial from friends accompanied the silver set. Clarence Q. Day had selected the set and was among those who contributed to the purchase. The silver was on display in the jewelry store of Haight & Wyer.

In 1877, Mr. George W. Perry presented Clarence Day with a new and elegant perambulator. The device was a miniature carriage that had springs and running gear. The body was handsomely finished and was monogrammed with a "D" on each side. The seat was upholstered. The perambulator was painted by Mr. George F. Wills, of the Wills & Horne Co., premier carriage manufacturer and painting company. Wills & Horne Co. made many of the apparatus pieces used by the Auburn Fire Companies over the years. The new wheelchair-like device was an artistic piece of work and a great improvement over the one that had been in use.

The Auburn volunteer firemen elected Clarence Day secretary of the department, and he was able to continue to participate in Fire Department activities. It was reported many times in newspapers that upon observing a fraternal convention parade in Auburn in the early 1870s, Clarence Q. Day remarked to several friends, "Why don't we organize a National Volunteer Firemen's Association and have our own conventions?" As secretary of the local volunteer fire department, he was a correspondent for the New York Mercury, a paper that devoted a special column to fire department news. In the column of that newspaper, he incorporated information regarding the idea of a firemen's convention and received many positive responses. The Fire Department formed a series of committees with membership to organize a convention, which was held in October of 1872. The Firemen's Association of the State of New York (FASNY) was rooted in that convention of 1872. Clarence Day was elected the first Secretary of the State organization and would remain in that position for almost two years. His inability to travel forced him to resign. He was able to retain his position as secretary of the Auburn Volunteer Fire Department until it was disbanded in 1894.

In March of 1881, the Hook and Ladder Company assembled in special session. Foreman Selover spoke of Henry Race in suitable remarks and presented Mr. Race with a rubber overcoat. Clarence Day sat to the side and took notes of the presentation that was made, no doubt he also reflected on the clever surprise Mr. Race had experienced. Foreman Selover's attention then turned to Day, and he gave a speech that acknowledged Clarence's efficiency and skill. Clarence Day was presented with an elegant gold badge. The badge was suspended from a gold bar, on which was inscribed "Logan Hook and Ladder". In the center of the badge was the monogram "A. F. D." and "Presented to C. Q. Day, Sec't. and Treas." and underneath read, "By members of his company, Auburn, March 18,

1881." The badge had been made by Alderman Bundy and the engraving was completed by Woodruff. Mr. Day was astonished at the present and responded, "You've got me!" and thanked the group for the gift. The special meeting concluded and adjourned. A group that had gathered for the special presentations to Race and Day remained, and there was music, dancing and food to celebrate the night.

Clarence Day opened a newspaper and cigar stand in Pomroy and Billiard's Restaurant in Auburn. He was forced to close when his disability interfered with his ability to run his business. Officers of the State Volunteer Firemen's Home at Hudson offered Clarence residence in the home, but he declined, preferring to remain in Auburn. Auburn residents were always supportive of Mr. Day. In 1873, the fire companies held a concert and hop at Tallman's Hall to benefit Clarence. Neighbors secured a phone that was installed near his bed so he could call for assistance when needed. Clarence Day became Clerk of the Board of Excise in 1876. In 1896, NYS Governor Morton signed the Raines Bill into Law, which among other things, abolished local Excise Boards and placed Excise Law under the jurisdiction of New York State. Clarence Day lost his job as Clerk of the local Excise Board.

Mr. Day spent summers at a little camp he leased on the shores of Owasco Lake at Long Point and would return to his home when the cold weather set in. He received $10 a month, $5 of which was needed for rent. During the 38th FASNY Convention, held in Watertown in 1910, it was decided that Clarence Day would be honored by the group monetarily. President Kyne addressed those gathered at the convention and spoke of Mr. Day, the first Secretary of FASNY and one of the oldest members of the group. A collection was taken up from individual delegates and $50 was presented to their friend, Clarence, as a token of their esteem.

It was reported that a February 1902 issue of the "Fireman's Herald" included a photo of Clarence Day along with an article that credited him with significant contribution to the formation of the New York State Fireman's Association. Clarence Q. Day wrote a column in the Auburn Weekly Bulletin in the early 1900s that listed facts and interesting events of the "olden days". It became a written record of many historical Auburn facts and events that may have otherwise been lost over time.

On September 10, 1912, Mrs. George Johnson, a neighbor, had prepared an evening meal for Clarence. Albert Chapin went to Day's home on Bradford Street to deliver the meal and found him dead in his wheelchair. He had been ill for several weeks prior to his death. Dr. Hyatt had already been on his way to Mr. Day's home for a regular visit when he was told of his death. Heart trouble had suddenly ended the life of the firemen's friend. Clarence Day lived alone and had no discernable near relatives. Funeral arrangements were delayed while efforts were made to locate distant relatives of Mr. Day. The Auburn Exempt Firemen's Association met on September 12, 1912, and appointed a committee to try and locate Day's relatives. He was buried in Fort Hill cemetery.

Following Clarence Day's death, a book containing the records of the Auburn Fire Department was turned over to Chief Jewhurst. Mr. Day's book contained a list of the charter members of the Auburn Exempt volunteer company. He had documented many fires and details of the Auburn Fire Department. He was a statistician of sorts for the Fire Department and his documentation ensured the rich history of the Auburn Fire Department would be available for generations to come.

Patrick F. Morrissey – Firefighter and Inventor

Patrick F. "Patty" Morrissey was a long-time fireman who began his firefighting career during the infancy of the Auburn Fire Department. By all accounts, Patty Morrissey was quite the character. An accomplished and brave firefighter and inventor, he also had a past that included a bit of trouble with the law. Patrick F. Morrissey was born in November of 1861, in Charleston, South Carolina, the same year Abraham Lincoln was sworn in as President of the United States, and the nation was in the midst of a Civil War. By the 1870's Patrick Morrissey was living in Auburn, NY. Patty Morrissey joined the volunteer Active Hose Company No. 7 in 1883. In 1885 he became assistant foreman of the company, and in 1886 he was promoted to foreman.

Patrick F. Morrissey

Patrick Morrissey ran into a bit of trouble with the law during 1896. On March 22, in self-defense, Morrissey shot his brother-in-law, James Bowe. Morrissey was employed as a night engineer at the prison and was on his way to his Underwood Street home on the evening of the incident. As he passed in front of the house of Mr. Daniel Larkin, of 5 Underwood Street, Morrissey's brother-in-law came out of Larkin's house. There was some bad blood noted between the two in the past. Morrissey and Bowe had married sisters, and Bowe and his wife had divorced under circumstances that included allegations of abuse and adultery from both sides. Bowe and Morrissey were about to pass each other on the street, when Bowe was reported to have grabbed Morrissey by the collar. After yelling and swearing at him, Bowe hit Morrissey in the head. A scuffle ensued, and Morrissey ended up on the ground with Bowe on top of him. Morrissey reached for and found his revolver and he shot twice; one shot hit Bowe above the left hip and the other in the torso area. Mr. Larkin, roused by the exchange, went outside and saw Bowe on top of Morrissey and the gun in Morrissey's hand. Morrissey gave himself up to police immediately following the event. Bowe had trouble with the law in the past and was on a $100 bond to keep the peace. Many felt that Bowe had been lying in wait for Patrick Morrissey and was looking for trouble. Bowe was taken for medical attention and it was thought that he might recover. However, at approximately 2am on the early morning of March 24, 1896, Bowe succumbed to peritonitis. It was found that one of the bullets had penetrated his intestine. Morrissey, who had been released on $5,000 bail, was arrested and jailed upon Bowe's death. Recorder Clark had managed to interview Bowe prior to his death and the story he told was materially different from that of Patrick Morrissey. Morrissey had taken care of his wife's sister (Bowe's wife) and her four children. Bowe was known to have threatened Morrissey in the past and had, just the week prior to the incident, lodged a threat to kill Morrissey someday. Morrissey was married with six children of his own at the time, ranging in age from 9 years to two weeks old. An autopsy was completed and the bullet was found in the muscles of the victim's back. The bullet was surmised to have entered from the front above the eighth rib on the left side and pursued a downward direction toward the center, through the transverse and descending colon, had pierced the intestine, traveled through the kidneys and lodged in the back. A Coroner's Jury ruled on April 8, 1898, that the death of Bowe was justifiable homicide by Patrick Morrissey.

On April 14, 1898, Patrick F. Morrissey was appointed as a callman with the permanent Auburn Fire Department with Hose Company No. 3. Patty Morrissey was partially disabled at the time he joined the Fire Department. A railway accident had claimed part of his foot, and he had only partial use of one hand. At the time of his appointment in the department, his disability came to light and was questioned. Morrissey was known by Chief Jewhurst and the Commissioners, and it was remarked that "he didn't limp very bad." Morrissey subsequently received the position. In April of 1899, he was promoted to a full-time firefighter position with the Chemical Company. Patrick Morrissey also enjoyed what little free time he had away from the station. He played baseball on the "Green Stockings" team in Auburn; he played third base and was a pinch hitter. During March 1901 he was transferred to Hose Company No. 3. A Civil Service examination was given on December 12, 1902, for the position of engineer of the steam fire engine that had been donated to the City of Auburn by the D. M. Osborne & Co. Patrick Morrissey was the only applicant for the test. He passed the test and was promoted to Captain of Hose Company No. 5 on December 18, 1902.

Throughout 1912, Captain Morrissey gave many exhibitions using his patented fire escape life belt. On one such occasion he scaled a five-story building in the Cady block of Auburn and amazed a large number of onlookers as he easily descended using his patented device. To further illustrate the safety and ease of its use, Morrissey "rescued" two Auburn youths, Joe Kinsella and Charles Smith, multiple times and in multiple ways from the top of the building. In November of 1918, Captain Morrissey transferred to Hose Company No.

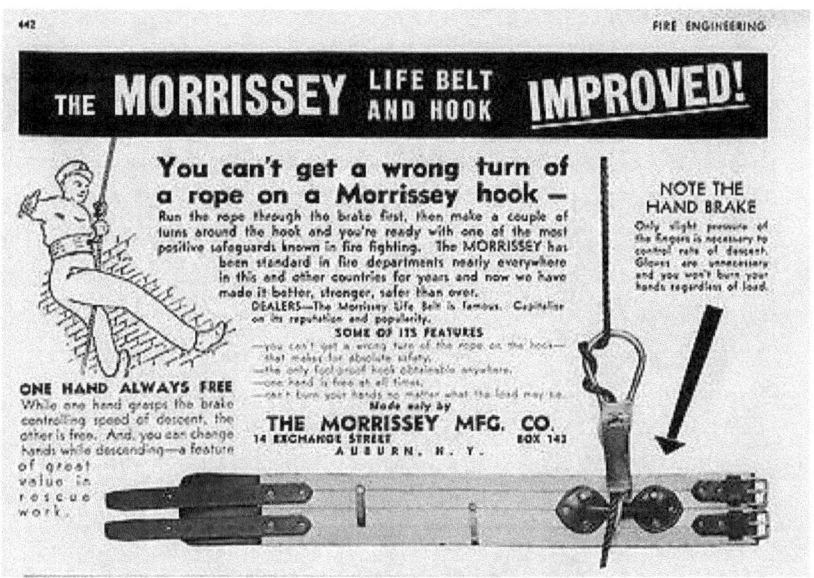

Advertisement for Morrissey Life Belt and Hook

3. In 1922, while assigned to Hose Company No. 3, Captain Morrissey braved the flume of the Owasco River raceway at the Dunn & McCarthy factory to remove the body of Leroy Baier, who had drowned in the water. For his valiant efforts, the Dunn & McCarthy Company awarded him a gold watch. That same year, Patty Morrissey took a trip with 300 other firemen from around New York State during his annual vacation time. The group traveled up the Great Lakes, from Buffalo to Duluth and back again. He maintained contact with friends in Auburn via postcards, and upon his return, said he would remember it for a long time. He was assigned to Hose Company No. 6 in 1925. In 1929, Morrissey received a bullet wound in the hand and scalp during the riots and fire at the Auburn Prison. In the beginning of the riots Morrissey and his men were cautioned by the inmate custodians not to enter the prison gate, but they insisted on entering and proceeded for force their way into the institution. They were met with resistance by the inmates. The convicts warned Morrissey to get out of their way in the melee, as they did not want to bump off a "nervy old-timer", but he stayed in the battle against the blazes, strong and steady. Captain Patrick F. Morrissey retired from the Auburn Fire Department in 1931, after a long and illustrious career.

Patrick F. Morrissey held several patents for his inventions. His most notable were a portable fire escape and a life belt hook. Known as the "Morrissey Belt" and "Morrissey Life Belt and Hook", the device included a patented figure-eight hook. Morrissey's fire escape belt was designed to be operated with one hand. Patented on August 10, 1915, to Patrick F. Morrissey and Herman W. Traub, the Portable Fire Escape forever changed rescue methods. Previous devices required two hands to operate. The device, Patent No.

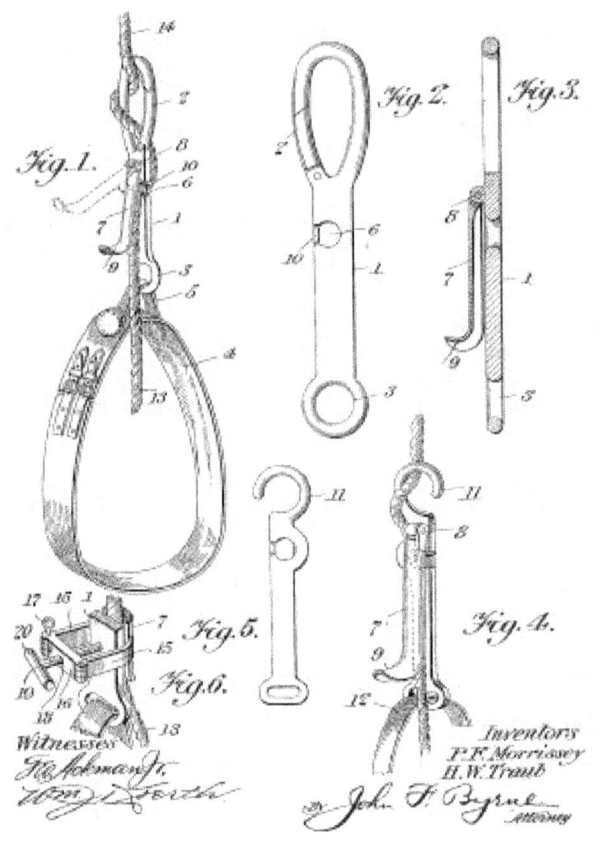

Patent – Portable Fire Escape

1,149,394, allowed for the speed to be controlled and to even stop in midair if necessary. A rope ran through the brake on the belt and then after a couple of turns around the hook it was ready for use. The device was friction controlled. One hand operated the brake to control the speed of the descent and the other was left free. The fire escape was operated by exerting pressure while sliding down. A steel brake was operated by hand and could control pressure of over 300 pounds. The fire escape could utilize any size rope up to 1 1/8". A person being rescued was placed in the loop during the descent. Captain Morrissey demonstrated his fire escape in many areas, including a descent from the top of the 22-story Flatiron building in New York City using ½" rope! The one-handed operation facilitated rescue work by firefighters, and the Morrissey Life Belt and Hook was quickly adopted as the standard in fire departments all around the country. The device was also wildly popular with travelers of the day, since it could easily be packed into a traveling bag and used to escape from a hotel or apartment house of any height.

In 1910, Patrick Morrissey developed a Twentieth Century Stall Trip for fire horses. As is many times the case, Morrissey had grown frustrated with the then-current stall trips that were not reliable and resulted in response delays. He set out to make a stall trip with improvements over any that the department had employed in the past. The Twentieth Century Stall Trip was created to ensure that a horse could not get loose when the trip was locked. It also made it nearly impossible for a horse to get caught up and result in a delay when the trip was open. The stall trip could be easily locked and was designed to be durable. Morrissey's stall trip was endorsed by fire chiefs across New York State. 1910 was a creative year for Patrick F. Morrissey, for he also developed and received a patent for a trolley wheel. Patent No. 968,876 was issued to

Patrick F. Morrissey, James Wise and Walter Byrne. The invention was a trolley wheel that was designed to last twice as long as other modern-day trolley wheels. The construction of the trolley wheel was such that it provided duplicate wire engaging surfaces. In 1916, Patrick Morrissey demonstrated his renaissance characteristics when he composed words to a musical composition. *"Mother's Picture in the Frame"*, was copyrighted with words by Patrick F. Morrissey and music by J. E. Andino. In 1926, Patrick Morrissey patented a holder for license and city name plates. Patent No. 1,573,087 was a license plate holder which allowed quick and easy securing of the plates and was simple, durable and efficient. Patrick F. Morrissey's contributions to the Auburn Fire Department via his service years and creativity certainly left an indelible mark on the department.

Augustus E. Hemrick – Born Fireman

Augustus E. Hemrick was born in Auburn, New York in December of 1861, to Antoine and Caroline Hemrick. Augustus was one of five children; William, Emma (died young), Edmond, Augustus and Frederick. Augustus "Gus" Hemrick was first associated with the Auburn Fire Department during the volunteer days in 1880, with Alert Hose No. 6. In 1887, he transferred to Letchworth Hose Company. He became a callman in the paid department in 1894, and was assigned to Hose Company No. 1. After less than a year, in 1895, his talent and ability convinced officials to appoint him as a permanent firefighter. He had a natural instinct to identify the origin of a fire. He was good at "knowing" a fire and being able to predict where it was and where it would go. The behavior of a fire was knowledge intrinsic to Hemrick, and he was a considered a valiant firefighter. At fires, Gus was always where the smoke was the thickest, wanting to be in the heart of the action. There were occasions when he suffered minor injuries, but he would return to the fire and his duties after he received first aid. At a fire at the Hanlon & Sheils Shoe store in 1904, Hemrick stepped on a live electrical wire and was knocked down unconscious for a moment. He quickly got up, shook it off and joked that he didn't want any more electrical treatments! He was made Captain in 1909 and assigned to  the Owasco Street station of Hose Company No. 2. In 1917, he was promoted to Assistant Chief of the Auburn Fire Department. Gus was described as a quiet and unassuming firefighter who had a steady resolve and much self-discipline. His orders were obeyed to the letter, as his men knew the expertise and knowledge behind them. He was an honorable firefighter.

Augustus Hemrick's retirement party was thrown at the hall of the Hook & Ladder Company on August 23, 1921. The event was attended by a very large number of people. So respected and popular was Hemrick, that the hall was filled to the rafters with well-wishers. Chief Jewhurst served as the toastmaster for the event, and there were many others who spoke to those gathered and shared stories and gave tributes. Augustus Hemrick was retiring from the Auburn Fire Department with almost 42 years of service. Tom Frost kicked off the event with three cheers for Gus! Songs and/or stories were shared by Cuckoo Kierst, Dick McClain, Timmy McCarthy, Bill Lynch, George Searing, Paul Flynn and many others in attendance. Gus was complimented on his physical condition and acknowledged for his long years in the harness. Chief Jewhurst's toast to Gus was something that every firefighter would surely relish to be said at the end of their career, when he relayed,

> "I have this to say, brother firemen, that I regret most deeply that we are to lose a good fellow and associate, and the department is to lose a faithful officer with the retirement of Assistant Chief Hemrick from service. I believe I express the sentiment of each and every member of the department. I am pleased to say that Assistant Chief Gus Hemrick has a clean and honorable record in the department. There has not been a single mark against him in his 42 years of service. Gus Hemrick was not a <u>made</u>

fireman, as the saying goes. He was a <u>born</u> fireman. He was always full of pep and firemanic ginger that goes to the making of a good and game firefighter. Years ago in the old volunteer fire department, Gus had the reputation of being some 'bunker'. Many a night he has slept with his rubber coat wrapped around him, the floor his bed, so that he might be the first away from the mark when an alarm came in. And ever since, he has shown that same spirit of a genuine fireman as he passed through the various changes of the department service. Gus Hemrick has filled with credit every position from private in the ranks up to that of Assistant Chief. His duties were always done with efficiency and satisfaction. At this time I want to say that I couldn't do justice to Gus if I did not say that I deeply appreciate the able assistance which he has rendered me at all times. Gus we deeply regret your leaving the department and now, on behalf of the entire department, I have the pleasure to present you with this handsome chair and rocker as a token of the esteem on behalf of a brother fireman and faithful friend. We trust your life of freedom will bring you years of good health, happiness, comfort and prosperity."

Following Jewhurst's speech, the crowd let loose a deafening round of applause and cheers. Hemrick was raised onto the shoulders of the firemen and he was set on one of the chairs he had been presented with. He was carried around the room for a bit, before they set him down to say a few words. Gus became choked up at the display of affections and kindness that his fellow firefighters had shown him. He humbly thanked the group sincerely and encouraged the men to continue where he left off and keep the good record and reputation of the Auburn Fire Department.

Following his retirement, Augustus Hemrick moved to McGraw, New York, in Cortland County. He enjoyed the fresh air and country living. Gus remained active in retirement, and although he experienced some health concerns, he was only confined to bed for one week. He frequently visited his old pals from the Fire Department, and his friends would make the trip to McGraw to see him. In 1926, he took a vacation through the Catskills. Gus suffered a stroke in 1941, and was bedridden for a period of time. He died at his home in May of 1944, at the age of 82. He had enjoyed more than 22 years in retirement.

Charles M. Kierst "Cuckoo"

There are people in our lives who are remembered long after they are gone. Charles Kierst is one of those individuals who is the subject of many a story that goes around the firehouse.

Affectionately known as "Cuckoo", Kierst was something else. Many of the stories that are told by the old-timers include a "Cuckoo" tale or two. Kierst began his career in the Auburn Fire Department in 1917 as a Callman. He was appointed as a permanent firefighter in 1919. He retired in 1959, after 41 years of service with the Auburn Fire Department. Charles Kierst served in the U.S. Navy during World War I and was a well-respected and much love firefighter. Stories of Kierst are plentiful and always told with a smile and a nod by those who knew him, and those who wish they had.

Charles Kierst enjoyed a good practical joke; sometimes more than the victims! In 1916, Kierst pilfered a balmacaan overcoat from Andrew Teneroch at a dance hall in a mischievous act intended to be comical. Unbeknownst to Kierst, in the pocket of the overcoat was a strongly scented fragrance bottle. When Kierst reappeared in the dance hall later, remnants of the strong fragrance clung to him and he was instantly identified as the culprit and the jig was up! However, the joke turned out to be on him when the police were summoned and "Cuckoo" was charged with petit larceny!

Charles Kierst was also active in the athletic arena. He was the Captain of the Auburn Fire Department handball team in 1926, when a handball league was formed with other Central New York fire departments. He was a pitcher on the Auburn Fire Department softball team and played golf as well. Charles Kierst enjoyed fishing and always had a line in the water for opening day of trout season. Kierst had an unlucky fishing experience on May 1, 1926, when he landed a nine-pound fish and a few smaller pickerel at the Barge Canal. He used a stringer for his catches, and in the process of getting the large one on, he failed to secure the stringer properly to the stick and the large fish thrashed about, and the stringer came loose. The nine-pound fish swam off with the stringer and other smaller fish in tow!

Charles Kierst was a big baseball fan. In fact, some say that he was Auburn's Number One baseball fan. Kierst attended World Series games for decades and made a habit of being first in line for the games year after year. Of course, some years provided more stories than others. His first World Series would prove to set the stage for all others. The year was 1921. The World Series would feature the New York Yankees vs. the New York Giants. It was the first World Series played entirely in one ballpark, the Polo Grounds in New York City. Charles Kierst and friend, Joseph "Johnny" Jakoud, left Auburn with $11 between the two of them. They got a ride from Five Points to Utica. There they met up with some friends before continuing on their journey, which reportedly included rides in a variety of vehicles, some with indication that they might be bootleggers. They stopped at fire stations and were provided bunks for the night. Long before the day of the game, people started to line up at the entrance to Brush Stadium for bleacher seats. It was cold, and it rained on and off. The line grew quickly. Charles Kierst was first in line! Johnny

Jakoud was second. Leslie Carpenter, a 15-year-old high school student from Jamaica, NY, was fourth in line, but Kierst and Jakoud allowed the young lad to squirm up between the two of them. They allowed him to stay there; in part to watch over the young lad, but they also sent him for coffee and sandwiches while they were in line! Twenty-eight hours in line they waited! By 8am, there were more than 1,500 people in line. Finally, the gates opened and Charles M. Kierst was the first one through! They had their pictures taken by newspaper reporters and movie cameramen. Kierst told reporters he was a "baseball bug ever since I was knee high." He went on to say, "The Giants are going to win, and the Babe will probably get himself two home runs." Kierst and Jakoud wandered around and shook hands with the Giants' Manager, John McGraw. They also shook hands with and got an autographed baseball from the Bambino, Babe Ruth! Others they encountered before the game included Phil Douglas, Carl Mays, Johnny Rawlings and more. The first game ended 3-0 in favor of the Yankees. Kierst and Jakoud remained in NYC to see the second game of the series, which ended 3-0 in favor of the Yankees. The two Auburn men headed for home, taking the same types of rides back. They arrived in Auburn with 90 cents remaining in their pockets and a lifetime of memories. Upon their return, the two went to the fire station and regaled the men with their World Series adventures and other New York City tales.

The 1921 World Series was not the only one that Charles Kierst attended, nor was it the only year that he came away with a tale! In 1953, he was first in line for bleacher seats yet again; it was his 17th World Series attendance. In 1955, he traveled to New York City to the World Series to see the New York Yankees play the Brooklyn Dodgers at Yankee Stadium. An acquaintance, Ralph Belcore, of Chicago, and he were in line outside the stadium. Kierst had gotten to know Belcore over the years, as Belcore was first in line many times for World Series games, and was sometimes Kierst's competition to getting to the front of the line. In 1955, Kierst was second in line. Kierst left his suitcases in the care of Belcore while he went to a nearby tavern. Belcore decided that since it was so quiet at that time of night, it would be okay to quickly leave his spot to mail a letter in a mailbox around the corner. But he was not quick enough. Upon returning to the stadium, both men's suitcases were gone! Vanished! Unfortunately, Kierst's suitcase contained memorabilia in the form of a collection of newspaper clippings about his first-in-line experiences along with other items dating back to 1921. He offered a $50 reward for the return of the suitcase, no questions asked. He also offered his place in line and a bleacher ticket as well. There was no report found that indicated whether his suitcase was ever recovered.

In October of 1964, at the age of 72, Charles Kierst was yet again reported by newspapers to be first in line for a bleacher seat at the World Series in New York. He watched the New York Yankees play the St. Louis Cardinals. During his lifetime, Kierst was first in line for bleacher seats at countless World Series games. If he wasn't first in line, one would not have had to look far to see him waiting patiently for the gates to open.

Charles Kierst and Ralph Belcore in line at the 1955 World Series; Yankees vs. Dodgers

Charles R. Hardy – Auburn's First Black Firefighter

Charles R. Hardy was born January 15, 1915, in Ithaca, New York. His family moved to Auburn when Charles was just a toddler. After high school graduation, Charles studied music at Ithaca College for three years. He had wonderful musical talent on the piano, as well as his singing voice, and felt there were future possibilities for him in the field. Mr. Hardy was Director of the choir at Thompson Memorial Community Church and men's choral club of the Booker T. Washington Community Center. Family responsibilities took hold in 1937, when Mr. Hardy returned to Auburn to help care for his grandmother who was ill. Charles married Eleanor Irvin in July of 1941, and the couple lived in Auburn in the family home on Chapman Avenue, a house that had been in the family for four generations. Charles and Eleanor Hardy raised two sons, John "Jack" and Leo. In 1942, he enlisted in the U.S. Army and signed up for Signal Corps training. Charles Hardy served in Central Europe, Normandy, Northern France and Rhineland. During his World War II service he earned the European-African-Middle Eastern Campaign Medal and ribbon with four service stars, Good Conduct Medal and the World War II Victory Medal and ribbon. Hardy was a clerk for the Aviation Gasoline Transport Battalion and later a Sergeant in charge

of a German civilian labor pool for Battalion Headquarters. He was honorably discharged from the Army in 1946. Following his military service, Charles Hardy worked at the Auburn Button Works as a tumbler for about a year before he was appointed as a firefighter in July of 1947; Auburn's first black firefighter. Hardy was assigned to the Hook and Ladder Company.

Charles Hardy was an Auburn Firefighter at the height of the Civil Rights Era and faced difficulties associated with being black during that time period. Intent on being a firefighter and executing the duties of his job in an efficient manner, Charles worked hard and was an asset to the Auburn Fire Department. Hardy took the Fire Lieutenant examination on May 9, 1953, and initially received a score of 89.55. His score was later re-adjusted due to a technicality with the application he submitted, as well as a review and ruling of appeals made by examinees on several exam questions. The final scores dropped Hardy from 3rd to 8th in the standings, a significant difference. Hardy felt he was discriminated against because he was black and filed a lawsuit to have the scores and subsequent rankings reviewed. The Civil Service Commission explained that Mr. Hardy's rating had been changed because he failed to fill in the section of the application to claim an additional 2½ points credit as an honorably discharged, non-disabled war veteran. Without the credit, Hardy's score was lowered by 2½ points, which resulted in the drop in his standing on the list. Hardy had attached papers to his application that showed he had served with the armed forces, but failed to fill the correct box on the application form. His intent appeared to be clear. The Commissioners indicated that correctly filling out the application form was part of the test.

Charles Hardy appealed his score, and the matter was sent to the New York State Civil Service Commission for a ruling.

On September 2, 1953, the Auburn Municipal Civil Service Commission ruled that the non-disabled veterans' credits of 2½ points, which were not previously allowed to Mr. Hardy, be permitted. The August 1953 Lieutenant list was revoked and a new list established, which ranked Mr. Hardy 5th. Three vacant Lieutenant positions were filled, but Charles Hardy did not receive a promotion. An additional Lieutenant examination was held in 1966, which ranked Hardy second in the standings, but he did not receive the promotion. Over the years Charles Hardy was actively involved in the Permanent Firemen's Association and the annual Muscular Dystrophy Drives held by the Fire Department. Charles Hardy made no bones about his feelings regarding his treatment by some members of the department and city officials. He was a member of the Auburn Fire Department for almost 30 years and reported there were some incidents of discrimination and disrespectful behaviors demonstrated toward him in the years leading up to his retirement in 1977. Hardy did not characterize his entire experience as unsatisfactory, for he had many true and genuine friends in the Fire Department. He was proud of his service with the Auburn Fire Department.

At the Tenth Annual Banquet of the Auburn-Cayuga branch of the National Association for the Advancement of Colored People (NAACP), Hardy was honored for his years of service in the Auburn Fire Department. Charles Hardy continued to demonstrate his musical talents through the years as well. He often performed soloist numbers with his melodic voice. In 2012, the Auburn-Cayuga Branch of the NAACP celebrated African American History Month by saluting 26 distinguished African Americans in Auburn who made significant contributions in Auburn and Cayuga County. Charles R. Hardy was among the Auburn Trailblazers honored that night. In 2013, the Cayuga Museum opened an exhibit called "They Stood Up: Civil and Human Rights in the Finger Lakes" which examined local historical figures and the issues they stood up for or against. The collection featured those who were influential during significant events and times in American history, including the civil rights movement and women's suffrage. Charles Hardy was one of the individuals featured in the exhibit.

Charles R. Hardy was an Auburn Firefighter throughout the Civil Rights Era and no doubt faced many struggles above and beyond the extraordinary tasks associated with being a firefighter. His perseverance in the department, and his demand for his legal rights, illustrated the strength of his character. His struggles in the department were real, but make no mistake about it, Charles Hardy was respected and well-liked by many firefighters, and he forged sincere friendships during those years.

April Amodei – Auburn's First Female Firefighter

April Amodei grew up assuming that she could do whatever she wanted in terms of a career choice. Her interests through the years were not dictated by how prolific the female gender was in any given area. Astronaut to pilot to firefighter, Amodei had the same dreams everyone else has. The sky was the limit. April's mother passed away when she was young, leaving her with her father and two older brothers. The opportunity to take a civil service test for a firefighter position in the City of Auburn presented itself, and Amodei was encouraged by a friend to take it. At the time, Amodei was a single parent and was working at the YMCA as the Aquatic Director. She had an interest in firefighting and felt that it would be a good fit for her. She took the examination and did very well.

She was appointed to the Auburn Fire Department on August 8, 1994. April Amodei was the first female firefighter in the history of the Auburn Fire Department. While not completely unheard of, female firefighters were few and far between. The first female paid firefighter in the United States was hired in 1973, yet women did not increase their numbers considerably until the 1980's. The 2000 Census reported approximately 11,000 paid female firefighters in the U.S., about 3.7 percent of all paid firefighters in the country. The 2010 Census reported approximately 14,000 paid female firefighters, representing approximately 4.8 percent of total paid firefighters.

Amodei attended the New York State Fire Science Academy and successfully completed the demanding training. April has always been physically fit and very athletic. Her initial introduction within the department was demanding, and there were certainly challenges along the way. Being a single parent, April had to work out the logistics of her new career, but she didn't ask for, or receive, any special treatment. Some of the gear was ill-fitted and made for a man's world; boots too large and gear proportioned for a man's body type. She made it all work, while the department worked out issues as they came to light. Previously comprised of all males, the department needed to institute some new rules in the department with the addition of a female. Some of the firefighters welcomed April into the mix and were of the mindset "as long as she can do the job, great". Others may have harbored a bit of trepidation having a woman in the ranks. April quickly exhibited her skill and talent as a firefighter. She didn't want to be pre-judged based on her gender; she wanted to prove herself as a firefighter.

At the beginning there was a bit of an adjustment period with the department incorporating Amodei as an Auburn firefighter. People would ask her, "Do you prefer to be called a fire lady, firewoman, firefighter?" She would smile and say, "I don't care what you call me, as long as I get paid every two weeks." April recalls her first night at the fire station. Lying in her bunk, she realized that she was putting her trust in this group of firefighters, and they were putting their trust in her. Their lives depended on each other, day in and day out. They were all in it together. It was both comforting and terrifying at the same time. April took her job seriously, and she was a capable and dedicated member of the Auburn Fire Department. The fact that she was a woman in a predominantly male field was obvious, but she focused on mastering the skills required for the job. She was treated the same as any other firefighter. April had a matter-of-fact approach in some matters. One officer tested the waters with her initially and said to her, "Don't get upset when we have a fire and I start yelling and screaming at you, cause that's just the way I am." Without missing a beat, Amodei replied, "Well, don't get upset when you yell and scream at me if I start to cry, cause that's just the way I am." But Amodei presents as anything but thin-skinned. April believed in doing the job well and giving the taxpayers what they expected and deserved. She was a perfect choice to be Auburn's first paid female firefighter.

In 1995, Amodei was called to battle her first major fire, a two-alarm blaze that required the rescue of family members from the second floor of a residence. The call came in as a box alarm and the crew arrived on the scene quickly. There was smoke billowing out of the structure and flames everywhere. She and another veteran firefighter worked their way up into the burning first floor of the structure while crews worked to get to the trapped individuals. She was unwavering in her approach to the blaze. At the end of the night, she got the nod from the veteran firefighter, who also told others that she had performed well and had done a good job. April was glad to hear the feedback, but also did not rest on those laurels. She thought to herself, "What did you expect?" Her job was to go in and fight fires, and that was exactly what she did.

Over the years, Amodei's character and skill as a firefighter became readily apparent. She was an asset to the department and a respected member. In 2002, Amodei was promoted to Lieutenant, another first in the Auburn Fire Department. She later became the department's Municipal Training Officer (MTO), a position she took much pride in, as it helped shape the firefighters' skills and performance in the job. As MTO, Amodei coordinated and provided training and certification skills to Fire Department personnel. Fire Department personnel are required to receive a specific number of both state and local training hours every year. Topics covered included basic firefighting, emergency medical services, building codes, hazardous materials and much more.

April Amodei retired from the Auburn Fire Department in 2014 with 20 years of service. She describes her career in the Auburn Fire Department as an amazing experience. Period. She is proud that no one was ever seriously hurt or killed during her time in the Fire Department. She is extremely humble when talking about her career, but the fact remains that she made a positive difference in the department with real and lasting contributions.

Mentors

Over the course of the more than 122 years of the Auburn Fire Department, firefighters have had mentors. A mentor's goal is to promote and teach positive career and life skills without regard for personal accolades. They are respected members who look to advance the Department as a whole. A good mentor could be a senior firefighter or an officer. During interviews, when current Retirees were asked about mentors in the Auburn Fire Department, the same names came up time and time again; Charlie Zambito, Joe Graney, Dick Walsh, Mike Harmon, Ed Bilinski, Pat DiNonno, Gerry Conway and David Diehl are at the top of many guys' lists. Of course, these names represent a snapshot in time; a list of historical mentors would include many more wise advisors. They were the go-to guys in the department, and they led by example. If you needed to know what to do or how to do it, any one of them could provide the answer. Well-respected by the department members, they were true leaders and educators in their field. In a position of honor and respect, these men didn't command attention and action. They were naturally recognized for their level of expertise and were approachable. They transferred knowledge to other firefighters and worked to ensure the success and expertise of the firefighters. With vastly different personalities, each one had his own mentoring method, but the end result was the same; they are remembered professionally as the wise advisors. On a personal note, Scott cites his father, Frank DeJoy, as a lifelong mentor as well as a professional mentor from the very beginning of his career, providing invaluable knowledge and guidance. Dave Kapcha was an instrumental mentor to Scott in his role as an officer within the Department. The mentoring relationship is extraordinary and treasured by those who are lucky enough to have had the experience.

New York State Fallen Firefighters Memorial

The New York State Fallen Firefighter Memorial is located at the Empire State Plaza in Albany, NY. Dedicated in 1998, it commemorates the memory and valor of NYS fallen firefighters. A ceremony is held during Fire Prevention Week each year. The names of individuals who made the ultimate sacrifice in service to their communities are inscribed on the wall. The NYS Fallen Firefighters Memorial Wall includes ten Auburn Firefighter names:

Lou Chadderdon	6/17/1880
Frank Murphy	2/1/1927
Irving W. Dwyer	12/21/1931
Joseph Anton	12/26/1932
James H. McGee	5/13/1939
John M. Gill	5/31/1942
Anthony T. Contrera	3/30/1960
Alfred H. Murphy	3/30/1960
John F. Searing	3/30/1960
Patrick J. LaGambino	5/12/1973

Auburn Fire Department Medal of Valor Award

In January of 1999, Fire Chief Michael D. Quill established the Auburn Fire Department Medal of Valor Award. The award recognizes heroic acts and deeds above and beyond the call of duty by Auburn Fire Department personnel. Upon establishment of the Medal of Valor, the first recipients of the award were recognized for dates up to and through December 1998.

The first Medal of Valor Award recipients were awarded on January 16, 1999:

- Firefighter Tom Hoff, for actions on April 27, 1993
- Firefighter Paul Baran, for actions on May 2, 1997
- Firefighter Dave Radley, for actions on January 12, 1998, involving a rescue

in 40-degree water in the Owasco Outlet with a swift current.

- Firefighter Scott DeJoy, for actions on January 12, 1998, involving a rescue in 40-degree water in the Owasco Outlet with a swift current.
- Assistant Fire Chief Dan Curry, for actions on September 14, 1998

Additional Medal of Valor Award recipients:

- Firefighter Jeff Dygert , for actions on January 29, 2000, involving a second floor rescue during a fire on VanAnden Street.
- Captain Terry Winslow, for actions on January 29, 2000, involving a second floor rescue during a fire on VanAnden Street.
- Lieutenant Edward Sherman, for actions on March 17, 2003, involving a second floor rescue during a fire on Easterly Avenue.
- Lieutenant James Lattimore, for actions on March 17, 2003, involving a second floor rescue during a fire on Easterly Avenue.
- Firefighter Samuel Giannettino, for actions on March 17, 2003, involving a second floor rescue during a fire on Easterly Avenue.
- Firefighter Richard Stabinsky, for actions on March 17, 2003, involving a second floor rescue during a fire on Easterly Avenue.
- Firefighter Christopher Logue received the Distinguished Service Award for actions on March 17, 2003, involving a second fire rescue during a fire on Easterly Avenue.
- Firefighter Shawn Stewart received a Fire Department citation award in 2002 for her dedication and support of a fellow firefighter during his illness.

Cayuga County Red Cross Real Heroes Award

In 2008, Michael Deyneka received the Cayuga County Red Cross Real Heroes Award for actions on September 4, 2007, during a fire that ultimately destroyed the Highland Park Golf Course. On receipt of the alarm, Auburn Fire Companies responded to the Highland Golf Course. Auburn Engine 2 secured a water source from the city. Lieutenant Michael Deyneka and Firefighters Adrian Humphrey and Kevin Donnelly entered the Highland Park building and made their way through the banquet hall toward the smoke-filled kitchen. They knocked out ceiling tiles along the way, looking for smoke and fire. They met up with three Owasco Fire Department crew members who were also attempting to find the fire. There was a lot of smoke, but fire was not yet visible. The fire was in the ceiling. Owasco firefighters ran low on air and were forced to exit. The Auburn trio remained and continued to track the fire. Unbeknownst to them, the fire had evolved and spread through the ceiling above and behind them. Radio communication problems prevented the firefighters inside from receiving any warnings. The fire had spread significantly; flames were working above and behind them. Firefighter Humphrey noticed fire coming out of the inspection holes made in the banquet hall. He alerted Deyneka of the fire that was beginning to surround them. Lieutenant Deyneka knew the lightweight construction of the building would result in the collapse of the roof in a very short period of time. The crew quickly evaluated the situation and Lt. Deyneka made the decision to remove him and his men from the building. They started to make their way out. Radio communication was restored and Deyneka was able to identify his crew as exiting the burning building, prior to another team being sent in after them. Within five minutes of exiting the building, the roof over the kitchen collapsed. Deyneka spoke of his recognition with appreciation, but stated he was only doing his job.

Honorary Members of the Auburn Fire Department

An Honorary Member of the Auburn Fire Department is a designation reserved for individuals who have contributed to the Fire Department in a unique and meritorious manner. It is a rare and prestigious honor that is afforded only to those who elevate the department in a significant manner. Honorary members have existed in the department dating back to the 19th Century.

Lyman Soule

Born in 1794, and affectionately known as "Uncle Lyman" to many who knew him, Lyman Soule was one of Cayuga County's pioneers. Mr. Soule was one of thirteen children. His family eventually settled in Sennett when Lyman was twelve years old. Lyman's family was poor and subsisted on scant and paltry provisions and goods. Lyman attended school and walked from Sennett to Auburn everyday with an older brother. At the age of fifteen, Lyman asked and received permission from his father, to try to make his own way in the world. In 1810, he apprenticed with Green and Remington tanners in Sennett. After a period of time, Mr. Soule traveled to the Rochester area and continued the tannery trade. Soon he had accumulated some $2,000-$4,000 and returned to Sennett. He and his brother, Howard, together bought the tannery. Due to health issues, he was forced to sell his interest to his brother and began to engage in the real estate business. Lyman was described as prudent, but not miserly. He was a man with frugal habits, a product of his meager early years; he saved his money and accumulated wealth. Eventually, Lyman's health issues resolved completed, and he lived in the family homestead following the death of his parents. Mr. Soule held several positions in Auburn and area banks and looked after affairs of the banks as he did his own, with close scrutiny and careful accounting. He was noted to be honest and decent in all his business dealings. He never married nor had children.

Lyman Soule was elected as an Honorary Member of the Logan Hook & Ladder Company in the Auburn Fire Department and enjoyed his association with the fire company. Mr. Soule owned much real estate in Auburn and Cayuga County. He was the founder and namesake of Soule Cemetery and donated the land on which the cemetery is situated. He also built, at his own expense, the receiving vault at its gate. He was charitable in many ways. In 1883, Lyman Soule was surprised when the Auburn "Hooks" and Geneva Hydrant Hose Company, along with Sutton's Band, showed up at his home on John Street to honor him as the oldest living honorary member of the Logan Hook & Ladder Fire Company. The band played a series of songs, and Mr. Soule spoke to the group expressing his gratitude. Lyman Soule passed away in November of 1885, at the age of 91, and is buried in Soule Cemetery.

Dr. Sylvester Willard

Sylvester Willard was elected as an honorary member of the Logan Hook and Ladder Company Co. 1 in 1844. Willard was born December 24, 1798, in Connecticut. He was educated at the New Canaan Academy and later graduated from the College of Physicians and Surgeons in New York City. He practiced in Connecticut until 1840, at which time he moved to Chicago. In 1830, he married Miss Jane Frances Case, daughter of Erastus Case. Dr. Sylvester Willard moved to Auburn in 1843. He was reported to be a good physician, although the later years of his life were devoted to other philanthropic and business activities. He possessed a genial manner and a kind spirit that made him many friends and commanded the highest regard of those who were merely acquaintances. He was elected President of the Auburn Savings Bank in 1860, and was interested in helping all classes of people to preserve their hard earned incomes. He served the remainder of his life as a public spirited citizen. His interest in the general business prosperity and advancement of the City of Auburn was illustrated in his active involvement in many businesses, associations and groups.

Henry Ward

Honorary member of Alert Hose Company No. 6, 1881.

Charles Haines

Lake Park Company President and Honorary Member of Westfall Hose Co., 1889.

Dr. J. M. Morris

Dr. J. M. Morris was elected as an Honorary Member of Fire Engine Company No. 1 and Niagara Fire Company No. 3 in Auburn in 1857. On the evening of May 13, 1857, Dr. Morris spoke before Company No. 1's foreman, Mr. Dyer and other firefighters and friends. He gave a heart-warming speech that bears repeating here:

> "Mr. Dyer, by the invitation of your Company, I am here to perform a duty for them and for myself. Your association with the Fire Department for so many years, has endeared you to the boys, as well as to the citizens of this, the loveliest, and, justly, one of the proudest cities in the State. I say proudest, because the feats this Department have achieved, stand number one. For, in all the contests you have entered into, you have come off with laurels. The nature of your occupation is one of peril. 'Tis true, I have not run with the machine, but I can imagine the excitement connected with it. It is dead of night, there is a sound borne on the wind's low swell. Listen. Murmuring voices in the distance break the calm of night's usual silence. Nearer and nearer it comes until audibly is heard the cry of fire! Fire! Hasten to the scene. What's that form seen along the corridor – now here, now there – goods and chattels are being borne as if by spirits amid the lurid glow. From the base, clouds of black smoke ascend - from the dome a flaming column lights the firmament for miles around. Are all the inmates safe? No! One is missing. The element seems stirred in its wrath. Just at that moment is seen descending that winding staircase, a manly form bearing in his arms a female form! Who is it that has been so hazardous? It is a Fireman. May this helmet protect your head, that your mind may be clear to carry out the promptings of your heart, to noble deeds and generous actions in the hour of peril."

Dr. Morris specialized in chronic diseases, including scrofula, a tuberculosis-like disease. Dr. Morris practiced in Syracuse and Sennett before settling in Auburn, New York. He devised an improvement on the system for telegraphing by signal lights at night. The system was installed on Genesee Street in Auburn in 1858. A large light was used and colors and figures were passed before it as part of the signaling process. The signals could be seen for great distances and in all types of weather. Signals could be exchanged at night, with the aid of a telescope, from over twelve miles away.

Helen Dauvray

Helen Dauvray was elected as an Honorary Member of the Auburn Fire Department on November 1, 1872. Helen Dauvray (born Ida Louisa Gibson), also known as "Little Nell, the California Diamond", was an actress who was best known for her presentation of the play, "Fidelia, The Fire Waif", which was wildly popular, especially among firemen. The play was a dramatization of one of Frank H. Stauffer's stories in which a young girl is separated from her father and kept away from him due to improbable events and circumstances. A fortune, murders and a fire scene were part of the play. On November 2, 1872, at the end of the second act of the play at the Academy of Music in Auburn, Little Nell was presented with her Honorary Membership certificate. During the play, "The Fire Waif", Little Nell performed as six different charac-

Helen Dauvray "Little Nell"

ters; fire boy, street singer, emigrant country girl, bride, a man of high social standing and the pet of a fire boy. Little Nell was a petite, beautiful actress who sang, danced, clogged and also played the banjo. She was more vaudevillian than dramatic in her acting, and she kept audience members engaged and entertained. During the fire scene, the Neptune Hose Company appeared with their stunning hose carriage. Auburn firefighters were requested to, and did, appear in the play as themselves in order to lend credibility to the scenes. Little Nell's singing voice was versatile and she was able to sing in character, which included German and cockney styles, among others. Her play included amazing stunts and special effects and thrilled audience members with her feats. A particularly noteworthy special effect of the play was known as the "nitroglycerine, galvanic battery scene" which she had copyrighted. Over the course of her career Little Nell performed numerous plays, but she was quoted as saying that "Fidelia, The Fire Waif" was her favorite. It is reported that Helen made investments in a Pacific Slope or Comstock Lode mine that netted her a small fortune within just a few years; half a million dollars by some accounts.

Helen Dauvray (aka: Little Nell) married baseball great, turned lawyer, John Montgomery Ward, in 1887. Ward was a shortstop for the New York Giants and is in the Baseball Hall of Fame. It is interesting to note that the first baseball World Championship trophy, coined the "Dauvray Cup", was made by the Gorham Silver Company, and was commissioned by Helen Dauvray in 1887. Helen Dauvray selected a trophy in a Grecian loving cup style, twelve inches tall, which was valued at $500. The cup was magnificent. The Gorham Silver Company modeled baseball bats to criss-cross and attach on either side with masks and ribbons on the top portion of the cup. It took more than 120 hours to fashion the Dauvray Cup and 36 hours to etch it to read "THE DAUVRAY CUP, PRESENTED BY, Miss Helen Dauvray, TO THE PLAYERS WINNING THE WORLD'S CHAMPIONSHIP." The total cost of the cup was $500. It was awarded to the winners of the World Championship series between the National League and American Association. The award was given prior to 1903, when the championship event was officially formalized as the World Series of Major League Baseball. Helen Dauvray also commissioned hardware, in the form of gold badges, for each of the winning team's players, as well as one umpire designated by the winning league. The rules associated with the trophy stipulated that it would remain in the possession of the winning team until a new champion was identified the following year. The exception to the rule was if any team won three consecutive championships, they would be able to claim the trophy permanently, and a new one created. Helen Dauvray was quoted regarding her offering of the cup, "I love the national game and desire to see whether the league champions are better than the association pennant winners. Of course, I believe the St. Louis Browns will be the association champions and I hope the New Yorks capture the league prize. If they do, I hope that they will win the cup, for I know them all from seeing them play, while I do not know the players of the Browns." Dauvray also spoke of

The Dauvray Cup

the notion of the award, "The idea of giving the cup was given to me by hearing so much talk about the Chicagos and Browns, and then I determined to give a prize to be competed for by the winners of the league pennant and the association pennant. I think it should be a perpetual prize not to be won outright, so that every year the clubs would have something unusual to strive for."

The Dauvray Cup was first won by the National League Detroit Wolverines, who had defeated the St. Louis Browns in 1887. It was won by the National League New York Giants in 1888, and 1889. In 1890, the American League Louisville Colonels won the coveted trophy. It was the Boston Beaneaters who won the Championship three years in a row; 1891, 1892 and 1893. The Dauvray trophy was turned over to the team permanently. Helen Dauvray and John Ward divorced in November of 1893, and a new trophy was not commissioned to replace the original. A replacement trophy, the Temple Cup, was provided by William Chase Temple, President of the Pittsburgh Pirates. Known as "baseball's lost chalice", the Dauvray Cup was last identified in November of 1893, in Newport, Kentucky, where Boston pitcher Henry Gastright had it on exhibition. The current whereabouts of the trophy are unknown. In 1896, Helen Dauvray married Navy Lieutenant and later Rear Admiral, Albert G. Winterhalter, alongside whom she is buried at Arlington Cemetery.

William Archie Goodwin

The history of the Auburn Fire Department cannot be told without mentioning William Archie Goodwin. Born October 24, 1874, and preferring to be called "Archie", Mr. Goodwin started out as a milkman in Auburn, but sought to become a member of the Fire Department. Regulations at that time required that fireman be at least five feet seven inches in height; Archie Goodwin was five feet two inches tall. Not allowing bureaucracy to stand in his way, Archie purchased a pony and built his own fire apparatus wagon. The wagon was painted red and outfitted with necessary tools. Daisy, his first pony, was later replaced with a black steed, Thelma, who was his beloved comrade and would pull the Goodwin wagon for decades. Archie fashioned his own fire uniform and maintained his own apparatus. He also had his own electric fire gong. At the sound of the alarm, the electrically released harness dropped onto the pony's back, and Archie and his horse and wagon were off to the scene of the fire. After a time, the firemen recognized Archie and allowed him to cross the fire lines to provide some assistance. If the fire bell rang in the morning hours, Archie's milk route had to wait until the fire was extinguished. Archie Goodwin also worked for the International Harvester Company in Auburn, but, again, his area was left vacant when the fire alarm sounded. Archie Goodwin became known for his "private fire department" and had worked his way into the hearts of many. In thirty-three years, Archie Goodwin did not miss a single fire call. He provided assistance when needed, and his presence at fires became as matter-of-fact as that of a regular fireman.

Before long, Archie and Thelma achieved nationwide recognition, and there were many newspaper stories written and visitors received by the duo. The Brooklyn Daily Eagle published a "Strange As It Seems" drawing of Archie in his wagon with Thelma in the lead. In June of 1924, Archie fell from the platform of an Auburn & Syracuse trolley car near the corner of Franklin and Foote Streets. He was knocked unconscious and suffered a fractured skull and collar bone that resulted in weeks of hospitalization and ended his "fire career". In 1932, Archie suffered another terrible blow when his beloved horse, Thelma, died in his arms at his Sherman Street home. The following morning Archie phoned the newspaper to report that Thelma had made her last hitch. Thelma had faithfully executed her duties beside Archie Goodwin for 27 years. Although he no longer responded to fire calls, Goodwin continued to follow and read everything he could about the Fire Department. In 1937, Archie Goodwin alerted the Fire Department to flames in a residence around the corner from him, at the Mulcahy home on East Genesee Street.

During Centennial Week in 1948, W. Archie Goodwin was visited by City Manager Train and Fire Chief Doyle and was made an Honorary Member of the Auburn Fire Department in recognition of his loyalty and services willingly given. Goodwin was presented with his appointment papers and a badge by the officials at his home on Sherman Street. The man, who for more than three decades had followed fire companies to fires, had attained, albeit in an honorary capacity, one of his lifelong dreams. It was a proud and shining moment for him. Archie Goodwin collected newspaper articles and photos of the Auburn

Archie Goodwin and Thelma

Fire Department apparatus and firefighters over the years. He Collected mementos dating back to the old volunteer days in Auburn and even had a copy of the original program from the New York Firemen's Association Convention in Auburn. W. Archie Goodwin died in April of 1949, at the age of 74. His memory lives on in the hearts of Auburn firefighters and the department received a portion of his collection of Auburn Fire Department articles and pictures. They are among the other valued Fire Department documents. William Archie Goodwin was an Honorary Member of the Auburn Fire Department and a bit of an archivist as well.

Leonard Volpe, New York City Fire Department

Leonard Volpe was a former Auburnian and Lieutenant in Ladder Company 148, at 12th Ave. and 42nd St. in New York City, when he became an honorary member of the Auburn Fire Department. Volpe was credited with rescuing four family members from a burning three-story home in Borough Park in 1968. Mr. Volpe retired from the NYC Fire Department and returned to Auburn. He led the Mercy Health and Rehabilitation Center's Fire Brigade in Auburn. A rescue specialist, Mr. Volpe directed and trained two five-person teams. The role of the hospital's fire brigade was to aid in rescue efforts and attempt to contain the fire until the Auburn Fire Department arrived. Auburn had additional fire-rescue teams at the Columbian Rope Company, Auburn Memorial Hospital, General Electric, ALCO, Procino-Rossi and Auburn Steel Company.

George Mercado, Washington D.C. Fire Department

George Mercado was a Lieutenant with a Ladder Company in the Washington, D.C. Fire Department. Mercado had an assignment in January 1961 that he would forever remember. John F. Kennedy's inauguration address was January 20, 1961. A fierce winter storm plagued the Washington D.C. area the day before the inauguration, with temperatures at 20°F and snowfall of 1–2 inches per hour. A total of 8 inches accumulated overnight. John F. Kennedy did not wear an overcoat when taking the oath of office and delivering his inaugural address, despite the cold conditions of 22°F and a wind chill at 7°F. During the inauguration, George Mercado was tasked with holding an electric heater toward Kennedy and ensuring that no fire occurred as a result. He was there on that history-making day and observed Kennedy officially become the 35th President of the United States. He can be seen in inauguration videos and photographs, wearing his Fire Department hat, imperceptibly completing his assignment that day. George Mercado retired from the Washington D.C. Fire Department and settled in Auburn, where he was the owner of Cap'n Quick Print and Copy Center.

John Elice

John Elice was part owner, along with Anthony and Yolanda Greco, of the Gem Automatic Car Wash Inc. located at 9 Lincoln Street. The car wash was located in the area where Wegmans currently stands. In 1970, Auburn Firefighters picketed Memorial City Hall regarding a pay raise negotiation. During the picketing, Elice opened his business to the firefighters and provided them coffee and snacks and a place to gather when needed. He was a friend to the firefighters and became an honorary member of the department. He was present at many department events over the years. The Gem Automatic Car Wash was closed in 1973 by the Auburn Urban Renewal Development Agency.

Thomas Anthony Southard

Thomas "Tommy" Anthony Southard had a life-long battle with cerebral palsy and passed away at the young age of 27. Although confined to a wheelchair, Tommy achieved much success and made lasting impressions throughout his lifetime. He was a member of Boy Scout Troop 385 of Centereach, Long Island and achieved the highest Catholic Scouting award, the Ad Altare Dei. Meaning, "To the Altar of God", the program's goal is to grow the Scout's spiritual experience and relationship to God and the church. Tommy was an outdoor enthusiast and received the Boston Council Freedom Trail Award following a 50-mile hike, which he accomplished without assistance. On November 7, 1987, Thomas Southard was elected as an Honorary Member of the Auburn Fire Department. Thomas passed away on April 13, 1988.

Kyle Scott

Each honorary member of the Auburn Fire Department is designated as such for contributions that elevate the department in a unique way. Kyle Scott is a special man who has made a distinctive contribution to the department. He has a sincere passion and genuine interest in the operations of the Fire Department. Kyle exemplifies the spirit of honorary membership. He has developed a working fundamental knowledge of the department, apparatus, members and processes through his frequent visits and inquisitive nature. Kyle always pays attention to details that would likely be lost on others. He possesses the uncanny ability to immediately pick up on anything that is missing or changed while he is at the station. Kyle's arrival at the station is usually announced with the rattling of four or five quarters in his hands; he paces back and forth repeating his excited phrase, "Oh my God." It's almost as if he is on an inspection of the department. He walks around and sizes up the station and its members, before asking his poignant questions, such as "Who's the new guy?" or "Where's Truck 2?" Once his tour is complete, he ends up in the kitchen to enjoy a cup of coffee in the company of the firefighters. Kyle celebrates the department and derives much pleasure from his conversations with its members. His candid awe and delight are endearing. He understands the serious nature of the job at hand and appreciates when time can be shared with him. Scott DeJoy would frequently remember one of Kyle's often-heard phrases when a fire call came in and he was going to his vehicle. When the bell would hit, Kyle would say, "Uh oh, General Alarm, everybody goes." Honorary membership is not something that one can apply for or request; it is, instead, recognition of an individual who is supportive of the department in a distinct manner. Kyle Scott certainly fits that bill.

Other Honorary Members

Other Honorary Members of the Auburn Fire Department include; James Plis (supporter and friend of the Department), Linda Spinosa (former Auburn Fire Department secretary), Tony Giannone (a fixture at the fire station), David Daum (involved in Sports Weekend activities), Bernard Simmons (firefighter's son and friend to the department in his support), Vincent DiMora (involved in multiple Fire Department activities and events) and Bob "Buzz" Reed (Code Enforcement Officer and friend of the Department).

HOT SPOTS

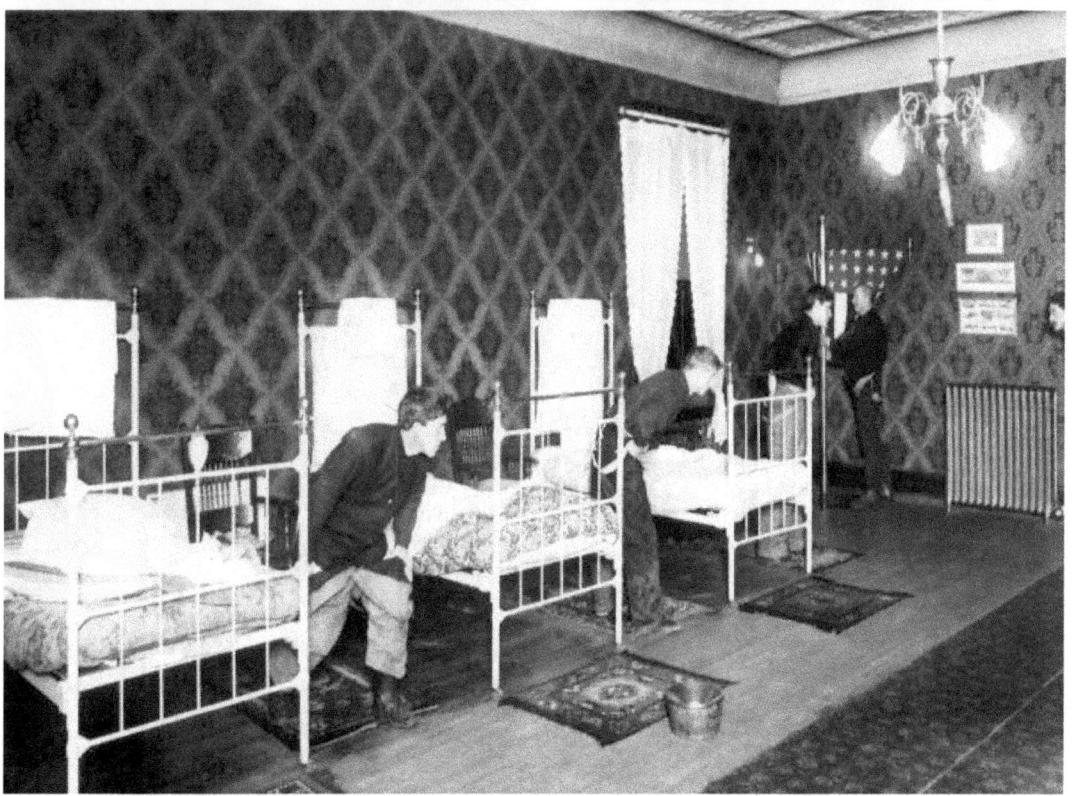

Top: Bottom to Top: Lucian DeSocio, Harry Mullens, Ralph Quill, Frank Fiore
Bottom: 1913, Engine 2 Alarm

Top Left: Fire exhibition jump
Bottom: 1958; Charles Kierst, Howard Shorey, Bud Maywalt

Top Left: Firefighter John Gill (young boy believed to be his son)
Top Right: Jim Monahan, Joe Graney

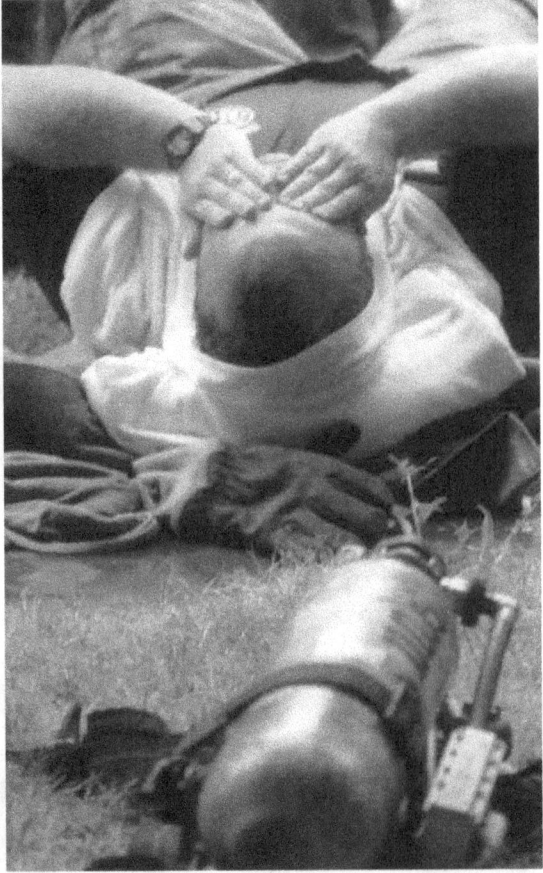

Top: L to R: Micky Burns, Joe Flynn (front facing camera), George Reidy, Dutch Soule, Frank Hawelka, Harold Murdock

Bottom Left: Photo courtesy of Christopher Logue

Top: Pete Mentillo, Frank Calarco, Joe Graney
Bottom: Engine 2: Mike Quill, Frank DeJoy, Angelo Tozzi

Top: 1947, New guys

Pranks, Practical Jokes and Funnies

Many firefighters took part in practical jokes and pranks over the years. Many of the same pranks are repeated from generation to generation of firefighters. Always good-natured and all in fun, these comedic events always amused those around the victim!

A firefighter had a habit of leaving his coffee mug out and not put away. After many requests and warnings, the mug disappeared one day. The firefighter looked all around, but was not able to locate it. A great deal of time went by before it was spotted by another firefighter, some fifty feet in the air and wire-tied to a light pole at Falcon Park! A photo of the mug was taken in its perch by the culprit. A print of the photo (before smart phones were prevalent) of the mug in its new home was left on the kitchen table for the firefighter to see. He was certainly surprised!

Ladder work is a requirement of the job for a firefighter. Some are more adept on a ladder than others. During a ladder training session the firemen had to demonstrate their ability to climb the aerial ladder extended at various angles. A veteran firefighter, who was very comfortable scaling a ladder, stepped forward and very confidently told them to put the ladder straight up to 100° and he'd climb it! The firefighters around him started laughing, and it was several moments before he realized that he had a mix-up in his math.

The windows at the Fire Department headquarters had no screens. On nights when the bunkrooms were very warm, the firefighters would sleep with the windows open. Occasionally bats would fly in at night and cause a raucous. Every so often a firefighter would pull a prank on someone by tying a black feather to a series of rubber bands connected together, with one end attached to the window shade. The feather was stretched to a pillow on a firefighter's bunk and tucked underneath it, held in place just so. When the victim went to bed and the pillow was moved, the "bat" would fly out toward the window and cause quite a scare!

A spare uniform can be a source of trouble. One of the firemen dressed a rescue/first aid mannequin in khaki pants and a chambray shirt, which was the regular uniform at the time. He waited until everyone went to bed, brought it into the bathroom and stood it in front of a urinal. In the middle of the night, one of the guys got up to got to the bathroom. No lights were turned on, and the man found that there was "someone" else in there as well. He started talking to the guy, but he got no answer. He continued to talk and ask the other "fireman" questions, but he only received silence in return. The fireman became annoyed and then ticked off. He was about to lecture the fireman, when he heard muffled laughter in the other room and began to put it all together. He realized he had been duped by a dummy that had been propped up in the bathroom!

Francis "Frank" Fiore was quite a prankster around the fire station and was known for the "dangling spider" trick (among others). He would put a fake spider on a string and dangle it out the second story window down to firefighters standing or sitting outside. Of course, the men would jump, and Frank would laugh!

During a rappel demonstration from a fully extended aerial ladder, Frank Fiore had made his way to the top and was sitting down, when all of a sudden he fell backward and slipped down! A collective gasp came from observers below, followed by a series of heckles and chuckles as they watched Frank lower himself down in a controlled manner; another of his pranks!

Some years ago, a few of the fellas liked to snack on limburger cheese in the evening. Someone sleeping in a chair at the firehouse is always considered to be a willing victim. Pete Mentillo had been watching television upstairs and fell asleep in a chair. The empty limburger wrappers were placed under the chair. After a bit of time, Pete stirred and repositioned and suddenly became aware of the odor. He jolted, looked around and yelled at one of the other firefighters, who had his shoes off, for having stinky feet! The others told him about the practical joke and soon everyone was laughing.

The funnel trick is infamous. A group of guys on the ramp would talk to a new guy about feats of skills. They would tuck a funnel into their pants and place a quarter on top of their head and then demonstrate how they could get it to go in the funnel. A new guy would usually say that was not hard, and he could do it as well. A friendly bet would ensue, and before long the new guy would be readied to show his own skills. Unbeknownst to him, someone was on the second floor, leaning out the window with a pitcher of water. As soon as the funnel was tucked into the guy's pants, they would let loose with the water. Roars of laughter resulted and the new guy learned in short order not to mess with the seasoned firefighters!

In the 60's it was not uncommon to find firefighters sitting outside on the ramp at the fire station. A new guy didn't notice when one by one the others left the area, until he was left alone sitting on the ramp. The rookie was unaware that another firefighter was upstairs in the bunkroom. He would fill a brown paper bag with water, lean out the open window above his intended victim and drop the bag of water onto the rookie's head. Splash!

Also in the 60's or 70's, during the 4th of July, Auburn Police were confiscating fireworks around the city. A firefighter managed to secure some of them from the Police Station. He snuck upstairs in the Police Station, lit a cigarette and stuck the fuse from the fireworks through it. He then went downstairs and joined some police officers and firefighters who were standing outside talking. After a bit of time, the cigarette burned down and lit the fuse and pop-boom-pop-pop-pop-pop! Everyone outside was startled and ran to see what the commotion was about! Of course, the culprit didn't get blamed because he had been standing with the group at the time!

Another classic prank, with a twist, was played on a firefighter who was sitting on the ramp one night, watching the downtown crowd pass by. The prankster was up in the bunkroom and had stunned a bat with a whack of a broom. A real bat. He tied a thread to its legs and lowered it down toward the ramp and right in front of the firefighter's face! The stunned bat came out of his stupor and started to wiggle around. Well, the firefighter was so startled by the prank that he jerked away from the bat and ended up smacking his head into the brick wall of the station and his chair went out from underneath him! Usually, a fake bat was used for such pranks. This one was a twist no one saw coming!

Following a fire on East Genesee Street hill, one of the firefighters was pulling out the wheel chock, when all of a sudden the fire engine left. Without him. He was dumbfounded and forced to walk back to headquarters! Engine four backed into the station and Chief Maywalt had come out to see what was going on. In the course of the conversation, they saw the firefighter walking down the street back to headquarters. The Chief demanded to know where the missing firefighter had been! He started to tell the story, and the Chief stated he didn't want to hear any excuses! The poor guy didn't have a chance to explain!

Bathroom cleaning detail is never a highly desirable chore and was oftentimes assigned to a rookie. Occasionally, a veteran firefighter would position a pair of turnout boots and pants in one of the stalls and then watch the new firefighter peer in, see that it was occupied and then walk away, only to return awhile later and still see the boots in place. Sometimes they would catch a look of concern or dread on his face as he waited for the bathroom to be vacated!

One of the firefighters had a ritual of calling his wife at 9pm every time he worked nights. The calls were brief and just a way to quickly check in. He didn't broadcast his activity, but everyone at the firehouse was aware of the nightly calls. Another firefighter decided to mess with him one night. He clued everyone at the fire station in on his plan so that they could watch it unfold. The prankster had been attending school in the evening, and on this night, he stopped at the firefighter's house after his class. He had convinced the firefighter's wife to go along with the prank. It got to be nine o'clock, and, sure enough, the phone rang. The prankster picked up the phone at firefighter's house and said "Hello". Well, the firefighter thought he had dialed the wrong number and started to indicate just that. The prankster proceeded to tell him that he had the right number and to hold on… his wife was just getting out of the shower and would be right there! Well, the firefighter stammered and stuttered a "What?!" and everyone at the fire station roared with laughter! The prankster had certainly pulled off the prank of the year! He got him! To this day, the prank is recalled fondly as a classic.

When a new firefighter walks in front of the truck at the station, it is not uncommon for the air horn on the truck to be sounded, startling the rookie.

It's easy to lose track of time and days; it happens, especially with a firefighter's work schedule. One day a firefighter showed up at 7pm in the evening, ready to start the day! Of course, he got quizzical looks from some of the other firefighters and then laughs, as they explained that he was 12 hours early for his shift! The poor guy thought it was 7am and not 7pm! Another time, a guy had been busy all day completing work assignments and cleaning the fire station. He sat down for a break toward the end of the day and was told by the officer in charge that it was very nice of him to come in on his vacation! He had completely forgotten his vacation started that day! He had donated his time to make the fire station sparkly clean!

Occasionally a group would get together and rig one of the metal beds in one of the bunkrooms so that when the victim went to bed, the mattress would drop through the frame, straight through to the ground. Short-sheeting the bed on a new guy was done time and time again too.

A television remote is usually controlled by one person, but one firefighter secretly brought in a universal remote one night and kept changing the channel on the firefighter who had the "real" remote. He would change the channel, and the other would change it to yet another channel; the volume got loud, then soft, etc. The unsuspecting fireman would extend his hand and point the remote directly at the TV and very carefully try to change the channel, only to be duped by the hidden one time and time again. He got baffled and increasingly annoyed. The hidden remote operator got such a kick out of the prank that he let it continue for two nights before the cat was let out of the bag!

Fire engines are heavy apparatus; combined with rain and other factors, it can lead to a messy situation. Such was the case one day when a fire company pulled up with a large fire engine, in a downpour, over an area that had just had street repair. The truck sunk to its floorboards. The Captain on duty was laughing at the scene, and he subsequently walked into the mud himself and got stuck. He asked for a hand to get out and one of the other firefighters pushed him further into the mud, sinking him almost up to his thighs! Only then did everyone find the situation comical.

New firefighters usually had to take care of the boiler at fire headquarters. The others would indoctrinate them by putting firecrackers in the coal bin. They would get tousled around and covered with coal soot and became indistinguishable from the coal. The new guy would grab a shovel, scoop up coal and throw it in the boiler. The next thing he knew, the firecrackers would start going off and would make a racket and scare the new firefighter!

What's Cooking?

Firefighters can cook. Some not well. But there are those who have stood out over the years with specialties of one kind or another. Working at the fire station through meals, many times the firefighters will eat together, family style, with each chipping in money to pay for the related expense of the meal. Or not. But that's another story. If you were not good at cooking, you were good at cleaning!

Culinary tales of the Auburn Firefighters date back to the 19th century. In 1878, the Geneva Fire Company was hosted at Ensenore by the Logan Hook & Ladder Company. They noted that the Logans had two or three men who truly understood how to bake clams to perfection. In 1887, the Protective Hose Company members were said to make superb Saratoga Chips.

Before a formal kitchen facility and supplies were available to them, it was not uncommon for the men to cook using the coal boiler. Hamburgers, chicken and an occasional steak were folded in between two pieces of screen and cooked over the coals. The boilers served double duty in those days.

One summer at Utt's Point on Cayuga Lake, a group of men gathered for a vacation. Firefighter Harry Orman was among them. He took on the role of cook during their retreat, and would later admit that he may have bitten off more than he could chew, especially when it came to cooking canned corn. One morning as he was heating an unopened can of corn on an outside fire, it exploded with a fierce blow! It was reported that the other men had to go all around the wooded point with a spoon to pick up enough corn to satisfy their hunger that morning!

Many times the culinary chores are divided up and each firefighter contributes based on their strengths and skills. James Gillooly was an all-around good cook; put him in the kitchen and the firefighters ate well! Ted Finizio was known for his culinary skills, including a great Deluxe Burger and delicious salisbury steak. Dave Kapcha was crowned the Wingmaster of Engine 3; his wings would rival any around town! Ed Reynolds was "keeper of the white cooker", a large rectangular, electric slow cooker that saw many great meals. The firefighters knew they were in for something delicious when Ed walked through the door carrying the cooker! Nick Luisi fed Truck Company well when he made his

Bottom: Photo courtesy of Jeff Clark

spaghetti and meatballs. Luisi also introduced Truck Company to an Italian sandwich that featured ham, salami, capicola and provolone on a half loaf of Caito's Italian bread. Frank DeJoy popularized "Creamed Cod Friday" at Engine 2 on Frederick Street. Frank DeJoy was also known for his 'YumYum' dish; a roasted sausage, kielbasa, onions, potatoes and peppers dish. Bob Tessoni made a mean Reuben sandwich! John "Butch" Delaney made an oyster stew that was legendary around the fire station. Dave Newert's turkey dinners were something to look forward to. Jack Curran made a great chili, among other specialties; but no one could come close to beating his chili. Other notables in the kitchen include

Jerry Conway and Mike Calarco. Bill Patrick's egg and olive salad was quite the elbow dripper. Bill DiFabio is generally known to be a good cook; however, his sausage gravy and meatloaf really gets the firefighters running… away from the kitchen! With an 'A' for effort, Bill's meatloaf meal was jokingly referred to as 'door stop' night and his sausage gravy tested even some of the strongest stomachs. Billy Hutson was known for his egg rolls. Larry Roberts made great tortellini.

Catchphrases

There are many sayings that are repeated over the years and which call to mind a particular person. Such catchphrases become popular either because they are funny, sincere or annoying. No matter the case, the Fire Department has had a variety of catchphrases over the years that became popular sayings:

Chief Jewhurst was often heard to say, "Get to the fire before the fire gets you."

Bob Regets coined the phrase, "A clean truck is a happy truck." Fire headquarters did not originally have a kitchen. The current kitchen area was a repair shop and had a pit and workbenches. Firefighters used to use the slop sink area, located on a wall adjacent to the Police Station, for their meal preparation. Bob noticed that the sink was frequently in need of cleaning. Every time the sink was cleaned, Bob would say, "A clean sink is a happy sink" which then morphed into "A clean truck is a happy truck." At the end of a run, when the firefighters were washing the truck, it brought a chuckle to the group to hear the familiar phrase. It became a classic saying around the fire station. The saying took on a life of its own and to this day can be heard on occasion, and is still received with a chuckle and a nod.

"Your chances are narrow when you buy from Darrow." Paul Kierst [Referring to Paul Darrow selling raffles tickets to the firefighters, and seldom did they win.]

The occasional single signal from the telegraph wire resulted in a phrase that every Auburn firefighter knows, "One blow, nobody goes" and "One blow, no go."

There are classic firefighter sayings that did not originate within the Auburn Fire Department, but have been heard over the years:

- Put the wet stuff on the red stuff
- I got mine
- Stay low and let it blow
- Train as if your life depends on it, because it does
- Too much…OK; not enough…No Good
- Gotta-getta Halligan
- Surround and drown

Automatic Hose Reel

Samuel F. Reynolds applied for a patent in 1883, and received Patent No. 357,154 in February of 1887, for his Automatic Hose Reel. While not a member of the Auburn Fire Department, Mr. Reynolds was a Supervisor of the 3rd Ward in Auburn. A noted inventor and musician, Samuel Reynolds devised a hose reel that automatically opened a valve and turned on the water upon unwinding the hose from the reel. The Automatic Hose Reel was exhibited at the State Firemen's Convention in Rochester and was well received. In 1887, Samuel Reynolds gave an exhibit of his hose reel during a steamer and water works test in Auburn. The Callahan shut off nozzle and relief valve were also exhibited at the same event. The hose reel sold locally for $4-8. In 1891, the effectiveness of the Reynolds Automatic Hose Reel was seen firsthand during a fire at the Columbian Cordage Company. Some cinders in the engine room ignited nearby waste. Workmen who discovered the fire in its incipiency were able to use the Reynolds Automatic Hose Reel to extinguish the fire.

Joseph Anton

Joseph "Joe" Anton served almost 30 years with the Auburn Fire Department. In 1894, he was appointed a callman with Hose Company No. 1. He became permanently installed in the Department in 1896 as a driver. In June of 1898, Joseph resigned in order to pursue other business interests. He worked for the D. M. Osborne & Co. and traveled to France and Germany as a representative of the company. He was reinstated as a callman in 1908, and again became permanent in 1909. He was one of eight Auburn Fire Department members who were forced to retire on pension by the City Manager in 1931, pursuant to a policy adopted by the City Council. On February 1, 1932, Joseph Anton was reinstated to the Fire Department. The day after Christmas 1932, the Fire Department was called to the service station and supply store, formerly known as Shirley's roadside stand, located at the intersection of the Auburn-Owasco Highway (East Lake Road) and the Koenig's Point Road (Rockefeller Road). The fire was significant, and the roadside stand was flaming. Anton was detailed to keep motorists and spectators away from the high tension wires that were a threat in the area of the fire. Joe suddenly collapsed while he was attending to his assigned task. He was immediately transported to the hospital, but it was too late. Joseph Anton had died. The sole source of water for the fire was a nearby well, which ran dry during the course of extinguishing the fire. They had to rely on backup sources of water to fight the fire. The roadside stand was ultimately destroyed, but Auburn Firemen were able to protect and save a neighboring garage and two small cottages from damage. John Anton, Joe's son, was at the fire as a spectator when his father collapsed. Francis "Bud" Maywalt was also on the scene as a spectator and was one of those who helped carry Joe to the vehicle for transport to the hospital; Bud would later join the Auburn Fire Department in 1943, and have a 30 year career himself.

Ross Duck

Ross Duck was born about 1877, in New York City. His family settled in Auburn when he was still young. At the age of 22, Duck enlisted in the U.S. Army and served with distinction in the Spanish-American War in the Philippines and China. He was initially assigned to the 7th Artillery, 16th Battery and fought with the famous fighting Ninth Infantry. He was discharged in May of 1902, after three years of service with an excellent service record. He intended to reenlist in the military. A carpenter by trade, Ross worked in Auburn for several months before he applied to be a callman with the Fire Department in October of 1902. He was put on a waiting list. In April 1903, he was appointed as a callman and was on probation for three months. He became a permanent callman in July of 1903.

November 26, 1903, Thanksgiving Day would prove to be a turning point in Ross Duck's life. On Thanksgiving morning, the men of Hose Company 1 set about their daily chores. Duck's good friend, John Clark, was a driver in the Company and prepared the team of horses for an exercise run. The horses were relatively new and had just recently been purchased by the Fire Commissioners. They were still in the process of being trained for work within the department. Duck accompanied Clark on the exercise run. They set off down Seminary Street at a good clip and as they turned onto North Street, the wagon slid around on the slippery pavement. The wheels struck the street railway tracks and the wagon overturned. Both passengers were tousled around and ejected from the wagon. Duck's head struck the icy brick pavement with terrible force, and he was instantly rendered unconscious. Clark was bruised and bumped up but suffered little damage, and he was able to hold onto the reins and stop the horses by guiding them into a telephone pole. Duck was immediately transported to a doctor's office and then to the City Hospital. Several surgeons attended to him and studied his condition. He suffered a severe concussion and fractured his skull just above his left eye. He also had injuries to his back. He was not expected to recover, and, in fact, was believed to be without hope.

Duck was unconscious for more than two weeks, hovering between life and death and his chances were seemingly slim. Just before Christmas Ross Duck became conscious and was able to take a short walk around the hospital grounds on December 23, 1903. By January 7, 1904, Duck was reported to have recovered greatly. He was discharged and returned to his callman position in the Fire Department. In September of 1904, the Municipal Civil Service Commission gave Ross Duck and Charles Adams a non-competitive examination for temporary appointment to the position of firemen in the Fire Department and certified them for appointment to fill two vacancies until a regular eligible list was available. Ross served as a temporary fireman on probation for six months with the Hook & Ladder Company and performed his work efficiently and was well liked and respected by those in the department.

At the end of his probation, Ross Duck decided that his interests were in the military. He submitted his resignation to Chief Jewhurst in March of 1905. The members of the Truck Company sent Ross Duck off with a gift of a cabinet maker's drill to assist him in his carpentry jobs. Ross went back to his carpentry trade for a time and then enlisted in the U.S. Marine Corps in February of 1906 for two years. He was assigned to Company 'D', 1st Battalion, Provisional Regiment at the Isthmus of Panama.

Backward Alarm

In February of 1938, the Auburn Fire Department received one of the most unusual alarms in its history. At just before 1am the firemen heard shouts outside headquarters. They looked out to find a blazing car and a man shouting for help. The inside of the car was a ball of flames. Engine Company No. 1 went to work with a large hand tank and a booster line to put out the fire. Once the fire was out, the firefighters questioned the driver regarding what had happened. The driver indicated he had been driving through Fleming, almost seven miles from the city, and detected smoke in his car. The exhaust pipe had set fire to the floor boards. His response was to drive fast to Auburn. His plan started to backfire when the seat he was sitting on caught fire, and he was forced to stand on the running boards of the vehicle. He continued to make the run to the fire station, pulled up and shouted for help. Rather than the Fire Department going to a fire, the fire came to them that day!

Distinguished Service Cross Recipient

Malcolm Britten Gott was appointed as a firefighter in 1940. He received military leave from his post with the Auburn Fire Department in 1942 to join the U. S. Army in World War II. Gott volunteered for overseas duty in March 1943 and left as a 2nd Lieutenant. He was promoted on the battlefield to 1st Lieutenant. Lieutenant Gott left England and made the invasion of France on D-Day with the First Infantry Division and the Fifth Ranger Battalion. On July 7, 1945, General Order No. 163 of the Headquarters, Third U.S. Army, awarded Malcolm B. Gott the Distinguished Service Cross for actions of March 18, 1945.

Second Lieutenant Gott, of the 39th Infantry Regiment, Company H, received the award for his extraordinary heroism in connection with military operations against an armed enemy while serving with Company H, 39th Infantry Regiment, 9th Infantry Division, in action against enemy forces in Germany. On March 18, 1945, in Rederscheid, Germany, Lieutenant Gott fearless advanced through intense enemy artillery fire, set up an observation post in a partially destroyed building, and with utter disregard for his own safety, called for an artillery barrage on two enemy tanks which had approached to within point-blank range of the building. Although subjected to devastating fire from both the enemy tanks and friendly artillery, he remained at his position and adjusted fire until the enemy tanks and supporting infantry were forced to withdraw. Lieutenant Gott's heroic actions and unflinching devotion to his duty were in keeping with the finest traditions of the military service. He was presented the Distinguished Service Cross from General George S. Patton. Lt. Gott also received the Purple Heart, Bronze Star, Combat Infantry badge and a Presidential Citation. Malcolm Gott decided to remain in the Army and submitted his resignation to the Auburn Fire Department in 1946. He served in the U.S. Army from 1942-1951, and again from 1957-1963. He died in 1984 and is buried at Arlington National Cemetery.

James McGee

James McGee had been a firefighter with the department for just under five years. He was 27 years old when he joined and was assigned to Engine Company No. 4. James had quite a reputation as an athlete in the Auburn area and was very popular among his co-workers and other friends. He had just recently been assigned to Engine Company 6 when they were called to a fire alarm at The Home on Grant Avenue at about midnight on May 13, 1939. McGee got in the truck and they were off! On arrival, he was seen to jump off the truck and begin toward his assigned station at the fire. James dropped to the ground. Firefighters went to his aid. He was conscious and complained of numbness in his arms and legs. He was rushed to the City Hospital. James McGee lapsed into a coma and died later that morning. The coroner reported that he had suffered a cerebral hemorrhage. He was only 32 years old. The fire was able to be quickly extinguished and was found to be caused by a rag containing furniture polish stored under a bathtub. The cloth burst into flames by spontaneous combustion. There was only slight damage to a first floor bathroom.

Bronze Star and Combat 'V'

James E. Byrne, a U.S. Marine Corps veteran of the Korean War, participated in the amphibious landing at Inchon, the "Nightmare Alley" engagement, and the infamous

Chosin Reservoir area evacuation. He was awarded the Bronze Star by General Lemuel C. Shepherd, Jr., commanding general of the First Marine Division. The battle became known as the "Nightmare Alley" engagement. His citation read:

> "For heroic achievement in connection with operations against the enemy while serving with a Marine infantry company in Korea on 7 November 1950. While his company was proceeding in convoy through a steep walled ravine, it was halted by an enemy road block and subjected to enemy small arms and machine gun fire. Corporal Byrne, serving as a rocket ammunition carrier, displayed outstanding professional skill and initiative.
>
> Observing that many Marines were becoming casualties, he occupied an exposed position and without regard for his own personal safety, covered the evacuation of the casualties by accurate and effective fire from his carbine.
>
> He repeatedly exposed himself to draw the enemy fire, thereby allowing the wounding Marines to receive medical aid and be evacuated. His actions were an inspiration to all members of his company and materially aided the wounded Marines in receiving medical attention much earlier than would otherwise have been possible. Corporal Byrne's courageous actions were in keeping with the highest traditions of the United States Naval Service.
>
> Corporal Byrne is authorized to wear the Combat 'V'."

James E. Byrne was promoted to Sergeant upon his return to the United States and was discharged in August of 1951. He joined the Auburn Fire Department on October 30, 1951. As part of the Armistice Day observances held in Auburn on November 12, 1951, a ceremony took place at Memorial City Hall, during which James E. Byrne was presented with a letter of commendation in recognition of his bravery on the battle front in Korea.

Making Movies!

In 1912, the Auburn Fire Department was filmed by the motion picture company, Motion World Theater, in association with Universal Pictures. A photographer employed by E. M. Day, of Motion World, filmed the firemen in action. The filming took place in the area surrounding City Hall and showed all companies of the department in an exhibition run. They attempted to make the run as realistic as possible and expected that they would be shown on local movie screens, and possibly in surrounding areas as well. As is the nature of movie pictures, news of the filming drew a huge crowd to Franklin Street. The photographer was situated in front of Hose Company 4 at headquarters and caught the firemen as they turned the corner of North and Garden Streets. Spectators all huddled into the corner area, trying to be captured in the filming efforts. Engines from Hose Companies 4, 3 and 5, as well as the Chief's car, were filmed as they traveled south down Garden Street. Hose Company 1, Hook and Ladder No. 2 and the Hayes truck were filmed as they turned the corner from Market to North Street. Fire Marshal Coneybear drove his car with Fire Commissioner Burgess as a passenger. There were plans to film the Pompier Corps, as well as the men at work at the training tower in order to demonstrate their spectacular feats. What a wonder it would be to see the results of the filming!

Metro-Goldwyn-Mayer Fire Prevention Cup

During the 1930 International Fire Chiefs' Association Convention held in Winnipeg, Canada, it was announced that the Auburn Fire Department had been awarded the coveted Metro-Goldwyn-Mayer Fire Prevention Cup. Chief Fred Washburn received notification of the award. The award recognized the Auburn Fire Department for having the best record among cities with populations between 20,000 and 100,000 for proficiency in fire prevention during 1929. The award was in the form of a very ornate and elegant trophy cup, about 24 inches tall and lined with silver and gold. It occupied a prominent location at headquarters and was admired by all who saw it. The cup stayed with the department until the following convention, held in Havana, Cuba, at which time it was turned over for the next recipient.

Smoking Is For The Birds

Chief James Doyle wondered if the birds in Auburn had taken up smoking cigarettes! The Auburn Fire Department was called out to a residence on Garden Street in March of 1950, after it was reported that flames were seen along a cornice of the home. Once on the scene, the firefighters found that the flames were confined to a group of birds' nests, dry leaves and feathers. The location of the fire was in a protected spot at the roof's edge, where apparently many birds gathered. There was no wire running in or around the immediate area of the cornice. There was no bonfire nearby that could have thrown off sparks. Firefighters concluded that a bird must have picked up a live cigarette and carried it up to the nesting area.

Music to Our Ears

The Cayugans, an orchestra under the direction of Mike Cervo, had Firefighter Frank Fiore as one of its members. Frank played a trumpet with skilled precision. Those who remember the Cayugans can probably recall some of the tunes they performed; *"Alfie"*, *"Cute"* and *"Moonlight in Vermont"* among them. The Cayugans drew large crowds wherever they performed and were a featured orchestra at many of the annual Firemen's Balls. Frank Fiore still enjoys playing the trumpet and can belt out quite a tune!

Alert Hose Company No. 6 had some musical talent in its ranks. At an Alert Hose picnic in 1885, entertainment was provided by members. John Hawley played the accordion. Nicholas Kierst and Joseph Clark each played harmonicas in an expert way. John Hawley, Joseph Clark, John Colbert and Peter McCoy sang many songs in quartette, duo, trio and solo fashion for those assembled.

The C. N. Ross Hose Company No. 5 had a quartette in the 1880s. The Hose 5 Quartette was quite popular at events. John Tyne (first tenor), Alex Chatelle and later William Beals (first bass), Charles Haigh (second tenor) and Andrew Howland (second bass) were members of the musical team. They sang at many banquets and social occasions. Also known as the Auburn City Pythian Quarette, they provided entertainment to many Auburnians over the years.

The Logan Hooks had "The Merry Twelve", a group of twelve fire company members and honoraries who entertained crowds with comic delights and singing. Some of their specialties included the "Charleston Blues" and a sketch of "Company B". The group was reorganized several times and members changed, but in 1886, The Merry Twelve was comprised of; John C. Winsor, Thomas Speares, Ed Smith, Herbert Walsh, John Flynn, Gilbert Goodrich, Matthew Flynn, Charles Adams, W. H. Weaver, George Bacon, William Moon and N. B. Gaston.

Central New York Champions

For three years in a row, the Monitor A.C. baseball team of Auburn held the amateur championship of Central New York title. The Monitors, a Stump City organization, played such teams as the Bone Yard Scouts, the Independents, the Swamp A.C., the Shamrock A.C.,

The Midnight Sons and the Hustlers. They won the 1911, 1912 and 1913 championships and had three future Auburn Firemen among their players. George Reidy (catcher), John Mohan (pitcher, center field and second base) and Charles Kierst were among the players in the amateur city league. The Monitor A. C. team was well known and celebrated for their talents on the field.

Mentillo Got the Boot!

"I have but one regret," said Assistant Fire Chief Peter Mentillo at his retirement dinner in January of 1968, "and that is that I'm leaving instead of staying. I wish I was just coming on the job. I hate to go, but as you know, all bad things must come to an end" he jokingly spoke to the more than 100 people present that night. Peter Mentillo had 43 years of service with the Auburn Fire Department. Many city officials and his fellow brother firefighters spoke of Mentillo and his career, remarking about his abilities and talents. Mentillo was known as the fireman's fireman, and he was very popular and well-respected among his friends and co-workers. He was presented with a "gold plated" firefighter boot, worn out at the heel and toe, which had been worn by Mentillo during his career. The boot was mounted on a wood stand and presented to him by Sid Burridge on behalf of the firefighters. The boot was presented to him jokingly, as he reportedly rarely spent his clothing allowance!

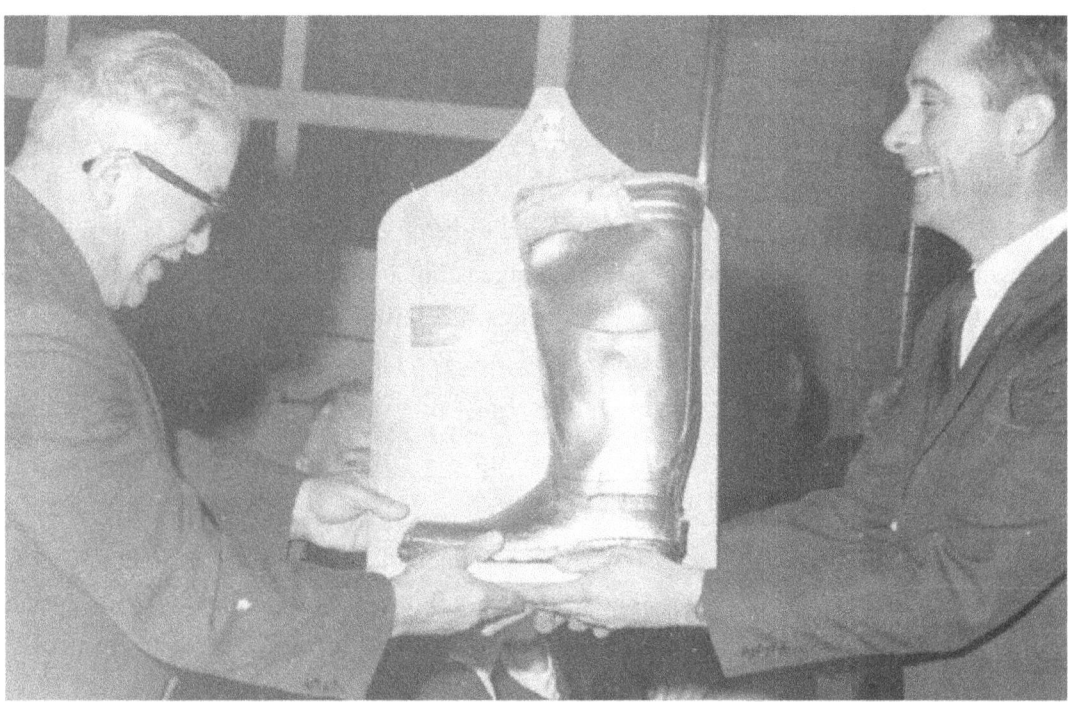

Baby of the Flock

John A. Colbert was the youngest firefighter at the time of his appointment as a callman in 1898; he was 20 years old. He was also associated with the department during the volunteer era during his teen years. Known as the "baby of the flock", John was the first firefighter appointed from a Civil Service List, having been added as a permanent fireman at Hose Company 1 on January 10, 1900. He was a member of the distinguished Pompier Corps and served 40 years with the Auburn Fire Department.

Bernard "Bernie" Simmons

With over 30 years in the Auburn Fire Department, Lt. Bernard Simmons was always active in community charities and events. He volunteered his time to participate in many money-raising activities for charities. Bernie Simmons was one of the organizers of the Auburn Softball Hall of Fame and spent years coaching youth basketball and baseball groups in Auburn. In 1987, Bernie received the Concerned Fire Fighters of the Year award for his many contributions to charitable causes.

Morgan L. Olmstead – 40 Years of Service and 2 Retirements

Morgan L. Olmstead was a 40-year veteran of the Auburn Fire Department when he retired in 1940. Olmstead was a member of the Westfall Hose Company in the volunteer days. He became a member of the paid department January 1, 1894, as a callman. He resigned in April of 1895 to start his own business. In April of 1899, he rejoined the department as a callman, and was made permanent on May 3, 1900. He served for 31 years and retired on pension July 1, 1931. However, he was recalled to duty January 9, 1933, and served until his 'second retirement' in 1940. Morgan Olmstead was 69 at the time his final retirement, but boasted that he could mount a ladder quicker than some of the younger men and had fought some pretty tough fires during his time.

Unruly Contest

In November of 1895, Auburn Police were notified of a furniture-smashing contest held in the quarters of Hose Company 2. What started the chaos was not disclosed. The incident was described in newspaper reports as "hilarious conduct of some persons unknown, recently, in the quarters of Letchworth Hose 2…" and was discussed by the Fire Commissioners at their meeting on November 8, 1895. The commissioners left the matter to the police after some remarks were made regarding the inappropriate actions taken by the men.

John Mohan

Firefighter John J. Mohan was elected as fifth Vice President of the New York State Permanent Firemen's Association in 1925. By 1929 he was first Vice President. He was appointed as President in 1930, during the annual convention held in Rochester that year. He retired from the position in 1931.

Frank E. Murphy

Frank E. Murphy, of Hose Company No. 6, responded to a fire on Wall Street January 31, 1927. The fire was observed by passersby who called in the fire alarm. The fire had started in a rubbish pile in the attic of the home. During the course of his actions on the scene, he suddenly fell to the ground while running up a steep bank. He was attended to and transported to the hospital, where he ultimately died; it was reported he suffered a ruptured blood vessel at the base of his brain. The owner of the home was later arrested by police and charged with having a revolver without a permit. The revolver was observed by officers during the course of the fire. The owner was examined by physicians to ascertain his sanity following the fire. He was found to be "incompetent" and was sent to Willard State Hospital.

The Branded Fireman

As one of firefighters was getting out of the shower at the fire station, an alarm came in. Knowing he had no time to spare, he sprinted, grabbed for his rubber coat and turnout gear as the crew raced out the door. They went to the fire and extinguished it successfully. Upon returning to headquarters and removing his gear, the bare-chested firefighter saw that he had a line of burn marks down his chest where each of the metal buckles from his coat had become so hot from the intense heat of the fire that they had burned his skin. He was not seriously burned, but it certainly branded him for the night.

Logan Drum Corps Founder Retires

Captain George A. Platt's 41 years of service in the Auburn Fire Department came to an end in 1917. His retirement gathering was, no doubt, long remembered by the very large crowd of people who descended on the Hook and Ladder Company on Market Street to say farewell to the longtime firefighter. It served as both a reunion and farewell, as the surprise gathering included the Logan Drum Corps marching down Market Street playing "The Charleston Blues" in honor of "Cappy" Platt. The Logan Drum Corps had been founded by Platt on October 22, 1882, and played at numerous firemen's conventions and other venues through New York State, Pennsylvania and Canada. The group that night was playing the original drum that had been used 35 years previously and was wearing the original Logan Drum Corps uniforms. Two of the original members played at the event; David P. Shute (bass drummer) and William C. Gates (fife). Captain Platt was given a standing ovation by those present.

Logan Drum Corp, c. 1883-1885, John Winsor in Center
(From the collection of the Cayuga Museum of History and Art)

Surprise Retirement!

William R. Strong started in the Auburn Fire Department in 1890 as part of the Hook & Ladder Company, and was promoted to Captain of Hose Company 3 in 1894. In 1911, he transferred to Hose Company 6. On July 15, 1919, William R. Strong was retired from the Fire Department, only he didn't know about it in advance!! He was placed on the retired

list because officials felt he had reached an age when he could no longer be as active as the hazardous duties of a fireman required. Strong was 57 years old. It was said by some that Chief Jewhurst was not consulted prior to Fire Commissioner McCarty's action, however, he declined to comment on the matter. Not only was Captain Strong surprised by the announcement of his retirement, but he was not given the customary 30 day-notice either. He served the City of Auburn for almost 30 years. He was quoted by reporters as saying "The retirement notice was a complete surprise to me today." Captain Strong declared himself to be in good physical condition and this was substantiated by many members of the department. He was broken up about his retirement and was not ready to retire. Chief Jewhurst referred to Strong as "a good, faithful fireman and a very competent company commander. He was one of the best firemen Auburn has ever had." In February 1920, City Manager John P. Jaeckel and the City Council members reinstated William R. Strong as a Captain with the Auburn Fire Department, assigning him back to his position as Captain of Hose Company 6. Captain Strong got right into the harness and led his company at the stubborn Y.M.C.A. fire shortly after his reinstatement. Captain Strong's retirement surprise was certainly not one that he was ready for!

Quite the Fish Tale

Auburn Firefighter Joe Flynn was said to have hooked a two-pound trout on Owasco Lake near Long Point. In the process of reeling him in, Flynn fumbled, and the fish got away and took Joe's bamboo rod and prize reel! FIVE days later, while trolling in the same area, Auburn Firefighter Tom Frost got his line caught in a small tree branch. As he worked to clear his line he discovered another line tangled up in the branches. He pulled the line clear and found a two pound trout, still alive, on the end of it! He continued to pull the line into his boat and brought a fishing rod to the surface. He recognized the rod and reel as belonging to Flynn. Newspaper accounts credited Frost with the catch and Flynn with the assist. The fish was reported to have been enjoyed at the Frost dinner table.

Clowning Around

Glenn B. Adams Jr. was a Captain in the Auburn Fire Department. He was also a member of the Circus Historical Society and performed as a clown. Glenn Adams was said to have a particular makeup design that he used regularly and may have taken steps to register his clown face. Several other firefighters were known to practice magic; a few of them were pretty skilled magicians.

Monsters!

Members of the Auburn Fire Department have a long history of active involvement in charitable and community events. In 1977, at the 2nd annual Auburn Jaycees haunted house, eight firefighters were transformed into monsters; Bill Patrick, Bob Tessoni, Bob Sloan, Dick DiSanto, Larry Roberts, Ed Laraway, Dave Kapcha and Bob Regets. The event was a success, with over 1,300 people attending the haunted house and it quickly became an Auburn Halloween staple for years.

Auburn's K.O. Artist and the Pride of Hackney

Howard "Cy"/ "Young Cy" Townsend joined the Auburn Fire Department as a temporary firefighter in 1945, and became a permanent firefighter in 1947. Prior to his firefighting career, Cy was a talented and noteworthy heavyweight boxer in the Central New York area and beyond. Cy stood 6'1" and started boxing when he was a featherweight. Often referred to as the "Pride of Hackney" and the "Hackney Idol", Cy was noted to pack quite a wallop with his speed punching ability. He was certainly a big and powerful man. He was an outstanding amateur boxer and a Golden Gloves Division fighter. He served in the Army during World War II and participated in campaigns in Africa and Italy. He boxed in the Army's Fifth Division heavyweight championship. Auburn's "K.O. Artist" was a chip off the 'ole block, following in his father's footsteps. Young Cy's father, Frank "Cy" Townsend, was a skilled boxer in the Central New York area and an Auburn favorite through the 1920s. Frank and Howard Townsend were among those honored in 1972 at the Auburn Old Timers Boxing Dinner, the two being awarded the Father-Son Award in recognition of their contributions to the sport. Cy Townsend fought many first-rate opponents over the years, including George 'Cyclone' Williams, Eddie (Kayo) Kowalski, Jack Finn, Jack Latrobe, Battling Atwood, Joe Muscato and Baldy Copes. In 1958, Cy left the Auburn Fire Department and became a Cayuga County Fire Dispatcher until his retirement.

Darrow; the Eclipse

Captain Paul Darrow was an imposing figure, both in physical stature and as a firefighter. Standing at well over 6' tall and with a broad physique, his presence commanded attention. One firefighter told a story of a time after a fire when he and Darrow were walking down a hallway in a scarred building, water dripping from the ceiling and everything black with soot and char. Six ceiling lights were still on in a row extending the length of the hallway. The two were in their turnout gear. As Paul walked down the hallway, his towering frame took up quite a bit of real estate. His helmet hit one light bulb after another all the way down, and the light bulbs each exploded with a pop, pop, pop and sparks flew. In the end, the hallway was dark, and Darrow had eclipsed it.

On the Hunt

Over the years, and even today, many of the firefighters were and are avid sportsmen. On the days approaching April 1st, the fishermen would get their gear ready for opening day of trout season. Secret fishing locations would be scoped out, new techniques explored and new lures picked out. In the fall, they prepared equipment for opening day of deer season. Guns readied, hunting grounds selected and all the necessary paperwork in order. The goal, of course, was bragging rights at the firehouse! There has always been a 'friendly' competitiveness among the firefighters in the area of hunting and fishing. In 1955, four firemen set off to hunt and all four got a deer; Edward Bilinski, Francis Bunnell and Paul Oliver, Jr. (all from Engine 3) and Reynolds VanScoyk (Engine 1). Engine 3 won that matchup. In 1997, Frank DeJoy (Engine 2) shot an award-winning 19-point buck. It ranks, even today, in the New York State Big Buck Club record book in the Gun, Non-Typical Category, with a Boone & Crockett Score of 176.1.

Rock 'n' Roll!

It was a quiet night in Auburn, but for the Return of the Warlord! A portion of Genesee Street was closed late one night for a music video to be filmed. Manowar, an American heavy metal band originating in Auburn New York, was to film a video for *Return of the Warlord*. The Auburn Fire Department was requested to stand by the scene; apparatus was used to block off a portion of the street. Firefighters stayed out of the way, but were soon recruited to be a part of the video. They stood in a line on the street and represented an antagonist presence in the video. Auburn Firefighters Christopher Logue, Dale Clark, Mike Deyneka, Rick Liccion and Fred Kerr all appear in the popular music video.

On another occasion, a group of fireman attended a Weedsport Speedway concert event featuring Bret Michaels, famed lead singer of the band, Poison, and successful solo artist. A connection was established via a "six degrees of separation"-type association and the group of firefighters were invited into the Bret Michaels tour bus. They met the rock star and all shared stories and laughs together. They had items autographed before the end of their visit as well. Tom Hansen, Sean Crehan, Terry Winslow, Mike Deyneka, Richard Stabinsky, Sam Giannettino, Jeff Clark and Jim Leonard walked away with a great experience and a great story!

Nicknames

Many firefighters acquired nicknames over the years. As a term of endearment, they are both amusing and funny. Below is a list of some of the nicknames that span more than a hundred years, from the infancy of the department to modern times. The true identities are not listed, but in most cases Auburnians will know them, since they were so commonly used in place of their real names.

Burrhead	Bingo	Cuckoo	Farmer
Nibsy	Paddy	Petey	Smokey
Spuds	Sprint	Jessie	Cheddar
Otso	Butch	Wally	Mother Superior
Punchy	Birch	Bud (x2)	Snuffy
Mr. Meaney	Rusty	Pinhead	Muckles
Chubby	Buddy	Tiger	The Bug
Nasty	Bucky	Mother	Lug-Nut
Chico	Tootsie	Socks	Jim-Bob
Poody	Dutch	Mongo	El-Gato
Maynard	Jethro	Bachi	Captain Bam-O
Junior	GiGi	Cy/Si	Julie
Quilly	Sprout	Lyme	Smoothie
Bres	Shorty	Banta	Barnyard
Sparky	Mooch	Leroy	Barrel/Barrel Head
Noodles	Rags	Dink	Patty
Wizard	Not-So	Whip	Cement Head
Dirty Harry	Dan-O	Knobber	Remer
Guber	Dingbat	Maxi	'Lil General
Trippy	BoBo	Nippy	Tom-Tom
Daddy	The Saint	Flash	Charlie Rabbit
Holy One	Cappy	Meat	

Special Deliveries

Every so often the Auburn Fire Department is called to respond to a call involving a mother in labor. Usually the calls result in delivery of the mother to the maternity ward at the hospital. Sometimes the calls have resulted in successful delivery of the baby during the call. The first known delivery of a baby by an Auburn firefighter was completed by Robert Regets. He and Lawrence Roberts also delivered a second baby the following year.

In September of 1995, firefighters Steve Parker and Jeff Dygert were involved in the delivery of a baby boy, born three months' premature. Unbelievably, the pair was again involved in the delivery of a baby in March of 1996. The fire call was received at 12:47am on March 15, 1996, for a woman in labor. Parker and Dygert were part of the crew responding to the call and were both Emergency Medical Technicians (EMTs) as well as firefighters. The baby girl was born healthy and both mother and daughter were taken to the hospital for evaluation and were later released.

Rookies

Almost every firefighter has a story from their rookie years. One firefighter shared a story in which he had arrived on the scene of an alarm, wearing someone else's boots. Boots weren't issued by the department in those days, and the firefighter had not yet bought his own pair. The boots were not quite a perfect fit and were a bit big. He put on his mask and as he began to walk, he tripped over the hose and went down flat! He scurried upright and quickly looked to see if anyone had spied his fall, just in time to see his buddy's wife standing off to the side, laughing and pointing at him!

Another firefighter described one of his first experiences at a house fire years ago. His crew was first on the scene and he was instructed by the experienced firefighters to grab the booster line. Energized, with adrenaline pumping, he was anxious to prove his worth. A kid came out of the side door of the house and yelled, "Over here! Over here!" The firefighter tugged the booster line and ran, following the kid, who led him all the way around to the back of the house, in the back door, through the house back to the front and then up the stairs. It was a long haul, and they were not wearing any air-paks at that point. The firefighter charged up the stairs! When the rookie got to the top, he was breathing quite heavy and was exhausted. That was it. He was done. The smoke condition and arduous journey to get to that point, in gear, while tugging the hose, took its toll. The veteran firefighters simply shook their heads a bit and guided the spent rookie down the stairs and got him out of the house.

Hennessy's Again

The asbestos cigar store, owned by T. J. Hennessy, caught fire so often that people in the city began to place odds as to how many fires it would take before it would finally be claimed. Others wagered that the store could not be burned, unlike their cigars. In April of 1918, the Auburn Fire Department was called to the asbestos cigar store on State Street for the third time that month. Each time the fires were determined to be accidental and had resulted from discarded stubs or rogue embers, and the Fire Department was able to quickly extinguish them before any notable damage was done. The Fire Department's presence at Hennessy's was so common that pedestrians were heard to say nonchalantly, "Oh, it's Hennessy's again" and continued to stroll past the store.

A Life Saved

Lionel Morris was saved from drowning in the Owasco River in the fall of 1854, when he was just a toddler. Oscar Darwin Owen rescued him from the cold water. Oscar Owen would go on to serve in Admiral Winslow's Naval Fleet in the Civil War. Lionel Morris would later serve almost two decades in the Auburn Fire Department.

Through the Looking Glass

While working in a residential fire, a firefighter was leading an interior crew. Navigating the hallway filled with billowing smoke made it nearly impossible to see. He was down low and crawling along the long stretch, when all of a sudden – Boom! His helmet crashed into a mirror and shattered it! In the thick smoke, a mirror at the end of the hallway had reflected a bit of light from the other side of the hallway, making it look like the hallway continued on. His forward momentum took him head first into the looking glass!

In One Door, Out the Other!

Neither Edward Laraway nor Gerald Conway could ever have imagined the events surrounding their first day on the job. They both started at the Auburn Fire Department on the morning of January 17, 1972. While Ed was getting ready for work, his wife told him there was a fire downtown. Ed wasn't overly concerned; they wouldn't send a guy to a fire on day one. Temperatures were near zero that morning, and the snow was building up. Laraway and Conway reported for duty at headquarters. They walked in the door of the fire station and were immediately led upstairs to the attic by a veteran firefighter. The attic was full of smoke that was trailing in from the blaze across the street. O'Donnell Electric was on fire and the heavy, thick smoke was throughout the Fire and Police headquarters building. Flames reached over 30 feet in the air at O'Donnell Electric. They had limited visibility in the attic and were already getting a taste of smoke. They were each issued a coat and helmet and told to go across the street and report to the scene! Somewhat stunned, they looked quickly to each other, donned their gear and proceeded down from the smoke-filled attic and went across the street. Conway and Laraway were given directions and tasks to complete, one of which was to help two experienced firefighters with a 35' ladder. Not having had any training yet on any equipment, they paid close attention to what the others were telling them to do. The O'Donnell Electric fire was only the second time that the department utilized both of their aerial ladders simultaneously. The blaze was a three-alarm fire and was raging. High winds played against the scene. The cold and snow was particularly biting, with the wind chill 25 below zero. Ice formed on the equipment and apparatus. Their streams of water quickly froze and made the area treacherous to maneuver. The roof collapsed from the weight of the snow and water that was icing quickly. The fire lasted more than two hours and was battled under tough conditions. The firefighters' helmets, boots and coats iced over during the alarm. The fire was brought under control. Ed Laraway and Jerry Conway ended up responding to multiple alarms that shift and never left the block! They never even got to ride in the fire truck! So began two long and successful careers within the Auburn Fire Department.

Captain Searing's On! Run!

There has always been a hustle in a firefighter's response to an alarm coming in, but when Captain Bernie Searing was on the truck, they really had to move at top speed to get on the truck or risk missing it as it drove off! Such was the thought one night when an alarm sounded and two firefighters made a mad dash through the old double doors to get on the truck before it left! Smack….Blam! The two collided into one another and down they went; one with his nose bleeding and rattled a bit. Lying in front of the ladder truck with a broken nose, he looked up and made eye contact with the driver of the fire truck, who had been poised to exit the station. The driver looked down at him and very matter-of-factly waved his hand for the injured man to move aside. He moved and the truck proceeded to respond to the call; a pickup truck had hit a telephone pole guywire and tipped over. While the fire crew responded, the injured man was taken to the hospital. The hospital staff asked what had happened and one of the firefighters, who thought they were inquiring about the alarm, proceeded to say, "Well, the truck tipped over…" but before he could finish, the hospital staff started to scramble, thinking that a fire truck had tipped over and that there would be more patients coming in! They were preparing for a large-scale event! The firefighters quickly explained the situation and only then did everyone share a laugh.

Fits Like a Glove….Sort Of

As the wheels of progress turned and fire apparatus became more and more technologically evolved, the trucks grew in size and complexity and were a bit of a tight fit in the bays at headquarters. Responding to a fire call one day, the driver pulled out and proceeded to the scene. On arrival, the firefighters noticed that all the compartment doors on one side of the truck were gone! Missing completely! Upon arrival back to headquarters, the crew pulled in, only to find Chief Maywalt standing in Truck Company's bay shaking his head and looking down at the compartment doors that were lying neatly on the floor. It was always a tight squeeze getting through those old bay doors!

Breathing Can Be an Art

Back in the day, the canister-type masks were the standard in the firefighting industry. They were difficult to use and many firefighters struggled with them. Lucian DeSocio is remembered as being one of very few men who could successfully wear the canister mask for long periods of time successfully. The masks did not provide oxygen, and instead, essentially only filtered out smoke particles. A firefighter knew the mask was working if they got hot; when the mask was removed they could see the outline of the mask on their faces.

Science Experiment Gone Wrong

After watching a television show that featured the science behind cannons, one of the firefighters decided he was going to try to make one. He gathered together and secured a stack of his favorite DJD/PBR cans and added a tennis ball and lighter fluid. He had apparently loaded the device incorrectly, because when it was lit, BOOM! A flaming tennis ball was launched into the air, high above the roofline. It drew attention from everyone in the area. At first there was awe and some chuckling, but what goes up, must come down. The fluid-soaked, blazing ball fell back to the ground with a splash, leaving behind a little fire where it had bounced down. The ball continued to bounce and leave behind a fire each time it landed! Everyone chased after it, stomping out the flames that were left behind! In the end there was much laughter and several lessons learned!

How in the heck did that happen?!

Boys will be boys. Some time ago, a young Auburn boy managed to get himself stuck in a tapered pail. He had climbed into the three-foot high, two-foot wide pail feet first and managed to wedge himself pretty good. He wasn't able to get out. His father's attempts to extricate his son were unsuccessful, so he picked up the pail and carried it, containing his son, to the fire station. The firemen were a bit perplexed, not only wondering how to get him out, but also curious as to how he had managed to get into such a pickle. Only the boy's head and neck were visible outside the pail. Firemen were able to free the boy in about 20 minutes. Using an electric saw and tin shears, with great care, they cut away the pail. He was successfully released from the pail and was not injured. The boy was allowed to ring the bell on the fire truck, as the firemen had promised at the beginning of their work.

Stuck in the Muck

Decades ago, the Owasco Outlet was dredged, and a deep pile of sediment and debris was piled in an area south of Fleming Street and Pulsifer Drive. A nine-year-old Auburn boy went to the area with his brother and a friend to look for possible fishing grounds. Upon walking in the muck, the boy's feet got stuck and he was not able to free himself. The more he tried to maneuver his way out, the deeper he sank. The boy's brother ran for help. A nearby resident threw a rope to the stuck boy and instructed him to hold on. When the Auburn Fire Department arrived on the scene, the boy's head was almost all that was showing! They quickly formulated a plan to extricate him from the muck. They laid a 24-foot extension ladder on the soupy mud and crawled across it to get to the boy and pulled him out. He was carried to safety, unhurt and with a lesson learned.

"Bring Me Home"

William D. Petrosino, "Billy", started as a firefighter in 1987. He graduated at the top of his class at the NYS Fire Academy in Montour Falls. His analytical nature, and ability to think on his feet, saw him rise through the ranks to become a Captain in the Auburn Fire Department in 2002. He had the respect and friendship of many fellow firefighters. Billy was diagnosed with a fast-moving lung cancer in 2006, and was receiving treatment in Illinois. The end was drawing near and Billy wanted to die at his home in Auburn. He was not able to fly on a commercial airline, and the prospect of his dying wish seemed slim. The fellowship of peers at the Fire Department is strong and Bill's family of firefighters came together, pulled some strings, and made arrangements for a Mercy Flight helicopter to bring their brother home to Auburn on March 14, 2006. William Petrosino died in his home on VanAnden Street, as was his last wish. He died March 15, 2006, just one day following his arrival. Captain William Petrosino's casket was carried to the cemetery on an Auburn fire truck. He received salutes from uniformed Auburn firefighters, was carried under a huge American flag suspended from two fire trucks and the Wheeler bell tolled. Bill was surrounded by family and friends and was in Auburn, where he wanted to be.

Loyalty Runs Strong and Deep

Firefighters depend on each other for their lives, in all situations and at every call. A fire in the Marshalls department store in Auburn in the early 90's was the setting for an event that evidenced that sentiment exactly. The basement area of the store had a heavy smoke condition with fire. A seasoned Lieutenant was with a relatively new firefighter, whose air-pak vibralert alarm actuated, indicating an upcoming end of service for his air flow supply. The Lieutenant told the younger firefighter to go ahead and head back. He indicated he would not leave the lieutenant alone. The Lieutenant told the new guy he had things underway and he could leave, but the rookie remained steadfast in his resolve, stating "You stay, I stay. You go, I go." He made no movement toward the exit. Seeing that the rookie was truly sincere in his thoughts and intended to stay with his Lieutenant regardless of his own air situation, the two exited together. It made quite an impression on the Lieutenant, who even today recalls the scene with true admiration and respect.

Poets Among Them

Artistic and creative firefighters illustrate their talents in many ways. On a cold Christmas Day in 1977, Bill Patrick reflected on a holiday spent working at the firehouse and composed the following poem within the handwritten logbook of the Auburn Fire Department:

Christmas Day

'Tis Christmas Day with Bob in the seat
and there's plenty of food all ready to eat;
Rudy's not hungry, and neither is Paul
'cause early last night they gave it their all.
Bill and Bill are walking around
settling the food they earlier put down;
George is in the kitchen where all the food is stored
sampling all the goodies and never getting bored.
The truckies are upstairs with pillows 'neath their heads
making sure the winds don't blow away their beds;
No bells have rung, besides one at eight
we're hoping for silence … it sure would be great.
Many dispatchers have passed in and out
shortening their workday, without a doubt;
Our chores are all finished, we've hung up the brooms
we've made all the beds in all six bunkrooms.
We're all here together, but lonely inside
'cause we're not with our families and wonderful brides;
It's our job with its rules, and sometimes it's hell
but we're ready to roll at the sound of the bell.
It will soon be over and we'll be out the door
when C Platoon arrives to relieve mighty Engine 4.

Engine 4 log entry from December 25, 1977
Auburn Fire Department, Auburn, New York

Assistant Chief George Bannon   *Firefighter Paul Baran*
Lieutenant Bob Flynn   *Firefighter Bill Hutson*
Firefighter Rudy DelFavero   *Firefighter Bill Patrick [Author]*

The 50th Anniversary Celebration of the organization of the Logan Hook and Ladder No. 1 Company was held in October 1874. Following the parade march, Lieutenant Colonel Terance J. Kennedy, organizer of the first Civil War Cayuga volunteers, addressed the crowd gathered at the old City Hall. His speech was compelling and its spirit stands the test of time. He remarked, in part:

> "Fire, destructive in its course when once rekindled, proves on many occasions, the destroyer not only of property, but life and limbs are also sacrificed to its flaming vengeance, and the fond hopes of many a helpless family, whom a few short hours before possessed a happy home and all its comforts, lie buried in the ashes beneath the dying embers of a destructive fire. To guard against such scenes as these, every well-ordered village or city provides a properly equipped fire department. All recognize the necessity. No good citizen, however poor he may feel, even objects to his just share of necessary expense. The life of a fireman when on duty is necessarily an arduous one. It requires brave hearts and willing hands, to be ever ready at the call of duty, by day or by night, in sunshine or storm. The daring of the true fireman is always equal to the emergency that requires exposure. Unawed by the burning timbers, or the crash of tumbling walls, he coolly places his ladder or plies his hooks or hose where experience has taught him he can do most good."

In years past, downtown was a bustling center of activity with a steady stream of pedestrians walking up and down the streets. Social networking in those days entailed handshakes, a nod and talking directly with people. Many can remember seeing the firefighters sitting in chairs outside the fire station, greeting people and watching activities in the area. It was not uncommon for the old-timers to sing songs and occasionally one might catch Guter playing his bass drum or Fiore playing the trumpet. Neighbors would gather to enjoy the evening music. A soda pop could be bought from the machine at the station for 5¢ a bottle. Of course, times change. A firefighter's duties are numerous, and while the specific tasks and equipment have evolved over the years, the core mission of the department has not. They work to prevent or minimize the loss of life and property from fire and natural and man-made emergencies. Many of those interviewed for the book, including past and present members of the Fire Department, cited the traditions that have always existed within the department. They are difficult to impart, but are expressed by many as important and valued. The heart of those traditions fosters camaraderie and trust; only the names have changed over time.

Being a successful firefighter requires so much more than passing a civil service test, a physical fitness evaluation and hours and hours of formalized training. A successful firefighter must also be courageous, caring and empathetic, quick-thinking and resourceful, honest and dedicated, assertive and accountable. Whether born or made, a successful firefighter embodies the spirit and dedication of the Crusaders, from which the Maltese Cross became their symbol of protection, honor and bravery.

The Auburn Fire Department holds decades of memories within its walls. A variety of fire trucks and other apparatus have been parked in the bays. There are items that you can see and touch, things that have seen firefighters come and go over the years; brass poles, bells, caned chairs, lockers, bunks, blankets, desks, tables and much more. The buildings, themselves, hold an unmistakable sillage, a unique combination of lingering smoke residue, rubber, grease, synthetic fibers, metal, oil, sweat, old coffee and other various materials. It is the patina of years of fire and rescue runs made by the dedicated men and women of the Auburn Fire Department. The scent is immediately recognizable for those who worked there and for their family members who had occasion to visit. It is a place that echoes with the accumulated years of joy and celebration, unbelievable grief and sorrow, laughter and joviality, both quiet and raucous times. Oh if those walls could talk!

The history of the Auburn Fire Department is extensive, remarkable and ongoing, but the common thread throughout the fabric of time is the dedication and bravery of the Auburn firefighters, who are always ready to roll at a moment's notice, to save and protect.

They are our hometown heroes.

*Frank De Joy gives the signal to "Shut it down."
(Photo courtesy of Christopher Logue)*

ACKNOWLEDGEMENTS

We would like to thank the Auburn Fire Department and its members for the support shown throughout this project. Access to the Fire Department archives and historical information proved invaluable, and this book would not exist were it not for the research that we were allowed to conduct there. Thank you to Fire Chief Jeff Dygert, who supported our venture from its inception. Special thanks to the Retired Firefighters Association of Auburn, NY, and its members, who actively contributed to the content of this book. These pages were brought to life through their willingness to share experiences and memories with us. We are very fortunate to have their support and appreciate their contributions.

Gathering together information, facts and other data would have been so much more difficult had it not been for Tom Tryniski's Old Fulton NY Postcards website. His website has an incredible collection of over thirty-four million scanned historic newspaper pages, mostly from New York State. It is an incredible and invaluable resource. Thank you!

Thank you to the Legends Room at Cayuga Community College (CCC) and Ormie King, who graciously met with us and provided additional information for the project. The Legends Room at Cayuga Community College is a gem! The Mary Van Sickle Wait History Room at Seymour Library proved useful in our research. Thank you to Auburn City Clerk, Chuck Mason, and his staff, who assisted in finding answers to our questions and inquiries. We appreciate the contribution of information and material by Mayor Michael Quill.

Thank you to Ryan and John of Downtown Books & Coffee and their independent book publishing services, who helped us realize our goal of getting this book ready to share with the world.

Thank you to the Auburn Citizen newspaper, which has chronicled Fire Department events and activities in detail, dating back to 1816, and has ensured that its history has been documented. They have provided 200 years of news stories, some of which have been reproduced in this book.

Thank you to the retired firefighters who allowed us an interview; each of you provided clarity and insight into your role and the department as a whole. Jeff Clark, thank you, for double-checking our apparatus information (and for the meals during our research ☺). To our sister, Debbie Blake, thanks for your assistance with proofreading! To the families and community members who provided access to personal scrapbooks, photos, memorabilia and other information – Thank you. Auburn is rightfully proud of its Fire Department, and we hope that we have produced a historical reference that the community will be pleased with.

To our spouses, Mark and Monique, thank you for your encouragement and support along the way, as well as your patience and understanding during the long hours we spent on the computer and at the fire station.

REFERENCES

Information was derived from many personal interviews conducted, as well as a large assortment of scrapbooks, photo albums, journals and personal collections that were made available by past and present Auburn firefighters, their families and members of the community.

Amodei, April. Personal interview. 6 Nov. 2015.

Ancestry.com Collections. Genealogy, Family Trees & Family History Records at Ancestry.com. Web.

Auburn Citizen, Auburn, NY. Print and Web.

Auburn Fire Department 1927 Souvenir. Auburn, 1927. Print.

Auburn Fire Department Souvenir Book. Auburn, 2005. Print.

Auburn Fire Department, History Archives. Auburn, 2015.

Auburn Fire Fighters Souvenir Book. Auburn, 1983. Print.

Auburn New York City Directories. Auburn. 1850-1980. Print.

Auburn, N.Y. 200 Years of History 1793-1993. Auburn: Bicentennial Committee, 1992. Print.

"Baseball's Lost Chalice." Our Game. 3 Nov. 2011.

Biographical Review; Sketches of the Leading Citizens of Cayuga County, N.Y. Boston: Biographical Review Pub., 1894. Print.

Bradish, Jay. "On the Job New York, Fire-Alarm Inferno Rips Auburn Factory Site." Firehouse. 1 Feb. 1995: 40-41. Print.

Brahney, William. "Auburn Water Works." Online interview. 28 Jan. 2016.

"Brief History – FASNY." FASNY Brief History Comments. Web.

"Chew the Fat Session." Personal interview. 5 Oct. 2015. Retired Firefighters Association of Auburn NY members.

"Chew the Fat Session." Personal interview. 2 Nov. 2015. Retired Firefighters Association of Auburn NY members.

"Chief Edward J. Jewhurst, of Auburn, Dean of New York Chiefs." *Fire and Water Engineering* 7 Aug. 1918: 100. Print.

City of Auburn Common Council Proceedings. Auburn, 1893-1929. Print.

"City of Auburn, NY – Apparatus." *City of Auburn, NY – Apparatus.* Web.

"Dedication of the Firemen's Monument." Rochester Fire Department 1817-1882. Rochester: Central Library of Rochester and Monroe County – Historic Monographs Collection.

Dygert, Jeffrey. Personal interview. 5 Jan. 2016.

Fiore, Frank. Personal interview. 10 Oct. 2015.

Hall, Henry. *The History of Auburn*. Auburn: Dennis Bros., 1869.

Henderson, Harry. "A Woman's Problem: How to Save Your Family from Fire." *Woman's Home Companion* 1 Apr 1954: 33, 70, 72. Print.

Jones & Company Bell Founders – Troy Bell Foundry. Troy: A. W. Scribner Book and Job Printer, Cannon Place. 1870: 1-66.

Legends, Local History Room, Cayuga Community College. Auburn, 2015. Print Material.

Lewin, Lori. "Auburn Firefighters Put Their Lives on the Line." *The Record* 19 Dec 1990, Vol. 1 No. 5 ed.: 1, 12.

"MDA Labor Day Telethon History." *Muscular Dystrophy Association.* Web.

Mary Van Sickle Wait History Room, Seymour Library. Auburn, 2015. Print Material.

Malone, Harry R., and William H. Arnold. A Sesqui-centennial Souvenir Describing One Hundred and Fifty Years of Progress: With a Complete Story of the Sullivan Campaign of 1779 and a History of the Towns of the Finger Lakes Region Settle by Veterans of that Exhibition. Auburn, N.Y.: Harry R. Melone, 1929.

Martin, William, William Lee, and R. Michael Harmon, III. Personal interview. 10 Nov. 2015.

"Meneely and Company Records: Manuscripts and Special Collections," New York State Library. 1825-1945.

Monroe, Joel Henry. Historical Records of a Hundred and Twenty Years, Auburn, N.Y. Geneva, NY: W.F. Humphrey, Printer, 1913.

Newman, Mark. "Dauvray Cup Was Once a Coveted Possession." MLB.com: News. 3 Nov. 2011.

O'Hearn's Histories. Auburn. Print. Web.

"Old Fulton NY Post Cards." *Old Fulton NY Post Cards.* Web.

"Overweighted." *The National Police Gazette.* New York 4 Sept. 1880: 4-5. Print.

Quill, Michael D. Personal interview. 14 Dec. 2015.

"Roll of Honor." *New York State Fallen Firefighters Memorial.* Empire State Plaza, Albany, NY. 2015.

Shepley Bulfinch Archives & Records Management. Boston. 2015.

Spicer, Adam, Bill Patrick. Personal interview. 9 Nov. 2015.

Storke, Elliot G., and James H. Smith. "Auburn Fire Department." 1879. *History of Cayuga County, New York,* Syracuse: D. Mason, 1879.

"The Bandwagon New Members." *Hobby Bandwagon – Circusiana Monthly* 1 Oct. 1949: 6.

Tozzi, Angelo. Personal interview. 4 Oct. 2015.

"United States Patent Office – Patents." Google – *Patents.* Web.

www.ingramcontent.com/pod-product-compliance
Lightning Source LLC
Chambersburg PA
CBHW080329170426
43194CB00014B/2507